10-

A Reporter In Sweet Chicago
Len O'Connor

Contemporary Books, Inc.
Chicago

Library of Congress Cataloging in Publication Date

O'Connor, Len.
   A reporter in sweet Chicago.

   Includes index.
   1. O'Connor, Len.   2. Journalists—Illinois—Chicago—
Biography.   I. Title.
PN4874.045A37   1983   070'.92'4 [B]   83-15093
ISBN 0-8092-7648-8

Published by Contemporary Books, Inc.
180 North Michigan Avenue, Chicago, Illinois 60601
Manufactured in the United States of America
Library of Congress Catalog Card Number: 83-15093
International Standard Book Number: 0-8092-7648-8

Published simultaneously in Canada by Beaverbooks, Ltd.
195 Allstate Parkway, Valleywood Business Park
Markham, Ontario L3R 4T8 Canada

For John, Paul, Meg, Bill, Leonard, and Patrick.

CONTENTS

A
Reporter
In Sweet
Chicago

CHAPTER **1**

"THEY WON'T COME BACK TIL IT'S OVER, OVER THERE"

NOBODY TROUBLED TO EXPLAIN IT to the younger children, at least not in our house, when grubby boys appeared in the predawn darkness of our quiet street that frigid morning in November 1918 with their shouts of "Great War ends! Extra paper!" There had been table talk for several days in our house about the likelihood that the war, which had become increasingly foreboding in our lives, might soon be over. Perhaps the older members of our family assumed that even the younger kids would understand that what the newsboys were saying was that peace, thank God, was now at hand. But no one gave any thought to reassuring the children who had been startled into shivering wakefulness by the raucous cries of the newsboys. At least not in our house. So we lay in our beds, fearful of what all this shouting outside portended.

Even the youngest of us had become accustomed to the excitement of the newsboys' unexpected appearances on our block, clutching bundles of newspapers and shouting, "Extra paper!" The fiercely competitive Chicago newspapers were ea-

ger to race to the presses to be first with the news of some
momentous development in the battles being waged on what
was referred to as "the continent." Mostly the decision to redo
the front page and go to press with an "extra" was inspired
by a few meager details that had clacked in on the Western
Union or Postal Telegraph wires. The editors slapped a commanding headline over what frequently was only a few crumbs
of information on a late-breaking story. Bundles of these "extra" papers would hastily be loaded onto circulation wagons,
and the delivery men would urge their horses into fast runs to
the various outlying neighborhoods, like ours. It was a not-
infrequent sight: newsboys in drooping knickerbocker pants,
socks slipping down their skinny legs to scruffy shoes, begrimed
faces looking cocky under caps that were askew, loudly hawking
their product in residential areas. But there were, this time,
some differences.

Newsboys did not come into the streets in the dead of night.
The customary hours for selling extra papers were limited, as
a practical matter, to the evening, before most people switched
off the lights, locked the front door, and went to bed. So it
was quite unusual to have newspaper boys in the street before
dawn with their loud cries of "Great War ends!" Moreover,
the regular newsboys would be appearing in another hour or
two, pushing two-wheeled carts packed with tightly folded *Chicago Tribune*s and *Herald-Examiner*s and tossing the morning
papers with all the latest news on the front porch of every
house listed in their delivery books. The sudden presence of
newsboys with an "extra" paper on a darkened block was a
sign that something of enormous importance had occurred.

It was likewise significant that on this occasion there was no
mistaking what it was that had been deemed of such moment
that it called for going to press with an "extra." Householders
had long grown wary of being tricked into buying "extras"
turned out with not a crumb of late-breaking news by editors
who simply were trying to boost the circulation of their newspapers. As if in league with the editors, or perhaps because
they realized no one would buy an "extra" if he knew how
little it contained, the newsboys invariably employed unintel-

ligible language in crying out the essentials of the big news story; the only understandable thing about their cry being "Read all about it!" This time, though, they were clearly shouting, "Great War ends!" It was as if they knew they were the messengers of great tidings. And even though the word *armistice* was new to the vocabularies of the newsboys, and to most of the householders who heard them shout it, the printed report of an armistice in Europe carried with it a promise that the fighting had stopped, or soon would, and that the young men in service who had not been killed would now be coming home.

In our neighborhood in Austin, the sparsely developed western region of World War I Chicago, first here and then there, and then down the block a little, houses were lighting up, signifying to the newsboys in the street that half-dressed men and women would soon appear on their front porches and hurry down the steps to buy a paper. Upstairs lights came on first in these two-story frame houses as men and women got out of bed to light a gas lamp or pull the chain of an electric fixture in the center of the bedroom ceiling. With no break in their shouting, the newsboys waited for those who would be coming out their front doors with coins clutched in their fists.

Being a rather large family, we had to share beds. There were continual complaints about a roommate's occupying too much of the bed or hogging the blankets, but the worst of the quarrelsomeness arose from the unresolved disputes between two occupants of the same bedroom over whether the window should be opened to let in the cold night air or kept closed to keep the room cozy and warm. In the bedroom that I shared, the windows were raised by mutual agreement of myself and my brother—which is why, on the dark morning the newsboys came into our block with their "extra" paper, we were jarred into wakefulness by their shouts.

It was family custom in our house to keep the bedroom doors closed. At least part of the reason for this was Father's belief that one's bedroom was his castle, but a more practical reason was that our parents did not want the occupants of one bedroom to be disturbed by a commotion that might occur between the occupants of another.

In the silence of the night, even in so well-built a house, sounds carried. Thus it was that if you had to get up to use the bathroom in the dead of night, you had best be careful to tread softly. Even so, the creaking of the varnished hardwood flooring gave you small stabs of panic. You could see your way from bedroom to bathroom, because a gas jet on the wall of the upper hallway was kept burning on a low flame as a night-light. When you remembered which boards in the flooring creaked and which did not, and if you were careful where you stepped, you could get to the bathroom and back to the bedroom quietly. But you had a guilty feeling when you opened your bedroom door and stepped out, because you could hear Mother stirring in her bed, and you were sorry that you were awakening her.

Mother was the lightest sleeper in the house. Thus it was that when one of the children was running a fever, or having a nightmare, Mother would quietly appear at bedside to see what was the matter. With her bedroom door left ajar, you could discern from Father's rhythmic snoring that he had not been disturbed. Sometimes, in her zeal to be protective, Mother would be in the room sprinkling us with holy water even before the sound of the distant thunder that had awakened her brought in the storm that would seem to shake the house as the flashes of lightning frightened us. When we awakened to the cries of the "Armistice extra" newsboys, it had been reassuring to know that whatever this calling out was all about, Mother would be close at hand. But this night, it was Father who got up.

The children who were awake were instantly aware that it was Father who had gotten up, because his movements in the night were noisier than Mother's. We heard him murmur something to Mother, and there were other sounds from the front bedroom to suggest that he was getting up to investigate the basis of the newsboys' clamoring. The brother with whom I slept was, like me, quite awake when Father stepped out into the hallway, carefully closing the front bedroom door behind him. We knew that he paused at the gas jet to turn up the light for better illumination, because the gas gave off a slight hissing sound when you increased the flow. Then we heard him un-hook the little gate at the top of the stairs, which was put in place every night to preclude the possibility that a child might accidentally topple down the steps. We heard the sounds of his retracting the accordion slats of the gate and starting down the stairs.

We knew from the creaking of the steps how far down the staircase Father was. We were familiar with the particular creaking sounds that each step made as you put your weight on it; the creaking sometimes betrayed us on the nights when interesting company was staying late or there was an all-night wake and we ventured down the stairs to sit on a step and peer through the spaces between the balusters, taking a grip on the mahogony banister, to observe what was going on. It didn't matter to Father when he got up to investigate the predawn cries of "Armistice!" that the stairs were sending out signals of how far down the staircase he was and how soon he would be turning the key in the lock of the front door and making his way outside to buy the "extra" paper.

When Father went out in the dark of morning, and before he had gotten off the front porch and down the steps, we heard him respond to a greeting from some neighbor who was on the same mission. We waited for Father to return to the bed-room to discuss with Mother the great news that had come at this extraordinary hour. Hopefully, his whispered digest would be loud enough for us to get a clue of what the great happening might be. To our regret, Father did not come back upstairs. We heard him turn the key in the front door lock upon his return from buying the "extra" paper, but he had elected to remain downstairs. Our guess was that he was sitting in the front parlor, at the table that held our Tiffany lamp with its clawed feet, reading the newspaper. Actually, having seen at a glance that there was nothing in the "extra" paper that he had not already read, he had gone to the kitchen for a bite of early breakfast. Moments later we heard Mother almost noise-lessly steal out of the front bedroom and go downstairs to join him.

The brother I slept with, every bit as awake as I was, reluctantly stayed with me in our bed, and the two of us speculated on what was happening. As we talked in hushed tones, the cries of the newsboys grew faint as they made their way down the street. Then, as the first glimmer of dawn began to wash away the darkness of the night, we heard the lamplighter on his bicycle, stopping and starting, stopping and starting, as he made his rounds from one lamp post to the next, turning off the gas jets. The porous mantles of the street lights that turned the greenish-golden hue of the burning gas into white light went dark, one by one. Only rarely had we been up early enough to observe this ritual of the lamplighter, but we knew he would be back when evening fell, this time with a torch gripped in one hand as he stolidly went from post to post, to direct his flame into an opening at the bottom of each lantern and light them up again for another night. With dawn breaking and with the lamplighter already on his morning rounds, my brother and I decided to chance venturing downstairs; the worst that could happen to us was that we would be sent back to bed.

Moving stealthily down the stairs and through the hallway toward the kitchen where Mother and Father were to be found, we paused in the dining room to listen to what they were saying. What we heard was Mother say, in a disappointed tone, "So the war is not over," and Father's reply, "No, only the headline of the *Evening Post*'s 'extra' says it is over. Everybody knows it's just about over." Father went on, "It's only a matter of time before the Germans accept the terms of Marshall Foch. Only the Austrians have surrendered, and that was in the *Daily News* last night." In reply, Mother said yes, she knew about the Austrians' having surrendered.

Puttering around in the deliberate fashion of a housekeeper who knows what she was about, tending to the preparations for family breakfast, Mother stopped to say, "There is a chill in the house, John." That was Mother's way of suggesting that he go into the basement and get the furnace roaring. "I think it would be best to wait a bit," Father replied. "The stoking makes a good bit of noise, and the children hear it through the registers, and I think it best that they stay in bed for a while." Mother nodded in agreement. "I'm famished for a cup of coffee," Father went on. "If you will make the coffee, I'll go up and shave and get dressed for work." Mother said she would take care of the coffee; it was nothing, really, she said. Then she urged Father to take a few minutes to have a bite to eat before he went upstairs to get ready for the office. Father smiled. "I've had a piece of your banana cream pie that I was lucky to find in the icebox," he replied. "I guess that will hold me for a while." With that, he got up and started out and immediately discovered my brother and me in the dining room. "Mother!" he cried out in mock alarm, "you'll never guess what I've found in the dining room!" We noted, with relief, that he was smiling and glad to see us.

There could be no denying that the families on our block had reaped a heavy share of the war's heartbreak. As a child, I had found it romantic and exciting when one of the older boys on our block suddenly appeared in uniform. Never imagining that any harm could come to a boy I had come to know, I had been proud in my childish way when I heard that one of our own boys from the block was now in France, "fighting the Huns!" When two or three kids my age would take our lead soldiers into a backyard, using a spoon to dig the trenches that we heard the older people talking about, we would give the names of the boys from our block to the lead soldiers that we credited with heroic feats as we "played war." We played "Kill the Kaiser," too, but only occasionally: nobody wanted his lead soldiers to be on the German side.

All too soon, it seemed—and all too often—a pall would settle on even the five- and six-year-olds in our block when some family got word from the War Department that a soldier-son was now a casualty. We never dreamt that our generation would be called upon to go through the same kind of thing, in the same France and the same Germany. Everyone on the home front seemed to believe that our boys were fighting a war to save democracy and that there would never be anything so frightening as this again. Even five-year-olds were grave as their parents read, line by line, the updated casualty reports in the morning *Tribune*.

I had heard my mother remark to someone that the shadow of death seemed to fall impartially on the rich and the poor. Able-bodied lads in some families had managed, in some way, to avoid the draft that had swept so many other boys into the Army. The relatives of young men in combat referred scornfully to those who had managed to weasel out of it as "slackers"; it was humiliating for a family to have a "slacker." My older brothers were too young to be drafted, and our household suffered no shame. Even as a child, it was vaguely apparent to me that the boys who got excused from the draft, for one reason or another, were the sons of men who had influence or were "well fixed"—meaning, they had money. But there were some wealthy families, such as the Kings who lived on our block, who seemed to think it was a matter of honor for young men to fight for their country, whatever the risks.

The Kings were the wealthiest people on our block. Mr. King was clean-shaven, firm of eye and jaw, and had an overall trimness of tailoring and figure. Mr. King owned a La Salle Street brokerage firm that bore his name, and he reputedly was worth a fortune, but he was too well bred to imply by word or gesture that he was a man of means. The Kings owned the large house at the very end of our block and the adjoining lot on the corner, at Augusta Street, which had been painstakingly transformed into a garden so beautiful it seemed out of place in our neighborhood.

From a story that appeared in the *Chicago Tribune*, we had learned that Mr. King graduated with honors from the U. S. Military Academy at West Point and that his promising career as an officer in the U. S. Army ended when he was seriously hurt in an accident while on maneuvers. Living so close to a man who certainly had done his bit for his country, the people on our block took pride in strolling down the sidewalk in the early morning to watch Mr. King run up the American flag on the metal pole, anchored in a concrete base, at the center of his garden. Mr. King had started doing this on April 7, 1917, the day following the United States' declaration of war against Kaiser Wilhelm's Germany. In the ensuing eighteen months, he had never missed raising the flag in the morning and lowering the flag and folding it triangularly in military fashion at sundown. Somehow, the vision of Mr. King raising his flag reassured everyone on our block that, as frightening as the news from Europe seemed to be, victory would come in good time.

A sadness fell upon our block when Mr. King was observed one morning running up a second flag on his pole. Directly below that of the stars and stripes was a much smaller flag, with a white field, a blue border, and one gold star in the center. A day or two later my father told the family at dinner that the Kings' youngest son, Dickie, had been killed in action. Dickie had served as an infantry lieutenant in the Rainbow Division, under the command of handsome Douglas Mac-Arthur. A photograph of the self-assured MacArthur sometimes appeared in our newspapers, the exploits of the Rainbow Division attracting rather frequent attention of the war correspondents. After dinner on the night that Father informed us of the disheartening news about Dickie, my father put on his coat and hat and, with somber face, left the house; no one had to be told that he was walking down to the Kings' house to extend his sympathies. Only later did we learn that Mother had sent a dozen white roses to Mrs. King, with a note that said, "God love you!"

This was not the first time that Mother had sent roses to a house on our block. She had done so when PFC Bobby Florian's name appeared in the "Killed in Action" column of the *Tribune*, and she had sent flowers to the Widow Kermit when the *Tribune* reported that Bobby Kermit had been wounded in action. My Mother felt particularly sad about Bobby Kermit's being wounded, because he was the widow's only son. It had been the consensus on our block that it was foolhardy for Bobby to enlist; his mother needed him at home. The Kermits were a threadbare family. The two daughters had quit high school to find jobs to keep the wolf away from the door, as the expression goes. On the day that Bobby Kermit's name was in the *Tribune*, Mother did more than send flowers; she called up Mr. Sorenson, who owned the big grocery and meat market on Chicago Avenue, and gave him an extensive list of staples and assorted treats she wanted Sorenson's delivery wagon to drop off at the Widow Kermit's. My younger brother and I couldn't help but hear these instructions, as we had wandered into the house while Mother was on the telephone with Mr. Sorenson. With quiet emphasis, Mother was telling Mr. Sorenson that the Widow Kermit was not to be embarrassed by being told who her benefactor was; Billy Barker, Sorenson's delivery man, was simply to ring the Kermit's back doorbell and bring in the boxes of meat and groceries, explaining only that they were paid for. As Mother put the receiver back on the hook of the telephone, she fixed my brother and me with a gentle look and said, "I think we will keep this a secret," and, young as we were, we understood this was a cross-your-heart-and-hope-to-die situation that obligated you never to disclose what had transpired.

There was yet another family with a son damaged in the war, but Mother did not send roses to them. She dearly wanted to make some kind of gesture of sympathy, and we heard her discussing this with our Dad, but his judgment was that any act of charity in this instance was likely to be misunderstood. The war-damaged boy was Kurt Gruetenberg, eldest son of Mr. and Mrs. Otto Gruetenberg, who had once been part of the social community of our block but, who had withdrawn in frigid seclusion when the United States went to war with Germany. The Gruetenbergs, who had come to the U. S. from some place in Bavaria, had been intensely pro-Kaiser. Otto, who had a good position in a brewery located on Goose Island, requiring that he leave the house early every morning for the long streetcar ride, had argued the cause of his fatherland with harsh good humor, the other men on the block enjoying his blustery responses when they joshed him—until war was declared. Otto Gruetenberg's misplaced patriotism was responsible for the immediate estrangement that set in when war was declared. Everyone had been startled, subsequently, when the eldest Gruetenberg boy appeared in the white cap and bell-bottom trousers of the U. S. Navy, having inexplicably gone into service to fight the Hun. Some of the men on the block, ashamed of themselves for having rejected the Gruetenbergs as traitors, tried to repair their relationship with Otto—but he would have none of it, responding to verbal compliments relating to his son with a guttural growl and scowl. Young Kurt, who was stationed at Great Lakes Naval Training station north of Chicago, came home on weekend leave only two times. The first time, he remained in the Gruetenberg house; the second time, he got drunk in Fogarty's saloon on Lake Street, and companions he had picked up at the bar had to walk him home. Thereafter, he vanished, and nothing was heard of him for many months, until his name appeared in a wounded in action listing in the newspapers. The details of how he had been hurt were never disclosed, but the gossip on our block was that a gun turret had blown up on the destroyer he served on, killing some of his shipmates and wounding others. Then, one September afternoon, Kurt came home. Those who saw him were shocked. He was on crutches, his empty right pants-leg folded up and fixed with a large safety pin at the hip. The right side of his face was blotched with scar tissue, and a livid scar ran from directly below his right ear to the corner of his eye. Kurt was maneuvering with grim confidence on his crutches, and those who saw him—and I was one who did—wondered how he had been able to make it home on the streetcars. In awe and some fright at the sight of this damaged young man, people on the block gaped at him as he made his way along the sidewalk. Kurt kept his eyes on the walk, in the manner of a man who desires to have no contact with anyone. As he neared the Gruetenberg home, his mother and a younger brother came out on the porch. She made no move to race down the steps and sidewalk to hug Kurt and welcome him home; she merely stood on the porch and stared, her thin lips compressed. Even when Kurt reached the foot of the steps and paused as if to gather his strength to make it up to the porch, his mother made no move to help him. The nextdoor neighbors heard Kurt say, "Ma, I'm home." The neighbors said that Mrs. Gruetenberg replied, "Ja, so I see." Mrs. Gruetenberg did not embrace her son when he got up the steps and raised his face to look at her. No words passed between them, the nextdoor neighbors said; Mrs. Gruetenberg merely opened her front door, watched Kurt swing himself in on the crutches, and then followed him, closing the door behind her. A sense of anguish weighed on all who had had a sight of Kurt Gruetenberg's homecoming. The war was going poorly for the Kaiser in September 1918, and the embittered Gruetenbergs had no empathy for anyone who had had a part in this, not even their eldest son.

If there was a hotbed of pro-German sentiment in our block in 1918, it was not in the Gruetenberg household; it was in our house. Working in our house were Buster Brown, a peglegged, mustachioed German who did the cleaning—scrubbing the floors and all of that—and Miss Louise Lerch, a practical nurse who was more German than Buster if you measured the gutturals of her voice and who got paid for doing God knows what. These two bothered me—the pro-Kaiser Buster and Miss Lerch. Both were Bavarian-born, and both had spent most of their lives in Germany. Late-life immigration to America had not minimized their devotion to the fatherland.

Buster Brown, which everyone knew was not his true name, was an erstwhile hobo who had gotten religion when he fell out of a boxcar on a moving freight train. The wheel of the undercarriage severed his left leg. And the Lord appeared to him and said, "Buster, I don't like how you are leading your life. I don't like it at all. Repent, Buster Brown." And he went to the mission and prayed, and the mission got him fixed up with the peg leg and found him jobs as a day worker. He had cropped auburn hair, a florid face with a bushy mustache, and a broad chest that seemed to be popping out of his tightly buttoned vest. He wore a red kerchief around his neck, and the sleeves of his striped work shirt were drawn up and held in place by elastic braces, leaving exposed his strong forearms, thick wrists, and large gnarled hands.

Miss Lerch had been a nurse in Germany. A large-bodied woman, she dressed in clothing that flopped about her and wore flowered hats that never got straight on her head, even though she anchored them with a hat pin. Lerch went home at night loaded with food and old rags and clothing that she would give to the poor, and she always protested when she was paid that she had no use for money and that she had done nothing to earn it, which was close to the truth.

It was part of the daily drill for my Mother to set out on the dining room table at mid-morning a pot of coffee and sweet rolls from Paesch's Bakery or doughnuts brought to a cocoa brown in her cast-iron kettle. Countless mornings, Buster Brown and Miss Lerch accepted Mother's invitation to sit down for a cup of coffee, but never did they look quite comfortable about doing so. It was as if they didn't think it proper to be sharing a repast with the lady of the house. Never did either one decline the invitation, but unfailingly they gave the impression of feeling out of place as they took their chairs at the dining room table.

Buster Brown always was clumsy in taking his place. The peg leg made it difficult for him to maneuver at the dining room table. He moved about the house with agility as he attended to his chores; even when he got on his knees to scrub floors, his handicap did not impede him. But getting into a chair, Brown anxiously looked under the dining room table to make certain he would not carelessly scratch a leg of the table. Invariably it was part of the ritual of the mid-morning coffee break that conversation ceased until everyone was assured that Buster Brown was settled. Mother did not pour coffee until he was fixed in his place with his strong forearms on the table.

Miss Lerch always wore a look of apprehension, her gray-green eyes peering at Buster Brown through the thick lenses of her eyeglasses, as he went through the ritual of sitting down. She would sigh in audible relief when he managed it. Then, fussing with the ankle-length black dress that was several sizes too large for her, she would turn her attention to the goodies that Mother had placed on the table. Miss Lerch expressed delight one might expect from someone who had never seen a cinnamon roll or homemade doughnut—although she was offered a treat like this every day.

It was only after they had helped themselves to rich cream from the small Waterford pitcher and had had a few sips of coffee and munched on pastry that Buster Brown and Miss Lerch would start talking. Without fail, their conversation would begin with mention of some victory the newspapers had credited to the Wehrmacht; their tone of voice suggested that this was great news. Quickly, Mother's helpers would project this modest turn of fortune into the decisive victories soon to come. Buster Brown and Miss Lerch vied with each other in patriotic optimism, but both were careful to specify that it would be the inferior French and British forces who would be taught a lesson. If only in the name of politeness, neither of Mother's helpers would dare offend her with indiscreet remarks that American toops would likewise be decimated. Their expression of criticism of American participation in the war was limited to stony disapproval. American involvement they blamed on misguided leaders in Washington, especially President Woodrow Wilson, who, they said, had been hoodwinked by such devils as Lloyd George of Britain. Americans did not perceive, they said, that war against Germany was not in our national interest.

Mother did not debate them. Her role seemed to be that of interested observer, but she found these morning sessions over coffee to be highly entertaining. Occasionally Buster Brown or Miss Lerch, both of whom professed to be deeply religious, would say with conviction that Germany would win because, after all, God was on Germany's side; Mother would giggle.

Lerch was a devout Catholic, leading to religious quarrels with Buster Brown, a devout Lutheran. Lerch said that Martin Luther was a renegade priest who had lost his soul, and how could you claim to be faithful to God, following the precepts of a renegade priest? Buster would explode. Baby Loretta in her lap, Mother would sit at the dining room table, a passive witness to the daily argument, giggling every now and then when one of the disputants put forth a particularly spurious bit of logic. Only when she decided that time was wasting and the house was not getting cleaned would she bring the argument to a close.

It made the kids in our house feel bad to gather from vague remarks that sometimes passed between our parents that part of Buster Brown's wages were somehow being transmitted to the Kaiser—although this was my father's little joke. It was likewise unpleasant to watch Miss Lerch set out for the street-car each evening with bags of food and clothing that Mother gave her to distribute to the needy in the economically depressed part of the city where she lived. Was Mother naively helping to feed and clothe German sympathizers? This was what our "Aunt Hannah" persisted in saying—and whereas Aunt Hannah was given to exaggeration, there seemed always to be a vein of truth in even her wildest statements. Her remarks about giving things to the enemy troubled the kids in our house. It troubled me, at any rate.

Aunt Hannah was known in our neighborhood as someone who relished an argument. She was married to a tall, taciturn policeman named Jack Kerr, who was an Episcopalian, but a very nice man for all of that. Uncle Jack was as tight-lipped as Aunt Hannah was garrulous. On rare occasions, when Mother took us on the streetcars to South Water Market, which was located along the riverfront downtown, we would get a glimpse of Uncle Jack dealing with the snarl of streetcars and wagon traffic at the Wabash Avenue bridge, which was his station. It was impressive to observe the authority he displayed in dealing with the chaotic jam that might have provoked despair in a cop who was less imposing or who was lacking in self-assurance.

Aunt Hannah and Uncle Jack appeared to be quite compatible, but they were direct opposites of each other. She was plump, and he was trim. She was inclined to wear colorful dresses, even to wakes, and he was neatly conservative. Aunt Hannah was a social creature who could not exist without people to mingle with; Uncle Jack was satisfied to keep to himself. She delighted in gossip and church bazaars and going to the picture shows; as a traffic cop who had to be on his corner every morning at an early hour, coming home in mid-afternoon when South Water Market was shuttering, Uncle Jack went to bed shortly after supper. He needed his rest for the rigorous day that lay ahead.

Aunt Hannah and Uncle Jack were actually not related to us, except in some distant way—being cousins of my mother's cousins. They were childless, which was possibly the reason Aunt Hannah made a fuss over the kids in our family, bringing us bags of penny candy and small toys, by way of maintaining her standing with us. They lived on the next block but spent a great deal of time in our house. My mother seemed to enjoy the frequent visits of Aunt Hannah, even though her presence interrupted the household routine when she dropped in unannounced. It was taken for granted that when Aunt Hannah stopped by she would say something outrageous to start an argument.

Mother would often giggle on those mornings when Aunt Hannah Kerr dropped in to have coffee. Aunt Hannah had a reputation for taking a stand in any discussion, her practice being to argue the minority position. Buster Brown and Miss Lerch would seem to draw back when Aunt Hannah appeared, as if getting prepared for her verbal bombardment.

On the days that she stayed, Buster Brown did not get his work done. Aunt Hannah followed him about the house in unrelenting continuation of the arguments that had started between them when they squared off at mid-morning at the dining room table. If Aunt Hannah remained at the table with Mother, Buster Brown passed to and fro with his mop and broom and cleaning bucket, passing low-keyed insults.

If there were a basis for Aunt Hannah's badgering of Buster Brown, it was her indignation over the rise in the cost of living that had resulted from the Kaiser's war. "Do you know that butter is twenty-seven cents a pound, Buster Brown? Do you know that pork chops are twenty cents a pound? Do you know that Mr. Sorenson is having a hard time getting sugar? This is what you have done to us with this war of yours!"

Buster Brown would cringe under the onslaught, but grimly he would reply that prices would have stayed the same if we had minded our own business and stayed out of a war that did not concern us. "It is the punishment of God, Mrs. Kerr, the high prices," he would declare. And Aunt Hannah would fling her arms over her head in frustration. It seemed to Aunt Hannah that every time she talked Buster Brown into a corner he slid out of it by attributing whatever it was she complained about to the will of God.

Sort of a student of continental intrigue, Brown had read

up on Bismarck and the War of 1871. He argued at great length that Germany was the salvation of Christianity and was merely doing God's work in fighting the heathenism of France and England. Aunt Hannah Kerr would be exasperated: "They are killing people. They are murdering innocent women and children. How is it God's work to kill innocent people?" Buster would stoically reply, "God works in mysterious ways."

Aunt Hannah got pleasure out of baiting Buster Brown and Miss Lerch about their pro-Kaiser bias. The two Germans sputtered protests that Aunt Hannah seemed to enjoy. But she could just as easily take the other side of the argument when an ardently pro-President Wilson lady dropped in to visit with my mother. I couldn't figure out, sometimes, which side Aunt Hannah was on. Aunt Hannah made my head ache. Being only six years of age, I didn't know too much about this Kaiser that everyone was always talking about. I understood, of course, that the Kaiser was a terrible man who was in charge of the German army. Even at age six, I was aware that the Kaiser was a very bad man, and it always made me uneasy to sit at our dining room table when Buster and Miss Lerch were having coffee and hear their ardent pro-Kaiser talk. My mother, sitting at her customary place at the end of the table, never disputed anything that Buster and Miss Lerch said in admiration of the heroic Germans. She simply smiled, sitting quietly with her cup of tea until she thought it was time for her "help" to get back to work. Then she would stand, and our pro-Kaiser Germans would hastily get to their feet, murmur thanks for what they always referred to as "the tasty repast," and hurry back to work. Several times, though, I overheard my mother expressing concern to my father about the pro-German bias of Buster and Miss Lerch. My mother was fearful that, if they did not exercise some discretion, Buster and Miss Lerch were likely to be arrested.

My father did not take any stock in the notion that the Kaiser was a devil who dealt in unspeakable atrocities. When the newspaper cartoonists depicted Kaiser Wilhelm as a butcher who sliced up children, my father had declared that this was patent nonsense. My father's view was that the Kaiser deserved blame for having launched a war that was without equal in history, but that even the Kaiser was constrained to conduct his war in a civilized fashion. My father was second to no one in deploring the suffering and waste of life of the Great War that lay on Kaiser Wilhelm's conscience. He bought greater numbers of liberty bonds than he could reasonably afford, holding that those who were not in combat were obligated to give financial support to those who were. He nonetheless expressed disapproval of the newspaper cartoons that bred Americans' hatred of the Germans by portraying the Kaiser as a bloodthirsty brute. My father's contempt for these cartoons was so freely revealed that it put him at odds with some of his superiors at the bank, judging from the disclosures, made to Mother at our dinner table, of cutting remarks that some of the men he worked for had made to him. These reports created a fear in some of us that he was in jeopardy of getting canned.

In our block, Father's outspokenness had troubled such good friends as Mr. King, even though Mr. King had a practice of asking Father for his opinion of developments in the war. In response to a question, Father would express his opinion, for example, that the Kaiser was probably no worse a man than the leader of any other nation that was struggling to survive in the bloodiest of wars. And it was not only to Mr. King that Father would be so candid. Many others shook their heads in grim dismay when they heard Father say, as he sometimes did, that they'd live to see the day when Germany would be welcomed back into the family of nations. Father was too highly regarded to admit any reckless notion on the part of the neighbors that his views were dangerously close to being treasonous. But some of the older kids in our family, taunted by classmates over something unpatriotic that Father had said, were disturbed by his candor.

On the morning of November 11, 1918, the telephone company's coin collector trotted up the steps of our front porch, breathless as always, on his monthly visit to empty the box of our telephone. Customarily, our collector came into the house with his cap on his head, his little bag of coins gripped in one hand and his account book in the other. Sitting at what we called our library table, in the front parlor, he dumped the coins from our telephone onto the table, spread them out, and with what seemed to me to be amazing speed, he started counting them out. Standing off to the side as he did this, I was transfixed, as always, as the fingers of his right hand deftly slid the nickels, two at a time, into his cupped left hand, pressed to the edge of the table. With dexterity, he effortlessly culled the slugs that my mother, as all housewives, had put into the telephone when she ran out of nickels. With speed and skill, he stacked the nickels and put them into rolls that he would carry away, and he made notations on the number of nickels and slugs in order to settle up the question of how much the phone company owed my mother as her percentage of the nickels and how much my mother owed the company for the slugs.

My mother never stood there to watch the count; she trusted the collector to give her "honest measure." However, my mother was particular, when the collector was settling the account, to get all of her slugs back; she needed the slugs for telephoning when she didn't have a nickel and the telephone company operator directed her to deposit one before putting her call through. When my mother had given the collector whatever it was that she owed the telephone company, and when the collector had given my mother her slugs, the monthly visitation was over. Picking up his bag and his book, the collector hastily went on his way to the next house.

Apart from mumbling hello and good-bye, the collector didn't waste any time in conversation. It being my mother's custom to offer a little something to anyone who came into our home, she would always invite the telephone company man to take a few moments to have coffee and taste her homemade doughnuts or something like that. The collector, always in a fret to get on with his work, invariably declined—tipping the peak of his cap by way of saying thank you. But on November 11, 1918, the telephone man unhesitantly said yes, that would be very nice. This was a very special day, which was why the collector decided that the telephone company wouldn't mind if he took a few minutes of working time to have coffee.

In making his rounds from house to house, the collector got to hear a great deal of the neighborhood gossip. At least with regard to the families on his route who had a telephone, he couldn't help but hear the good news, the scandals, and the family problems as he hurried from house to house emptying the coin boxes. Servicing so many phones on a regular basis, the collector got to hear private conversations he wasn't supposed to hear. But like a priest in the confessional who is bound to secrecy, our telephone company collector was the soul of discretion. He never, to my knowledge, revealed anything about anyone. This day then, when Mother served this man coffee and sat down at the library table with him to have a cup of her Oolong and Gunpowder tea, she was startled when our tight-lipped collector took a sip of his coffee and said:

"I hear there's gonna be a war celebration on the block."

It was apparent that my mother hadn't known about this, and she said so.

"I didn't hear who started it," the collector went on, "but the celebration's all that everybody's talkin' about in the houses I was in before I got here. They're gonna have a bonfire—right out there on the street. The women are gonna bake pies and cakes and things. Sounds to me like they're plannin' a big night to celebrate the end of the war."

When the collector left, my mother hurried off to get our copy of the *Chicago Tribune* to read about the ending of the Great War. The same as other families on our block who were well fixed, as the saying went, we got home delivery of the morning *Tribune*. At night my father would bring in a copy of the *Chicago Daily News*, which he had paid his two cents for downtown and had read on the elevated on his ride home from work at "the bank." It was my mother's custom, when the dinner table was cleared and her kitchen was spotless again, to sit down in "her chair" in what we knew as the "back parlor" to read the *Tribune* and the *News* from front page to back, skipping only the sports. I was impressed by the importance of the telephone man's information when I observed that my mother immediately wanted to have documentation about the ending of the war.

My mother was disheartened to discover that the home-delivered edition of the *Tribune* didn't have any news about the ending of the war. There was a great deal of information in the *Tribune* about the "False Armistice." And I guess there was a story or two on the front page that said that, even though the first announcements had been premature, the "real" Armistice was imminent. But there was hardly enough reason in that to justify a big celebration over the ending of the war.

Our household had had a painful experience with the False Armistice. My father had been late getting home from work the previous evening, having had trouble getting through the mobs of revelers, many of them drunk. My father had looked harried. We had been shocked to see that his suit and his overcoat, my father being meticulous about his clothes, were blotched with the stain of something that someone had spilled on him. Coming in, and being greeted by my mother and all the kids, my father had walked directly back to the dining room, uncapped the decanter of whiskey that he kept on the sideboard, and poured himself a stiff drink. He had downed his bourbon, taken off his overcoat and hung it on the hall tree, and walked to his chair in the front parlor, where he sat down to recount the details of the problems he had had trying to get through the mobs downtown to the elevated station. Having learned before leaving the First National Bank that the widespread report of the war's being over was false, he said it infuriated him to be jostled around by a mob of drunks who were making fools of themselves over an historic event that had not occurred. My mother, supportive of my father, as always, dismissed the matter of someone's having soiled my father's suit and overcoat and excused herself to go put dinner on the table. My two older sisters went off to help her. It saddened me to see my carefully groomed father sitting there in his soiled suit.

Dinner that evening was much the same as always. The table was set on a freshly ironed white linen tablecloth. There was a silver setting at every place, and my father's bone-handled carving set at his. There was a fresh linen napkin for each one of us. A Waterford goblet, with fresh water and ice, was at each place. There was a dinner plate of mother's best china in front of everyone, my father moving his away to make room for the platter with the roast of prime beef that Mother carried in from the kitchen. But a pall hung over all of us that evening. The kids felt bad about what had happened to our father. My father had put the matter out of his mind and dominated the conversation with his customary reports on the interesting things that had occurred during the day at the bank. My mother, who had spent hours preparing this meal, was gracious and cheerful as always. But one of my older brothers complained that the roast beef didn't "taste good," and I thought there would be a flare-up of tempers. My father looked annoyed, but the crisis melted away when my mother said that she was sorry but the meat had been in the oven too long.

On that day when the telephone company collector gave us the news that there was to be a victory party in our block that night, my mother soon received confirmation that there was nothing "false" about *this* Armistice; my father called from his office at the bank to tell her it was official now—the war was over. I remember thinking it strange that the First National Bank had information that the home-delivered edition of the *Chicago Tribune* did not have—but, of course, all of the newspapers had the story now; they simply hadn't had time to get their updated editions off the press, loaded onto the circulation wagons, and out on the street. A short time after my mother got the phone call, the newsboys of all the newspapers were in our block with their "extra" editions about the ending of the Great War. By that time the ladies who were striving to get the block celebration organized came up our front steps, put a finger on our bell, and told me, when I answered the door, that they wanted to see my mother.

This was proving to be a most exciting day. For some reason—possibly because I had been upset over the problems my father had had the previous evening in trying to get through the False-Armistice crowd and because I had been awakened before dawn the previous day by the cries of the newsboys— my mother hadn't sent me to school on November 11, 1918.

When the neighbor ladies came in and told my mother about

the big victory celebration that the families on our block would have that night, my mother expressed her pleasure at hearing of the plan and went to the telephone to call Mr. Sorenson, at our grocery, to ask that Mr. Barker, the delivery man, put twenty dollars worth of frankfurters on the wagon and bring them to her for the celebration. The neighbor ladies had been astounded. Twenty dollars worth of frankfurters! My mother ordered all the hot dog buns that Mr. Sorenson had available and asked politely, if he didn't have enough, could he send Mr. Barker over to Mr. Paesch, at the bakery, to see if he had any to spare. The neighbor ladies were beside themselves at hearing of this extravagant spending. When my mother told Mr. Sorenson that jars of mustard would be needed and relish and I don't remember what else, all of it to go on her bill— the ladies squealed with delight. I had no idea what my father would think of all this spending—the total adding up to fifty dollars or more, which was a considerable sum in those days, when the average working man was fortunate to be making twenty a week. But I heard my mother mention what she had done when my father telephoned late in the day, which was his custom when he was leaving the office, and he hadn't said anything negative to upset my mother.

My mother was perhaps the most generous soul on the block; she gave to everybody. The kids taunted us that the hoboes who came to the back door, pleading for something to eat, regarded my mother as such an easy score that they had chalked the word on our back fence. Investigating this, we discovered it to be true that somebody had chalked a mysterious message on the alley side of our fence.

Buster, as always, took delivery of the stuff my mother had ordered from Sorenson's Grocery and Meat Market when Mr. Barker came to the back door with his big boxes. Buster, as always, put the nonperishables neatly on shelves in the pantry and got the things that needed refrigeration into the icebox. He chopped up a small block of ice to cover the boxes containing the great quantity of hot dogs. But it was evident from his dour expression that this day of defeat for the Kaiser was a bitter day for Buster Brown. At mid-afternoon, Mother got her purse to give the two-dollar-per-day wages to both Buster and Miss Lerch. My mother made a special effort, it seemed to me, to be kind to them, and she earnestly invited them to the victory celebration. But she had paid them early, an indication that they would be free to leave as soon as they had finished the most important of their chores, and I could tell from the energy with which they went about their work that they were eager to leave. And, with looks of bitterness, they soon did. My mother, I think, had expected that they would do so.

I was relieved when our "help" left for the day. Buster went out the back door, and Miss Lerch went out the front, on the apparent assumption that this was her privilege by reason of her higher station in life. Even as a kid it fascinated me that although they both reached the sidewalk at the same instant, they did not socialize, walking apart as they set out to Chicago Avenue, a block and a half away, to get the streetcar. It puzzled me that their pro-Kaiser comradeship did not carry over when they left our house. Even as a boy, it was evident to me that Buster Brown and Miss Lerch were not too bright—but I guess they had enough sense to keep their mouths shut, their heavy German accents being a dead giveaway in a neighborhood where a considerable number of gold stars were on view in front-parlor windows. On the joyful day when the people on our block were celebrating the military defeat of the Kaiser, I imagine that my mother was glad to get her German-speaking "help" out of sight. If dirty dishes and pots and pans accumulated from Mother's contributions to the celebration, Buster Brown might have to pay for his time off by cleaning up the mess first thing in the morning, though my mother was not the kind of homemaker who could abide having a dirty kitchen, and the chances were that she and the girls would wash everything and put it all away before going to bed. But even as a kid, barely able to make a judgment about something like this, I thought my mother showed relief at having sent Buster and Miss Lerch on their way; Lord knows what kind of unfortunate remarks they might have made, if they had mixed in with the jubilant crowd that was celebrating the defeat of the Kaiser.

My mother had some reservations about the propriety of our block's having a grand celebration to mark the ending of the Great War. I heard her tell my father "it didn't seem right" to celebrate when the war had placed "so heavy a burden of sorrow" on so many families. "It doesn't seem right to be joyous," she said, "when so many families—right here on our block—have lost a son or have had him come home a cripple." As always when my mother showed deep sadness, my father didn't say much in reply; he simply put his arm around my mother and squeezed her gently. Even though I was but a child, it made a deep impression on me to witness this; it is a rich experience for a child, I think, to see that two people who love each other can give support to each other, with neither of them saying much.

It eased our anxieties over Mother's distress when we observed our father going to the telephone, on the night of our block's celebration of the Armistice, to invite the Kings to come sit on our porch for a good view of whatever exciting things would be going on. It pleased me, at any rate, when Mr. King seemed to be thanking my father and accepting the invitation. Even as a child, I thought this was no small gesture. I was certain of this when my mother smiled with pleasure as my father told her the Kings would be coming to our house. My mother had been terribly upset about the Kings, because, just a month or so earlier, Mr. King had run up yet another small white flag, with the gold star in the center. The people on our block had felt terrible about this, because they knew it meant that the Kings had been notified that yet another of their sons had been killed in action. I had been listening when my mother called the florist on Chicago Avenue to order another delivery of white roses to Mrs. King. My mother had had trouble speaking, and tears had welled in my eyes. A family with two sons getting killed in a war!

All morning and well into the afternoon the older boys on our block worked at the task of preparing for a huge bonfire that would extend across the frontage of five or six houses. Big, strong boys had managed the herculean task of hauling the trunks of dead trees from new housing lots in the next block to the asphalt pavement of our street. The timbers were so heavy and large that it had taken about a dozen of the older boys to get the job done. They had managed, somehow, to inch the trees along—with much huffing and groaning—and a couple of the incorrigible boys scandalized the ladies of the neighborhood with occasional bursts of swearing. In anticipation of broiling juicy hot dogs and baking potatoes in the coals, makeshift grills were fashioned on the front lawns, at a safe distance from the long bed of timbers and tree chunks that would be blazing in the street. When the older children of our family returned home from Our Lady Help of Christians School for lunch and saw this work in progress they were mystified and then delighted to learn that preparations were under way for a grand celebration of the Armistice. And they did not return to school that afternoon. Before my mother had gently suggested to Buster Brown that he might like to leave early for a change, he glumly carried out the boxes of Orange Crush and other bottled refreshment that had been delivered by Mr. Barker to our house. In due time my older brothers would carry out the boxes of frankfurters and the rolls and the relishes and mustard.

The lamplighter man came along, laboriously pedaling his bicycle, as dusk was falling. With the four- or five-foot ladder on his shoulder, one hand holding it in place and the other hand guiding the bicycle and gripping his torch, he gazed in silent disbelief at the trunks of trees and kindling on the pavement. Showing unusual interest in what was going on, the lamplighter man took a moment to watch the preparations before he set his little ladder against the lamp post, climbed two or three rungs to reach the gas vent, opened it, and ignited the gas with his torch.

Ladies of the block had pretty well finished their chores of setting up tables for the celebration treats and bringing out the huge galvanized pans that they boiled their laundry in, by the time that the lamplighter had appeared. Food would be spread in generous quantity on the tables, and the laundry pans would be filled with blocks of ice, to be chopped into small chunks with ice picks to chill the soda pop that Sorenson's, the patriotic merchant on Chicago Avenue, had provided.

Some of the old gentlemen of our block, smoking their pipes and cigars, stood in little groups on the sidewalk, soberly observing all of this. One of the old-timers declared over and over again that this was going to be the grandest celebration that a man could hope to see. And everyone was saying that it was amazing how thoroughly everything had been arranged in so short a period of time.

When it started to get dark the older boys splashed some kind of flammable liquid on the timbers and set them afire with torches; it was grand to hear the crackling as the flames swept through the dried felled poplars. The fires were glowing nicely when "the men who worked downtown"—and this included my father—returned from work.

At supper time—and I never could figure out why our evening meal was "dinner" and most other families had "supper"—the scene went sort of dead. Most of the families had gone into their houses for the evening meal, leaving only a few of the older boys to keep their eyes on the fires, for safety's sake. But people started coming out of their homes in short order, and the sidewalks and the clear parts of the street soon crowded up. My father, in coat, vest, and tie, leaned on the banister of our front porch.

A huge log out in front of our house was glowing when, as darkness fell to usher in our block's night of celebration, the Kings arrived. My parents were happy to see them and placed them in the most comfortable chairs on the porch, my mother making a special effort to make Mrs. King welcome. Apart from the wakes in our house when one of the children had died, the Kings had never been in our home. We all felt honored that they had come. My mother brought out a silver tray with a pitcher of root beer on it and poured some into one of her best glasses for Mrs. King and urged her to try some homemade cookies. My father produced his very best whiskey in a decanter, but informed Mr. King that there was also some good Scotch if he preferred that. The Kings and my parents settled in for a pleasant evening, and I slipped down the stairs to mingle with the crowd, my mother cautioning me to be careful.

There was a great deal of feasting. The smaller children were permitted to get close enough to the fire to roast "weenies" impaled on the end of a stick that one of the older men had whittled during the day. A sizable number of these sticks were available. There were tables of cookies and cakes and cheese and cold cuts and a seemingly endless supply of bottled pop to wash it all down. When my father and Mr. King came down for a closer look, my father brought along two quarts of his Waterfill & Frazer whiskey, to provide a little nip for the men who might want something "a bit stiffer" than Orange Crush and Coca-Cola. Our block had a grand time on the night the Great War ended.

Here and there, as the hours sped by, the celebrants took to singing songs. At first two or three shy voices could be heard, singing the lyrics of the war songs. Then the volume would swell, as ten or fifteen individuals lent their voices to the chorus and everyone sang with more confidence. Soon there were several groups, here and there on the block, their voices raised in different selections. It sounded discordant to me, the melody of one song clashing with the melody of another. Then, as if all of the groups came to realize that this was a night of reconciliation, everyone joined in together, and soon the whole block, on the sidewalks and the porches, thundered out the words of "Keep the Home Fires Burning," and "It's a Long, Long Way to Tipperary," and "Over There." A glorious, memorable, wonderful night—that night our block celebrated the end of The Great War.

I heard one of the old-timers say, as he gazed into the glowing embers in our street with a soulful look in his eyes, that it was an honor to be present because this was an historic occasion. Everyone within earshot nodded when he said, "We shall not see this again, because the nations of this world have found that getting locked in the combat of a great war is not the sensible way to settle their differences." The people around him murmured their agreement and slowly began to drift away, returning to their homes. I wasn't sure that I understood what the old-timer had said. I was tired and headed for home, because I wanted to go to bed.

Except for the pavement of our street, where the asphalt had bubbled up under the heat of the celebration night fires, things in our block quickly returned to normal. The damage to our street was a matter of concern to my father and other householders. My father sometimes went down from our front porch to join in discussions with the other men as to how to go about getting the city to repair it. Someone apparently telephoned the alderman, because he came over one day to inspect the pavement. He brought a couple of other men with him, and a group of us small boys tagged along as the alderman led his companions from spot to spot. We didn't dare get too close to them, but I got close enough to hear the alderman say, "Damned shame!" and "Damned reckless!" My impression was that this man, with his grim look, thought it had been terrible for our block to have celebrated the ending of the Great War by building fires on the pavement. In due time, Mr. Smith or Mr. King, or someone who was not timid about such things, called City Hall, and trucks came out and workers fixed up our street and most everyone seemed to forget about the damage our fires had done. But I hadn't much liked the alderman's swearing about our celebration; everyone had had such a grand time. When—in due course—he came to our house to ask my father to help him out on something, it made me mad, as the kids would say, when I answered the door and had to let him in to talk with my father. What good, I wondered, is an alderman who doesn't want people to have a good time celebrating the ending of a terrible war!

CHAPTER 2

WHERE YOU CAME FROM
IS WHAT YOU ARE

A T OUR HOUSE THE DAY BEGAN, so far as the children in their second-story beds were concerned, with the sounds of Father's stoking the furnace. The clanking noises carried from the basement to the cast-iron registers that were recessed in the flooring of the bedrooms. The grinding of coffee invariably was the next sound that those of us who lingered in our beds would hear. We didn't get up right away, because experience had taught us that, if you delayed for a few minutes, the heat would then be wafting up from the registers. But the pleasant sound of Father's grinding the coffee alerted us that, wanting to or not, we would soon have to get out of bed. We competed among ourselves for use of the solitary bathroom; all the children wanted to dress there, because it seemed to be the first room in the house to get warm. Father, of course, had first call on the use of the bathroom. But another morning sound alerted us that Father had finished shaving and the bathroom would soon be free; the signal was the slap of the case as he put his straight-edge razor away.

It was in the kitchen, though, that the day began for all the family. For about a half hour every morning, our kitchen was the center of activity in our house. Mother was well along in her preparations for breakfast by the time the first of the children put in an appearance. Almost always, my two sisters were the first to be scrubbed and dressed and ready for the day; the two older boys generally had to be sternly ordered by Father to get up and get dressed.

Breakfast was substantial. The kitchen table would be set by the time the kids came downstairs. The coffeepot, kept hot over a low gas flame on the stove, would give out occasional burps, as if trying to call attention to itself. At every place setting at the kitchen table would be half a grapefruit, each segment having been cut loose by Mother and her paring knife, or a generous glass of orange juice, extracted from fresh oranges on the pointed, ribbed cone of the glass strainer. A loaf of homemade bread, the bread knife alongside, would be on a small cutting board. There would be a dish of butter on the table and dishes of homemade strawberry jam and grape jelly. The quart bottles of golden-colored milk, delivered to our back door by Mr. Foster of the Borden Dairy, were kept in the icebox. The kids who preferred milk to coffee would help themselves, fetching the milk bottle out of the icebox; the cream in the neck of the bottle would have been poured off for use in the coffee or for later use in the preparation of dessert for dinner.

Sizzling in the frying pan would be slices from the big slab of bacon that Father brought home from George F. Harding's, downtown. A large iron frying pan, with a bit of pure lard simmering, would be ready to accommodate those who wanted French toast; quickly, yet seemingly unhurried, Mother would whip up an egg into which she'd dip slices of homemade bread before slipping them into the frying pan; a glob of butter melted on each piece as it was placed before the child along with a can of Log Cabin maple syrup. In winter months there would be Cream of Wheat or oatmeal in the double boiler. A pan of water might be simmering so that eggs of good size could quickly be boiled. If one of the kids wanted scrambled eggs and toast, Mother would smile and whip up the eggs and let the child make the toast; the child would pull down the sides of the toaster, which sat on the stove, place a slice of bread on each side, then let the springs snap up again; then everyone would be on the alert that the gas flame under the toaster was not too high, because burning toast created a disagreeable odor— and led to vociferous objections by the other children.

Within the hour, all would be out of the house. The first to leave was Father, who would walk to the Laramie Avenue station of the Lake Street Elevated. Father was almost always well on his way by the time any of the children appeared in the kitchen. The children who were present when he got up from his breakfast, wiping his chin with the cotton napkin, would get a peck on the cheek from Father, after Mother, whom he called "Dear Heart," had received hers. Father didn't trifle with dour warnings to the children to work hard at school and behave themselves; the children were aware of what was expected of them. As the first to leave, Father was spared the aggravation of witnessing the minor panics that seemed to arise every morning as the kids scurried to get out of the house. One of the kids seemed always to have misplaced something. There was often a frantic search for hats or gloves. There was near-hysterical alarm when a child could not find homework that had been placed somewhere for safe keeping, the child unable to remember where. In this momentary chaos, however, everything would be found, and, with a kiss from Mother, one by one the children would be on their way. My two sisters generally were the first to leave, invariably with a departing word to my younger brother and me to help Mother and be good boys. The four older children set out with various degrees of enthusiasm on the five-block walk to Our Lady Help of Christians School, our parish grammar school, where BVM nuns wore large, black birdlike hats, with starched white crusader bonnets underneath; flowing black habits that extended to the tips of their shoes; and around their waists, huge strings of rosary beads, with a four-inch bronze crucifix.

The house was lonesome when my father and the four older children had gone. There was much to keep Mother occupied until they all came home again. But my younger brother and

I felt left out of things when the others had gone. We had not much to do except invent ways to entertain ourselves until the kids came home at noon for lunch; and then we had the long afternoon, interrupted only by our mandatory naps. However, being too young to be flying out the front door every morning for school, I had the pleasure of spending the day with my mother—getting a chance to learn something about what was going on in the neighborhood, to listen to the conversation of the various women who came in to visit my mother, and, as Christmas approached, to study the boxes that would arrive from Marshall Field's.

I very much enjoyed spending the day with my mother, sitting alongside her in the kitchen as she cooked or ironed. She was not a person to pry into anyone's affairs, not even a child's, and she kept me entranced with her matter-of-fact remarks about her brothers and sisters—or her mother and father, both of whom had been born in a place called Bannon-outside-the-walls of Cork, in the early 1800s and had come to the United States in the 1840s on separate sailing ships. Sitting alongside my mother, I learned many things. She told me that her father, who lived not far from us, had as a young man developed skill at the highly dangerous work of setting dynamite. My mother said it was treacherous stuff to work with—"the slightest mistake likely to blow you to Kingdom Come"—but that her father had believed that a man had to take some risks if he had ambitions to make something of himself. My mother made a point of telling me that her dynamite stories were hearsay. "This was in Ireland," she told me, "and I was not there, nor have I ever been there, being born right here in Chicago. But we had the house on Dekoven Street, you know—across the street from Mrs. O'Leary whose cow supposedly kicked over the lantern? Friends of your grandfather or your grandmother, *my* mother—and *her* maiden name was Murphy, too—would come sit in the kitchen and talk about Ireland as they sipped coffee or whiskey. And someone would mention the dynamite, and they'd all start talking about it. That's how I came to know about the dynamite."

From what she had gathered from the conversation of the

men sitting around the kitchen table at her father's house on Dekoven Street, my mother told me, her father's skill with dynamite had been very much in demand by those who were building factories in Cork and warehouses in the dock area of the port city of Cobh, and that her father had earned good wages. Unfortunately, however, his reputation for being skilled with dynamite was his undoing; it had made him suspect in British eyes and he had been forced to flee Ireland in the 1840s with a price on his head.

In Boston, my grandfather had been discouraged by the anti-Catholic bias that he found. At so many employment offices he encountered the sign: "No Irish Need Apply." Her father, my mother said, felt bad that having escaped from the British in Ireland, he had come face to face with the same bigotry in Boston, Massachusetts. And so, she said, he moved on to Chicago—in hope of better fortune.

At a very tender age I sat quietly at my mother's side—entranced by her little stories of what my roots had been. A hunger to know about my beginnings seemed to have taken hold of me on those many afternoons when I sat alongside my mother as she did her ironing and I listened to her tales of what used to be. My mother seemed to realize, from my rapt attention perhaps, that I was fascinated by her little stories of the past. Her stories filled a need in me. Sometimes she would pause, her hand gripping the handle of the "flat iron" that had been heated on our gas stove, and gaze out the window as if looking at some distant place. I used to wonder: where had she gone?

As I got older and got into the business of checking up on information, I would smile when I chanced upon confirmation of something my mother had mentioned to me in the long ago. It pleased me greatly to come upon evidence that substantiated one of my mother's stories. It made me proud to discover that my mother had been what we call a highly reliable source. I have thought of her with gratitude, these many years, as I struggled to get information and tell it straight.

I had no idea of what Father did all day at "his" bank. It had not been by chance that my father had gone to work at the First National Bank of Chicago. My grandmother, née Sullivan, had insisted. The story was that Grandfather O'Connor, as a lad in Cobh, had run away from home and enlisted as cabin boy on a sailing ship bound for America; the story was that my grandfather, one of 11 children, was not missed until it was time to outfit the kids in a new pair of shoes, and his parents found they need pay for only 10 pair. That was the story, but I cannot attest to its accuracy. Be that as it may, my grandfather did, in fact, spend his adult life as a master of sailing ships. And because of his work, my grandfather had been away from home most of the time. Even when he gave up the oceans of the world and confined himself to running ships on the Great Lakes—making his home at Taylor and Halsted streets, near downtown Chicago—he was gone a good deal of the time. And in bad weather the waters of Lake Michigan are quite as treacherous as any ocean; old-timers frequently talked about the great number of ships that had been lost with "all hands" while attempting to bring down to Chicago the bulky rafts of timbers needed to rebuild the city after the Great Fire of 1871. My grandfather had been lucky enough, or skillful enough, to get safely into Chicago with his rafts of logs. My grandfather, it was said, had "made a decent living" with sailing ships—but my grandmother, the story was, wanted her two sons in less dangerous and "more respectable" work. So she insisted that my grandfather get employment for my father and his older brother Michael at the First National Bank when they were in their teens.

It frustrated me, across the years, that I was unable to discover my grandfather's connections at the First National Bank. The closest I came was one old-timer's recollection at a wake. He told me that my grandfather and a pal of his named Captain Hickey had been important sea captains and would have known the big bankers, and "it was quite an ordinary thing for a man to ask a friend to do a little kindness for him."

The impression I received as a child was that my grandfather was not altogether pleased with the arrangement he had worked out. However, my father was. As children, my father and his brother had had to spend a month every summer with my grandfather on a sailing ship. My father, in terse recollection of these summers, told me the worst part of it was getting becalmed for days, or even weeks, when the winds died out and the big sailing ship lay almost motionless on the water.

My father was the only breadwinner on the block who rode the El each day; the elevated was faster than the streetcars, but it entailed a one-mile walk to get to it, plus a steep climb up the stairs at the station. No one else on the block shared my father's notion that it was worth the effort. Winter and summer, in sunshine, rain, or snow, my father left the house precisely at 7:30 every morning and returned exactly at 5:00 P.M. Neighbors would often be heard to say that a person could set his watch by John O'Connor.

Once each year, my father set out, after having had his dinner, to pay a call on Clamitz & Pfetzing, the Jewish tailors at Madison and Laramie. In good times or bad, even when extraordinary medical expenses disrupted his carefully calculated family budget, my father bought a new suit in the autumn. Every three or four years, he bought a topcoat or a heavy dress coat instead. Each new suit or coat was almost identical to the one it replaced. His taste ran to oxford gray or black, with perhaps a faint pencil stripe in the fabric. Occasionally, my mother would gently suggest that he might consider a suit a bit more dashing. He remained firm, however, and he felt justified in this when, after several fittings, the new suit was ready, and my mother expressed the opinion that the subdued material was indeed best for him. My father wore stylish dark leather gloves in cool or wintry weather—thin gloves that fit tightly. The gloves contributed to his appearance as a man of substance. He wore Bannister shoes, which were expensive—costing more than twenty dollars—but worth it if measured by the comfort they provided him on his long walks. There was something distinctive about his choice of hats. Again, his tastes ran to dark gray or black, and he fancied a wide-brimmed felt hat that was creased on top from front to back. In an era when many men wore caps, there was something special about a man who wore a hat. My father doffed his hat when he chanced upon one of the neighborhood ladies or a priest or the unsmiling minister of the Lutheran church at the end of the block.

My father would bring home corned beef and slabs of bacon from Harding's. He and some of the senior members of the family regarded brisket of corned beef as a treat, when boiled with cabbage in a big pot; but some of the younger kids were not so fond of the combination—mostly because of the "scum" that could be seen bubbling on top of the water when you raised the lid of the pot to take a look. The rest of our meat came from Sorenson's or, later, when Sorenson went out of business, from Morbach's Meat Market. Occasionally some other kid on the block would make critical comments about how much meat we got from Sorenson's, not to mention the boxes of other edibles that the neighbors could see being delivered to our house. Sometimes, after the first of the month, when Mother and Dad would sit down together at the dining room table to sort out the bills and write the checks, one or the other would express a word of reproof at the extravagant eating habits of our household. Invariably, though, Father would then say that he would rather put good food in our bellies than pay out money for doctor bills.

People were delighted to be invited to have dinner at our house, because my mother, who was particular about buying the best meat and vegetables, was truly a great cook. Frequently when we had guests, one of the men would turn to my father and say, "You set a great table, John"—which is as nice a compliment as can be paid to a host. Our evening meal was a special occasion—and I always enjoyed it when, after his last bite of some extraordinary dessert my mother had served, my father would light up a cigar. Life has gotten to be too busy now to allow for such nightly rituals as this.

The arrival of cold weather inspired my mother to bake beans. She would have laid in a supply of beans almost as an afterthought in telephoning her order to Sorenson's. These were Michigan beans, which are smaller than navy beans and contain much less starch. In her preparations for a Saturday night dinner of baked beans and sirloin steak, with a lettuce and tomato salad on the side and some family-approved dessert to follow, she would enlist the help of one of the kids. It was an honor to be selected to spread the beans on the kitchen table and pick out the tiny stones and any beans that were not perfectly white; to let a blotched bean go into the big metal pot in which the beans would soak overnight was to run the risk of having someone at the dinner table make vomiting sounds when he bit into one.

Saturday night was a family night at our house. Some daring soul might start a penny-ante, penny-limit, poker game in the dining room; cheat-sheets had to be written out for the girls to remind them that two pair beat one pair and three of a kind beat two pair and so on. Some nights, my father would sit in on the game, and it did not seem to matter to him whether he won or lost; but we had some poor losers in our house. There were arguments over who had bet what, and disputes over some unorthodox manner of dealing—leading my father to throw in his cards and go off to some activity that was less aggravating.

Saturday night was also the night that the younger children were fated to be plunged into hot water in the bathtub and thoroughly soaked. On Saturday night, needing it or not, the younger children got taken upstairs to the bathroom and put into the well-filled tub. To make it tolerable, a young boy might be given a new bar of Ivory soap and a pencil and a sheet of stout writing paper to put together a sailboat. In summertime I preferred watermelon rind to Ivory soap for the hull of the boats.

As the final ritual of a winter evening Father would announce it was "time to hit the hay," and he would go down into the basement to bank the fire for the night. Every householder seemed to have his own ideas as to how this should be done; at our house, the procedure was to shovel the ashes out of the furnace into a metal ashcan that only a strong young man could lift; Father mixed coal with some of the ashes and encircled the heart of the fire with this combination to slow the burning and ensure that the furnace would not go out during the night. He used a long, heavy metal poker to get the fire banked to his satisfaction. We took it for granted at our house that this job was expertly done, because the fire was still glowing every morning when Father went down the basement steps to get a good blaze going to warm up the house and keep it warm throughout the day.

At an early age the children learned that the big black pile in our coal bin was a mixture of Pocahontas and Coke and Pennsylvania hard coal. There was a good deal of discussion among the men of our block as to what kind of coal and what combinations produced the best and most even heat. You would hear them talk about quality and price per ton almost every time someone got a delivery from the coal company. The coal would be delivered by horse and wagon and shoveled out into a pile on the asphalt paving in front of your house. Sometime later in the day, if your family could afford it, a begrimed worker would arrive, pushing a huge wheelbarrow with a big shovel in its bed. Having inquired as to which basement window opened to the coal bin, he would methodically scoop up a load and wheel it to the window, propped open with a stick, and dump it in. When there was a ton or more of coal to be moved from street to basement and the day was hot, householders regarding it as a matter of both pride and prudence to lay in a good supply of coal long before the bad weather set in, the worker would sweat profusely, and the coal dust would settle on him, and nobody cared to look at him, because it filled you with a sadness to see him suffering like this. Sometimes the kids would fill up a glass pitcher with water at the kitchen sink, chop off some ice from the 50-pound block in the icebox, and take it out with a drinking glass to the poor man who was wheeling in the coal. If it were a terribly hot day and my mother had some lemons, she would whip up a pitcher of lemonade and have one of the kids go out with this. There was a generous return for these acts of kindness, although no one was motivated by the desire to get something in return for giving the sweltering coal man a chance to quench his thirst; the benefit was that, when his task was finished and the last of the coal dumped into the basement, the man might ask for a broom and carefully sweep up the path of coal dust and spillings that extended from street to basement window.

On Sundays all of us gathered at the dining room table for

breakfast. If there were something Father felt obliged to say to the children—an admonishment to start watching something called "p's and q's,"—it would be on Sunday that we were likely to hear it. Father scheduled his disciplinary pronouncements for Sunday, because he believed such things were best delivered early in the day, and Sunday was the only day the entire family was gathered for breakfast. Father's rule was that nothing disagreeable was to be discussed during a meal, so it would not be until after the plates and silver service had been cleared away that he would reluctantly get around to whatever admonishment was on his mind. It was another of his rules that no one, including himself, was to leave the table until he had asked to be excused. In the event, however, that Father had something of a personal nature to discuss with one of the children, he would detain the one and excuse the others, by way of not embarrassing the child whom he deemed in need of a talking to. Customarily, whether it was one child or all of us who were to receive a word of Father's disfavor, Mother would excuse herself on the pretext of having something to attend to in the kitchen. Father's rebukes made her uncomfortable. In principle, Mother was in accord with Father's discipline; it was being witness to the display of it that disturbed her.

There was such great compatibility between my parents, I think the kids got an exalted view of what being married and raising a family was all about; it frightened me when I witnessed a bitter exchange between the parents of some kid I was pals with. I can't remember a solitary time when something so terrible occurred in our house. My mother and father occasionally had conflicting points of view. But they clearly loved each other and went far beyond the call of duty to maintain a joyful setting for the family.

My mother loved opera and theater, but I don't think my father had much interest in either. They'd go off together to performances, but sometimes my mother would go to a matinee to spare my father the tedium of sitting through something he didn't really like. My father enjoyed long walks and an occasional baseball game, but my mother had no interest in either, so, with an excuse that there was something important to be attended to, Mother would stay home and Father would go off alone. There was unfailing tolerance between them on the matter of spending free time. My mother loved being on a ship. Several times in the course of the summer, she would pack a big lunch and off we would go on the streetcar to the excursion boats docked on the Chicago River. The Christopher Columbus, the whaleback which had been built to carry passengers from downtown to the World's Fair of 1893 on the South Side, was one of our favorites. It was grand when the ships moved outside the sight of land on the four-hour crossing of Lake Michigan. Sometimes, our dad would go along with us. And my mother loved the water so, he would take her on a week-long voyage on a "luxury ship." Mother enjoyed every minute of the luxury-ship holidays, and Father made an effort to be agreeable, but the trips bored him.

My parents went to all social affairs together. And they went to Mass and other religious ceremonies together. Mother and Dad used to go off to Ash Wednesday services in a little black taxicab; why, I wondered, would they go to church in a taxicab? It was actually their daring little habit to play hooky on Ash Wednesday, going off to see the movies instead. About one night a week, they would go to the movies. Generally, they went to the Iris or the Plaisance. After the movie they would stop in at what we called "The Greek's Ice Cream Parlor" and have a chocolate soda.

We kids preferred the Weneeda movie theater, described by some as "a hole in the wall." The Weneeda had gotten its name in a contest the owner sponsored as a promotion for its opening. The winner of the ten-dollar gold piece prize was a woman who lived on our block. She had realistically hit upon the name "We Need a Theater!" For short, everyone took to calling it "The Weenie." The kids in our neighborhood were faithful Saturday afternoon patrons. The owner, a tiny Jewish man with placid face, methodically took the tickets. The price was eleven cents: ten cents plus one cent war tax, which we thought unfair because it wasn't our war and besides it was over and we had won.

"The Weenie" wasn't much of a place, really. It had a narrow entrance on the sidewalk and a ticket booth set into a wall about midway down the entrance aisle; this little corridor blossomed out into three sections of serviceable wooden seats. The first thrill was simply seeing the large silver screen on which the "picture" would be projected. Even before the house lights were dimmed and the first reel of the movie began to roll, a lady on a piano stool was pounding out mood music on the upright. For the best-known pictures, the owner would employ a violinist. When you spotted a man with a violin you knew this was supposed to be a "good" picture.

Mostly, though, the kids were a little dubious when they spotted the fellow with the violin; it meant we had wasted our ten cents, plus the penny war tax, to see a movie that was meant for grown-ups. The movies the kids wanted to see starred such sterling characters as Tom Mix and William S. Hart and other he-men who were clever and brave. A good cowboy movie, followed by an installment of a terribly exciting serial that ended with the helpless heroine lying on the railroad tracks as the locomotive came thundering at her—this made for a really exciting Saturday afternoon. The kids all shouted and vowed that they would certainly come back to the Weenie next week, which is what the tease at the end of the installment urged them to be certain to do.

Kids with a little money in their jeans always came into the "show" with a bag of candy, purchased at shops near the Weenie. Greek stores seemed to be the best places to buy your treats; there were metal trays of chocolate and hard taffy—big, wide strips of candy the Greek would lift off the tray and break with a tiny hammer. The Greek would scoop up the pieces and slide them into a peppermint-striped bag, casually weighing your quarter-pound on a tiny scale. Some of the kids bought the Greek's dark peanut brittle. This was harder to chew than the taffy, but not so sticky. You could break a tooth, chomping down on the peanut brittle, and all the kids knew that you had to move it around your mouth for a while before you started grinding away at it. Some of the kids preferred what we called "store-bought" candy—sticks of licorice, strips of paper dotted with tiny mounds of white and pink sugar candy, and little tin dishes of sugar candy that came with a tiny spoon to dig out the candy. Stuffing yourself with sweets was a common practice at the Weenie. So, too, was constant conversation and catcalling from the moment the kids gave the little man their admission tickets until they filed out when the lights came up. These were the days of silent films, and the gabbing didn't seem to bother those who wanted to read the insertions of dialogue on the screen.

It was only on the rare occasion that something wholly unexpected—and shocking—appeared on the silver screen of the Weneeda that the kids fell silent. There was a Tom Mix cowboy picture one Saturday that contained a scene that stifled every kid in the house. It was a dining room scene; numerous friends of a wealthy rancher were gathered at the table of his big home on a big ranch in some part of the Old West that was not otherwise defined. Ranchers and cowboys and a few friendly Indians were there to enjoy the fabulous spread. Tom Mix, who had already done his heroics, was the guest of honor. The kids crowded into the Weenie were hollering their disapproval of this "sissy stuff" when, incongruously, a huge cake was wheeled into the big rancher's dining room, and a hussy, stripped to the waist, jumped out of the cake. The kids watching the Tom Mix movie gaped—and gasped. The girl's immodest display was on screen and gone in such short order, it was almost subliminal. But the kids simply sat there, stunned, as if not believing this risqué bit in a Tom Mix movie. When the movie ended and the lights came up, all the kids started talking. There was a good deal of wide-eyed discussion. Some of the bold ones grinned and boasted that the movie was great. Some of the kids, looking ashamed, scurried out of the theater. The flash of the girl who had no shirt provoked a great deal of comment and opinion. The prevailing judgment, as I remember it, was that a girl who wore no shirt did not belong in a cowboy movie. I agreed with this. I had no brief for the notion of half-naked women showing up in cowboy movies. The kids I ran with had come to accept the standard close of the hero's kissing his horse as the sun faded in the western sky.

But a lady with no shirt showing up in a cowboy movie? No way were we going to approve of that!

On our block, when I was a kid, everybody knew a good deal about everybody else: what kind of house they lived in, what kind of job the husband had, what kind of things they bought at Sorenson's, which families were stretching their credit, what family crises were arising. There was, despite all of the eyeing of one another, a genuine neighborliness. When someone died, the ladies of our block would don their hats and their Sunday coats and set off on a mission of ringing doorbells, spreading the word and soliciting funds for a floral piece festooned with a ribbon on which was imprinted, "With Sympathy, The Neighbors."

It was déclassé, in our neighborhood, to hold a wake at the funeral parlor. The neighborhood mortuary was equipped for this solemn occasion, but it was generally agreed that funeral parlor wakes were simply too cold; a man was entitled to be stretched out in the casket in his own parlor in his own house; a woman was entitled to be waked in her own home; and would a family do less for a child who had never known any other home?

Neighborhood ladies would arrive at the back door of the house of mourning, arms laden with hams and beef roasts and loaves of fresh-baked bread. These benefactions would be accepted gratefully by some member of the family and then carefully stowed away in the icebox. The meat and bread would be sliced and placed on platters for the grieving family and those close enough to be invited, as the wake went into the night, to have a cup of coffee and a bite to eat. Constant watch was kept to replenish the platters and the garnish, and the cakes and the cookies on the dining room table. In the kitchen, coffee was continually being boiled in large blue enamel pots. Someone would be pressed into service to grind the coffee beans in the grinder attached to a kitchen wall. A decanter of whiskey and glasses would sometimes be found on the kitchen table. Rather self-consciously, male mourners would help themselves to a stiff drink—most of them finding it necessary to explain that they were "bushed" or otherwise in need of a medicinal pick-me-up.

There was a ritual to attending a wake. To begin with, an obligation to put in an appearance rested upon everyone in the neighborhood and upon all friends of the deceased or members of the family—even if it meant a long ride on the elevated or the streetcar. It was required that you show up in your best clothes, neither gaudy nor colorful, and that you reflect a mournful demeanor as you walked up the steps of the front porch. Walking past the basket of flowers placed as a mark of mourning beside the front door, and into the front parlor, you would go up to the widow or widower or whomever the senior mourner happened to be. Customarily, you would murmur, "Sorry for your trouble," or something like that; it didn't matter how you expressed your sympathies, because no one really listened. If you looked as if you were someone who expected to be embraced, you were embraced. Then, as others crowded in on you from behind, as if it were now *their* turn to console those in sorrow, you solemnly directed your gaze to the mortal remains. Reflectively, you studied the face, the hands, the posture of repose. If this were a Roman Catholic wake, a prie-dieu would be before the casket, and even a "fallen-away Catholic" would kneel and move his lips in prayer for the soul of the dearly departed.

At what were called "big" wakes, many people crowded in to pay their respects and the floor of the front parlor groaned under the weight of so many people. An effort would be made to hurry along a line of mourners, who got no more than a quick glance at the departed in the front parlor before being moved into the back parlor, then into the dining room and the kitchen and out the back steps.

It would not be until about 11:00 P.M. that the crowd would thin out and not until about midnight that the family and close friends would be left alone to flop into chairs and davenports, able at last to get off their feet. Those who had stood sentry long hours near the casket—greeting all who appeared, embracing close friends, weeping with some, or recounting the sad details of how death had come—were now urged to have something to eat. An exhausted widow or mother of a dead child would gently be advised to go upstairs and try to get a bit of rest. Some of the men would announce the intention to stay up all night to keep vigil before the casket, and the widow could take solace in hearing this. Three or four men, perhaps, would declare an intention to keep the corpse company, and in a short time, they would be left alone to spend the night in telling stories and sneaking off to the kitchen for a sandwich and a cup of coffee or a splash of whiskey. The men carried on Irish Free State arguments in the kitchen and periodically paid an inspection visit to the casket. They fought off the compelling desire to lay back in an overstuffed chair and close their eyes—and thus the vow would be kept to "Spend the night with Charley" or "Dad" or "Mom."

On burial day, in an air of urgency and dread, members of the family walked self-consciously into the front parlor for a private last look at the departed. Aunts and nieces who had taken charge of the kitchen urged everyone to eat, warning that it would be a trying day and one had to be sustained to get through it.

The man who ran the mortuary, where the body had been embalmed, arrived in his dark clothes and grave demeanor. He brought the gray gloves the pallbearers would wear. At the grave, the pallbearers would toss the gloves on the casket as it was lowered on straps through a blanket of ferns that concealed the rectangular hole where the loved one would remain until the Day of Resurrection, when, as every parochial school child knew, all the dead of all the ages would rise from the grave as perfectly formed mortals. A priest or two—friends of the family—would arrive to say a few prayers prior to the closing of the casket. In a businesslike manner, the undertaker supervised removal of the floral pieces to the tonneau of the "flower car," which had been drawn up before the hearse at the curb out front.

The family fought back the tears as the pallbearers gripped the long handles on the sides of the casket and started to the front door, down the steps and to the hearse. With unsteady steps, the family would then be escorted out and solicitously helped into the rented limousine. Everyone made an effort not to weep and to appear brave. The neighbors were on watch at a respectful distance, making their judgments as to how the family was performing.

There could be no quarrel with the neighbors; in some cases a neighbor might even have taken the day off, losing his wages, in order to be present. Even some who had a lifelong aversion to the Papacy and the Roman church actually sat through the mysterious requiem Mass, as a compliment to the good Catholic neighbor who had died. Some of the neighbor ladies waited near the house until the last of the funeral cortege had pulled away and then scurried into the house to clean it thoroughly from front door to back. They would raise the front parlor shades, run the carpet sweeper, wash the floors, and put the dining room and kitchen in order. They would restore the home to its accustomed state of cleanliness—striking the set as stagehands would do and making the home appear as if it had never been the scene of death or wake or heartache. It was an act of charity to the family that would presently return from the cemetery.

The parish priest, in black vestments, and flanked by two candlebearers who looked to be bored, would greet the casket at the door of the church. He would intone prayers for the dead and sprinkle holy water on the casket and then lead the processional down the center aisle to the foot of the altar. The family followed the casket to the front pews, where they would genuflect and file in. Six candelabra, three on each side of the casket, would hold bleached wax candles, whose flames symbolized life eternal. After intoning the somber *Requiescat in Pace*—the stabbing words of finality in the requiem Mass—the priest would lead the recessional to the door of the church.

The cortege would form quickly. The pallbearers returned the casket to the hearse, the family got into its limousine, and all who were going to the cemetery got into cars the drivers maneuvered into line in the procession. The open car with the flowers had vanished, having sped off to the cemetery, where the driver placed the floral pieces around the gravesite in preparation for the committal service that would follow the Mass.

If there were a delay in moving away from the church, it was because the celebrant of the requiem Mass had been fasting since midnight, in accordance with the law of Holy Mother Church, and the poor man had need of a sip of coffee and a bite of something before the long trip to the cemetery. The waiting could be tedious for the grieving family.

If there were a period of waiting, most likely an adult member of the family would say something appreciative about the sermon the priest had given. Mention would be made of unexpected persons who had been spotted in the congregation. All present in the family car would withhold judgment on how the undertaker, the priest, and the choir had performed until the senior member of the family expressed an opinion. The family was relieved if the opinion were, "It was very nice; everyone was very thoughtful and kind."

If there had been difficulty of some kind—if a relative had felt slighted—there might be hurt feelings resulting in lasting distrust or estrangement. It might have been that the relative had offered advice not heeded, regarding what kind of casket should be chosen. It might have been that the relative who felt slighted had brought a cake or cookies or a casserole that the family had regarded as unappetizing. Or perhaps the relative had not been urged to linger and have a bit of supper with the bereaved after the wake. Or it might have been that in the family council on who should ride in a limousine, the relative had been overlooked as one who ought to have a place in a limousine. It might have been that the relative's family had been passed over in the selection of pallbearers. Whatever, the many decisions that a wake and funeral entailed carried serious threats to family harmony.

A melancholy settled on me when I witnessed, as I did many times, the casket of someone I loved, someone who had been part of my life, being lowered into the grave. Sadness welled up in me as I stood with our family at the gravesite of someone I would never see again. There was something profoundly final about the priest's reading the Latin prayers for the dead and flicking holy water on the casket as it slowly disappeared into the bed of ferns. Invariably, as mourners drifted away to give the family one last moment of privacy in their grief, the priest would come over to say something that might lessen the agony of the family's loss. At one of our burials in Calvary Cemetery, a priest said, "I know it is hard to accept the sorrow of losing someone who is dear to you. It is only with the passing of time that we become reconciled to God's plan that living on this earth is transitory. But it is also part of the Plan that eternal joy is the reward of those who have led good lives. And I would hope that you might find some comfort in this, as you contemplate the sorrow that has been placed upon you." It is difficult to adjust to the concept that death is part of the scheme of things and that there can be a happy side to it. But there would not be much purpose in living, as far as I am concerned, if this were not true.

Because we were no longer part of a cortege, the limousine that took us home from the cemetery moved at a much faster speed than the cortege had moved on the way out. The uniformed policemen who had been stationed at all busy intersections to hold up traffic on the route to the cemetery had gone off to other duty; the driver of our limousine had detached the little purple flag from the radiator cap, and he observed all traffic regulations in taking us home. There were no expressways, and our limousine was now in the flow of traffic, heavy because of the narrow streets. Some of us kids complained about being thirsty or hungry or having need to go to the bathroom. We were tired out from the wake and the requiem Mass and the burial. At least for the kids, the ride home from the cemetery was tedious. A sorrowful silence would have settled on our parents—and whatever other adults were in our limousine. In miles, the ride home from Calvary Cemetery was not great—ten or twelve miles, at most. But, after a burial, the ride home was always terribly long.

The limousine did not return us to what could be called a "fashionable" neighborhood. There was a scattering of families in our neighborhood who were known to be "well fixed," but hardly anyone had the bad grace to "put on airs," as the saying went; men "of position" were quite as friendly and agreeable as men who had only modest jobs and modest incomes. The most reliable gauge of a family's affluence was the quantity and the quality of the food delivered to its back door by wagon from Sorenson's.

On our block in Austin, several houses, including ours, dated back to 1903, when developers began transforming this prairie section of the burgeoning city into a residential area. Our house had been built at a cost of $4,000—a tidy sum of money in those times. The homes had become increasingly expensive, and the price of those built after 1914 zoomed to $8,000, a result of rising labor and material costs in the inflated war economy.

Three or four individual builders had a hand in the project that eventually put a house on every twenty-five-foot lot on our block. Outwardly, not even those constructed by the same builder were identical in appearance: the wood siding of one was different from another—or perhaps the windows were unlike those in the house next door, or the front porch was larger or smaller than the one next door. In conformity with the zoning code, all were set on precisely the same line at the prescribed distance from the sidewalk; all had the same small porch leading off the kitchen at the rear of the house; and all had a backyard ending at the alley.

On the interior, no matter which contractor had built them, the houses were very much the same. The front door opened into a hallway that ran almost to the rear of the house; a staircase was just inside the front door; there was a front parlor, with its gas-burning fireplace, the back parlor, the dining room, and the large kitchen. There were three or four bedrooms in every house on our block. In our house there were four, and Mother and Father occupied the front bedroom which had windows facing a small porch, complete with balustrade, to which Father had attached a bracket to hold the pole of the American flag he faithfully displayed on the Fourth of July and other national holidays.

Our neighborhood was a friendly, peaceable, decent place to live. And on our street, everyone seemed to know everything about everyone. Sorenson's wagon driver was a young man named Barker, who was considered a wild one, but he was very good about making his deliveries, even in bad weather, and he was especially nice to the kids. He got into trouble of some kind and was arrested and locked up with a couple of boys of poor reputation, from the eastern side of the neighborhood—which was considered the "not nice" part of the neighborhood. When Mr. Barker fell into company with his "evil companions" and the lot of them got arrested for robbery or something like that, the whole neighborhood seemed to be alive with gossip about the shocking affair.

Living down the street from us were the Towne brothers, who were youthful and trim. They kept their place up, but for some reason, they were only tolerated by their neighbors, who seemed to want to make it clear to the Towne brothers that they didn't belong on our block. The Towne brothers had an orchestra that played in the big speakeasies. We never knew for certain which of the Townes played the piano and which the saxophone. They were friendly with the kids on our block, though the kids knew you weren't supposed to get too close to the Towne brothers. Their major fault appeared to be occasionally having a crowd of people in their house at some ungodly hour of the night. Invariably they started up a noisy session of music that disturbed the whole neighborhood, and never did they apologize to the neighbors for having disturbed everyone's sleep.

Freddie Houseman, a gifted coronetist—and really a wild one—had been trained by the Towne brothers. Freddie was the stepson of Mr. Bergstrom, the plumber. Helen Houseman Bergstrom preferred to call her husband a sanitary engineer. Freddie went off to Japan and married a Japanese girl and was very subdued when he got back home.

After dinner in our house the children were free to remain at the table, provided we were quiet, to listen to our parents' conversation. Rarely, we were excused when there was something scandalous to be discussed—such as the officer at my father's bank, who deserted his wife and children, and ran off with a stenographer. We were excused the night Mother reported three policemen had that day marched up the long flight of steps at the shabby little house across the street. That house was occupied by a queer, unkempt couple who seemed to be resentful of everyone. The police had come to investigate the frumpy housewife's wild howling. Her husband had come home drunk in midday and beaten her up.

It was painful to every other family in the block to have such neighbors as this, and occasionally, some of the wealthy men on our block would come and visit my father on our front porch and vow that they meant to buy that sorry-looking house, dispossess the trouble-makers, and have the place torn down. Only rarely did we get a glimpse of the sullen man who lived there, or his unkempt wife; when chanced upon, they did not respond to greetings, except to glare at whomever had the temerity to speak to them. No one knew what kind of work the man did, or anything about the origins of this couple; all anyone knew was that this small frame house, greatly in need of paint and other repair, had once been well-kept by the widow of a retired policeman. The antisocial couple who now occupied it ignored broken windowpanes and weeds. The only sign of life within this strange place were the angry voices of man and wife, who apparently hated each other. The children on our block kept their distance from this house across the street from us; even the most audacious was not so brave that he would chance an encounter with this man or woman. The violence and loud shouting within this house not infrequently impelled close neighbors to call the Austin police station. Everyone in the block would have been grateful if one of the rich men *had* bought the place and reduced it to rubble; but no one ever did.

The two richest men on the block, Mr. Smith and Mr. King, came calling on my father occasionally to talk about the problem of the shabby house across the street and its abominable occupants. They would sit in chairs on our front porch, gazing at the shabby house, and talk about getting possession of it. Mr. Smith, his red cheeks turning purple and his mustache quivering, did most of the talking. He expressed his displeasure in tones so loud they easily carried across the street. Mr. Smith had a habit of swearing—goddamning this and goddamning that in his explosive outbursts—and quite frequently, in presenting his opinion of the shabby house on our block, he would declare, "It is a goddamn insult to all the decent, God-fearing people who live here!" Mr. King, on the other hand, rarely had much to say. His presence on the porch during these conferences seemed to be his way of indicating his concurrence.

It was quite untoward for anyone to swear in our house, and the kids would have received a lick from Father's razor strap if they had done it, but Mr. Smith seemed to have special privilege. Father was not visibly disturbed by his cursing, even if some of the children were present to hear it; it seemed that accepting Mr. Smith's practice of calling upon God to damn something was a condition of having him for a friend. And at least Mr. Smith never employed vulgar or obscene words. However, sometimes when he and Mrs. Smith would be over for a game of 500 and the cards fell unexpectedly against him, Mr. Smith would involuntarily explode the name "Jesus!" He would be embarrassed as Father frowned, Mother fixed him with a stare, and Mrs. Smith reproved him, saying, "Watch your tongue, Dan Smith!" Immediately, Mr. Smith would murmur a flustered apology, invariably adding, "It's just so goddamn exasperating; those goddamn jacks in your hand! I didn't figure you to be holding the jacks."

The Smiths were the neighbors most frequently in our house. They came every other Monday evening to play cards with my parents, the husbands paired off against the wives. On intervening Mondays, they played in the front parlor at the Smiths'. They played until 10:00 P.M., at which time they would settle up the pennies, and my mother would bring out coffee in her silver service and plates of meat and cheese sandwiches, with all manner of garnish on the side. There would be two bottles of beer for Mr. Smith. If he and Father had lost, Mr. Smith would loudly declare he was getting a bargain for his money: so much to eat and drink to compensate him for the pennies he had surrendered to the ladies. The kids, who wandered in and out of the front parlor during the game, found it tedious to hear Mr. Smith say the same thing about his bargain, in precisely the same way, on so many Monday nights. Some of us suspected that Mr. Smith contrived to lose, by way of setting the stage for his remark—although we gathered from comments that my father made to my mother, when the hats and wraps had been fetched from our hall tree and the Smiths had made their noisy farewell, that my father didn't think Mr. Smith was too bright, even though he had a successful business.

Mr. Smith owned a small company that engraved and printed bonds and other securities. The company prospered because his people did good work, and there was little competition in this business. Mr. Smith was not an engraver, and it was never explained how he got into the business of printing securities. All we knew was that he spent most of his day visiting banks and brokerage houses and sometimes stopped off to see my father at his bank. Occasionally Father came home with a cheerless report for Mother: "Dan brought up the matter of my going into partnership with him." My mother would reply, "Oh, not again!" and Father would shake his head at Mr. Smith's inability to get it through his head that Father *liked* working at the bank; he also regarded it as a more secure job for a family man—even though Father would sometimes admit there was a great deal of money to be made in the business of printing securities.

Mr. Ganey, the tall, spare nextdoor neighbor who had a fine job as engineer of a public high school—and more authority and a larger paycheck than the principal—had been the first in our block to invest in a car. And what a car! It was an imposing Pierce-Arrow touring car, painted black with red stripes.

Mr. Ganey's purchase of the Pierce-Arrow created a problem that intrigued everyone on the block. At the back of his lot, at the alley, Mr. Ganey had a red barn, and it was here that his touring car, with its canvas top and its tufted leather seats, was kept out of the weather. But the car was longer than the buggy Mr. Ganey had once owned, and the rear of the touring car stuck out a couple of feet into the alley. Unable to close the big door of the barn, in which hung Mr. Ganey's impressive assortment of tools, he was concerned that the junkmen or the Greek peddlers who came down the alley hawking their wagonloads of fresh fruits and vegetables would pilfer his possessions. Having to go off to his school every weekday morning at seven, and not getting home again until about five in the afternoon, Mr. Ganey enlisted the kids to keep watch on his property, giving a few of us five- and ten-cent bribes.

Employing the kids created a new problem. Pretending that the duty of being on watch made it necessary to be inside the barn, the kids were forever swinging open the metal doors on the Pierce-Arrow, climbing in to make believe, gripping the steering wheel, and manipulating the brake and driving levers. Frequently, a youthful watchman would bring his friends into the barn, and they would climb into the back seat, sharing the thrill of pretending they were whipping along in Mr. Ganey's car, the breeze in their faces. Not infrequently, having come into the barn after playing in the mud, the kids would soil the leather seats. Even worse, their shoes would scuff or cut into the leather. It annoyed Mr. Ganey, who kept his car in more immaculate condition than he kept any other possession, to find mud on the leather seats. It infuriated him to discover damage had been done to the leather, and he would get angry and mutter swear words like "goddammit," which made the Catholic school kids feel terrible, knowing that anybody who talked like that was in danger of losing his immortal soul.

There was no danger, of course, that anyone could accidentally start Mr. Ganey's car. It had to be started by cranking; Mr. Ganey entrusted no one but himself to crank his Pierce-Arrow. Spreading his legs for leverage, and bending over with one hand braced on the hood, he gripped the handle of the crank with the other. If the engine coughed or sputtered but did not start, Mr. Ganey would leave his crank to make an adjustment on the spark lever, "giving it more spark," before trying it again. Invariably, if anyone were watching this performance, Mr. Ganey would say you had to keep your cranking arm flexed and the thumb of the cranking hand safely tucked in alongside the fingers; the engine was prone to "kick," which could dislocate the thumb or fracture the forearm.

The same as other proud owners of automobiles in those early days, Mr. Ganey spent more time puttering around his car and wiping it clean than he spent driving it. There were few roads that could safely be negotiated in those days, and legislatures, apprehensive about the accident potential of these early cars, imposed restrictive speed limits—not exceeding ten miles per hour in populated areas and perhaps fifteen in open country.

It was a thrilling experience to go riding in Mr. Ganey's touring car. On a Sunday afternoon, he might knock on our back door and ask my mother, who was preparing dinner, if the family would care to go for a drive that evening. I thought these occasional invitations were Mr. Ganey's way of repaying my mother for the cups of sugar and the eggs and the other things she was continually doling out to Mr. Ganey's daughter-in-law, who lived with her husband and children in Mr. Ganey's house. The young Mrs. Ganey had the habit of explaining that she had unexpected visitors and had nothing in the icebox.

I was sort of lukewarm, as the saying went, about the Ganeys. It didn't particularly bother me that young Mrs. Ganey was always running short of things in her icebox—although I used to wonder why she didn't remember to get what she needed from Sorenson's, the way everybody else did. But the Ganey family's disinterest in enjoying our kind of lifestyle perplexed me. Christmas, for example, was just another day for the Ganeys, as far as I could tell; nothing exciting seemed to attach to their house at Christmastime. If they bothered to decorate a tree, it would be a skimpy thing that had shed its needles, with few ornaments and only one string of lights.

At our house, Christmas officially began shortly after Thanksgiving Day. It was then that the State Street stores began their full-page Christmas advertising campaigns. My father would come home with the *Chicago Daily News*, and we would spread it open on the front parlor rug, frantically turning the pages until we came to the toy advertising. We would scrutinize the picture of every item that was advertised and read every word of the description. It was a nightly ritual, even though there was a great deal of repetition, as the same toys were advertised night after night.

The other signs that Christmas was approaching were the night my father came home with "Sparkling Gems" and the

night he announced he thought it was time to start checking
the Christmas tree lights.

The Christmas tree lights were packed away in their original
boxes in a closet upstairs, and no one dared to touch the boxes,
from the day the Christmas tree came down until two weeks
or so before the following Christmas, when my father brought
them out to check the electric cords for fray, inspect each
socket, and test every bulb. Checking the Christmas tree lights
was an all-evening affair. There were ten bulbs to each circuit,
and if one light were defective, none would light. After loading
up each of the sockets with a bulb, my father would utter a
sound of dismay if he plugged the string into a wall socket and
the bulbs did not light. A search then began to identify the
bulbs that had burned out. Father's method of doing this was
to test each bulb in the string that did not light in a socket of
a string that did light; the defective bulb identified itself by its
inability to complete the circuit and light up the string. The
children's method was to replace all bulbs in the dead string
with live ones. In the early evening father was tolerant of our
haphazard system, but he would start to lose patience as the
clock on the mantle chimed nine. And Father could get quite
impatient if the hour were late and one of the kids inadvert-
ently mixed bulbs from the pile of dead ones that were to be
replaced with bulbs from the larger pile of those that had been
tested and determined to be in working order. To mix up the
bulbs meant that no one knew which ones were dead, and the
whole process of testing had to begin again—although, remarkably, this could be done in jig time if the hour were late.
In any case, Father would place the dead bulbs in a sack and
place the sack on a table near the clothes tree on which his
overcoat hung on its hanger. In the morning he would buy the
replacements. Having the old bulbs made it convenient to buy
new ones of the same colors—red, green, blue, white, and yellow—the family having settled over the years on the balance it
liked.

Generally, inspection of the Christmas tree lights would follow the arrival of "Sparkling Gems." Sparkling Gems were
Christmas candy—hard candy of such delicious taste and va-

riety that no one ever made better Christmas candy than this. It was made in Harrisburg, Pennsylvania, and how my father ever discovered there was such a treat, and found out how to order it, was a mystery. "Pure sugar," the printing on the can said, "Pure Flavors." Sparkling Gems came three pounds to the can, and my father would buy perhaps nine cans. The nuns got a couple of cans, and a few of our "needy" neighbors got a can. After dinner, the head of the house would announce that we had better test the candy to make certain that it was as good as last year's; Father would pry the lid off one can, and Mother would fetch dishes and pour a generous quantity of Sparkling Gems into each, placing them strategically within reach of everyone. Mother did not have much of a taste for Sparkling Gems, and Father would have stopped off at Mrs. Snyder's to buy a two-pound box of chocolates. Mother would open the box, offer some chocolates to everyone, then settle in her favorite chair—the chocolates on an adjacent table—to digest the *News*.

Our Christmas tree was a thing of beauty—or so we thought. It was lovingly decorated and aglow with many lights. We had a traditional feast at our house on Christmas Eve; meatless, of course, with oysters and shrimp and baked fish, and homemade Christmas cookies that we all raved about, pleasing my mother. Then we all gathered in the front parlor, where the lighted Christmas tree stood in the bay window—in the spot where the casket was placed when we had a wake. Members of the family exchanged gifts, and my father gave each of us a ten-dollar gold piece. These were memorable nights, these Christmas Eves.

Santa Claus paid his visit to our house late at night, when all of the younger children were asleep. It was always a matter of regret to us younger kids when we awoke and raced downstairs to discover we had missed him again—the old fellow had come and gone without our knowing he had been in the house.

Christmas at our house was a joyful time. My mother and my father were always painstaking about getting the toys and other things the kids had been hoping for. Christmas was a hard day on my mother. She had to spend a couple of hours plucking pinfeathers out of the turkey she had personally selected at Sorenson's. And she was occupied for a long time in the kitchen, making her dressing with Bell Seasoning, stuffing the bird and getting it ready for roasting. The turkey and the mince pies did not go into the oven until the family came home from Mass. On Christmas Day, it was our family custom to troop over in a body to the red brick building that housed Help of Christians Church on the main floor and the parish school rooms on the two floors above. We went to what we called "the eight"—eight o'clock Mass—because those who were old enough to go to Holy Communion had been "keeping their fast"—meaning they had not tasted food or drink since midnight—and they had been up for hours. Generally, on Sundays and Holy Days, we went to "the ten," always taking our places in the pew that had our family name on it—five rows back from the communion rail. This had been "our pew" since the day the church was built. My father had had the choice of where he wanted to sit, by reason of having made a generous contribution to the construction costs. Sometimes it was a good place to sit, putting you close enough to have a good look at anything interesting transpiring at the altar. But Christmas Day was not a very good day to be sitting so close up, because this was a day our pastor, a cadaverous-looking man with blue veins on his nose, gave the sermon. And Father P. J. O'Reilly gave the same sermon every Christmas.

The truth was, I suppose, that I didn't like any of his sermons; Father O'Reilly was one of those preachers who continually plays on moment-of-doom themes. My mother always sat patiently through his strident orations about mankind's flirtation with eternal damnation. But Mother embarrassed herself once, when she giggled during one of Father O'Reilly's thunderous sermons. She was unable to contain herself when the priest wagged his finger and declared that lest the sinful man mend his ways, he would wake up one morning and—reading the *Chicago Tribune*—find his name in the death notices. But my mother managed, somehow, to sit quietly during Father O'Reilly's tedious homily on Christmas Day. It was my father who couldn't abide the Christmas Day sermon. My father drummed his fingers on a knee from beginning to end of the sermon. With the sober look of a judge about to pronounce sentence, Father O'Reilly would clear his throat and begin, "Under the Starlit Skies of Old Judea. . . ." My Father would groan quietly and say, *sotto voce*, "Oh, not again!" Every Christmas we got that line about "Old Judea."

One Christmas, as he was carving the turkey, my father startled everyone by unexpectedly reciting the line, "Under the Starlit Skies. . . ." Our Uncle Phil Devitt, who was always invited to our holiday dinners, thought he had to say something in response to this queer mention of Old Judea; he turned to my father and said, "If no one else has a call on it, John, I will be obliged if you will reserve me the pope's nose." Some of the kids thought it was sacrilegious for Uncle Phil to refer to that lowly part of our turkey as the "pope's nose." I got a reproachful look from my father when I boldly asked Uncle Phil why he called that private end of the turkey the "pope's nose." Uncle Phil looked a little uncomfortable and said, "What do you call it?"

With all eyes on me, I gulped and said, "The kids call it 'the part that went over the fence last.' "

Uncle Phil nodded. "I've heard the expression," he said, "and I must say that there is some logic to it. I suggest, though, that if you study the pictures of our Italian popes, you'll discover a striking resemblance between the pope's nose and this particular part of the turkey's anatomy." Then, turning to my father, he said, "No offense intended, John." My father nodded politely and continued carving, and nobody had the bad manners to bring up the question again.

One Christmas, when I was about five years of age, one of the older members of our family thought it would be a great thrill for the little kids if they got a look at Santa Claus, and, before any of us had been sent to bed, one of my older brothers dressed up in a Santa costume, white beard and all, and made a great deal of stomping his feet as he ho-hoed on our front porch. Someone shouted that this must be Santa, and we younger kids went racing to the front porch—and there he was! But, with one careful look, I drew back and did not join in the effusive cries of welcome. When my father, worried about my distrustful reaction to this visitation, asked me why I wasn't happy to see Santa, I grimly pointed at this impostor in the beard and the red-and-white suit, and I said something that members of my family were never to let me forget: "If this is Santa, why is he wearing my brother Bill's shoes?"

CHAPTER 3

MY SISTER'S
RED SWEATER

I DON'T THINK I COULD BE ACCUSED of resistence to education, although some of my brothers and sisters seemed to think I "wanted to be ignorant" all my life. It was true, as they were a long time in letting me forget, that I had gone on strike one time, refusing to go to Our Lady Help of Christians grammar school for a period of two weeks or so. But the issue had simply been my refusal to wear a red sweater that had been handed down to me when one of my sisters grew out of it. I didn't mind wearing a hand-me-down; all the kids I knew did this. Without the slightest objection—probably with pride—I wore my older brothers' knickerbockers and caps when they outgrew them. But the humiliation that I felt attached to wearing a *girl's* sweater was too much to bear, as far as I was concerned. Whatever the penalty, I would not put it on.

My grandfather—my mother's father—who then lived with us, was fascinated by my refusal to wear the red sweater. I guess I hoped my grandfather, who had risked his life for principle in Ireland, would take my side; but apart from telling my mother that his judgment was that I would never wear the sweater, my grandfather remained neutral. My brothers and sisters were scornful of me, but neither my mother nor my father reproached me or threatened me. On the tenth day or so of my "strike," the other kids came home with the news that the students of Our Lady Help of Christians were being cast in a play to be performed for the entire parish. The enticing part of this news was that a few of my first grade class were to be chosen for parts. The desire to be one of those selected welled up in me. And that night, with a feeling of shame, I told my mother that I wanted to be in the play and that I would like to go back to school, even if it meant wearing the red sweater. Next morning, I did.

I learned a couple of things from this experience. I learned from the patience my parents had shown that there is no better way to deal with someone who is being stubborn and outrageous. I learned that there comes a time in any crisis when it serves your own best interests to capitulate. And I guess this was my first brush with the proposition that every man has his price. The old BVM sister who taught first grade selected me for a walk-on part in the great play—and I thoroughly enjoyed it. And perhaps I learned from my classmates' disinterest in my unexplained absence from school that others are not particularly interested in your personal problems. It hadn't mattered at all, so far as the first graders at Our Lady Help of Christians School were concerned, that I showed up wearing my sister's hand-me-down red sweater.

I was only six years of age, and I had scarcely gotten started in first grade. I was aware, I think, that being in the lower half of seniority of the nine children in our family, I was not entitled to regard myself as amounting to very much. I didn't mind. My father had a good position at the First National Bank, and I found a lot of comfort in that; it was all right if I weren't important, so long as my father was. As for having a lowly place on the family totem pole, the first grade sister did harp at me that I wasn't doing as well as my older brothers and sisters had done—and I thought she was "mean" to keep mentioning it.

I rather liked going to school. I liked the three- or four-block walk down Iowa Street, pausing always at Laramie to gaze at a weathered, wooden-frame walk-up set at the rear of a lot. This was a respectable part of our neighborhood, but it was common gossip that two mysterious Italian men, referred to as "Mustache Petes," resided in this little house. The story was that in the middle of the night the Mustache Petes had strange visitors. The women who lived nearby were scandalized at reports that, in defiance of the Federal Prohibition Act, these men "made wine" in the basement; it was true, I guess, because the odor of fermentation was inescapable for anyone walking down the sidewalk of Iowa Street.

Hardly anyone ever spoke to the two Mustache Petes who lived in the old house. The kids were given frightening warnings to keep a safe distance from this house. But the two Mustache Petes came out one morning while I was walking to school, and they smiled and said hello to me. I had been in dread of coming close to the two Italians, but they looked all right to me, and I said hello to them. It got so I tried to time my walks to school to catch them leaving their house, because I enjoyed saying hello to these Italians that everyone seemed to fear. I didn't dare mention the chance encounters to anyone, as the entire neighborhood was apprehensive about the Mustache Petes; even when one of my brothers or sisters was babbling some shocking gossip of what these two "outsiders" were up to, with their visitors at odd hours, I kept silent. Who would believe me if I said that I had come to know these two men and that they looked all right to me? Then, a terrible thing happened.

In the dark of one night two or three men had gone into the little house at Iowa and Laramie and murdered the Mustache Petes. How these homicides were discovered, I never knew; one story was that a policeman walking his beat had observed that the front door of the shabby little house was open, and that he had found the bodies when he went up to investigate. It took a day for the newspapers to gather and print the sordid details, and it was several days before the horror that swept our neighborhood subsided. The story was that the two Mustache Petes had had their throats slashed by assassins of the "Black Hand." The newspaper stories explained that this Black Hand was a secret society, tracing back to the "Old Country," and that the Black Hand dealt in all manner of evil things and assassinated those who double-crossed or defied it.

I felt awfully sad about the two Mustache Petes' being murdered by this Black Hand. No one ever discovered why they had been assassinated in such a grisly way. Subsequently, a haunting fear was always with me, in all of the years that I walked along Iowa Street to and from school. It was not a fear that something terrible was going to happen to me; it was sort of a foreboding, I guess, about the frightful violence that seems to be part of the human condition.

There is a piece of music, lovely in itself, that has always been identified in my mind with the brutal murder of the two Mustache Petes. The night that this terrible thing occurred was the memorable night that my father uncrated the magnificent Victrola he had bought for our house. Carefully, my father set aside the ten free records that had come as a bonus. Then, with all of us gathered around him, he cleared his throat and read the instruction booklet on how to use our new machine and how to take care of it. Only after he had emphasized all of the dos and the don'ts did he raise the mahogany lid of our Victrola, put a record on the turntable, and wind up the spring by turning the handle on the outside. Then, carefully putting a needle in place on the playing head, he gently set it down. All of us were enthralled by the beauty of the music.

In its selection of the ten free records, RCA had provided a little something for all tastes. The kids' favorite turned out to be "Freckles," and we never got tired of hearing the voice of a brassy tenor belting out the lyrics about poor Freckles; he got blamed for every broken windowpane. My mother was delighted to find records of Galli Curchi and Enrico Caruso, plus some orchestral records. One of her favorites was a symphonic rendition of "Humoresque," and it became one of mine also, as Mother played it over and over again on that first night we had the Victrola—the night the two Mustache Petes were slaughtered. The lonely lilting of "Humoresque" was grooved in my memory—and to my last day, I guess, the sound of just a few bars of it will nudge my thoughts into remembrance of the horrifying night when the Black Hand slashed the throats of two Italians who lived in the little walk-up house in our neighborhood.

The Victrola changed the pattern of our family life. An impressive piece of furniture, it was given a place of its own in a corner of our back parlor. The upright piano seemed suddenly out of place, though it had been the center of after-dinner activity, everyone gathering around to sing as one of my sisters played. The Victrola crank had to be turned to wind the spring that drove the turntable and the cranking had to be attended to regularly. One winding would keep the pace of the revolutions constant for more than one side of a record. But there would be groans of complaint if the child operating the Victrola got careless about the winding, because the sounds would slowly come to a halt, the final notes being no more than a growl, as the turntable went slower and slower and stopped as the spring "ran out." For a while, at least, we had the most expensive "playing machine" in the block, and the neighbors made excuses to come calling to admire it and listen to the beautiful music. It was commonplace to hear a neighbor tell my father: "That is a magnificent instrument, John. A truly remarkable instrument." We were all proud to hear that.

The Victrola had been delivered to us in a large packing crate imprinted on one side with the RCA trademark: an intelligent-looking dog, resting on its haunches, its head cocked toward the megaphone of a tabletop phonograph. Printed in large letters below the picture of the dog were the words "His Master's Voice." The kids I ran with talked a lot about this smart dog, because I had hauled the crate into our backyard, and the kids like to crawl into it and gab about something to create the impression that *they* were the "master's voice." With my mother's permission, I would sometimes bring a couple of kids into the house to admire the Victrola and crank it up and play "Freckles" for them. It made me feel proud to show off something that nobody else on the block had.

I don't think that my father was greatly impressed by this

wonderful machine he had bought for us. He missed the family singing, as my sister infrequently played the piano now. I think it annoyed my father when one of the kids played the same record over and over again; but he only expressed his disapproval when somebody forgot to crank the machine and the music fell into a grumble as the turntable slowed down.

There were a few times when it was regarded as untoward for someone to use the Victrola. Nobody ever said anything, but we all understood that no one was to use the Victrola when one of the kids had some "hard" homework to do. More importantly, we were all acutely aware that there was to be no music or loud conversation on the nights that my father and my mother sat together at the dining room table, with all the household bills and the checkbook in front of them, to settle up the family accounts. It was, of course, unthinkable that anyone would dare to play records on the Victrola when there was a wake in our house.

Other kids liked to come home with us after school, supposedly to play, but actually to snack. Some days there would be freshly cooked doughnuts. We'd find Mother standing at the stove carefully slipping flats of doughnut dough into an iron pot and turning the doughnuts over with a spatula as they expanded and browned. She lifted them out at precisely the instant when they were properly cooked, the simmering lard never penetrating the crust. Mother had the practice of testing the heat of the lard by deftly inserting a small strip of white wrapping paper into the hot liquid. Mother had the gift of all good cooks of knowing when conditions were right and when they weren't.

Sometimes we would arrive home from school as the doughnut dough was being mixed. Mother sifted the flour into a bowl and added the milk and the lard and the salt and whatever else her recipe required. With practiced fingers, she would knead it, adding a splash of milk or sifting in a bit more Ceresota flour. Then she would plop the glob of mixture onto a board and roll it with a rolling pin covered with a white cloth to keep the dough from sticking. With the mixture flattened out, and the lard now hot in the cast-iron pot, she would take a tin doughnut cutter and deftly press out the doughtnut shapes, gathering up the holes and all the trimmings, rolling out the dough once more, and using the cutter again. Sometimes, especially if you had come home with a friend, she would scoop up some of the circular bits and slip them into the pot, giving the kids an unexpected treat and giving herself a reading on whether the lard was hot enough—or too hot—for the doughnuts.

I had a sister who liked to make gingerbread, but only when she felt like doing so. She made a mess of the kitchen, in contrast to the neat manner in which Mother managed to keep everything in order, cleaning up the pots and pans almost effortlessly as she went on with the cooking. But if my sister's methods defied neatness and order, her gingerbread was exceptional, and it delighted her to have kids sit at the kitchen table, gorging themselves on her creation and washing it down with huge cups of rich Borden's milk.

I had a brother who made fudge, but only when he felt like doing so. He also made a mess of the kitchen, and his ability to make fudge left a lot to be desired. Either my brother's fudge was cooked too much and would crystallize or it was not cooked enough and would not harden. The trick of knowing just when to add the vanilla extract—being careful not to put in too much if you would avoid having fudge with cloying sweetness—was to check the consistency of the bubbling ooze in the pan by dropping a bit of this liquid off the end of a spoon into a glass of tap water; if the drops disintegrated in the water, the stuff needed more cooking; if the drops gummed together, it was ready to be taken off the heat, whipped furiously, and poured into prebuttered tins before it started to congeal. My brother's fudge remained mushy, no matter how much it was whipped, but the leavings in the pan quickly firmed up, creating the contradiction that his fudge was undercooked and overcooked at the same time. The best part of being present when my brother cooked his fudge was cleaning up the pan by scraping away with a spoon at the crystallized remains.

During my grammar school years, my grandfather came to live with us, and a nice friendship developed between my grandfather and myself. One day I came home with materials I had purchased at a hardware store and announced that I was going to build a newfangled thing called a "crystal set." My older brothers and sisters scoffed, but my grandfather stood by me and declared that he was certain that I would be able to build it. I was only twelve years old and had no skills to suggest that I could manage to put this crystal set together. But my grandfather, in one of his rare displays of asserting an opinion, declared, "The boy will get it put together—and when he does, everyone in this household will be teasing him to let them put on the earphones and listen to the music that is miraculously coming to us through the atmosphere."

Because I had only a vague idea of how you went about building a crystal set, I didn't deserve this vote of confidence. But I pored over the instructions that I had been given at the hardware store, and I had some serious discussions with an older boy named Vernon Smith, who worked with his father in the securities-printing business. Vernon Smith had built several crystal sets. He told me that the first thing I had to do was transfer the large spool of copper wire to an empty cardboard Quaker Oats box—being certain to place one loop of the wire directly alongside the previous loop and, once finished with this difficult chore, to brush the whole coil with clear shellac, by way of keeping the wire in place. This I did, and, with Vernon instructing me on every step of the project, I finally got the thing built. I was enormously proud of this accomplishment. But my humiliation was that it didn't work.

I had put in the tiny crystal, with a wire that Vernon called a "Cat's Whisker" poking into it. I had managed to clear a track at the top of the coil that the "station selector" could slide over. But when I plugged in the earphones and worked the selector and the cat's whisker, I didn't get anything. I was terribly disappointed and fearful of the razzing the other kids would give me. When I confessed to Vernon Smith that my crystal set didn't bring in any sounds, he carefully examined this thing I had built and said it looked OK to him. He said he would take it home and try it out. The next day, he brought it back to me, saying, "You've done good; it works fine."

Dolefully, I shook my head, and then he said, "what kind of an aerial have you got?"

Well, I scraped up what money I had and borrowed some more from one of my sisters, on the promise that I would pay her back out of my weekly allowance, and I went to the hardware store to buy a reel of "aerial wire" and two glass insulators and some coated "lead wire" to bring the sound down along the side of our house, from the aerial to my crystal set. My mother was aghast when I announced I was going to climb up to the peak of our roof and install an aerial. She raised such objections that Vernon Smith said *he* would do it—and he did. My mother died a thousand deaths, as the saying goes, watching Vernon Smith crawling along the peak of our roof and installing the aerial. When the ordeal was over, Vernon brought the lead wire into the house and attached it to my crystal set. My mother was ecstatic when Vernon, having insisted that she wear the headphones, slowly moved the selector and brought in a station that was playing music!

My grandfather had frequently looked in on me as I sat at the kitchen table working on my crystal set. He never said anything to me but always gave me a look of approval. He came into my bedroom the day the aerial was installed and put the headset on. He nodded when he discovered that my project had turned out successfully. But he showed little liking for this newfangled thing his twelve-year-old grandson had put together. He became an addict, though, when some ingenious communications people figured out a way to give the nation instantaneous coverage of the 1924 presidential nominating convention of the Democratic Party.

One of radio's first major demonstrations of its ability to cover a great news event was its prolonged, on-the-scene reporting of this nominating convention in old Madison Square Garden in New York City. On NBC, Graham McNamee gave his lengthy, breathless accounts of the melodramatic deadlock in which the delegates found themselves. In roll call following roll call for several days, no candidate could get enough delegate votes for nomination to run against Republican Calvin Coolidge in November. The newspapers seemed to regard radio coverage of a political convention as sort of a stunt, and there is no indication in the old papers I've seen that the newspaper people of that era were apprehensive that this upstart, radio reporting, might grow up to do a lot of them in.

My grandfather frequently congratulated me for having put together a crystal set that allowed him to listen to what was going on in faraway New York City as the Democrats battled day after day. My mother, thinking that it would hurt my grandfather's back to sit hour after hour on the edge of my bed, asked me if I could get the crystal set to work in our back parlor. Adding on to the lead wire from the aerial on the roof, I managed somehow to do so. My grandfather, the earphones on his head, sat comfortably in his rocker listening to Graham McNamee's reporting from the Democratic convention. I sat on the piano stool—watching my grandfather, who let me listen only occasionally. Lulled by the monotony of the convention reports, my grandfather dozed now and again, but whenever I suspected there might be something exciting going on at the Democratic convention and tried to remove the headphones from my grandfather, he invariably woke up and protested it was "his turn" to listen. Sometimes my grandfather would remove the headpiece and, with the earphones in his lap, give me his views about politics and politicians. He didn't seem to have too high an opinion of politicians. I found it to be awfully exciting to discover how the Democratic Party was going about its serious business of selecting a candidate to run for president of the United States. I was eager to find out everything I could about the convention, and I read all the accounts that appeared in the *Chicago Tribune* and the *Chicago Daily News*. My grandfather helped me when I came upon words like *delegation* and *constituency* that I didn't understand. Listening to the convention broadcast from New York, I developed a great desire to get a firsthand look someday at a presidential nominating convention. One of my older sisters ridiculed me when I mentioned that someday I was going to be present at one of these grand affairs. There would never come a time, my sister told me, when they would ever let someone like me inside a hall to witness something as important as the selection of a candidate to run for president. Well, I said, there was no harm in wishing.

Having brought the crystal set radio into our home, I was pleased to find that I had gained status with my brothers and sisters. I had one sister who persisted in saying that she found it difficult to believe that her no-account little brother had been able to put such a thing together; it annoyed me that she frequently tacked on this qualification. The truth, of course, was that I never would have been able to construct this thing if Vernon Smith hadn't guided me from one step to the next. I suppose what really bothered me about my older sister's making a point of taking her little dig at me, when she felt obliged to join the other members of our family in their little compliments to me, was that this particular sister zealously insisted on having "her turn" at putting the headphones on.

There were only a few pioneer radio stations at that time. The two favorites, as far as my family judged it, were WDAP, which broadcast from a studio in the Drake Hotel, and WEBH, which was set up in the Edgewater Beach Hotel, a fashionable place on the lakefront on the North Side. Both had programs of popular music. Both stations broadcast the music of the famous orchestras that played in their dining rooms for dancing. There was no such thing as "radio news," although stations started taking items out of the major newspapers—with no mention of the source of these items that an announcer read into the microphone. Even as a kid, I thought it was silly to broadcast stories everybody had already read in the newspapers. The Graham McNamee broadcasts of the Democratic convention had provided a clue as to what the potential of radio might be, but I cannot recall anyone even mentioning this.

Broadcasting in the early 1920s was more of a curiosity than something to be taken seriously. There was a good deal of bragging among those who owned a little radio set about having tuned in on station KDKA in Pittsburgh, Pennsylvania, or some other faraway place. Late at night we could pick up one of these signals on my crystal set. The programming of distant stations was no better than what we could get locally. But "getting distance" was a big deal to those who owned a set. By way of clearing the airwaves to make it possible to "get distance," a "silent night" was instituted. The local stations had to cease broadcasting on Monday evenings in order that people in our area could go searching around the kilocycles for such far-off stations as KDKA.

The one local-area station that was not precluded from broadcasting on silent night was WTAS, which was set up in a Prohibition-era nightclub on a highway that led to the little city of Elgin, about forty miles west of Chicago. Our family had a particular interest in WTAS because it was owned by a famous criminal lawyer named Charles Erbstein. He was a boy-hood friend of my father. The two of them had palled around together when they both lived in the area of Taylor and Halsted. Every once in a while Charley Erbstein would come to our house for dinner. He was an exceedingly gracious man, who always arrived with a big box of chocolate candy for my mother, and he told a great many jokes and was nice to all of us kids. I have no idea what it was that prompted him to start a radio station in a dubious nightclub called the Purple Grackle. Mr. Erbstein was a regular performer on his radio station. The nightclub orchestra pounding out its music in the background, Mr. Erbstein, who had a gift for gab, would take the micro-phone and talk away at length on any subject that came to his mind. It was pretty interesting to hear a man who came to our house for dinner talking on the radio. He was a very nice man, Mr. Erbstein, and we enjoyed having him come to our house for dinner.

My father had a great deal of affection and admiration for his boyhood chum, but sometimes it appeared that my father was concerned about some of the "crazy" things Mr. Erbstein would say or do; my father, for example had serious misgivings about Mr. Erbstein's choosing the first letter of his children's names—Willie, Tommy, Annie, and Sammy—for the call letters of his radio station in the Purple Grackle. I heard Father tell Mother that it was a "failing" for a man not to show "discre-tion" in things pertaining to his children.

My father seemed to be quite upset with Mr. Erbstein one

night when he told a joke. It turned out all right, but it was touch and go for a few moments. Mr. Erbstein's joke had to do with two Irishmen who stopped off in what was called "A Blind Pig" to have some drinks, before proceeding on their way to the wake of a Jewish friend. The two Irishmen, it seemed, were pretty loaded when they finally staggered up the steps of the Jewish fellow's house and went in to pay their respects. Stumbling around in the crowd of mourners, looking for the casket, they finally decided they had found it and knelt down at the piano, blessed themselves, and moved their lips as they said a prayer for the repose of their friend's soul. As Mr. Erbstein told it, one Irishman pointed at the piano and said, "Ah, but he looks good! If it weren't for him bein' dead, I would say he never had a sick day in his life." The other Irishman kneeling there at the keyboard of the piano nodded his head in agreement and said: "Never saw him lookin' better. And, my, didn't he have a grand set of teeth!"

It was an old joke, I suppose, but I wanted to roll off the dining room chair laughing. My father had a mirthless look, and I didn't dare—until my mother started to giggle and my grandfather, who sat across the table from me, exploded in laughter. Then we all laughed, Mr. Erbstein and my father laughing more than anyone else. I guess my father decided that this was a great joke, because he added it to the repertoire of jokes he told at the end of Thanksgiving and Christmas dinners. It became one of the jokes that I was raised on.

Mr. Erbstein was not always a source of enjoyment at our dinner table. He was always up to something, judging from the frequency of my father's after-dinner anecdotes about him. Thus it was that I heard the Erbstein story that put me in awe of the man.

My father came into the house one evening visibly upset. He walked directly to the sideboard in our dining room and poured himself a drink of whiskey; this didn't happen very often—and, when it did, it was a sign that my father was terribly upset about something. Sensing that something awful had happened, my mother hurried in from the kitchen to embrace my father and ask him what was wrong. My father shook his head and gave a great sigh. "Erbstein tried to kill himself today—in Criminal Court," he said.

My mother was thunderstruck.

"It's true, I'm sorry to say," my father went on.

"What happened?" my mother demanded.

"They were doing what they call 'the closing arguments,' and Charley was on his feet, trying to persuade the jury to set his client free," my father said.

"Set him free on what?" my mother interjected.

"It was one of Charley's murder cases—and they had his client dead to rights," my father said. "This fellow that Charley was defending stood accused of having poisoned his wife, and it seems Charley couldn't use any of his usual tricks to get him out of it. The state had introduced a little bottle that contained the leftover portion of the poison. So Charley picked up this little bottle and held it up for the jury to see and mocked the prosecution's argument that it contained the poison that Charley's client had managed to get into his wife. Before anybody could stop him, Charley uncorked the bottle, raised it to his lips, and drank what was left of the poison."

"Good Heavens!" my mother declared.

"It was bedlam in the courtroom," my father said. "Members of the jury stood up and cried out. The judge stood and called a recess, pounding away like fury with his gavel. The state's attorney was shouting. The bailiffs were running around, not knowing what to do. It was bedlam."

"Did Charley die?" my mother asked anxiously.

My father shook his head. "No," he replied matter-of-factly. "Charley didn't die. He stood off to the side, smiling as if he were getting a lot of pleasure out of all of this commotion he had caused."

"Then it wasn't really poison?" my mother asked.

"Of course it was poison," my father said, getting a little testy. "It was the same concoction that Charley's client had used to do in his wife."

"But it didn't kill Charley, you said," my mother replied.

"No," my father said. "It seems Charley simply walked into a little cloakroom. He had a doctor there, or a nurse, or someone trained in dealing with this kind of emergency, and they pumped his stomach out."

"Good Heavens!" my mother said.

"So when order was restored in the court, and they brought the jury back in, and the judge asked the jury if they had reached a verdict, well, of course they had reached a verdict. The verdict was that Charley's client was not guilty."

I could tell by the look on my mother's face that she thought this was a terrible verdict. But she asked another question: "When the jury announced that the man who poisoned his wife was not guilty, did Charley embrace this awful man?"

My father looked at my mother as if she had suddenly gone daft. "Of course he didn't embrace the man who poisoned his wife. He did a very clever thing to get the man out of it, but Charley doesn't associate with someone he manages to get off a murder charge. Charley Erbstein is not a man who would care to maintain a relationship with a man who would poison his wife."

It hardly ever happened that I heard my father getting cross. My mother never gave him the whisper of a reason for getting cross. But she obviously was not able to deal instantly with the bizarre business of Erbstein's drinking poison. She sighed and turned away. Being only a kid, I couldn't handle the moral complexities of this, either. But I would have to say that from that day forward I lived in awe of Charley Erbstein.

I never learned what my grandfather thought of Erbstein's cunning. I suppose that, being a man of unwavering high standards, he did not approve of employing deceptive tricks to help someone guilty of serious wrongdoing escape paying the penalty he deserved. My grandfather was one of those morally courageous individuals who would go to the bridge with you on a matter of principle, but he was not a man to condone actions that were intrinsically wrong. If you were on the side of what he considered to be "right," I don't think you could ask for a more loyal friend. You wouldn't have much chance with him, though, if his judgment were that you were wrong.

The thing that I remember about my graduation from grammar school is that my grandfather wasn't alive to see it; he had died and been buried at Mount Carmel Cemetery, west of the city. Never having known my father's father, the ship captain, I had developed a great accord with the only grandfather I had known. I don't remember anything about his wake, except that it was in our house. What I remember is that he suffered a great deal of pain before he died, and it had added to my mother's grief that he steadfastly refused to cry, accepting the pain like a Spartan.

Father O'Reilly, sitting on a big red chair on the stage of Our Lady Help of Christians hall—a lineup of BVM nuns behind him—officiated at my graduation from grade school. He had never done an unkindness to any of the school kids; he would have to be judged as a good man and a good priest. But his grim outlook on life had not endeared him to any of us. When the eighth grade sister called my name and I walked over to Father O'Reilly to get my diploma, I joyfully accepted the parchment document, bowed, and turned away—feeling a little silly as the nuns and my parents and the families of all the other kids politely applauded. I .was glad to be getting out of what the kids called "Help."

I wanted to go to DePaul Academy, which was a considerable distance from our house in Austin. I wanted to go there because a couple of boys I ran with had received "scholarships" from DePaul Academy. Every kid in the neighborhood knew these two boys were not "scholars," but muscular boys likely to develop into good football players. The best students in my graduating class were enrolling in St. Mel High School. I was not enthusiastic about it, though I had no serious objections, but I was sent to St. Mel's.

Most of the Christian Brothers at St. Mel's were pleasant and well educated and apparently enjoyed teaching. They were easy to get along with. But the principal was not. He was a burly man who continually sniffed snuff and whose cassock was dusted with crumbs of snuff. He was constantly on patrol of the corridors with an accusatory glare for every boy who happened by. His name was Brother Francis. Not without reason, he was wryly referred to as "The Bear." His favorite pose was to stand with feet spread and hands on his hips, as he scowled threateningly at every boy who passed by. I very much disliked being a student in this school that was run by Brother Bear.

At St. Mel's, each kid received a report card every Friday. The report card had to be returned on Monday morning with a parent's signature on it. It was part of the procedure at St. Mel High School for Brother Francis to storm into every classroom on Friday afternoon and dispense the stack of report cards on the teacher's desk. He seemed to get pleasure from the students' looks of dread. The kids who did exceptionally well, and had the grades to show for it, might get a nod of approval from Brother Francis. Kids like myself, who got B-minuses and C-pluses, frequently were accused by Brother Francis of being lazy and not trying; he was always on me for not getting As in Latin and history and whatever. The kids who got Fs on their weekly report cards were not infrequently whacked on the side of the head by Brother Francis, who further humiliated them by reading aloud their bad grades. The poor kid receiving this abuse looked down at his shoes in shame. I don't think I ever complained to anyone about this cruel behavior of Brother Francis—to whom could I complain? Even when I hit the books—by way of escaping his wrath—and raised my grades a little, he continued to rag me about being lazy. My freshman year at St. Mel High School was dismal. I used to pray that Brother Francis would get transferred to some other Christian Brothers' school; I used to pray that Brother Francis would gag on his snuff and die. To my deep regret, Brother Francis didn't die. But *I* almost did—and that was how I got away from him.

What happened was that in early September, just before I was doomed to return to St. Mel's for my sophomore year, I went swimming one night with some of my pals. It was a chilly night, but we had gone to a club on Madison Street with an indoor pool. When it came time to get dressed we discovered there were no towels. We tried drying ourselves with toilet paper, but, still wet, we pulled on our clothing and headed for home. During the night, I became terribly ill. It was an illness that lasted a long time.

I came down with an extremely bad case of pneumonia. Effective antibiotics were not then available, and the pneumonia spread from one lobe of my lungs to the next. By day and by night, I felt that my blood was alternately boiling and then icy cold. An infection set in, and a quantity of some kind of evil liquid built up in my chest. In a moment of consciousness, I heard the doctors diagnose my problem as empyema—which I learned later, much later, was an accumulation of that evil liquid at such a rate that my system couldn't get rid of it.

Very early in this ordeal, my father brought in a registered nurse from St. Anne's Hospital. Her name was Miss Davison. She was beautiful, and she was an angel. She lived with us for weeks. There was not a solitary thing that Miss Davison could do to make me comfortable that she did not do. I think I was wise enough, even though I was just a kid in pain and frightfully ill, to make things a little easier for her; I tried not to complain and I did not cry.

I thought I was going to die, because everyone else seemed to think I was going to die. This was what the doctors seemed to be saying when they whispered to each other and to Miss Davison. I could tell from the look in my father's eyes that he thought I was going to die. The other kids in our family made an effort to joke with me when they were permitted to come in on brief visits, but—sick as I was—I could sense that they were terribly sad.

Father O'Reilly came into the room one evening and with exceeding gentleness administered the sacrament of extreme unction. I had learned in catechism class at Our Lady Help of Christians School that this was what the priest did when someone was about to die.

The doctors came in one evening acting strangely professional. They pulled up the top of my pajamas and thumped my chest and my back and then rolled me over on my side so that my bare back faced them. I knew they were getting ready to do something serious to me, but I didn't know what. Miss Davison came over and gripped my hands, and I could see she had tears in her eyes. When I asked her what the doctors were going to do to me, she calmly replied, "They are going to aspirate that bad liquid that has built up in you. It is going to hurt a little, so I will stand here and hold on to your hands."

I had never heard the word *aspirate* before. I got to know it well, because they did it three times. Miss Davison had been right; it hurt. What they did was insert a large needle into my back, press it through the space between ribs and into the pleural cavity—where it drained off the soupy stuff inside me. Looking over my shoulder, I could see the greenish-gray pus flow out of me through the rubber tube and into a sterilized glass jug. My parents and Miss Davison had fixed their eyes on me with sadness, and I had managed not to cry out when the wide-mouthed needle had been pressed into me. My serious physical condition had precluded the use of an anesthetic to kill the pain. But there wasn't too much pain, once the needle was inserted—and I felt immediate relief when that stuff started to flow out of me, relieving the pressure that had been building up on my heart and my lungs.

My mother was in agony. She relaxed only when I managed to say that the doctors were making me feel better. But a few nights later, when the doctors came back and gravely said they had not arrested the building up of this fluid in me, I had a sense of terror about having to go through this draining once again. Miss Davison tried not to cry; I remember that. But the repeat performance of the aspirating seemed to be more than my mother could stand.

The door of my bedroom was ajar, and I caught a glimpse of my father with his arm around my mother. I felt terrible, hearing my mother sob in a rare display of grief. Having stood up bravely to the deaths of four children—James, John, Loretta, and Bernard—the imminent loss of yet another was simply too much to ask her to bear. I heard my mother tell my father that she knew I was going to die; that the doctors had been quietly getting her prepared for my dying; that her dear friend, Miss Davison, had admitted there seemed to be very little chance that I could survive. I felt bad that I had gotten so sick and was causing heartbreak to the one person I loved the most. I had an overwhelming sadness the night my mother was engulfed by sorrow at the horrifying prospect that I was to be taken from her. Enduring high fever and pain was one thing; being the cause of having your mother in great despair was far worse.

I was carried to an ambulance and transported to St. Anne's Hospital. There a surgeon made a large incision in my back and removed a section of a rib in an effort to release the green-ish-gray stuff that was building up in me and threatening to snuff the life out of me. I managed to come out of it, and I became a sort of miracle boy for the nuns, the doctors, and the nurses who came into my room for a look at the boy who didn't die. I had a pretty good time being the center of atten-tion at St. Anne's Hospital.

It took many months for the surgical wound to heal. But slowly and steadily, I began to recover. I read a great deal and listened to the radio my father purchased—broadcasting, like myself, trying to get on its feet and develop into whatever it was fated to be.

I took to rereading some of my freshman class books from St. Mel High School, and I became ashamed of myself for not having worked harder to get better grades. My father began to talk about my getting back to school. It pleased me that I was getting strong enough to return to school, though I was dismayed at the prospect of being surrendered once again to the jurisdiction of Brother Francis. One evening, after the fam-ily had had dinner, my father asked if I were up to paying a call on Brother Francis—by way of discussing the possibility of my resuming classes at St. Mel's. I said I would like that—and it was true, because I sorely missed the company of the class-mates who had become my good friends. So off we went, in a taxicab, to the Christian Brothers' rectory on Washington Boulevard.

Brother Francis seemed to be a little wary of my father, a man of imposing stature who was direct but invariably cour-teous. My guess was that Brother Francis was a little nervous about having to deal with my father. Brother Francis kept looking at his wristwatch, as if to suggest that he had more important things than this to attend to. I suspected that my father, who dealt daily with important people in our city, read

Brother Francis quite well—but my father was pleasant and gave no sign of what his impression of this Brother Francis might be.

My father showed no response when Brother Francis volunteered, "It is not even remotely possible that your son can rejoin his old class. They are sophomores now and have already completed their first semester."

"I take it, then," my father said, "that this terminates our conversation. There is no place for my son in your school."

"I didn't say that," Brother Francis replied aggressively. "Provided that certain conditions are met, I am willing to accept him as a member of the present freshman class."

"And what would these conditions be?" my father asked in a gentle voice.

"The primary condition," Brother Francis replied, "would be that his tuition be paid—even though we are now in the second semester—for the entire year."

"Would there be something else?" my father asked.

"Well," Brother Francis responded, pointing at me, "he would be required to behave himself and not cause any trouble."

My father nodded. He said, "Have there been instances where he did not behave himself and caused trouble?"

Brother Francis looked flustered. "I didn't say that," he replied. "I got the feeling from watching him, when he was a freshman, that he is inclined to be scornful of how things are done in our school. I don't want any more of anything like that. Otherwise, he can come back—provided you are willing to pay full tuition."

My father did not indicate his opinion of what had been discussed. He simply nodded and thanked Brother Francis for his kindness in giving us some of his "valuable" time. Then we left.

I wasn't privy to the private discussion that ensued later in the evening between my parents, but apparently they decided that the best they could get out of a bad bargain was to send me back to St. Mel's. That's how it was that I got to be a high school freshman twice.

I didn't last very long at St. Mel's: a couple of months, I guess. For a while The Bear ignored me. For the first few weeks I got high grades—As and B-pluses—and Brother Francis didn't say anything to me. Then I got bored with going over the same schoolwork I had done the previous year. I told myself I already had passing grades in Latin, English, and ancient history and all of that stuff. I didn't see much point in doing my written homework assignments. In class examinations I was fine; but it irritated some of my teachers that I wouldn't turn in the written work and, consequently, they started giving me Is, for "incomplete." The more Is that I got, the more disdainful Brother Francis became when he handed me my report card. I was an unhappy boy.

It was late April, I guess, when I had a final confrontation with The Bear. I was in a corridor on some pretext or other when I unexpectedly encountered Brother Francis. He scowled at me as he strode toward me, his fists clenched, as if he intended to beat me up. I wouldn't want him beating me up under any circumstances and certainly not when I was still convalescing from serious surgery. He made motions as if he were going to belt me, but all he did was roar at me that I was too lazy to do my work and a disgrace to the school. The Bear roared that what I needed was a firm hand and that he intended to give me one—"even though your father wants to baby you." I figured he was going to beat me up, as he had beaten up other kids. I was scared, I am sure. But I made an effort not to let him know it. I loathed him. I longed to tell him that he was a son of a bitch, but I didn't dare. Unexpectedly, he turned away.

Except for the part about wanting to call Brother Francis a son of a bitch, I gave my parents a factual report on all of this as I sat with them at the dinner table that evening. I had gone directly to my locker after my run-in with The Bear and had returned home in midday, with all of my books. My mother, I could see, was really angry about Brother Francis; she referred to him as a "beast" and declared that no one so vicious as this should be entrusted with running a school for boys. My father was impassive; he simply puffed on his evening cigar as

I recounted my sad story. When I finished, he smiled at me and said, "All right, you are well rid of him. You are not going back to Brother Francis; we will find you another school. Unfortunately," my father went on, "this has been an unhappy experience for all of us. But at least you have come face to face with the knowledge that there are people like this in high positions in this world."

I came face to face with Brother Francis only once more. Many months after I had walked out of St. Mel's, I walked back in again to see a basketball game. DePaul Academy, my new school, was playing St. Mel's one night, and I went over there to see the game and meet some of the kids I had gone to school with. And whom do I encounter but The Bear! When I turned to get away from him, he hurried over to me and took his threatening stance. With so many people crowding into the game, I was sure he wouldn't take a swing at me, but I didn't want to talk to him. So he talked to me. Did I miss St. Mel's? No? Well, did I miss my old friends? Not really? Well, was I disappointed in having to go to a "dumb" school like DePaul Academy?

I was only a kid, but I knew he was getting his jollies in sticking it to me. I was getting angry, but at least I had enough sense not to get into an argument with him. He threw me off guard when he suddenly said a few polite things—even wishing me well. "Though that isn't much of a school, that DePaul." And then he asked me to do him a favor. He was running out of snuff, he said, and he would be much obliged if I would do him the kindness of running to a shop down the street to get him a can of snuff. I stared at him.

With Brother Francis glaring at me, awaiting my reply, I said, "I don't go to St. Mel's anymore, Brother Francis. You had better ask one of your own boys to go get you the snuff."

"You don't have to attend St. Mel's to get me the snuff," he grimly replied. "The shop is only down the street a little ways. I am asking you to go get the snuff." I could see he was getting mad. His voice was rising. People filing into the basketball game could see he was angry and hear what he was saying.

I shook my head. "I won't do it, Brother Francis. You want snuff, you can go get it yourself."

He stared at me in utter disbelief. His face turned red, and the muscles on his neck twitched. With the basketball fans gawking at Brother Francis and me, I gave him what I hoped was a look of disdain and joined the crowd that was going in to see the game.

I guess it doesn't matter much, my remembering so vividly my last encounter with someone I had reason to dislike. I shouldn't brag about it, but I guess there is a little bit of Mafia in me. It may take me a while to settle a score with someone who wasn't on the square with me, but I have this urge to get around to it, when I can; how else are you going to live in a world crawling with folks like The Bear?

DePaul Academy was part of DePaul University. It was run by the Vincentian priests. The same as any other school, it had good students and bad ones; decent kids and wild ones; learned and skillful teachers; and teachers with impressive degrees but little else to qualify them for teaching anything to anybody. I really enjoyed my three years at DePaul Academy. The kids were much more relaxed than the kids at St. Mel's. There seemed to be genuine friendship between the priests and the students. They would flunk you if you didn't do your work, or refuse to promote you a grade if you didn't deserve it. But neither the principal nor any of the "profs" ever hollered at a kid or beat up on a kid.

The principal at DePaul Academy was a gracious Vincentian priest named J. J. Edwards. If you came late to class or if a teacher got annoyed with you and kicked you out, you had to go to Father Edwards' office to get his signature on a little card that would get you back in. Just about every kid in my class, including myself, got kicked out every once in a while. I got kicked out of a Spanish class one time when I was called on for a translation but couldn't respond, because, while my head had been turned for some reason, some crazy kid had grabbed my textbook and thrown it out the third-story window. The teacher was mad as the dickens because I didn't even have a book, and he told me to leave the class and not come back until I had Father Edwards' signature on a readmission card. As I got up to leave, I looked at the kid sitting next to me, a friend named John Cortelyou, and asked him if he knew who had thrown my Spanish book out the window. John Cortelyou shrugged, indicating he didn't know anything about it. I figured he knew something but didn't think it was wise to tell me. So down I went to J. J. Edwards' office, and then I forgot about it. Decades later, I was invited to take part in a convocation of some kind at DePaul, the last convocation of DePaul Academy, I think it was, in 1968. I went to make an appearance at the academy's closing ceremonies. I stood off to the side as a long procession of men in caps and gowns started down the sidewalk. At the head of this procession, with the bunting of his various degrees around his neck, was my old classmate, John Cortelyou, now president of DePaul University. Spotting me, he raced over in an unprofessorial way and shook my hand and urged me to march with him and go into the graduation ceremonies with him and otherwise play the role of distinguished alumnus—this honor to be mine, I guess, because I had managed to stay out of prison and politics and had succeeded, somehow, in not getting convicted of libel or otherwise bringing disgrace upon my alma mater. Honor or not, I wasn't getting involved in a couple of boring hours of kids' getting their diplomas, and I begged off. I told my old chum, Cortelyou, that he had better hustle back to the front of the parade because, university president or not, the procession was continuing on its way without him. Cortelyou didn't seem to care about losing his place at the head of the parade. Instead, he looked at me penitentially and said, "Every time I run into you or see you on television I have a feeling of guilt. There is something in the dim past that has gnawed at me for all these years. I have been wanting to apologize to you for a long, long time—but, frankly, I'm afraid I haven't had the courage to do it."

I was surprised to hear the president of DePaul University say something like this. I gently suggested to Cortelyou that he must have slipped a cog in his head, talking so seriously about something in the past, but he shook his head and said,

"You remember when we were in Spanish class in the academy—sitting side by side? Well," the priest said, with a sad sigh, "*I* was the one who threw your book out the window."

I simply stood there, on the lawn of DePaul Academy, and stared at him. He looked to be as repentant as any sinner who has succeeded in working up courage to confess an old sin. Then, suddenly, with this priest looking into my eyes so earnestly, it dawned on me! Yes, the book being tossed out the window! The whole affair, so long dormant in my mind, came back to me. I grinned at the memory of it. Poor, sensitive Cortelyou—standing there in his scholastic gown, the insignia of his scholarly achievements around his neck and the mortarboard on his head. Why, of course it had been Cortelyou who threw my Spanish book out the window! I looked at him full in the eyes and asked, "What in the hell did you do that for—throw my book out the window?"

He replied, "I honestly don't know. I imagine I thought it was a good idea at the time." Then we both laughed, and I told him he had better get moving, and he scurried away to take his place of dignity at the head of the procession.

What I am trying to say is that that was a great place for a kid to get a high school education, DePaul Academy. The building it occupied is still standing and is still in use for something or other. I go look at it occasionally when I'm up in that area. I've got a couple of bittersweet memories of the place, of course; it had been a great disappointment for me, when I tried to get some small job on the student newspaper, that the kids who had control of it looked at some copy I had written and handed it back to me, telling me I was a good kid but I would never make it as a newsman. The terse turndown had me feeling bad for a while. But not even student editors know everything, I guess—and I owe something to a lot of people, including Brother Francis the Bear, for making it possible for me to go to DePaul Academy.

I spent my last two years at DePaul Academy—1929 and 1930—as a protected young man in stormy economic seas. The frightful stock market crash of October 1929 provided the ominous signal that the world we had known was on a very steep slide into disaster. By the time I graduated, in 1931, the nation was struggling to survive—and slowly losing the battle. Many a man on our block and in our neighborhood had lost his job, with utterly no prospect of finding another. The small banks in our neighborhood closed their doors; people we knew with savings accounts in these places gathered forlornly outside—knowing the nest eggs they had scrimped to put aside for emergencies and their old age had been devoured by an economic monster that came to be known as the Great Depression. People we knew lost their homes because they had no money to make the monthly mortgage payments; the irony of this was that the lending institutions that foreclosed on them subsequently filed for bankruptcy. These were terribly hard times.

The onslaught of the Great Depression had minimal effect on our household. Except emotionally. Because of the drastically lower prices on everything, the Depression—we all came to realize—was a boon to families like ours that had a steady income. But we came to suspect that some of our friends and neighbors didn't have enough to eat; I was away at DePaul Academy most of the day and didn't get to see what was going on in our block, but kids who lived near us began to thank me, with looks of both gratitude and shame in their eyes, for the staples and meat that my mother was casually providing the neighbor ladies. One woman, for example, regularly came to our back door to "borrow" a cup of flour and went home with eggs and butter and homemade bread and meat and all manner of edibles that my mother gently suggested the other woman "might like to try." I was not able to get it out of my mind that people who were our friends actually did not have enough to eat, and I felt guilty when I sat down at our dinner table. I think my mother and father and the other kids felt the same way. Sometimes, when the dessert plates had been cleared away, we heard grim tales of banks "having a run" on them. Depositors, fearful of the safety of their money, were lining up at the tellers' cages to close their accounts. Dinner time at our house, as far as I could judge, was turning into an unending recounting of frightening stories. Who ever heard of such terrible things—people losing their jobs and their homes and their savings, people not having anything to eat?

The only grown-up I knew who had firmly predicted a depression was my father. Throughout 1928 and well into 1929, he persistently preached the gospel that the American people were in what he referred to as a "fools' paradise." He protested constantly that "ordinary people" were squandering their savings on investments in the stock market. He deplored the national infatuation with buying stock on "margin"—ten percent down. He warned us at dinner every night that even if initially you were fortunate enough to get rich without working for your money, almost certainly you would stay in this suicidal game too long. Yet the stock prices continued to rise, and the daily newspapers carried front-page stories about people "making a killing" on "tips" provided wholesale by the stock brokers. My father took to bringing to our dinner table the annual reports of major corporations, and, having lit his after-dinner cigar, he would summarize these reports—always concluding with his personal calculation of what the reports came down to: dismal earnings per share.

One evening after dinner, my father, with a reassuring smile on his face, announced that we would now have to "tighten our belts," because he had been notified that day by his superiors that everyone at his level of earnings at the bank would be obliged to accept a ten-percent salary cut.

Not too long afterward, Father came home one night, walked directly to his decanter of whiskey, and—after downing his drink—told my mother: "Dan Smith's lost his money, and it doesn't appear he can save his company." Mr. Smith was broke! Whoever would think something like this could happen! My mother simply could not believe it. My father, speaking softly, said, "I'm afraid it's worse than that. Dan has been accused of embezzlement of some kind; gambling away someone else's money on stocks. It's a federal matter, but I don't have the details."

As they sat together at the dining room table that evening, I heard my mother ask my father if things were so bad with Mr. Smith that he would wind up in jail. "I don't know," my father replied. "I expect he thinks he might. He stopped by the office today, and he told me that while he was prepared for the worst—he *did* get reckless with someone else's money, I think—he had no intention of going to prison. He pulled a little silver box out of his pocket and showed it to me, and all that was in the little box was one tiny pill. I asked him what it was, but he wouldn't say; poison of some kind, I think." I was depressed, hearing that Mr. Smith was ready to swallow poison.

Some weeks later it came to pass. Mr. Smith had been found guilty in Federal Court. On the morning that he was due back in court for sentencing, as one of his sons waited outside the house to drive him downtown, Mr. Smith apparently decided the moment had come to take his pill. His son told my father that when it seemed his dad was taking a long time to get dressed, he had gone upstairs to see what the delay was—and found Mr. Smith sprawled out on his bedroom floor. My mother and my father, both looking grieved, exchanged knowing looks when my father recounted this story.

I had more or less become accustomed to hearing that wealthy men my father had done business with were driven to suicide by losing their money in the stock market crash. Some of those who killed themselves were men my father frequently had talked about; they were "society" people, home builders, and men of prominence in one thing or another, all of them now stone broke. It was a tenet of our religion that killing yourself was defiance of God and one of the most awful things a person could do; sometimes I would think about the certain damnation that had awaited Judas when he hanged himself after having set up Christ for a payoff of silver.

In such terrible days, I completed my high school education. On the night I graduated from DePaul Academy I went alone to get my diploma. I hadn't told my family about the graduation ceremonies, because my mother was seriously ill in Passavant Hospital, and my reckless judgment was that the commencement would only cause inconvenience for my family. My mother was genuinely shocked when I walked into her hospital room the next day and showed her my diploma. But then she giggled. One of my brothers and my two sisters were furious

with me, and one of my sisters told me I was not "civilized."
I was afraid my father would be upset with me, but he seemed
to regard my private graduation as amusing. My father asked
me if I had celebrated, and he howled (although I didn't think
it was funny) when I told him that one of my classmates, Harry
Bauler, had taken me over to his dad's speakeasy, and his old
man—Alderman Paddy Bauler—had bought me a couple of
beers and cooked up a pan of hot dogs in the kitchen at the
rear of the place.

I didn't do much of anything during the summer of 1931.
We played softball for hours and hours at a time. I went on
the Lake Michigan excursion boats with my mother. I went to
Wrigley Field a great many afternoons, as one of my uncles
had a gate pass and little interest in whether the Cubs won or
lost. Now and again, there would be a discussion at our house
about where I would go to college, everybody assuming that
this was what I would be doing for the next four years. With
the nation deep in its Depression, a kid with reasonably good
high school grades could get into any school, because few families could afford to send someone to college. But it began to
appear that I wouldn't be going to college. As the summer
wore on, I hadn't received a letter of admission from a solitary
institution. My father was annoyed.

It was my fault that I was not getting accepted; my parents
had left it to me to fill out and mail the application forms, and
I had procrastinated. The reason I hadn't applied anywhere—
not a very good reason—was that I had little interest in going
off to college. Some of the best-known men in our neighborhood—educated men—were out of work. A couple of bright
and college-educated young men who were longtime friends
of my eldest brother took to dropping in at dinner time to
gulp a few drinks and have a big meal; they were marvelous
storytellers with a seemingly endless string of funny stories
about what Wall Street had been like when the stock market
crashed, and they had simply walked out of their stock brokerage businesses without bothering to lock the door. They
had been "paper millionaires," and now they were broke. And

the newspapers wrote about "important" men who were now selling apples on the downtown sidewalks.

But as the summer months drifted by, I became painfully aware that I had wise-guyed myself out of something I should have recognized as important to me. Then, one August afternoon, a recruiter from a college in Davenport, Iowa—St. Ambrose College—came calling on the families of high school graduates in our neighborhood. He talked to the kids, he talked to their parents, and he even had some kind of plan to make a college education available to a boy of limited means. I was invited to meet with this priest from St. Ambrose College, but I had never heard of the place and didn't have any interest in being enrolled there. I don't remember where I drifted off to, but when I came home, there was this priest from St. Ambrose College in conversation with my mother in our front parlor.

I don't remember how the arrangements were worked out; probably, I never heard. I certainly had not been involved in the negotiations. But a few weeks later, not without some mental reservations, I was taken with my luggage to the LaSalle Street Station and put aboard a Rock Island Railroad train that was taking off for the four-hour trip to Davenport, Iowa, and points beyond. Like it or not, I was off to college.

I hadn't been too joyful about getting sent to St. Ambrose College. On the train ride to Davenport, I felt sorry for myself for not having applied to Notre Dame or Northwestern or some such big-time place. I was depressed that I had put myself into what some of the kids referred to as a "cow college." Many times, thinking back on all of this, I have admitted to myself that I had been a snob. St. Ambrose was probably the best thing that could have happened to me.

Situated on high ground on the outer reaches of the city, St. Ambrose was a lovely place. Save for a couple of new buildings, the physical plant consisted of large red-brick structures with ivy on the walls. Healthy oak trees of considerable size were spread out nicely on the campus.

Hard times had compelled major universities to terminate brilliant young professors, and those talented men subsequently found work at the small colleges. St. Ambrose had an exceptional faculty. The head of the Chemistry Department, for example, was a feisty young man named Jeremiah Goggin, who invented luminous paint and one of whose students eventually invented synthetic fabrics and got rich in the process. A priest named Ulrich Hauber, the head of biology, was an agreeable man who held that the available textbooks were harmfully tedious, so he wrote his own. I had, in short, lucked into a place that had some very special professors. One of my favorites was a fashionably dressed Bostonian sort of man named Tom Lally, who was exceedingly particular in the matter of deciding which students he would permit to take his courses; he limited his class in economics, for example, to only six or seven of us.

We had a priest, a Father Henry Takkenberg, who rated with me—and still does—as one of the most erudite men I ever met. He was a slick, bald-headed little man who snapped his eyes around with the confidence of a blue jay—a man who had picked up PhD's in such disparate subjects as English and physics and chemistry. "Tacky," as we called him, taught freshman English, drama writing, and short-story writing. I took all three courses, doing poorly in freshman English and getting top grades in the other subjects. It might be a little much to say that Father Takkenberg had a greater influence on me than any other teacher I ever had, but I know I enjoyed his classes more than I enjoyed any others, anywhere.

Father Takkenberg was repelled by having fifty or sixty students in one class, which was the burden he had in freshman English. Tacky preferred his writing classes, where he arbitrarily limited to five the number of kids he would deal with. It was his pleasure to conduct his writing classes in the little cottage he lived in. His writing classes were supposed to be limited to forty-five or fifty minutes but invariably ran on twice as long and frequently even longer than that, and not one of the students complained.

It annoyed me that while Takkenberg was pleased to give me top grades in his "exclusive" writing classes, he had weighted me down with a string of "Incompletes" in freshman English. These "Incompletes" eventually threatened to preclude my receiving a degree. My deficiency in freshman English was that

I hadn't bothered to commit to memory, as required, considerable amounts of classic poetry. I told him once, when he politely inquired about my refusal to memorize the poetry, that I thought it was "silly." He had smiled and said, "I couldn't agree with you more. But in this intolerable situation in which they have placed me, how else would you suggest that I keep all of those healthy young minds occupied?"

It was with much pleasure that I would hurry over to Tacky's cottage for the writing classes. He would bring out ashtrays and bottles of beer and we would have a great time. Takkenberg had personal friendships with successful Broadway playwrights and professional writers, and he occasionally would go off to New York to see the plays and have dinner with his old friends. By way of establishing his credentials for teaching us short-story writing, Tacky had written four or five magazine stories that were published under *noms de plume* in *Collier's*— no small feat. Takkenberg enjoined us to keep quiet about his literary moonlighting, but it came to the attention of Bishop Henry P. Rohlman, and Tacky wryly told us he had been called down to the chancery office to explain. Father Takkenberg told us that the bishop, whom we all knew as a decent man, had congratulated him on his professional skill. However, the bishop ordered Tacky to cut it out—on the grounds that these were hard times and it ill-behooved a Catholic priest to deprive professional writers of an opportunity to earn a living. Takkenberg merely shrugged when his writing class protested the bishop's naked display of censorship. But when I thought about it, it pleased me very much that I knew a bishop who had such judgment of things.

I never got the slightest clue, nor did the four others in Father Takkenberg's class, as to what he thought of our short stories. The students dissected one another's stories in bitterly candid critiques during class. Then, having retyped the manuscripts, we mailed the things to the best magazines. Occasionally, one of us would get a letter from an editor who said the story showed "promise" and, "Please let us see anything else you write." But not a solitary one of us was lucky enough to sell a story—and the funny thing about this, I think, was that at least three of us subsequently spent our lives in writing. One of the guys wound up as an editor of *The New Yorker*. But it didn't seem to bother Takkenberg, one way or the other, that we were unable to do what he so casually had done.

When I got into my third year at St. Ambrose, I unexpectedly was selected to be editor of the college newspaper. I had gotten into the practice of writing for the college paper, and it pleased me that the guys running this weekly thought I was pretty good; at least, they used everything that I wrote. There had been a great deal of speculation, at the end of my sophomore year, as to who the new editor would be; one of the likely choices for the editor's job—and I thought he deserved it, if only because he carefully went over the copy and was dependable in getting it down to the printer—was a guy who had expressed dissatisfaction with my stories. I really thought this kid, who was to be a senior, deserved the job, although I figured that if he got it I wouldn't be working for him. Some of my friends said I should be the editor, but we all understood that this was a job to be given to a fourth-year man. It was pretty startling when the president of the college announced that *I* was going to be the editor.

It was no small thing to be the editor. The college policy was to "reward" the editor by remitting half of his expenses— tuition, board, fees, and I don't know what all. I hadn't known about this, and I was delighted. I thought my father would be proud of me. My father was enormously pleased that I had been chosen for a job so prestigious. But he frowned when he heard that I had fallen heir to a rather substantial financial benefit. "It pleases me very much that you have received this recognition," he said. "Yet it disturbs me that the sum in question might well be that which makes the difference in whether a lad in financial need will be able to stay in school or be compelled to leave it."

I can't say that I shared my father's concern about the plight of a hypothetical kid's having to leave college because I would benefit by a sum he might desperately need. I hadn't thought of that contingency of my good fortune. But I had more or less programmed my father to make this response. Not infrequently, I mentioned in my letters home that kids that I had been going to class with had vanished overnight, their parents no longer able to carry the costs of keeping them in school. The kids were generally too embarrassed to suffer the pain of sticking around to say good-bye. In later years, when I read the stories of innocent people in war-torn Europe disappearing overnight, this provoked sad memories in me. It wasn't that a kid unexpectedly leaving St. Ambrose could be compared to the individuals dragged out of their homes in France or Germany or Poland or some such place—never to be seen again—but there was a faint and disturbing similarity to the kids' vanishing from my college residence hall in the dead of night.

If I wondered what had happened to the kids who were compelled to leave school, I suppose I had reason to wonder where life would have taken *me* if I had not been placed in a college job that seems to have directed my life; I wouldn't be writing any books, I am sure, if I had gone into dealing in stocks or bonds or manufacturing shoes or something like that—though I might have done a lot better with stocks and bonds. Who knows?

I got so involved in trying to produce a college newspaper that the students and faculty might enjoy reading that I more or less neglected my scholarship. Sometimes the president of the college would drop by my room to ask if I could find time to write a speech he had promised to make and didn't have time to prepare. I did some publicity work for the college. I kept busy and had a grand time, to be honest about it. But I was always playing catch-up on my class assignments, and my grades suffered.

I lived next door to a small corner suite occupied by a priest who taught me in English literature. The constant pounding of my typewriter as I worked late into the night annoyed the hell out of this priest; I guess I kept him awake. One day the priest demanded an explanation as to just what it was that had kept me at my typewriter the previous night. My reply was that I had been working on a term paper for him. This was true. This priest had a heavy hand in doling out his assignments. For reasons that might have related to my nocturnal typing, he didn't have high regard for my writing; I continually received a mediocre C from him. I didn't mind. There were three or four kids, not especially bright kids, who consistently got A's from him on their written work. Our private joke, which partially explained my being at the typewriter at ungodly hours, was that I wrote the reports of the kids who got A's. Why not? These kids were friends, though they did slip me two or three dollars to get them out of a tight spot. Father Takkenberg caught me at this one night and thought it was hilarious. His counsel was that I should be careful to reserve the best report for myself. This I tried to do—but I still got a C on what I judged to be the best paper, and the other kids got an A on the stuff I had written but didn't regard as being quite on the mark. Well, you can't win them all, as the saying goes.

Father Takkenberg came calling one evening to ask if I could find time to write a play. Tacky had set up a class to teach a few of us how dramatic stuff was put together, and somebody had put the arm on him to come up with an original play students in the Speech Department could perform. I told Tacky I didn't think I could do it, but I would try. With Takkenberg using a heavy pencil on the stuff I wrote, I dreamed up a plot about a renegade wire service reporter giving up his life to save that of a bad priest in Mexico. Our play went over very well in its limited engagement. It was a great thrill for me to have characters on a stage reading my lines. I wrote a couple of other plays that were not so good but were staged anyway, and I got to daydreaming about being a dramatist. Nothing came of that, but thanks to Tacky, I learned a little bit about it—enough to make some money later writing radio plays.

I was having a good time, but getting an education was interferring with my extracurricular activities. Father Takkenberg occasionally would urge me to memorize some of the classical poetry so he could pass me in freshman English. But I never managed to get around to doing it. I would argue with him that I was too busy. He told me that I had to get rid of that "Incomplete" legitimately and that he couldn't simply eliminate it, or members of the faculty who didn't think much of me—such as the priest who lived next door—would raise hell. So I would promise to try to memorize some of his poetry to get out of this jam; but I never got around to it.

Part of my problem was that St. Ambrose College, as part of its struggle to stay alive, was getting good in football and basketball, and I was getting terse telegrams from the *Des Moines Register* and the *Chicago Tribune*, asking me to file tiny stories. It made me feel important—not to mention the little checks that would come in the mail, in payment for the fifty or seventy-five words I had sent them. The *Tribune* sometimes sent me five whole dollars!

I got to be a stringer for both the *Davenport Democrat* and the *Davenport Times*. They were rival papers—although both were owned by the Lee Syndicate—and they didn't much like the idea of my writing for "the enemy." A very nice man named Ralph Leysen, the managing editor of the *Times*, called me in one day to talk about my "lack of propriety" in stringing for both papers; I thought he was going to can me, but he stopped short of that. Anyhow, for a kid who was supposed to be getting a college education, I was terribly busy with other things.

Late in my senior year, Father Takkenberg came to my room one night to restate his thoughts about my "Incomplete" in freshman English. Well, I was getting close to graduation and I had been worrying about the "Incomplete." "I know you have been preoccupied with one thing or another," he said. "But my thinking is that we should attend to that deficiency, and I have called on you to take an examination. I mean, take an examination right now."

I should have known that the day of accounting would come. But it had been a long time since I had looked at his obligatory poetry. For an awful moment—wondering how I was going to explain to my folks that I wouldn't be getting a degree—I thought, well, here I go.

Looking quite serious, Father Takkenberg said, "I trust you will understand that the content of an examination is entirely at the discretion of the professor who teaches the course. In accordance with this principle, I have arrived at a formula of scholastic inquiry that I would like to think will satisfy the deficiency that confronts us. So I place the question to you:

can you recite for me, in its entirety, the poem entitled, 'Mary Had A Little Lamb'?"

I looked at him in disbelief. I said, "Is this supposed to be a joke, Father Takkenberg?"

He firmly shook his head. "I am quite serious," he replied. "This examination is well within the parameters we have just discussed. So, again, I ask you: Are you familiar with the words of this examination poem? If so, I ask that you give me a recitation."

Embarrassed and perplexed, I cleared my throat and said: "Mary had a little lamb, with fleece as white as snow. And everywhere that Mary went, the lamb was sure to go. . ."

"Excellent!" declared Father Takkenberg.

So, if anyone ever raises the question of how it was that I managed to get a degree in English from St. Ambrose College, well, there you go.

My family drove in from Chicago for my convocation. Not having paid a great deal of attention to the matter of who was getting citations for scholarship, I had been as surprised as my family when I was called up to the bishop a second time and—would you believe this?—given a citation for scholastic honors. My mother and father thought this was just grand. Later we had a celebration lunch at the Blackhawk Hotel. I broke it up early, having a date to do an interview in the early afternoon with a crude heavyweight prize fighter who went by the name King Levinsky. My father, having read somewhere that King Levinsky had been a fishmonger on Chicago's Maxwell Street before pursuing a career in the ring, took a dim view of this job that I had found for myself.

"We spend all of these years providing a son with an education," my father said, "and what does he do with it? He gets a degree and goes off to interview King Levinsky!"

My father was a little disappointed, I'm afraid, that I had taken a job with the *Davenport Times*. Personally, I thought I was lucky to have a job to go to on the day of my graduation; there weren't too many in my graduating class who had much chance of finding a steady job. Some of what we called "the churchies" were going off to seminaries to study for the priesthood. We had a few kids who were going off to big eastern schools to get master's degrees and PhD's in literature and history and business. A couple of the young guys were going to medical school, and a couple of others were going into law. Against this background, I could see that it wasn't much to be going off to get a story out of King Levinsky. But you have to begin somewhere, and when Ralph Leysen of the *Davenport Times* had offered me a spot on his staff, I had taken it.

The *Davenport Times* was a good newspaper. But you had to work for your money. The rule was that the editorial people showed up at seven-thirty in the morning and, with a brief period for lunch, you were lucky to get out by four-thirty in the afternoon. We published three editions, six days a week. When President Roosevelt was yammering about making the forty-hour work week the law of the land, Leysen—who was a fast and fine writer—did an editorial that tore Roosevelt apart: how absurd was this "New Deal" going to get, limiting American workers to a mere forty hours of work? I worked pretty hard, but I would have to say that if you wanted to learn how a newspaper gets to press, this was an ideal place.

They put me on what they called "the state desk," which meant I had to edit piles of amateurish news items that had come in overnight from what we grandly described as "correspondents" in a great many small communities in eastern Iowa and western Illinois. A lot of this stuff was so bad that I couldn't believe any newspaper would be willing to pay ten cents an inch for the stories I had to patch up before sending to the composing room. If I complained that I had never even heard of the towns this garbage was coming from, the news editor sitting across from me would irritatedly say, "It doesn't matter if you've never heard of these places; fix it up to be set in type."

The editor I was shaping this stuff up for was an irascible character who knew his business and was regarded with fear by all of the reporters. His name was M. A. Fulton. He was a gruff old bastard. In moments of weakness he would own up to being a deacon or something like that at a Methodist church in a community north of us on the Mississippi. Occasionally at

deadline, he would get so upset at what he judged to be am-
biguity in a story that he would curse and throw it back at me
or holler for the reporter who had written the piece to provide
a translation. I kidded Fulton once when he was in one of his
rages, telling him it was offensive to me to be working with a
church deacon who used such shocking language. I was only
kidding him—trying to get him to calm down, I guess—but I
never did it again, because he took my remonstrating seriously,
apologized for his bad words, and vowed he would try to control his "un-Christian" temper. Of course, he did not thereafter control his temper, but how is a good editor supposed to
get copy together, if he doesn't holler at somebody every once
in a while?

I got pretty fond of "Fult." He was an exceedingly nice man,
granting that he roared and threw a paste pot at me every now
and then. M. A. Fulton was a purist in the matter of writing
accurately. He drilled into me the lesson that, if you are going
to write something, you might just as well get the facts straight.
In his despair at the bad writing of some story he was anxious
to send to the composing room, he would turn to his typewriter
and rewrite the thing with great speed. There was not much
style to anything that he wrote, but he invariably did a work-
manlike job. One thing about him was that his copy was "clean,"
with no X-ing out or anything like that. One afternoon, when
the Goss press of the *Davenport Times* was grumbling out the
final edition and a copy boy was running up the stairs with
samples of the final edition under his arm, plopping one on
every desk for reporters to quickly scan their stories for accuracy, Fult walked over to me with an evangelical look in his
eye.

"You're a good writer," he said matter-of-factly, "and I don't
want you to take any offense at this. But you are getting into
a bad habit of turning in dirty copy. I suggest you start watching
yourself on that—because it increases the chances that a linotype operator will misread something and give us a bad mistake
in your story." I was a little offended at this suggestion. It was
true that, having to turn out so much stuff, I was handing in
copy marked with penciled corrections. I had been schooled

on the virtue of producing "clean" copy; Father Takkenberg had drilled into me the precept that a heavily edited manuscript is a telltale sign of the writer's muddled mind. So I had been aware of what I was doing. But from that day forward, although I never worked in a place where "clean copy" was characteristic, I have always been reasonably careful about putting temptation in a linotyper's eyes.

I got to know a goodly number of the farm wives in Iowa and Illinois who served as our "correspondents"; I was on the phone with these gals a lot, and not infrequently my rewrite of their information produced much longer stories than they would have dared to send us, and the extra length added to the "inches of type" that they would get paid for. But the day came, not too many weeks after I had gone to work on the *Davenport Times*, that I was moved out of my job with Fulton.

What happened was that one of the paper's top reporters had the bad luck to die. I hardly knew the man, and I certainly did not expect that I would wind up with his "beat"; there were two other young guys with seniority who were more likely candidates than I for the dead man's assignments. It was understood that the replacement would not be announced until the guy who had died was buried. It was more or less obligatory that everyone on the editorial staff attend the funeral. The pastor of the fellow's church scheduled the church services for late afternoon—to permit all of us to attend, as the final edition was now on the press.

Then the pastor, looking frightfully morose, gave his little talk about our reporter who was dead. Except for this pastor's not seeming to know much about the man who was dead—and I had been at requiem Masses where the priest obviously didn't know a damned thing about the guy he was preaching over— it seemed to me that this religious send-off went well. But one of the *Davenport Times'* mourners didn't think so.

Outside the church, as the casket was being placed in a hearse for the journey to the cemetery, our people were gathered in little groups—hats off and looking solemn. Our publisher, E. P. Adler, was standing with Ralph Leysen. Leysen turned to the publisher and said he thought the funeral had gone very well. E. P. Adler grunted. Leysen, getting a little anxious, asked, "Don't you agree with me, E. P., that the service went very well?"

E. P. looked glum. He didn't respond immediately. Finally he pointed to the pastor and said, "The son of a bitch didn't mention the *Davenport Times* once! Not even once!" Into each life some rain must fall, I guess.

A couple of days later Leysen called me into his office and told me that he was giving me the dead guy's job. I was aware, I'm sure, that the two young reporters with seniority would be madder than hell, but I was glad to get the job. There would be an automatic raise in my pay, the managing editor said, because of my "added responsibilities." I was glad to hear about the raise in pay; God knows this newspaper didn't pay its reporters very much. But I was also just about fed up with helping M. A. Fulton put together three or four pages every day about the fascinating happenings in Muscatine and Strawberry Point, Iowa, and the other exciting places that got space every day in our "farm edition." Getting the dead man's beat was like getting paroled.

My new job required that I attend the morning press conference of a tough old guy named Colonel A. G. Gillespie, who ran the Rock Island Arsenal. The big story there, our city editor told me, was the Army's supposedly secret work on developing a mobile tank that would be terribly important in the next world war—"if there ever is one." And I had to pay a daily call on the U. S. Army Engineers' Rock Island District offices, to see if there were anything new in their enormously expensive program to control the Mississippi with locks and dams that would extend all the way down to New Orleans. When movie stars and other assorted big wheels came to our area, I had to do long interviews with the notables. You worked for your money, meager as it was, at E. P. Adler's *Davenport Times*.

The sports editor, a fat little guy named Leo Kautz, discovered that I had once had a passion for major league baseball, and he conned me into covering the minor league games in Davenport's riverfront stadium. The worst part of this assignment was that they were night games. With my regular schedule, it was a sixteen-hour work day before the game was over and I had written my report and hung it on a hook near Fulton's desk for the night-shift composing room guys who would set it in type and leave galleys on Kautz's desk. It was good baseball; the Davenport team was about the best there was in the Western League, which was but a step below the major leagues. But on the nights Davenport's team played a double-header, it grieved me to watch a paddle-wheeler—with a band playing and a joyful crowd aboard—heading downstream early in the first game. I figured I would be lucky if we were in the fifth or sixth inning of the second game when the boat came back again, heading for the dock. A couple of times Kautz sent me to Iowa City to cover football games at the University of Iowa, which had one of the best teams in the Big Ten.

Every reporter on the paper was obligated to come up with three or four lengthy feature stories for our Thursday paper. Thursday was the day we published a "fat" paper, filled with food-store advertising. And management had a notion that these editions should be puffed up with reading material, to preserve the delusion that *this* was a newspaper. Nobody seemed to care what kind of stories you put on the hook for the Thursday food section, and I took to dreaming up some pretty wild stuff. I wrote one tongue-in-cheek story about a taxicab's driving through the streets of Paris, France, with the head of a horse sticking out of the roof. My explanation was that the horse, panicked by something or other, had jumped onto the cab and had crashed through the canvas roof. The driver in this little story of mine was blithely unaware that a horse sat in his cab. I enjoyed thinking up crazy stories like this and seeing them printed in the *Davenport Times*. But one day Leysen called me into his office, and I thought, well, it was fun while it lasted.

Naturally, I expected that Leysen was going to raise hell. But he shocked me. He said he had been reading with great interest the "unique" stories I had been writing for the Thursday food section. And he said he had hit upon a great idea to have me write a column, three days a week, on any subject matter that interested me. This would be in addition to my other assignments, the managing editor said, but he would add an extra five dollars to my pay, if I would agree to do this. I mildly protested that five dollars wasn't much compensation for three columns a week. He said it would be a great opportunity to display my ability, as editors in all parts of the nation—or so he said—scrutinized the small-town papers. I was about to say no, thanks, but then I figured—oh, what the hell; why not give it a try?

Some days it was easy, and some days I really bled. The worst part of it was that some of my colleagues, with a good deal more seniority than I had on the paper, were bitter about Leysen's giving me the column—but their dismay eased up a bit when they discovered that often I was so hard up for something to write that I frequently was forced to spend evenings in the city room trying to think up something.

We didn't have much of a "morgue"—a reference library—at the *Davenport Times*. But nicely bound copies of old newspapers, going back a long way, were available. I took to thumbing through these almost daily. In time, I learned more about the past of Davenport, Iowa, than I had really cared to know. A running story that fascinated me, going back a great number of years, had to do with the founding and growth of an inventive enterprise called the Palmer School of Chiropractic. The motherhouse of this extraordinary adventure in "medical science" was in Davenport. It was ruled—and owned, I guessed—by a bearded gentleman who liked to be referred to as "Colonel" B. J. Palmer. I had been sent up there by our city editor, a competent newspaperman named Bob Klauer, to do a long piece on Colonel Palmer, and this assignment triggered a great interest in this place that taught the "science" of making ailing humans feel better by moving their spinal cords around.

If Colonel Palmer were an educated man, he successfully deceived me. He was loquacious, but he didn't seem to say anything. I tried, for example, to find out how he had come to be a "colonel," but to no avail; he blissfully ignored my questions about that. Colonel Palmer, who prided himself on being a "world traveler," interrupted our interview to do his

weekly travel broadcast for his radio station, WOC, which had
its studios in the Palmer School. He invited me to sit by as he
did his broadcast. "You will find this very educational," he
said—and he was right; I did. The colonel's program began
with his unashamedly reading some copy intended to explain
what a brilliant man he was. Then he got into his travel copy,
which consisted of travel agency brochures spread before him.
I wondered how in hell you could get away with doing something like this on radio, but I decided that nobody would holler
if you owned the station.

The star announcer at WOC, by the way, was "Moon" Reagan. Moon's brother—Ronald—was a sportscaster at the other
B. J. Palmer radio station, WHO in Des Moines. There was a
little talk about the Reagan brothers being in pretty good shape
with Colonel Palmer, the spine mechanic.

I tried not to be petty or mean when I wrote a long story
about the great Colonel B. J. Palmer. But when I handed it in
to Klauer, he scanned it and then, imperturbably, asked, "Do
you want me to drop this in the wastebasket, or would you
prefer, as the reporter who wrote this beautiful piece, to do
that yourself?"

There were a couple of us on the editorial staff who didn't
seem to have much luck with our Palmer School of Chiropractic stories. Part of the problem was that our publisher was
a personal friend of Colonel Palmer. I should have suppressed
my curiosity about B. J. Palmer, but I kept finding interesting
little items in the old papers about the Palmer School of Chiropractic and—just for the pleasure of it—I kept writing little
stories, but they always wound up in the city editor's wastebasket. One day Klauer called me over to his desk and, in one
of those man-to-man conversations, said he was tired of reading
my items about the Palmer School. "You don't seem to realize," he said, "that that old bird is a community asset. It is not
our practice to take sly little shots at community assets."

"The established medical profession doesn't seem to regard
the Palmer School as an asset," I replied.

Klauer nodded and said, "Yeah, I know what they say about
B. J. Palmer—and that's not my concern. My concern is that

B. J. Palmer has a homecoming for the school's graduates once a year. Thousands of them come here—and they spend a lot of money. It's big business for the hotels and the stores, and, because we run the advertising, it is big business for us. I admit I get a charge out of some of your stories. But, you know, it doesn't make sense to keep throwing little rocks at the bird that is laying the golden eggs. You get what I mean?"

Yeah, I got what he meant, and I stopped bothering him with my fascinating little items about the Palmer School of Chiropractic. You live and learn what it is that makes the world go 'round, I guess.

I didn't have much more traffic with Klauer, because the spokesman for a group of well-heeled Davenporters unexpectedly offered me a job that would pay more than twice what I was getting from the *Davenport Times*—and I took it. I accepted the job of editor of a privately published weekly called *The Catholic Messenger,* which the group of monied guys were buying from an old-line family that had published the thing for decades and decades, without even attempting the slightest change in its makeup.

Leysen thought I was making a big mistake. He went so far as to say that his judgment was that some day I would have his job; it pleased me that he would be nice enough to pay me a compliment like this—although inwardly I cringed at the prospect of winding up with his job. Fulton simply said he had never expected I would stick around very long.

As for *The Messenger*, Fulton said, "You've had the training to do a good job with it—although my advice to you would be to make haste slowly, because the readership of *The Messenger* is accustomed to the old-style format and won't be pleased if you change its content and its appearance too quickly." He was a smart guy, that Fulton, and I should have followed his advice.

I had a nice talk with Fulton. But he surprised me when he said, "I think the people who bought the paper have made a good choice in selecting you as editor, but I hope they're smart enough to know you won't be working for them very long. There are some people in our business—Leysen, for example, and perhaps myself—who are quite content to earn their spurs in a small city like Davenport and spend their lives in the one place. I don't know where life is going to take you, but I expect you'll wind up in Chicago or New York or Washington. You've got newsprint in your blood, and you'll never get rid of it. So, I wish you well, and my hope for you is that you find a lifetime of good stories to cover." He was a marvelous man.

In later years I saw only one of these guys who had taught me how to put out a newspaper. I ran into Klauer, a die-hard Republican, at a presidential nominating convention one time. It was a Democratic convention. It had been more than twenty years since I had seen Klauer, and I was quite surprised to see him. Was he covering the convention for somebody? "No," he replied, grinning at me, "I'm a delegate—from Arizona." I said I thought he was a died-in-the-wool Republican! "Yeah," he said, laughing. "I was. But let us say I finally saw the light and converted to the true faith. You've heard about things like that, haven't you?" Yeah, I had heard about things like that. Strange things happen in the space of twenty years or so.

Fulton had been right. I immediately, and drastically, changed the writing style and the format of the Catholic weekly. The new owners were ecstatic, but the faithful readers who loved their old paper, having read it every week all of their lives, were deeply offended. Overnight, you might say, I had jazzed it up typographically. I drastically cut the tediously long reports from the Vatican and from the Catholic bishops in the United States. I ran a great many spot news pictures. When I got a tip that a bloc of Communist party card holders were planning a surreptitious pro-Spanish War meeting in Rock Island, I slipped into the meeting and shocked the drawers off my elderly subscribers with an exposé splashed all over the front page! Yeah, I really did a job of revamping a venerable old newspaper. I was so insistent about making it dance that I damned near killed it.

I stuck with it for about a year. The guys who owned the thing were dismayed at the undercurrent of resentment I stirred up, but they didn't fire me. I quit. It had been my practice to spend my weekends in Chicago, catching the late-afternoon

Rock Island train on Saturday and coming back on the milk train that got in at six A.M. Monday. It was an extravagance, spending money in Chicago—but I sorely missed living in the city.

On one of my short weekends I had a talk with a fascinating guy named Ed Condon, who was the bright, handsome director of public relations for Sears, Roebuck and Company. It mystified me that a retailer I regarded as dealing in work pants and milk pails would have any need for public relations—which provides a clue as to how ignorant I was about these things. But Condon offered me a job. He introduced me to a rather young man named Bass Yarling—a brilliant guy with a solid background in the newspaper business, who told me that he had agreed to be head of publicity at Sears, Roebuck when Condon offered him "a bunch of money"; he couldn't resist the temptation. "You could say," Yarling told me, "that I sold my soul for gold. I have a lot of trouble saying 'no' when somebody makes me a good proposition; if I were a good-looking gal, I guess by now I would have forty-two children." Sears had offered me a generous sum of the work pants and milk pail money, and I said, OK, I would take the job. Yarling said, "If I size you up correctly, you will develop some acute rectal pains working in public relations. If it comes to that and you suffer a chronic desire to vomit, all you have to do is come and tell me, and I will arrange to set you free."

It came to that a little sooner than Bass Yarling anticipated. I took the work pants and milk pail money for about a year— longer that that, I guess; I don't remember. Some of it I liked. Yarling had conceived a new kind of house organ for the Sears, Roebuck employees, and I spent an awful lot of time on it. I wound up as the annointed editor of this thing—a job that entailed the duties of reporter, writer, makeup expert, and get-the-coffee go-fer. The trick that Yarling had turned, in dreaming up a house organ that Sears, Roebuck employees actually read, was to publish a company newspaper that had the look of a big-city tabloid. It was heavily weighted, as it was intended to be, with milk pail company propaganda. Sears' executives puffed up like poulter pigeons when the business magazines praised it.

I did other things in public relations. I wrote some speeches. I set up press conferences. I put together publicity stunts—some of which even worked. The chief executive officer at Sears, Roebuck was a retired Army general named Robert E. Wood. He caused a bit of a problem, because he had a habit of hollering at news photographers who took his picture during press conferences. How was I supposed to get the chief executive's picture in the newspapers when he kept hollering at the camera guys? I finally figured out what was bugging him; the general had a stupid habit of looking directly at the flashbulb, and his vision was thereby blurred when he went back to reading his text.

Fortunately, I had no part in the publicity stunt that led to Bass Yarling's having a nasty quarrel with a wire-service photographer. Our work pants company, which was already very deep in what was quaintly referred to as "hard goods"—stoves and refrigerators and all of that—had made a deal with a farm-equipment manufacturer to produce a house-brand tractor for Sears, Roebuck. Our office had the assignment to thump the drum for the unveiling of this tractor, and Yarling was mother hen of a group from public relations that went to a county fairgrounds in Indiana somewhere. Everything went splendidly. The distinguished guests loaded up on a big spread, washing down the food with good booze. Then their attention was directed to the beautiful new farm tractor that was driven out on the racetrack of this county fairgrounds. Overwhelmed by the applause, I imagine, the driver of the tractor didn't slowly circle the racecourse, as he was supposed to do. No, he started cutting this way and that way on the track, stirring up clouds of dust as he skidded along in his extemporaneous demonstration of the tractor's mobility. Everybody applauded. Then the tractor turned over—and everybody gasped.

I was told that General Wood looked as if he wanted to race down and grab the driver by the throat and choke him to death. But good old Bass Yarling was right on the scene. He had been scurrying along behind the tractor. "I was hollering at that bastard to quit making a goddamn fool of himself," Yarling told me later. When an AP stringer came racing up with a camera and started shooting pictures of the overturned tractor, Yarling grabbed the film holders, pulled open the slides, and exposed the film. The photographer got so enraged, so the story was, that he started swinging his Speed-Graphic camera at Yarling's head, and it required uniformed policemen to get Yarling safely away. Yarling slipped two fifty-dollar bills to an aide to pass on to the cameraman to pacify him for the "inconvenience" he had suffered.

As Yarling had predicted, I felt a little like throwing up when I got this lesson in big corporation public relations. I began to think this wasn't my game. I began to think of quitting, although I feared I would end up on the bread line if I kept walking away from opportunities. I was nudged a little closer to getting out when I was assigned to handle a publicity stunt with a young Hollywood movie star named Judy Garland. It looked innocent enough, this Judy Garland stunt, but it wound up making me feel rotten.

The scenario simply called for me to take a cameraman to the basement floor of the Sears store on State Street to get some pictures of the young singer opening the door of a Sears, Roebuck refrigerator. When I got to the scene of the crime, as the saying goes, everything was in order. The young star stood off to the side waiting for her cue to step in and give a loving look to our refrigerator. What bothered me was that Judy Garland looked miserable. I knew she would put on the charm when it came time to take the pictures, but her sad look bothered me. Her mother was there, and a press agent from her Hollywood studio and a couple of other people—all of them jammering away, making a big deal out of nothing. Hearing the authoritative instructions these loudmouths were directing at the girl, I got the feeling she was treated as if she were some kind of a trained dog that had to be told firmly what was expected of her. She did OK when they moved her in for the pictures, and it was over in a matter of minutes. The camera guy got good shots of her, and Sears, Roebuck got a lot of mileage out of her picture. But the whole affair fed my private doubts as to what in hell I was doing in this business.

I more or less have had a policy of fixing my eye on a better nest before I flee the coop. So perhaps it was a growing disenchantment with corporate public relations that led me to try something else. Spending my evenings at my typewriter at home, I started writing for radio. I had gotten to know a fellow named Murphy, who was the continuity editor at NBC-Chicago. He encouraged me to try writing soap operas. Over a period of several months, I wrote more installments of soap operas than anyone would care to read. I don't know if they were any good; probably not, because I couldn't get an advertising agency to sign me up for one.

Somehow or other, I was lucky enough to sell some one-act radio plays, and the pay for this was surprisingly good. A couple of the small advertising agencies gave me jobs, for pretty good fees, writing one-minute commercials. One night, with a party going on in our apartment, I sat at a table in the kitchen and knocked out ten one-minute commercials for an agency that was peddling maps for Rand McNally. This entailed writing about places I had never seen, but the advertising agency, which paid me five hundred dollars to write this stuff, seemed to think my commercials were great. Maybe; but when I got into the Army, I heard those commercials over and over again on small-town radio stations; they irritated the hell out of me, because they reminded me of happier times—such as the night I took time out of a good party to write this stuff, having forgotten that I had promised an advertising agency to deliver a set of air-ready commercials the next morning. Well, so it goes; you do what you have to do to make a dollar.

After splitting with the public relations business, I didn't do too well in the freelance jungle. Overall, I guess, I did all right—but, when you lead a chancy existence like this, you get reckless with your money when it's handed to you in one big chunk. I mentioned this to a guy I had come to know at NBC-Chicago—Ken Fry, the news director, a former sports editor of a Chicago newspaper. All I got in reply was a sassy grin. No. I got more than that.

I was sitting chatting with Fry one day at a big table in his newsroom as he hastily edited wire copy. Fry was in kind of a bind, because the staff guy who should have been doing this was late for work. Suddenly Fry tossed a piece of the wire copy to me and asked if I would put a pencil to it. This I did, as we talked along, and I tossed the copy back at him when I finished. Fry glanced at it and put it on his pile of material for the upcoming broadcast.

"We prefer that it be rewritten," he said, "but with a small staff, we don't have much chance to rewrite a lot."

"Why do you want it rewritten? Isn't Associated Press's writing good enough for you?" I asked.

Fry grinned. "I didn't say it was necessarily any better when it's rewritten," he said. "It's just easier to read, if the copy isn't all marked up. The guys who read this aren't newspeople, you know. They just read good. You give one of these guys a fifteen-minute show and he will read it on the air without a bobble. The guy will come back in here after telling the world everything that's going on and say: 'What's new?' "

I said I didn't believe a professional announcer would do this. Fry replied, "No?" And then he said, "I think you should do something respectable for a living. Listen: You want a job in here—putting news shows together? It'll keep you humping; we've got two local stations and two networks that we've got to keep feeding. It doesn't leave much free time for scratching your ass or anything. But, you want a job, I'll give you one."

I didn't think Fry was serious. But he certainly looked like he was serious. So I said, yeah, I'd like a job in his newsroom. "When would you want me to start?"

In reply, he scooped up all of the wire copy and plopped it down in front of me. He said: "You had better hustle; this stuff has got to be ready to go on the air in ten minutes."

CHAPTER 4

THEY CALLED IT
RESPECTABLE WORK

I WORKED MY TAIL OFF PUTTING TOGETHER NEWS SHOWS FOR NBC. We had two local radio stations, WMAQ and WENR, and two networks to service—and hardly half a dozen guys to do the work. But I wasn't strictly involved in straight news. I was given the opportunity to make considerable amounts of extra money writing specials and half-hour dramatic shows. I even wrote some advertising copy for one of the ad agencies that bought time on NBC. And one of my primary assignments was to produce a sports show.

This assignment arose out of a dispute between NBC's two radio networks—the "red" network and the "blue" network. The Federal Communications Commission ultimately forced NBC to divest itself of the blue network, the argument being that the National Broadcasting Company had too much control of radio in the USA. But in the early '40s, when NBC operated both networks, there was a great deal of competition between the two. The blue network carried a sports show hosted by a guy named Bill Stern. The people running NBC, concerned about protecting the red network's claim to being the big cheese of broadcasting, wanted to show Stern that he wasn't as indispensable as he seemed to think he was. So I got dragged into sportswriting.

I didn't know all that much about sports reporting, though I'd done a bit of it in Davenport. Covering baseball in a stadium alongside the Mississippi, covering some football, some tennis, and a Monday night wrestling show that was pure hokum—that was about all the experience I had in writing sports. Apparently, it was all the experience my superiors at NBC thought necessary to dream up a program that would teach a lesson to the great Bill Stern. And that's what they told me to do.

The sports show that I dreamed up for NBC was called "The Fort Pearson Sports Show." It was on the air every evening, originating at WMAQ Radio in Chicago, the biggest moneymaker of NBC in those days, and broadcast live from coast to coast. The bosses were deadly serious about making a success of this thing. All it was, really, was an up-to-the-minute summary of the major league baseball games or some struggling new adventure called pro football. If we could dig up a guest who had something interesting to say, we'd have an interview in the studio. I would supply the questions that my "talent," Fort Pearson, would ask. In the concluding section of the show Pearson would read an editorial piece I had written. The editorial would raise a little bit of hell with somebody like George Halas of the Chicago Bears. The show drew a whopping audience—and phone calls of outrage from people such as George Halas.

Fort Pearson had a beautiful voice and a convincing style. He was one of the best news readers in the nation. Pearson was not, however, what you would call bright. He could read the words I had written for him, but if somebody like George Halas called to raise his own holy hell, Pearson would look at me in dismay and hand me the phone.

Pearson came to be regarded as an authority on major league baseball. The irony was that while I was writing him into this reputation, he never set foot inside a major league baseball park. Stern, who worked out of New York, periodically visited Chicago and broadcast his sports show out of our place. He generally made an effort to be cordial to Pearson, and Pearson was polite to Stern. But it was evident that they regarded themselves as rivals, and, on one occasion, Stern suggested to Pearson that it might be a good idea—his sports reputation resting on his "expertise" in baseball—for Pearson to find time to see a major league game. This infuriated Fort Pearson, but he wasn't bright enough to make a damaging reply, though there was an obvious retort. Bill Stern, the celebrated football expert, had never seen a pro football game. Such was radio sports reporting in the good old days.

Having become a great sports authority, Fort Pearson was exceedingly well paid. He was getting something like $300 a show, or $1,500 a week—for reading what I wrote on a show I had dreamed up. When I got into this thing, we had a verbal deal that we would go fifty-fifty. That was a great deal of money—not exceptional in later years, certainly, but one-half of $1,500 a week was a breathtaking amount of money in those days. But I never got my half. NBC, regarding the payment of big fees to a mere newswriter as bad economics, decreed that I was not to be compensated.

But the sports show was only a sideline. I earned my keep as a newswriter. By way of bringing a degree of order to the chaotic newsroom, NBC had put me "in the slot"—a phrase borrowed from newspaper city rooms. Being in the slot in our operation meant that you not only wrote your share of the copy, but you also parceled out wire service copy to the other guys for rewriting and double-checked what they had written. You had to tell the writers how long you wanted the story to go. Every sheet of copy that came back to the slotman was marked in the upper right corner with a penciled number of how many lines the story contained. You had to keep a running count as lines of copy piled up for any particular news program, because there was a limit to the number of lines a staff announcer could read on the air in a five-minute, ten-minute, or fifteen-minute program, and each announcer had his own pace. You had to make fast cuts in your own copy and the other guys' copy, if the line count started to run long.

As the guy who had the bad luck to be "in the slot" of the

NBC-Chicago newsroom, I got a reputation for being disagreeable, because I came down hard on anybody who gave me a piece of copy that started off with a bass-ackwards lead—especially if he were a new guy trying to impress me. I suppose I should admit that I am addicted to writing convoluted leads; as with reformed drunks who talk a lot about the virtues of abstinence, it takes one to know one.

In those days, we'd get calls from outraged professors or teachers of English, if I had let copy get by with split infinitives or sentences that ended with prepositions. With depressing regularity, we were hollered at by listeners convinced that we were part of an evil scheme to undermine the grammatical foundations of the English language. It now seems unreal that there actually was a time when careless writing infuriated listeners. Mispronunciations, over which the newsroom had little control—some of the staff announcers having their own quaint ways of reading the names of persons, places, and things—would touch off more complaints.

We had some talented news readers at NBC-Chicago. These guys sounded "sincere" when they read the news. Likewise, they were first-rate in reading commercials about bath soap and peanut butter. In the early '40s, announcers—not newsmen—read the news on local radio stations. Not all of NBC's announcers were "permitted" to read news. And only those who had been cleared to read news were admitted into the newsroom. But, as always seems to happen when you impose restrictions—and *I* didn't set the rule; management did—not everyone got the word.

I was sitting at my desk in the newsroom one Saturday afternoon when a rather big guy with horn-rim glasses walked in and looked us over. I asked him if he was looking for anything in particular.

"No," he replied, working up the smile you see on the face of a cat that has lunched on your canary, "I just wanted to look around."

It was so unusual for someone to walk unannounced into our newsroom that the writers stopped typing to look at this guy.

"Who are you?" I asked.

"Oh," he replied, "I'm a new announcer. I just came in; I drove in from Pittsburgh, where I was working—at KDKA—before they hired me. I was driving along that road at the southern end of the lake, and I was listening on my car radio to station WMAQ, and you know what I told myself?"

"No," I said. "What did you tell yourself?"

"Well, I told myself that *this* was *my* station—WMAQ-Chicago. It was a thrill to drive along listening to WMAQ—listening to the music, hearing the voices of the announcers I'll be working with. So here I am—reporting in."

"It's nice to see you," I said. "I hope you like working here. But I'm afraid you're on the wrong side of the house; what you're looking for, I think, is the announcers' lounge. It's on the other side of the foyer—the other side of the elevators. There'll be a page boy out there, at a desk, and he'll show you."

With apologies for interrupting us, he said he would be off.

"What's your name?" I asked, toying with the temptation to put him on the list of announcers barred from the newsroom.

"Garroway," he replied. "The name is Dave Garroway—and I'm sure you're going to be hearing a lot from me."

"Oh, sure," one of the newswriters said. "We'll be hearing a lot from you."

"That's right, Tiger," Garroway said, "I'm going to make it in this business."

And with that, he left.

Garroway did make it in the broadcasting business. So did the guy he got to be pals with at NBC-Chicago—Hugh Downs.

On the networks, this was the golden age of radio news for well-informed guys with untrained voices—men like John W. Vandercook of NBC and Edward R. Murrow of CBS. NBC News had a doll of a guy named Earl Godwin, a thoroughly experienced reporter who was widely regarded as having more inside information about the Roosevelt Administration than the best-informed members of the U. S. Senate. He wrote brilliant copy. He had marvelous sources of information, and he possessed a magnificent talent for banging out his copy on any available typewriter with quickness and clarity. His weakness was that he had a raspy, rather high-pitched, country boy voice.

He didn't trifle with the voice-of-doom delivery style of Gabriel Heater, who started off each of his news performances with the pronouncement that "There is good news tonight!"— even when all hell was breaking loose and civilized man seemed to be falling into the fiery hole. Nor did Godwin rattle off the news staccato style, as Walter Winchell did to encourage acceptance of his superconfident scam that he had the inside poop on just about everything. This was not Earl Godwin's method. All that Earl Godwin was interested in was putting out accurate information that nobody else had.

Earl Godwin had one weakness of delivery that was the despair of the upper echelon of NBC News. He had a mysterious habit of transposing *t*s for *p*s while reading, on live broadcasts, significant stories about the status of U. S. shipping to Europe and the Far East. Godwin, immediately aware of having said "shitting," instead of "shipping," would compound his mistake with a short giggle.

I got to know Earl Godwin on his periodic visits to NBC-Chicago. Word had drifted to our newsroom that at the first presidential press conferences, which took place in the Oval Office, Godwin had the boorish practice of dragging up a leather chair to Roosevelt's desk and using a corner of the desk as a writing table. The story was that President Roosevelt invariably clinched his long cigarette holder in his teeth and glared at Godwin.

I asked Godwin about this one day when he was working out of our newsroom in Chicago. Was it true that he had the nerve to use Roosevelt's desk as a writing table?

"What is wrong about my doing that?" he replied. "My, God, a man calls reporters in for a press conference, the least he can do is provide us with a place to take our notes."

"Is it true—as some of your colleagues have said—that when you sit down, you push Roosevelt's knickknacks out of your way?"

"Yes, I do that," Godwin told me. "My, God, this man's desk is cluttered up with all sorts of little things. I often wonder how a man with the fate of the world on his shoulders can work at a desk loaded up with toys and junk."

"Mr. Godwin, when the Roosevelt press conferences are over," I asked, "do you straighten up the desk before you leave?"

Earl Godwin look at me with astonishment. "Do I do housekeeping? No, I don't do housekeeping. The President of the United States has sufficient staff to fix up his desk. I am a White House Correspondent; I am not a housekeeper."

Another of the men with whom I worked was H. V. Kaltenborn, then one of the nation's favorite news broadcasters. Kaltenborn was an imperious guy who demanded attention to his needs and had the annoying habit of fingering the Phi Beta Kappa key that decorated his vest. He had come to fame on network radio after having been editor of a bold and notable newspaper called the *Brooklyn Eagle*, and he had the demanding manner of a tough newspaper guy who wants his own way. Unlike most of the other famous national radio news guys who visited our shop, Kaltenborn declined every offer of a private office where he could be alone with his great thoughts. No, Kaltenborn insisted on writing his copy at the big desk where the news was flowing, the telephones were ringing, and the newswriters were working. He would check the teletypes to bring himself up to date on the wire service reports, but he handled the copy carefully to assure that it wouldn't pile up and jam the teletype keys. He was never so brash—again, unlike other famous visitors—as to rip off a piece of wire copy that interested him. Kaltenborn would simply say that when one of us found time to cut the wire-service copy, he would like to have another look at the news item. Some of our famous visitors—Lowell Thomas, for example—always brought along their own writer and never even bothered to look at their news copy until they walked into a studio to read it faultlessly. But Kaltenborn wrote his own stuff.

I don't recall how it was that, even when they had me writing a network sports show, NBC pressed me into service as Kaltenborn's editorial flunky. My recollection is that, for some reason, I was the only young man in our newsroom who was acceptable to him. I lay no claim to being someone of irresistible charm. He simply found me more tolerable than any of the other guys in our shop, and even though it was known that I was getting a $25-a-day stipend for working with the great Kaltenborn, the other guys seemed to be damned glad that I was the one who got stuck with him. On the occasions when I was having judgmental difficulties with Kaltenborn— my being too Irish, I guess, to acquiesce to Kaltenborn's every opinion—the guys I normally worked with would look up from their typewriters and exchange knowing smiles. On these occasions the other guys seemed to share the thought that I earned my $25.

As Kaltenborn's baby-sitter or boot-boy, or whatever phrase might please you, my job was to keep wire service copy in chronological order, with the latest leads on big stories on top of separate files on international events, Washington developments, Wall Street and financial stuff, and so on. Kaltenborn was particularly concerned about getting accurate information and the latest details on whatever story he was writing. While writing a piece, his whole being seemingly was concentrated on the story. Then, having filled as much space as he chose to lavish on a particular story, Kaltenborn would toss all of the wire copy on that story into a wastebasket and go on to something else. Kaltenborn kept a meticulous count of the number of lines he was producing. Once he reached his line count limit, Kaltenborn would push away from the typewriter—his daily task of writing a news summary completed.

I was always relieved when Kaltenborn had finished his script; he would start making an effort to be civil again. But while Kaltenborn was writing, I continued stacking late wire copy. And invariably, once the news summary was completed, Kaltenborn refused to read the late wire stories. When I gently chided him, suggesting he had better have a look at the stuff, he would grandly wave me off and tell me it was of no importance. So I would shrug and watch him dump the neglected wire copy into the wastebasket. But we had a clash over this one time.

My little dispute with H. V. Kaltenborn occurred early in

1943, as I recall. Once again, when he finished writing his script, he refused to scan the pile of leftover copy. "There's an AP story in there, Mr. Kaltenborn," I said, "about the possibility that the Japs have torpedoed an American ship—and I think you ought to take a look at it; you haven't mentioned it in your script."

Kaltenborn's face clouded. He glowered at me. And then he said, "I read the report when it was coming in on the ticker. It is pure speculation, and I do not deal with the speculative." His tone was unusually frigid, so I shut up. If a story that the Japanese had sunk an American ship loaded with valuable war materiel didn't interest him, who was I to tell him he had better think it over? But when he returned from the studio where he flawlessly read his script, the Great Man said, "I am disturbed that you let me go on the air omitting a major story." He looked at me accusingly, and I wondered what in hell he was talking about.

"My engineer," Kaltenborn said, "asked me why I made no mention of the 'big story' of the day—the Japanese sinking one of our important ships."

"Mr. Kaltenborn," I said, "I called your attention to that story, and you told me it was too speculative to bother with."

"You didn't advise me of the importance of this Japanese action," he replied, although the accusatory tone of his voice was modifying. "If I am going to depend on you when I am here in Chicago," he went on, his indignation cooling down still more, "it is necessary that you emphasize to me the importance of any major development that I possibly have overlooked." And with that he picked up his coat and stalked out of the newsroom.

That was the first of two occasions when I was so infuriated with Kaltenborn that I wanted to tell him to go to hell and walk out on him. Our grand old bird got his hackles up again a couple of weeks later.

Kaltenborn sailed into our newsroom on his next visit with an uncharacteristic display of good fellowship. I was wary of him on this day that he returned to us. When, in a highly unusual gesture of generosity, he pulled out a little black purse and then a dollar bill to pay for coffee for the newsroom—announcing in a grand voice that this would be his "treat"—I said I didn't want any. But if I made a point of keeping my distance from him, Old Man Kaltenborn was the soul of cordiality. He even nodded his head in agreement when, his script written, I stayed his hand when he made a move to sweep the neglected pile of wire copy into a wastebasket. "Sir," I said, "to be on the safe side, I think you should give a glance to this stuff." Somewhat to my surprise, he nodded and said, "Yes, I quite agree with you." And, having had a look at every page of the throwaway pile, he marched off to the studio to broadcast his network news show.

Kaltenborn had no sooner walked out of our newsroom, heading across the hallway to the little studio where he sat at a small table facing the microphone, than the teletypes of all three of the wire services stopped click-clacketing. They were not silent, because news wires that are suddenly brought to a stop sort of tug at their leash like sheep dogs—panting in a mechanical way, eager to be turned loose to get on with the story they were transmitting before they were interrupted. Teleprinters that are idling make a petulant, impatient, throbbing sound as they wait to be fed some more of the punched-out tape that will let them resume their transmissions. And this is what our machines were doing, all six of our printers—three of them carrying Associated Press reports, two of them United Press, and the sixth, the International News Service report.

Newsroom guys quietly gather around teleprinters when the machines cut off in mid-sentence and then throb as they wait to get back into action. It wasn't often that the printers of all three wire services were simultaneously idle and tugging at the leash; it hardly ever happened that even two of the wire services came to a halt at the same instant, as they scrambled to "get there first" with a big story. With all three of our wire services obviously in a contest to be first to break this story, it had to be something very big. If AP, UP, and INS all skidded to a halt in their transmissions at the same moment, something extraordinary was happening somewhere. A series of bells sounds when something of importance is about to be transmitted. And if there is anything that instantly brings a lethargic newsroom to life, it is the cessation in mid-phrase of whatever has been moving on the news wires, the tinkling of those bells, and the slow but deliberate beat of the keys that click out the few words of a "bulletin" or "flash" that give first notice of an event that will force the replating of front pages and the interruption of network programming.

H. V. Kaltenborn was taking a last look at his copy in the studio across the hall, waiting for the cue that he was on the air, while all of our newsroom guys crowded around the teleprinters, eager to find out what in hell was up. I couldn't help but wonder how I was going to break in on Kaltenborn when the printers came to life and disclosed this big news story.

Kaltenborn got his opening cue, and I could hear him on the newsroom speaker as he went into his customary up-and-down style of delivery, when the printers came to life and gave us the flash:

CHURCHILL IN WASHINGTON.
CHURCHILL AT WHITE HOUSE.
CHURCHILL, FDR CONFERRING AT WHITE HOUSE.

Reaching to one of the machines, I grabbed the top copy of this astounding story and ripped it off. I raced out the door with it to get it to Kaltenborn, who was about one minute into his broadcast.

I was pretty noisy, barging into the studio. I made enough of a racket to draw a dirty look from Kaltenborn, but I didn't care; like it or not, Kaltenborn had to be informed that Churchill had done the near-incredible: flying the Atlantic to confer with Roosevelt. Nowadays transoceanic flights are accepted as a routine aspect of modern life, but at that time, Churchill's flying to Washington, DC, was breathtakingly daring. Even though Air Force planes were flying the Atlantic to Britain, it was mind-boggling that the British prime minister would dare to take such a grave chance. But as I approached Kaltenborn's desk, clutching a ripped piece of wire copy, I couldn't help wondering if the great man of NBC News would believe it.

Kaltenborn glared at me with loathing as his voice went up and hung there for an instant before dropping down in emphasis. He continued reading his copy as confidently as you please, and I placed the wire report on top of his script. Without so much as glance at it—and this annoyed me because I had encircled the word "flash" with a thick copy pencil—he picked it up and tossed it to the floor. I stooped and picked it up and put it back in front of him. He gave me a dark look as he picked it up off the table and flipped it to the floor again.

From the control booth, the engineer and the producer frantically motioned me to get away from Kaltenborn. But I picked up the Churchill flash again, slapped it on the desk under Kaltenborn's nose, and fixed a fist on this bit of copy, by way of insisting that he read it. When he picked it up, tilting his head and adjusting his eyeglasses to read the flash, I stepped away from him.

With a slick ad lib to explain to his listeners the obvious pause on the air, Kaltenborn said that he had just been handed a late-breaking item. Then he intoned the big news that Churchill was visiting Roosevelt. He read the flash on the air a second time, pushed his entire script off the little desk on to the floor and went into a faultless, brilliant analysis of the prime minister's courageous and historic visit to Washington. Kaltenborn wound up with the fascinating suggestion that a feat such as this would instill fear into Adolf Hitler and his crowd. They might read into this, Kaltenborn declared, a fateful sign that Germany was losing its grip on the world. Never, in my entire career did I hear anybody speak off the cuff with such poise, so smoothly, or with such brilliance as did Old Man Kaltenborn that evening in a little studio at NBC-Chicago.

Suspecting that this old bastard wasn't going to forgive my interrupting his show, I got out of the studio before he finished his spontaneous oration. A couple of our newsroom guys, aglow with excitement over the professional skill that Kaltenborn was displaying, had come out into the hallway to await Kaltenborn and congratulate him on what a great job he had done; our news director had come out to pass on the praises of the NBC-New York executives who had called to express their amazement at the speed and aplomb with which Kaltenborn had beaten CBS on one of the big stories of the war.

When Kaltenborn strode out of the studio, animated at having pulled off a big coup, he was showered with compliments. He broke loose of our guys and called to me. I wondered what in hell he was going to holler about now. But Kaltenborn held out his hand and said, "There are two things I am obliged to say to you: I would first of all like to apologize to you for my impatience with you when you were trying to be helpful. And, secondly, I want to say that I am grateful that you insisted on forcing the Churchill story on me; it would have been foolish, indeed, if I had neglected to deal with so vital a piece of news as this." I don't know what I said in acknowledgment of his apology for having given me a hard time, but it impressed me that he was big enough to give me credit, in front of the newsroom guys, for saving his ass on a big story. It has been my experience in the news business that the big wheels are not noted for apologizing or giving credit to underlings.

In the stylish and sanitized climate of modern-day radio and television reporting, the young men and women who have attained renown for their slickness in presenting the news would consider those of us who trace back to the old school naive and crude. Perhaps this is an apt description of what we were— but you have to make a beginning somewhere.

Radio news came of age in World War II. The best radio news shops were getting the same wire service reports upon which the newspapers were dependent. And the networks and the best local radio news operations were quick to develop methods of interrupting on-air programs to break the big news. In radio there were no linotype machines, no front-page replates, no need to delay getting the big story on the air. It was in the early days of World War II that radio news fattened up on the grand opportunity to beat the hell out of the newspapers.

The people who have fallen heir to the good news jobs at NBC-Chicago owe something, I think, to Ken Fry and Bill Ray. They were hard-news guys who hammered the NBC-Chicago newsroom into a top-grade operation. I learned a great deal about broadcasting from both of them. They were way ahead of their time. Fry had come to NBC from a newspaper—the

Chicago Evening Post. Ray had come to NBC from the *Chicago Journal*, an exceedingly good newspaper and another of the first-rate Chicago newspapers that had gone belly up. Ray had been hired originally to run the NBC-Chicago publicity office, which was a big thing at that time. However, the outrageous but highly capable Ken Fry got swept up by patriotic fervor and quit to become a director of the nation's War Information Service. And he recommended Bill Ray, a skilled and experienced newsman, for the job of news director. Bill Ray eventually went off to the Federal Communications Commission as head of the complaints division, dealing, in part, with complaints about me—would you believe it?—and Ken Fry became the public relations director for the Democratic National Committee.

A.A. Schecter, a pal of Ken Fry, ran NBC-New York in the early '40s. Abe Schecter laid the foundation for the NBC News capability of the present day. He hired correspondents, set up communications systems, and opened bureaus in all parts of the world. It didn't bother Schecter to reach out and hire a star writer or reporter away from CBS or the *Christian Science Monitor* or any other news organization. With the lure of big money and generous perquisites, A.A. Schecter generally got whomever A.A. Schecter wanted. But I know of one time that he was shocked to have someone say no.

Sitting at Fry's desk one day, Abe announced that he wanted to transfer me from Chicago to New York.

"No way," I said.

"Look," Abe said, "I'll double your pay and pay all of your expenses, and I'll give you an expense account to help you out in New York."

"No, thanks," I replied.

Fry grinned at Abe Schecter and said, "I warned you he'd tell you to go to hell."

Abe looked at me and said, "Are you telling me to go to hell?"

"Not exactly," I said. "All I'm telling you is that I don't want to go. My roots are in Chicago—God, my grandfathers were here a hundred years ago. I know the guts of this city—how it works, how the gangsters and the politicians and the business-people operate. What do I know about New York? Nothing. That's what I know about New York."

"So you won't go," Abe Schecter said.

"That's right, Abe; I won't go."

"Suppose," Abe Schecter replied, "that I told you that I might have to fire you if you won't go to New York?"

"Then I guess you'll have to fire me," I said.

Ken Fry laughed. "I told you, Abe, that he'd tell you to go to hell."

Schecter shook his head. "I don't understand you," he said. "I thought you would jump at a chance to work in New York. New York is where the money is. You'll be sorry you turned this down. But if staying in Chicago is what you want, I won't push it anymore."

Despite my bravado, my days in Chicago were numbered. Early in 1943, I accepted the U.S. Army's kind, if forceful, invitation to join its ranks. God knows I had had plenty of opportunities to make the grand gesture of resigning from NBC to take a commission and write speeches and hammer out propaganda of some kind for the Army, the Navy, or one of the special services. I didn't have much appetite for something like that—but, to be truthful, there were many moments during my time in the U.S. Army when I felt I had been terribly stupid to have let myself drift into the misery of a combat unit. However, my stint with Uncle Sam gave me a good view of a great many dramatic things that would be imprinted on my mind for all of my days.

CHAPTER **5**

MESS KIT LOUIE'S BLUE PENCIL

I HAD A FEELING THAT I WAS MIXED UP SOMEHOW in something quite serious, the day I walked into Battalion HQ and found a phalanx of officers waiting for me. I thought they were going to court-martial me or something. This was in the earliest days of my training with the U.S. Army in pot poor Mississippi, and already I was being called on the carpet for God knows what. The major cleared it up for me.

"The Army," he informed me, "is based on the willingness of all personnel to produce their best efforts for the common good. And the reason you've been called over here is that you have been found to have a special talent that is needed by the battalion. And I am talking to you personally to make you understand that we are entrusting you with an important assignment. Starting right now, or as quickly as you can get to it, I want you to prepare a daily summary of the news that we will distribute to all personnel of this battalion."

I was stunned into silence.

"Battalion will provide whatever facilities you might need," the major went on. "And Battalion will handle the distribution of your news reports. Now, do you have any questions?"

"Yes, sir," I replied, "I have some questions. First of all, there is no source of news around here; no Associated Press, or United Press, or International News Service, or anything like that. I don't see how anyone can produce a daily news report, if he has no source of news."

"Take it off the radio," the major replied.

"Radio doesn't seem to transmit very well down here in Mississippi, sir."

"Oh, you'll make out. From what I've been told about you, you've had enough experience to make out."

"Yes, sir," I said, wondering what Old Man Kaltenborn would think about something like this.

My encounter with the battalion brass concluded with the major's issuing an order relieving me of KP and other assignments routinely parceled out to recruits in the Infantry. It was supposed to be good for the recruit's soul, or something like that, taking his turn cleaning up the skillets in the mess kitchen, but the major seemed to think I could make my way to paradise without trifling with the pots and pans. "I don't want this man assigned to any special duty that conflicts with his primary assignment. Do you all get that?"

That's how I got involved in turning out nightly news reports for the 363rd Medical Battalion of the 63rd Infantry Division at Camp Van Dorn, Mississippi. And that's how I was freed of the chores that customarily are assigned, in the good name of humility and discipline, to Army recruits. A Captain O'Neill wryly revealed to me, months after it occurred, that it was *he* who persuaded somebody in Division Headquarters to issue an order to Battalion to assign me to the task of turning out a daily news summary of national and world events for the officers and men of the 363rd Medical Battalion. This Captain O'Neill was an intelligence officer who was short on knowledge of military intelligence. He was a genial, educated man who had little respect for many of his fellow officers and who democratically and persistently violated the U.S. Army's social barrier between officers and so-called enlisted men. It was O'Neill to whom I owed my freedom from washing trucks and peeling potatoes.

"We weren't getting any news at Camp Van Dorn," O'Neill said, when finally he told me how I got assigned the job of providing it. "We had no newspapers. Nobody seemed to have a radio that worked, or time to listen to it. So one day I was down at Division Headquarters, and I was giving a report to the colonel in Personnel, and when he asked me if I had any ideas about improving morale—well, I knew from the information in your personnel jacket that you had come into the Army from NBC and that doing news reports was right up your alley. So, this colonel said it was a great idea to take advantage of this and assign you to the job of putting together a nightly news report. I told the colonel I didn't have the authority to give you this job, and the colonel says, 'I'll mention it to the general and my guess is we will be sending your battalion an order.' And that's what happened, and that's why the major called you over and told you he had this bright idea about assigning you the job of writing the news reports. I told the major that, yeah, we had to comply with this order that came from Division, but we'd have to take you off KP and things like that—because it would use up a lot of your time, doing the nightly news reports. And the major tells me we had to do what Division told us to do, and he said, 'By God, I want it done right.' "

So that's how it was that, in a crude sort of way, I was put back into the news business. It was easy, to tell you the truth. Even on the best of nights I had trouble on the Battalion HQ radio dialing in a station that I could read—and I had a hell of a time finding reports I could understand on the nights when the long-wave band seemed to be cluttered with static from the bottom to the top of the dial. But I managed to come up with a nightly report of maybe twelve hundred words, and when I was finished, one of the battalion clerks would cut a mimeograph stencil and grind out a few hundred copies, which were delivered to the mess halls and officer dining rooms. It was mildly gratifying to go up to our mess area for breakfast and find a lot of guys with their eyes on my news summary, though hardly anyone ever said anything much to me about my reports.

A squat little Italian guy named Alberico seemed to be more interested in my news reports than anyone else. Alberico was our mess sergeant, with hands so large he could pick up six eggs at a time, three in each hand, and deftly crack them open on the rim of a big pan and set them to fry without breaking a yolk.

The swarthy Alberico had the self-assurance and confidence of what we used to call a "tough Dago," meaning he was a poor Italian or Sicilian kid who could take care of himself. He had come out of the same mold as kids who had been my friends when I was a boy, and he seemed to sense it. The story on Alberico was that he had learned the restaurant business in New York and had been running his own place, serving up such delicacies as squid and linguini, when they drafted him. The story was that he had had to turn his place over to his wife and his brother-in-law and that his place was going to hell without his being there to take care of it. There was no need for a story to be told about how miserable Alberico was about being a U.S. Army mess sergeant; you could tell how grim he felt merely by looking at him. "It's a son of a bitch to be turning out this slop in the U.S. Army," he would grumble. "It's a real son of a bitch."

I hit it off pretty well with this Alberico from the time we first set eyes on each other—the day six or seven other recruits and I had been sent to his kitchen to do menial chores for him. With one hand on his hip and another pointing to each recruit in turn, he said, "You do pots, you clean the stoves, you do potatoes," and so on. His buck sergeant cooks watched silently as he made his assignments; there was something ominous about the no-nonsense manner in which he softly made these assignments. I had the feeling, standing off to the side and observing this, that Alberico was issuing orders like a Mafia chief who regarded what he said as quite beyond any possibility of negotiation. I wondered, when he turned and looked me full in the face, what menial work he would be telling me to do. When he spoke to me, with no change of expression, he surprised me.

"You know how to peel potatoes?"

"No," I replied.

"You had any experience in cleanin' a stove?"

I shook my head.

The other recruits had wandered off to go about their jobs. The cooks had turned away, going back to whatever it was they had to do in preparing the noon meal. This left Alberico and myself standing there, measuring each other. I didn't say a word, because I couldn't think of anything to say. Besides, who starts up a conversation with a Mafia chief? After he had taken a very careful look at me, Alberico smiled and said, "Well, if there ain't anythin' you can do around here, maybe we should sit down and have a cup of coffee." And like a good host, Alberico went off to fetch a couple of mugs.

My fellow recruits, busy with their pots and pans and potatoes, would occasionally glance at me in disbelief. I guess it was a little unusual, seeing a guy who had been assigned to KP sitting at a plank table on what appeared to be an equal basis with the mess sergeant. Alberico observed the questioning glances but they didn't seem to make the slightest impression on him.

"I hear you're from Chicago," Alberico said, without indicating where he had heard this or that he needed confirmation of it. "I'm from New York," he went on. "I have a little place there that does pretty good; it did all right, that is, until I got my ass dragged into this Army—and now I don't know how we're doin'. They don't care what happens to your place when they drag your ass into this Army. You notice how they don't have any interest in what you had, when they get you into this Army?"

I nodded. It struck me that Alberico had me mixed up with someone else from Chicago. He mystified me further when he said, "You know, I got a couple of my brothers over there in Chicago, and they tell me it's a nice place; I would like to go over there some time. I was thinkin' about goin' to see 'em before I got grabbed into this Army. But I wind up over there in Florida, and then they put me in this cadre and they move us over here, to this Mississippi. This Mississippi is the asshole of creation, if anybody is askin' me. But here I am in this

Mississippi, drinkin' coffee with a guy from Chicago. It's a funny world, ain't it?"

I got to know Alberico pretty well as the weeks went by. Dropping in for coffee with Alberico got to be a regular thing, even after the job that they had given me to write news summaries had taken me off the list of GIs burdened with KP duty.

There were two things that invariably put Alberico in a sullen mood. He had the look of a man who was grossly insulted when he had to stand naked at his bunk during our Saturday morning inspections and have his private parts scrutinized by a group of battalion and company officers. And he looked to be at the brink of uncontrolled rage when an inspection team invaded his mess hall, searching for evidence of careless housekeeping. In one way or another, Alberico managed to tolerate most of the Army's methods of imposing its will and standards on all personnel. But it infuriated him to have a doctor from battalion bend down and peer at his penis or, in the kitchen, to have officers put their hands on his pots and pans.

As far as I was ever able to find out, every GI on the roster is subjected to the periodic inspection of his body. It is standard operating procedure, as they say in the Army, to require every enlisted man to stand at attention at the foot of his bunk in the barracks, wearing socks and freshly shined boots and nothing else, their genitals being scrutinized for the slightest indication of venereal infection. In the human adventure, there are more humiliating experiences, perhaps, than standing naked at attention in the barracks, as a party of officers from Battalion looks you over to determine that you're marriage-bed clean. Yet, in its zeal to make certain that everyone is in condition to fight, the Army seems to be infatuated with this ritual of examining the personal parts of the troops which Army procedure demands be put on display. And these "short arm" inspections, as they are called, are so much a part of the regular drill that only those who are fearful of being caught with the first indications of gonorrhea or syphilis have any feeling of outrage over having their privacy invaded.

There is more resentment to be found, although I don't know why, among the mess sergeants and their three-stripe cooks who are regularly subjected to inspection of their kitchens. One meal of contaminated food, or one tainted dish on the menu, can inflict an acute condition of what is called "the GIs" on an entire company, and it hardly seems unreasonable for the Army to stipulate the frequent inspection of utensils and cooking equipment in all mess halls. A quiet kind of terror spreads through the complement of an infantry company that falls victim to vomiting and diarrhea, transforming the latrine into the most popular place around. And, in passing, it might be observed for the ex-GIs who have gone through life thinking otherwise, that the contraction, "the GIs" does not imply that the intestinal malady we are talking about is "government issue," which is the phrase that defines the source of Army underwear, gas masks, rifles, prophylactics, and such other items that a thoughtful Army might provide. Nor is the government conceding any responsibility for a plague of vomiting and diarrhea. No, having the GIs is in no way to be taken as "government issue." To clear up any misconceptions that remain, the GIs is merely an abbreviated way of saying "gastrointestinal."

I tried to explain this to Sergeant Alberico one afternoon while having a cup of coffee with him and a buck sergeant named Rhem, who used to run a bakery in Jersey City or some such place before the Army drafted him. "You shouldn't take offense," I said, "when some lieutenant shows up from Division to inspect the kitchen. You're feeding 165 men three meals a day, and they've got a right to make sure this place is clean."

"You gotta be crazy," Alberico replied. "They can't trust me to run a clean kitchen, they should get me out of here. My food makes the guys sick, they should lock me up in the stockade. I don't need no young punk from Division comin' in here, tellin' me how to run my kitchen. In New York, I make somebody sick on my food—well, I can lock the goddamn door; somethin' like that happens, your place is finished."

"Same wit' me," Sergeant Rhem put in. "People get the shits on stuff I make at the bakery, they ain't comin' back next mornin' to buy some more."

Alberico glowered at Sergeant Rhem, which seemed to be Alberico's way of telling Rhem to shut up. Then, turning to me, he said, "I ain't against inspections. The way some of these guys are sleepin' it up with these Southern girls, it's a good thing they come around every Saturday morning to find out who's caught a dose and who ain't. Every week, that young captain shows up at the motor pool to check out the ambulances and trucks and everythin'. That's different; there ain't any reason to complain about that. God Almighty, we got our big mess truck down there. Without this young captain from Division makin' sure they clean it up, our big six-by-six that we cook in when we go out into the field, who's to say we won't give everybody the GIs the next time we take it out to feed the men on bivouac? I'm all for it; anythin' that guarantees me a clean truck to get our food out there to the men on three-, four-day bivouac. I ain't against inspections. Any dumb bastard knows—in the Army you gotta have inspections."

"You holler like hell, though, when they come in to inspect your kitchen."

"That's different," Alberico replied. "Bits of meat and stuff fallin' on the floor of our mess truck, rottin' away and nobody cleanin' it up—that's one thing. I'm all for it, havin' Division sendin' this young captain to the motor pool to check up on if it's clean. Havin' this guy tearin' into everythin' in my kitchen, scrapin' with his fingernails to find somethin' that he can report me for—that is somethin' else."

I laughed. Alberico glowered at me.

"You think it's funny? You think it don't mean nothin'? Let me tell you: You take that officer, runnin' his finger over the carvin' knives, lookin' for somethin' that's stuck there and ain't been cleaned off, diggin' with his fingernail in the crevice where a blade fits into the handle. You know what would happen back home if this guy tried that in his old lady's kitchen? She'd grab that knife away from him and boot his ass out of there."

I laughed again, thinking of the buck sergeant cooks' certainty that some day Alberico would blow his stack, grab the knife, and jab it into the officer who was trying to catch him with unclean carving knives. Alberico never went that far, actually, but I was sitting there having coffee with him one day when it looked for all the world as if Alberico was about to put a knife into an officer from Division.

It was a major from Division who came close to getting stabbed by our mess sergeant. Inspecting mess halls is not the usual function of an officer of this rank, but the major had dropped into our mess hall with a four- or five-man inspection team one day and, sensing Alberico's resentment, had given Alberico a hard time. This major found reason to make complaint about everything, triumphantly waving a pan that he had discovered on the range—and not up on a shelf with the other pans, where it belonged. Alberico, having no explanation for this, had tightened his lips and said nothing in his own defense. Army mess sergeants are not personally responsible, I don't believe, for making certain that every pot and pan is in its proper place. But all that Alberico said was, "Well, Major, I guess you got me there." He didn't say this in what could be called a respectful way. As Alberico explained later, when the major from Division was gone, what he had really wanted to say was, "Major, you make my ass tired. Why don't you get outta here and leave us alone?" But, watching this clash of personalities and listening to the frigid tones of their voices when they spoke to each other, it appeared obvious to me that we hadn't seen or heard the end of this. Indeed, when the major strode out of the mess hall he looked at Alberico and said, "Sergeant, I'll be back." With not the slightest note of apprehension in his voice, Alberico smiled and replied, "Yeah, you do that, Major; we'll always be glad to see you." And then the major from Division was gone.

I stuck around with Alberico for a few minutes, because I thought it isn't right to be in a hurry to part company with a guy who seemed to be having a problem. But I was anxious to be on my way, because I was having a little problem of my own and I wanted to sit down somewhere to think about it and reassure myself that I had done the right thing. The same as Alberico, I seemed to have gotten myself in to a little fix with one of the officers in Division. My problem was not with a major; it was with the colonel in charge of personnel—and my problem appeared to be that I had offended the sensibilities of our commanding general, Louis B. Hibbs. I had done so in the course of my second writing job for the U. S. Army.

Firmly established as battalion news writer, I had received an order to show up at an appointed time to see the colonel in charge of personnel. This order had come down "through channels," as people in charge of things in the U.S. Army like to say. I had been as surprised as anyone else by this order. But it had caused quite a stir, an unknown recruit being told to show up at Division. Our first sergeant, who had braced me with this order, was a good old southern boy who did not conceal his fears that something was going wrong.

"You can't get away with this," the first sergeant warned me.

"I can't get away with what?" I replied.

The first sergeant shook his head, as if he found it useless to discuss this further. "They want you over at Battalion. Right now. And all I can tell you is you better not be lippy with 'em, or it's gonna go hard on you."

Mystified, I crossed the road to Battalion HQ. The brass was waiting for me: our company commander, who seemed to be nervous; the major who was battalion commander, who seemed to be grim; and a couple of young officers, who had the look of guys who devoutly wished that they were somewhere else. When I saluted, figuring that this was what I was supposed to do—and making a stab at being "military" about it—they didn't bother to salute me back. The only response I got was that the major pointed a finger at his office and we all walked in. The major started to interrogate me.

"What are they calling you down to Division for? What kind of trouble are you in? We're trying to build a good reputation here," the major declared, "and I sure as hell don't want any-body lousing that up."

I added to their fears and disquietude, I guess, when I sighed and said, "Sir, I don't know anything about this. All I know is that the first sergeant handed me this order to show up at ten o'clock this morning at Division, and unless you want to give me an order to skip it, I had better get going."

Chancing nothing, which seems to be the way you hold your

Army command at any level, the major said he would have his jeep driver take me down.

"It's not far; I can walk."

"No. I want to be sure you get there. You're supposed to report to the colonel in charge of G-1. If the commander of Division Personnel wants to see you, you're goddamn well gonna be there."

"Thank you, sir."

"Thank you, sir, my ass," snapped the major.

Ten minutes later, at Division Headquarters—which was located on a grassy knoll, in a wooden building not much fancier than the tar-paper shacks that were the barracks of the enlisted men—I was escorted by an Army clerk into the office of G-1's top man. Surprisingly, he smiled, told me to take a seat, and went directly to the matter at hand.

"The general has been anxious to get us going on preparation of a 63rd Division history," the personnel colonel said. Then, glancing at some papers on his desk, he continued, "We've been going through the background sheets on the men of this command, looking for someone who is qualified to write the history. Judging from what I've seen in these personnel records, you're the man."

The colonel tried to sweeten the pot by telling me that the general, finding it demeaning to entrust the writing of his division's history to a lowly corporal—which I then was—would certainly elevate me to tech sergeant or master sergeant or something important. I gathered from the colonel's look of expectation that he thought I would be joyful to hear that I might be promoted to the top deck of what they called noncommissioned officers, and I guess it annoyed him that I didn't show much interest in being promoted. Some of the most experienced and knowledgeable GI's in our outfit were never going to make it to private first class, and none of them appeared to be troubled by it. The way it looked to me, even the most-decorated first sergeants I had business with did not seem too bright and, while they got paid a good deal more than the rest of us, they didn't make much money as far as my appreciation of decent compensation went. Maybe there was something wrong with my sense of values, but it didn't make a hell of a lot of difference to me whether I was locked in as a corporal or got pushed up to having a lot of stripes on my sleeve. After all, I could write the 63rd Division's history just as well as a corporal as something more important on the Army's scale of grade and rank. Word got around about my having turned up my nose at a promotion to master sergeant. The surprising result of this was that it enhanced my status with the intellectual set of our company. But the hillbilly kids, apparently disappointed at being associated with someone who was too stupid to take advantage of an opportunity that was offered him, did not conceal their dismay. Whatever, my talk with the colonel at Division HQ did not appear to have relieved me of the job of writing the glorious history of a combat division that had yet to see combat; all I had succeeded in doing, it appeared, was to shut off my promotion to master sergeant.

With the stipulation that the general would be too busy to be interviewed, the great project of writing the history of a division that didn't have a history was launched. Just for openers, on this project of writing the history of a division founded at the outbreak of World War II, it seemed like a sensible idea to find out who in hell was this "Van Dorn" who had been posthumously honored by having his name on this miserable place where healthy young men were being conditioned and trained to go to Europe to kill Germans. The problem about Van Dorn was that nobody seemed to know who he was or what his claim to fame might have been. Not even the colonel in personnel at Division knew anything about him, except that Van Dorn had been a general on the Confederate side in the War Between the States and must have been famous if they'd remembered him long enough to name a World War II camp in his honor. Finally, a private in our company proved helpful—at least, sort of helpful.

The private was named Hipple. He had been drafted right after he graduated from Ohio State University. This Hipple was one of those Civil War buffs and had gone up to Vicksburg a couple of times to walk over the hills outside of the city where a fearful battle had been fought. In the course of getting his

mind straight on precisely where this terrible fight had occurred and who was involved on both sides, studious Private
Hipple had done some research in the Vicksburg public library—or so he said. And, in thumbing through volume after
volume, he came upon some interesting discoveries about a
Confederate general named Van Dorn. And while he, alas,
could not remember the title of the book in which he had found
this stuff about General Van Dorn, it contained the biograph-
ical information that I was seeking. Or so he said. In any case,
with the special intention of paying a visit to the Vicksburg
public library to check out Hipple's story, I took a weekend
pass and went up to Vicksburg on the Illinois Central.

My mission was not too productive; I was not able, at the
public library or anywhere else, to find confirmation of the
most fascinating part of the story that Hipple had given me—
the circumstances of General Van Dorn's unfortunate demise,
which is what I had gone to Vicksburg to establish. I was not
able to find the book that Hipple had referred to as the source
of his information on how General Van Dorn had died. I got
the slightest hint of corroboration of Hipple's account of Van
Dorn's passing from a couple of ladies who were on duty at
the counter of the Vicksburg public library. These ladies were
visibly upset by my line of inquiry about the death of General
Van Dorn, though I had been at pains to state my question as
delicately as I could. I had more or less anticipated that these
two Southern ladies would take offense when I asked if they
could lead me to a source of information on the circumstances
of how a Confederate general had died; it wasn't every day, I
guess, that a young soldier from the North walked into the
public library of Vicksburg, Mississippi, to seek documentation
of a story he had heard that a great Southern general had
been, alas, shot to death by one of the girls in a whorehouse.
I was not so stupid that I didn't realize that two Southern ladies
in the Vicksburg public library would be a little disturbed by
a question of this kind. I was not too comfortable putting my
question. But it appeared to me then, and still does, that these
southern ladies were a little strong in their indignation—their
instant expressions of outrage inspired suspicion that they knew

something more than they were going to tell me about the sad ending of General Van Dorn.

I had phrased my question as politely as I was able. My recollection is that I said something about General Van Dorn's having met an untimely death in "a house of ill fame"—something like that. My remembrance of what the southern ladies said in response is imprinted on my mind. What one of them said was, "You ain't fixin' to sully that poor man's reputation, are you?" When I explained that I was merely attempting to search out information on a general whose name identified the camp of a U. S. Army Division that was preparing for combat, one of the southern ladies giggled and said, "Well, I do recollect reading some of the scandalous goings-on of prominent men in those times. I believe we have a book in this library which dwells somewhat on the sordid details of Mr. General Van Dorn's passing—"

"But the book has disappeared," the other lady librarian cut in. "And I declare I don't know where it has gone off to. So, while we would like to be helpful and accommodatin', I'm sorry to say we can't do anythin' for you."

And that was the end of my effort to confirm that a famous Confederate general named Van Dorn was brought to his demise by a bullet of a derringer, fired at him in anger in a cathouse. I never did establish whether the shooting of General Van Dorn in a cathouse ever occurred. I couldn't find anyone else in Vicksburg who could, or would, throw any light on this question of how General Van Dorn had died. Maybe he died in church, telling his rosary beads, for all I can prove. But the story of how this General Van Dorn was sent packing to a better world got into rather wide circulation among the men of the U. S. 63rd Infantry Division—and it seemed to me that the men were proud to be training in a place that had been named for so dashing a character as this. Well, why not? God knows, there wasn't much else at our dreary place in Mississippi that you could brag about. Being stuck in a camp as isolated as a Trappist abbey, named for a Rebel general who purportedly had been shot to death in a whorehouse, we figured we were paying for his sins.

I had gone to Vicksburg with the intention, or so I told myself, of scratching up a little material that might add a bit of life to the division history that I had been condemned to write. Failing that, at least I had hoped to find enough documentation to establish that General Van Dorn was being maligned and that he had behaved honorably "110 percent" of the time, to use a good old boy expression. So, having come up empty on both sides of the question on General Van Dorn's private life, I brooded a little as I sat looking out the window of the Illinois Central day coach that I rode back to our camp.

The truth of it was, I suppose, that I hadn't gone to Vicksburg with a realistic thought of pinning down a juicy item for the 63rd Division history. I knew in my heart that there wasn't a chance that I could get away with even a parenthetical reference to General Van Dorn's having been caught in a compromising situation and put out of business with a bullet. Wanting to include something like this in the history was one thing. But getting away with it, well, that would be like digging up the facts of a scandal that involved your publisher's wife. There wasn't a prayer—and I knew it going in—that I would ever get away with something like that.

Besides, the details of General Van Dorn's passing hardly mattered, because I soon managed to jeopardize my position as division historian.

My first draft of the division history carried an account of the casualties that had occurred during the 63rd Infantry Division's training. The inadvertent killing and serious wounding of young men being schooled to go off and kill the enemy is a tragic but quasi-secret consequence of combat training; subjecting recruits to drills under what they call "live" ammunition—machine gun or artillery shells fired over them—sometimes results in kids' getting killed or maimed. It is part of the price, the Army people claim, of turning out troops who are combat-ready. My error in judgment was that I included reference to this in the preliminary copy of the division history that I submitted to the colonel at Headquarters. The colonel was outraged.

As I recall, I didn't dramatize our misfortunes in killing some of our own guys. I made mention in my manuscript of what had happened a couple of times on what was called the infiltration course, because it seemed to be a valid part of the report on the agonies of getting an infantry division into fighting shape. There were no reports that I saw on what the body count of the dead and the wounded had been, but when something tragic happened, there came a call to our Medical Battalion for "all available ambulances," and it didn't take a mathematical genius to figure out how many had been killed or wounded; our own guys were driving the ambulances, and they had to fill out reports on how many terrified and hemorrhaging GIs they had picked up. My recollection is that they had picked up about a dozen and, whatever the totals on dead and wounded had been, this is the information I included in my copy about the tragic results of combat training. But the personnel colonel really blew his stack, leaving me with the distinct impression that I wasn't proving to be the kind of division historian he had had in mind. I can't remember that I cared very much, one way or the other, what this colonel's judgment of my choice of subject matter might be; if anything, I suppose I was relieved that he didn't like my work. But, finally, he got tired of preaching at me about loyalty and morale and stuff like that, and I was able to salute him and leave.

Under the heading of "morale," it seemed to me that you run into some queer situations when you are a GI in the U.S. Army. Our medics who had made the ambulance run to pick up the casualties at the infiltration course had come back with a story that had cast a pall over our camp on the outskirts of an already dreary place called Centreville, Mississippi. The medics' story was that a group of GIs—crawling out of a trench and worming their way over the bare ground, as machine guns fired over their heads—had been hit when the two-by-four braces nailed in place under the barrels of the machine guns broke loose. The kids got shot up when the barrels dipped before the gunners could stop firing. There was a good deal of discussion in our battalion about this, with our GIs expressing apprehension over the dangers when next it was our turn to crawl on our bellies under the machine gun fire. Would we, too, get shot up and maybe killed if the machine guns broke loose of their moorings?

Having coffee with Alberico at our company mess hall one afternoon, I was not surprised at his fuming over the grim news that the brass had succeeded in killing some of our own guys.

"They claim," I said, "it was just one of those unfortunate things."

"Like hell," he snapped back. "You fire over a bunch of guys with live ammunition, you goddamn well better be sure them guns are locked in place and don't drop down and tear up your own guys."

But before our discussion went any further, Alberico's antagonist—the major from Division—made a grand entrance into the mess hall.

The major walked directly to the door of the mess hall cooler, put his hands on his hips, and fixed his eyes on the printed menu for the day, which had been posted on the door with a thumbtack. Slowly, he turned to Alberico who was guardedly watching him.

"What are you serving today at the evening meal, Sergeant?" the major asked.

"We're servin' meat loaf," Alberico replied.

"You mean meat loaf, *sir*?"

"We're servin' meat loaf, *sir*," Alberico replied.

"Ever occur to you, Sergeant, that the men of this company might be getting a little tired of your meat loaf?"

"Did somebody complain about my meat loaf—*sir*?"

"I didn't say that," the major snapped. "All I'm asking you is why you're giving them meat loaf, when the menu calls for steak. You find time to read the menu that we send you every day, don't you? The menu calls for steak."

"Major," Alberico replied, "I know the menu calls for steak. But they don't give me enough goddamn steak, so I got to grind it up with bread—to make it go further—and cook up some meat loaf. Sure, I'd like to serve up steak, but they don't supply me with enough steak, so I got to make out as best I can with what they give me—and that's why we give 'em meat loaf."

"Have you complained to your officers, or Division Supply, that you're getting short rations?"

"God Almighty, Major," the mess sergeant replied, "*this* is the *Army*, and you got to make out as best you can with what you get. I got 165 men to feed, three times a day; who you gonna argue with when they tell you to serve steak and they don't give you enough steak?"

"So you give them meat loaf."

"It ain't so bad, Major. It's a lot better than the men had it when that order came down to all the mess sergeants in the division, a couple of months ago, that all we could serve at the two main meals was "C" rations. You ever look at any of them canned "C" rations, Major? You ever *smell* that stuff? God Almighty! The order that came down from the general said we couldn't even heat this stuff in the mess hall kitchen; we had to set up a tent, outside, and heat up the cans in boilin' water out there. They wouldn't even let the men bring them cans into the mess hall to spoon that stuff; the men had to eat outside, whether it rained or the wind was blowin' dust all over the place or it got cold or what. I'll tell you the truth, Major, me and all the other mess sergeants thought the general had gone nuts. God Almighty! Somebody of bigger rank than the general must have heard about what was goin' on in the 63rd and sent down an order to cut it out. And when we get the order, wherever it comes from, to cut it out, do they tell me and my cooks it's all right now to start operatin' again in the mess hall kitchen? Like hell they do! What they tell us is to cook in the tent outside, where it's a miracle if you can keep that goddamn Mississippi dust out of the meat loaf, servin' up the stuff into mess kits—with one of the noncoms standin' there near a pail of boilin' water to make sure each guy dips his mess kit in water before he gets somethin' to eat—and after he's done. God Almighty."

The major pursed his lips when Alberico concluded his lament. "I think I understand how you feel, Sergeant," the major said. "It has to be tough for you and your cooks to feed the men under these conditions. But what you don't seem to understand is that this is a very important part of the training program. The general is *simulating* actual combat conditions. He's giving the troops of this division a chance to experience what they will be up against in an actual combat situation."

"Major, you think you got to train somebody who's hungry to eat somethin' like 'C' rations when there ain't anythin' else to eat—or eat it out of a mess kit, instead of off a plate, when there ain't no other way to eat it? It's like this thing of marchin' everybody down to the infiltration course—me and my cooks and everybody else—and make us crawl around on our bellies while they fire machine gun bullets over us and explode dynamite near us. You think a guy has got to *learn* that he better keep his head down or he's gonna get hit right between the eyes?"

"It's part of the training routine, Sergeant," the major replied. "Recruits have to learn the sounds and the dangers of close combat, and the only way you can teach them is by exposing them to training under live ammunition. It's for the same reason that infantry companies are taken into the field and division artillery fires live rounds over their heads. The same reason that everybody in the division—you, the cooks, officers, *everybody*—has to have training in how to react in the event of chemical warfare; it is terribly important that everyone know what to do if the enemy fires phosgene shells at us—get the mask on, make certain it is working all right, and so on. Don't you understand the importance of all this?"

The mess sergeant shook his head. "Some of it is pretty important, I guess, sir. Goin' out to the rifle range and learnin' how to save your ass if they throw poison gas—that kind of stuff is important, I guess. I don't know about the infiltration course; it's only a real dumb son of a bitch who doesn't know enough to keep his head down when they got machine guns firin' over you. Havin' them teach you how to eat 'C' rations— that's crazy, if anybody's askin' me. You run into mess sergeants in other divisions, and you tell 'em how we've got to heat up the cans of 'C' rations in a tent outside—mess sergeants you meet from other outfits can't even believe it. All they say is, 'Who's the goddamn fool who dreamed that up?' "

"Do you tell them? Do you tell them that this is an order that came down personally from your division commander?"

"Yeah, Major. I tell 'em. I tell 'em our general even shows up at the mess halls of this division, just before chow, to make sure we're followin' orders on the 'C' rations. I even tell 'em, these other mess sergeants, we've even got a name for Major General Hibbs."

"What do you call him? What name?"

"Sir, you may not like it. But seein' as how you want me to say it, everybody is callin' the general 'Mess Kit Louie.' "

For some moments, the major was silent. Finally, he said, "Well, it's all behind you, Sergeant. As you mentioned, someone has shut off the 63rd Division's allocation of 'C' rations; I imagine they are running short and need what they have for the divisions already in combat. There's no reason, now, to be upset about it."

Alberico scowled. "They've still got us cookin' in that goddamn tent," he replied. "We got a mess hall that has to be scrubbed with soap and bleach, and the general says we can't use it; we gotta feed the men outside, rain or shine. They made us rewash every plate, every dish, every cup and saucer, every knife, fork, and spoon and stack it all away in bags. There ain't a man in the company that doesn't have to eat out of a mess kit. The morale in this outfit is lower than a snake's ass. And who is to blame? Mess Kit Louie; that's who. So, Major, don't tell me there ain't nothin' to get upset about."

"Sergeant Alberico, they can bust you for that."

"Yeah, I know, Major. They can put me in the stockade. They can kick me out of this goddamn army with a Section 8, and everybody knows you're bananas if they kick you out on a Section 8."

"You wouldn't want a discharge like that."

"Oh, yes I would, Major. Try me."

The major shrugged. "Well, that'll be all, Sergeant. Thanks for your, ah, cooperation."

Getting a half-assed salute from Alberico, he got into his jeep and was driven off.

Alberico, with a look of hate, watched the major from Division pull away in his jeep. Turning to me, he said, "They musta had a collection, the people runnin' this Army; they musta went out lookin' all over for the biggest son of a bitch they could find, to make life miserable for the rest of us. That major—he's one of the biggest son of a bitches of 'em all."

"You came on a little strong with him, Alberico," I said.

"Why not?" he replied. "He don't mean nothin' to me."

"He can take away your stripes," I said. "He can bust you to private."

"So let him bust me. It don't make much difference to me."

With that, Alberico walked over to a wooden cabinet in his kitchen, pulled out a bottle of Kentucky whiskey, and came back with his bottle and a couple of glasses. He poured whiskey into the glasses, raised his, smiled, and said, "Salute!"

Wiping his mouth with the back of his hand, after tossing down his drink, Alberico said, "You think that stool pigeon will bust me?"

"I wouldn't be surprised," I said.

A couple of days after Staff Sergeant Alberico had his face-off with the major from Division, I went into the mess hall for a cup of coffee and discovered that Alberico had been stripped of his stripes. He was deceptively passive, sitting on a bench with his cup of coffee. And none of the cooks was saying anything. But there were conspicuous marks on the sleeves of his fatigue jacket, where his staff sergeant stripes had been. By way of calling my attention to his loss of status, he pointed a finger at one unfaded spot where his staff sergeant grade had been, and in a casual way, he said, "That major from Division took care of me."

I felt bad about Alberico's losing his stripes. I was not surprised, because I had heard Alberico pop off to the major and you learn quickly in the Army that you don't have much chance of getting away with that; they make you pay a price, if you dare to take a stand on something that is contrary to what an officer tells you. It doesn't take much in the U.S. Army to create

the grounds for a charge of insubordination or something like
that against an enlisted man. Even now I would have to concede
that Alberico—by the tone of his voice and the language he
had employed—had gone a little far in making a case for the
defense of his meat loaf. He had, I think, challenged the major
from Division to demote him. And the major was quick to stick
it to him. Even so, it annoyed the hell out of me that a first-
rate man like Alberico was vulnerable to the whim of an officer
who, in civilian life, probably was not qualified to tie Alberico's
shoes.

I was in a similar fix. I, too, had stirred up the disapproval
of higher authority. The reason I had gone over to have coffee
with Alberico on that particular day was that I had just received
notice from the company first sergeant that he had just received notice from Battalion that Battalion had just received
notice from Division that I was no longer division historian.
Alberico, for some reason I did not understand, had taken a
degree of pride in my being assigned to write the division history. But when I walked in to discover that Alberico had been
demoted to private, I didn't say anything about the demotion
that had been dropped on me; I guess I didn't think my news
would be of any consolation to him.

Having offended the sensibilities of the personnel colonel at
Division, I had expected that they'd find somebody else to write
the glorious history of a division that hadn't been around long
enough to have a history; the colonel was upset over the copy
I had submitted about our infantry guys getting killed and shot
up by our own gunners on the infiltration course. The colonel
seemed to believe that I was slyly attempting to put responsibility for this senseless business on the brass, and the truth is
that this is exactly what I had intended to do. I knew in my
guts, of course, when I handed over this part of the manuscript,
that I was likely to get drummed out of the noble profession
of historians.

The only one who seemed to suffer any humiliation over this
was the major of our battalion. The order from Division, taking
me off the writing assignment, had come down through Battalion, and I didn't like the prospect of having to explain to

the major what had happened to me. But he never did call me over to get a confession out of me about whatever terrible thing I had done to get me fired. The only words that passed between the major and me came in a chance meeting outside Battalion HQ. He grinned at me in an evil sort of way, or so I thought, and said, "I had an order from Division today, telling me to reassign you. You hear about that?"

"Yes, sir," I replied. "The first sergeant told me."

"Well, we're taking you off the news summary assignment, too. If you're not good enough for them, naturally you're not good enough for me."

I nodded.

"You're going to be a medic," the major went on. "I don't know whether you're qualified for that. I have my doubts. But that's what you're going to be—a medic."

CHAPTER **6**

THE GORY LIFE
OF COMBAT MEDICS

I WAS NOT EAGER TO GET INVOLVED in the treatment of the raw casualties of battle. Quite the contrary, I had privately brooded over the problem of having to hold myself together to treat young soldiers who had sustained severe wounds. I had walked the deck of our transport ship on the way to France, trying to put down this terrible fear that I was into something that I simply couldn't handle. I was so haunted by the fear that I would not be able to deal with young men crying out in pain, that I couldn't even lie on my bunk and rest. It was a peculiar kind of terror; there was no fear that I might be maimed or killed—only dread of a tentful of young soldiers, staring at me with pleading eyes, in desperate need of my help. It was a persistent fear that, when called upon to treat the mangled bodies of young men like myself, I would simply fall apart.

At the staging area outside Marseilles, where our medical battalion was getting itself together to go into action, I had been assigned to Company D—the clearing station that would handle the wounded of the entire division. Procedures for the emergency treatment and transportation of combat casualties, so carefully put together in peace time by logistical theoreticians, had been drummed into all of us at the combat medic training school in Springfield, Missouri. A wounded man was dependent on a front line aid man to keep him alive on the field of battle. He'd receive further treatment at the aid stations, set up close to the combat line. From the front line aid stations, the wounded were to be transported to the regimental collecting station a mile or two behind the combat line. From there, casualties were to be taken to the division clearing station. At each successive stage, capabilities for medical treatment became more sophisticated. The clearing stations—the on-scene hospitals of every division—were better manned and had better equipment than either the company aid stations or the regimental collecting stations. On paper, the theoreticians' logistics made sense; in practice, as things turned out, the clearing station often was set up much closer to the combat line than the theoreticians had anticipated, and the wounded were carried to us directly from the front line aid stations.

In an area south of Lyon, I was first confronted by the thing that I had dreaded—a flow of gravely wounded infantry guys. We had been moving north cautiously. Every once in a while the retreating Germans would pause to fire their 88mm guns at us. Occasionally, the Germans would dig in and take a defensive position to delay our advance. But they didn't inflict any casualties until they laced a field south of Lyon with antipersonnel mines.

Our clearing station had been set up in a tent, with huge red crosses imprinted on the canvas, in a field on the southern outskirts of Lyon. Holding down the fort were three medics—myself; a marvelous Jewish kid named Herbie Strumpf, from New York; and a southern boy, Tom Fagg. They were efficient, low-key guys. Strumpf was a registered nurse in civilian life, and by the Army's caprice only a staff sergeant, though his wife, another RN, was also in Army service and was a first lieutenant. My recollection is that Fagg was a county farm agent or something like that, back in Asheville, North Carolina.

A handsome Irishman named Jim Nolan was the duty medical officer. Nolan's claim to fame was that he had been an All-American quarterback on a top-grade Syracuse University football team—or so everybody said. When I had heard that I would be working for Captain Nolan, my suspicion had been that this guy, still glowing in the status of All-American quarterback, would be insufferable. He proved to be quite the opposite. Nolan had the handsome, happy look of the Irish. He had a few scars on his face, and he had the impudent bearing of a man in top physical shape. Nolan was Irish enough to blow his top on occasion. But he was the best doctor we had, really skillful. He had great hands, this Captain Nolan—not for throwing footballs, but for doing what a surgeon is supposed to do when somebody's life is at stake.

In our medical tent that day, Jim Nolan was giving his three medics a friendly lecture on the dangers of infection from contaminated instruments, when two litter bearers came into the tent with the first seriously wounded American soldier I had seen. The kid on the litter had been covered to his neck with an olive-drab Army blanket. His face was ashen and contorted with pain. I was horrified at the prospect of what we would see when we pulled the blanket away. As the litter bearers placed their stretcher in place, the two handles at each end set on upended medical chests, one of the soldier's feet came clear of the blanket.

In a shredded boot, the foot was nearly severed from the leg. The stub of the leg was a matted mass of flesh and shattered bone. What was left of the kid's leg oozed blood through the dirty, ripped cloth of his trousers. The ugly, traumatic closure of the wound had shut off the arteries, saving the guy from bleeding to death. I stood transfixed as Captain Nolan leaned over to study the wound. Nolan then handed me some surgical shears and signified with his fingers that I would have to cut off the kid's foot.

Nolan looked at the kid with a little smile. In the gentlest of voices, he said, "You're having a rough time, son, but you're going to be all right. We'll give you a little injection of something for the pain and we'll clean you up where you've been hurt and we'll have you on your way back to a good hospital in no time." The confidence in Nolan's voice reassured the kid; and the half-grain of morphine Strumpf shot into the kid began to take effect.

Nolan gave me a commanding glance. Strumpf was already busy, setting up a bottle of plasma, and Fagg was gathering together the instruments Nolan needed to close the wound. At my end of the litter, the surgical shears poised and another medic standing at my side with a plastic bucket, I searched with my eyes for the tendon that held the damaged foot to the kid's leg. Slowly, I partially closed the shears to make certain that I had the right place to make the cut, and then I firmly closed them. The plastic bucket had been moved below the booted foot to catch it as it dropped. Some of the tissue in the torn stub of the leg quivered, but the kid's face showed no physical reaction—the morphine had taken hold.

It was a considerable while—a half hour, at least—before the ordeal was over. It took that long to get plasma into the kid and for Nolan to dig around in the stub of the kid's leg to tie off the severed veins and arteries. Throughout all of this, Nolan kept talking to the kid. I don't remember much of what Nolan said. What I remember is his reassuring kindliness.

When the kid who lost the foot—smiling at us now—was carried out of our tent to an ambulance that would take him to the evacuation hospital, other ambulances from the combat area south of Lyon were pulling in. A steady stream of casualties came in on the medics and doctors of Company D all that day and into the night. When, finally, it was over and we had sent the wounded on to a field hospital or the evacuation hospital, about twenty or thirty miles back, Nolan and the three of us—Strumpf, Fagg, and myself—were really bushed.

Sitting around our tent that night, Nolan critiqued our performance. He said a couple of nice things about me that embarrassed me; I wondered if he had known about the fears I had had. Having gotten through the day without caving in to panic, I felt pretty good about myself. With this day behind me, I felt, I'd be all right now—come what may. When Nolan came up with a bottle of bourbon and poured us drinks in paper cups, the whiskey felt very good inside me.

I guess it was the booze that made me bold. Or maybe it was Nolan's display of camaraderie. Whatever, I had been deeply impressed by Nolan. It was not just the professional skill that he had displayed. It was the kindly way in which he had chatted with the wounded men—pacifying their fears, building up their confidence, praising their courage, assuring them that everything would work out all right. I had never seen a doctor so gentle. Nolan had a gift for empathizing with wounded kids. There was something special about Nolan's ability to convey his sympathy and optimism to these kids. Whatever it was that prompted me, I had something to say—and I said it.

"I apologize if this offends you, Captain," I said. "But I've seen doctors work on people who have been badly hurt or wounded by gunshots or something like that. It has always made me sick to look at it, to tell you the truth, but now and again in my work in civilian life it has more or less been my job to horn in on things like this, to see what's going on. So I hope you don't take offense at what I'm going to say."

Strumpf and Fagg looked at me with apprehension; I could see that I was making them uncomfortable. But Captain Nolan looked at me rather solemnly and nodded his head and seemed willing to hear me out. So I went on.

"What I'm trying to do, Captain—in my own way—is pay you a high compliment. It's a question I have to ask you, but it's important for me to know. And what I want to know, Captain, is how it is you have this patient, gentle way of dealing with wounded men. Frankly, I've never seen a doctor with a bedside manner like that."

Nolan studied me. He lit a cigarette, never taking his eyes off me. Then, he said, "OK, that's a fair question—and I think I should answer it." And, with that, he opened his shirt and pulled up his undershirt, putting his chest on view. And I don't think I ever in my life felt that mortified.

Nolan's chest was mottled with patches of ugly, red scar tissue.

Boy, had this man been through something! "Captain Nolan," I said, "I apologize. I never should have asked you."

"Don't apologize," he said. "You would have found out about

it sooner or later. Only"—pointing to the scar tissue on his chest—"this isn't all. I've got it on the legs, too." And standing up, he lowered his trousers. His legs were covered with scar tissue.

"Captain, I'm sorry," I said. "I never should have said what I said." I felt ashamed.

"It's all right," he replied. "And, seeing as how I would have got around to telling you sometime, I guess I'll tell you now. I was just out of med school and I had just got married. I was on my honeymoon and, like a damned fool, I rolled over in a car. My wife came out of it all right; I got trapped, and, when the car caught fire, I got burned. I don't recommend it, but if you want to teach a young doctor how to deal with a patient who is in terrible pain and despondent, well, put him through an ordeal like that and I think you might straighten him out." Then he laughed and poured us all another drink. We loved the guy.

At the other end of the scale of our affection was a psychiatrist from New York City. I don't know how the guy ever made it through medical school. He was bright enough; there was no question about that. But he was inept. At first, Strumpf, Fagg, and myself figured that the reason he did such a sloppy job was that he was working too fast. Eventually we realized our psychiatrist had something in his head, a block of some kind, about blood. The shrink couldn't stand the sight of blood.

And he was as lazy as they come. On the nights that the shrink was duty officer, he resisted all urging to get out of the sack to attend to some wounded kid who had been carried in. Propping himself on one elbow, he would ask us what the soldier's problem was. And when we gave him a quick diagnosis, his response would be, "Give him the usual treatment." Having said this, he would roll over and go back to sleep. He was really something, this shrink.

Somewhere in Germany, many days after we had gone through Kaiserslautern, at the eastern extreme of the Siegfried Line defenses, the shrink did himself in with Strumpf, Fagg, and myself. German artillery units, which had calibrated distances so precisely that they were making direct hits on tanks, poured a lot of fire on our infantry guys. Shells from the German 88s shattered into jagged fragments on impact, and a lot of our guys were wounded. In a medical unit you never get accurate information on what is happening at the combat line; but you get a definitive understanding of the results of enemy action. In this particular case, ambulances streamed in from the front line with numerous GIs bleeding from shrapnel wounds. We had so many casualties that all the medical officers in our unit were summoned—even the shrink with an aversion to blood.

We ran out of ambulances to transport the patched-up soldiers to the rear; a lot of the kids we had treated had to sit where they could, or lie on litters outside, waiting for ambulances to take them to Evac. When things eased up in the medical tent, Fagg and I went outside to check up on the kids who were waiting for transportation. We came upon one kid whose bandage was wet with blood, and then another, and another. "My God," Fagg said. "What's happenin' here?"

What was happening here, obviously, was that somebody had fumbled the job of tying off the bleeders. Reflexively, we looked at the medical tags, which recorded the nature of the wound, what the treatment had been, whether the wounded man was entitled to the Purple Heart and—the key thing—the name of the attending medical officer. Fagg and I knew, before looking for the name at the bottom of these medical tags, who the doctor was: our old buddy, the New York shrink. We hustled the bleeding men back into the medical tent for repairs.

Fagg and I raised hell that night when we were sitting around our tent with some of the officers, drinking grapefruit juice splashed with ethyl alcohol. "It's a goddamn outrage," Fagg declared, "the Army allowin' that chicken-shit SIGH-chiatrist to work on these men." And I was at pains to let the doctor-officers know that I was as hot about this as Fagg. It's mutiny or insubordination or something like that if you denounce Army officers to other Army officers, but Fagg and I were beyond having any inhibitions about this—and, not surprisingly I guess, the shrink's fellow officers didn't speak up for him. As well as I can recall, the only one who said anything was the commanding officer of our unit. All he said was, "We've been through another bad day and what's over is over. I think you all understand that in the Army you do the best you can with what you've got. And now, if you'll excuse me, I'm going to hit the sack." As I remember, Fagg's outburst finished off our grapefruit juice and alky happy hour, but it didn't finish off the SIGH-chiatrist.

Our shrink had another peculiarity: he used to disappear. Nobody ever knew where in hell he had gone off to; the most we ever knew was that the shrink had been seen climbing into a jeep and driving off to the rear. We all thought it was a queer way for even a medical officer with the rank of captain to behave, but everyone was pleased, rather than outraged, when the shrink went off on one of his holidays. One of our guys— Fagg or Strumpf, I think—came up with the theory that our shrink was deliberately acting nutty in the hope he'd get transferred to some unit far from combat. Dealing with crazies was this guy's civilian trade, and you couldn't say that a conniving shrink would not contrive a scheme like this.

Well, if it was a transfer out of the combat area that he wanted, he had to wait a long time for it. Our division had been in a running fight with the fanatical kids of Hitler's 17th S.S. Division. The fight began outside of Heidelberg and carried on down the banks of the Neckar and then eastward into the heart of Bavaria. Things had started off quietly on our shrink's last night with us.

But, some time after midnight, all hell broke loose on the combat line. The concussion of the big guns on both sides of the line shook our medical tent, where the shrink—who was duty officer—was in the sack. Strumpf, who was working with me that night, laughed when he saw the shrink pull his Army blanket over his head. But not long after that, ambulances started to pull up with casualties, and the shrink had to get up from his cot.

Despite all the artillery banging away, we didn't have too many casualties. So few of our kids were brought in that we started getting the 17th S.S. wounded not long after silence fell on the front.

According to the Geneva Convention or some such gentle-man's agreement, American doctors—and German doctors—had a moral obligation to do all they could to save the lives of wounded enemy soldiers. There is a touch of madness attached to the practice of having your medical people work their tails off to help troops who got wounded in their effort to kill or maim your own guys—but this is the noble procedure of all civilized nations. We did everything possible for the German casualties—but our wounded got first priority and we didn't work on German casualties until we had taken care of our own. And this, I think, was an understandable course that did not violate the gentleman's agreement. On this night, having treated our own guys, we went to work on Germans.

Before the night was out three outsiders came in. They were from Corps or Seventh Army or some big-daddy outfit like that. They were G-2 officers—intelligence officers—and they had a particular interest in two or three of the Germans. The G-2 guys didn't say a damned thing to anyone; they simply stood there and watched. We thought that the presence of two majors and a lieutenant-colonel would knock our shrink off stride, but he just puffed up and strutted around to impress them. And then he disappeared—off to the latrine or some-where. One of G-2's Germans was as cold as a clam when Strumpf and I went to work on him. The G-2 officers stood off to the side. Strumpf set up a bottle of plasma and hit a vein with the needle—which is tricky when your patient's in shock—to get the plasma dripping into the German. Pulling back the blood-soaked blanket that covered the German guy, Strumpf saw the wide gash in the fleshy part of the guy's thigh, blood bubbling out of the wound. The G-2 officers were expression-less, but there was a grim look on Strumpf's face. Having to handle this as best he could, all by himself—our psychiatrist having disappeared—Strumpf grabbed what we called a "flat"—a sterile gauze bandage—tore open its package with his teeth, placed the bandage over the wound, and pressed down. Futilely searching the tent with his eyes in the hope of spotting an available medical officer, he finally rested his eyes on me and said, "Get a tourniquet around the upper part of this man's leg." I moved as quickly as I could, not knowing, really, what I was doing. I got the tourniquet around the guy's leg, and somehow it worked. Strumpf gave me a nod of approval and said, "Good!" But I thought to myself that we were one hell of a long way from saving G-2's pigeon; what we needed was a doctor.

The German kid was on the litter in front of us for quite a while before he started coming around. His cheeks turned from ashen gray to pink, and his breathing became regular. Strumpf, the palm of his hand still pressing down on the flat, looked up and said, "We'd have a good chance with this kid if we had a doctor to tie off the bleeders." The G-2 guys were as poker-faced as professional gamblers.

The flaps at the end of our tent came open, and Jim Nolan walked in. "Thank God," Herbie said. You didn't have to waste any time explaining a situation to Nolan; he took it all in with one glance at Herbie's pressure bandage, the tourniquet, the nearly empty bottle of plasma, and the G-2 observers. Nolan told Strumpf to get another bottle of plasma started, and then Nolan said, "When he comes out of it, Herbie, I think he could stand a little bit of your refreshment"—more morphine.

Nolan went to work on the open wound. He always worked fast, but worked particularly fast on the German guy, uncovering the bleeders, washing them off with saline solution, tying off the severed veins and arteries. It is a fascinating thing to see, a skillful surgeon closing a wound, and the more you see of doctors working on bad wounds, the greater becomes your admiration for a guy who really knows what he's doing. Nolan was really good.

The German opened his eyes as Nolan was placing a wide bandage on the guy's leg. Gazing up at Nolan, the kid had a look of gratitude in his eyes. Nolan grinned, gave the German a wink, nodded to the G-2 officers, and said, "It's been a hard night and I'm on overtime; if it's all right with all of you, I'll bid you gentlemen goodnight." And out he went.

And then in walked our friend the shrink. He waved a hand of greeting to the G-2 guys, who did not seem overjoyed that he had come back. He strutted over to the German on the

litter and ran his eyes over him. Then, turning toward Strumpf
and me, the shrink said, "I'm sorry to say he looks all right to
me." The guy on the litter mumbled something in German,
and the shrink gave him a cold stare.

"Doesn't this man speak English?" the shrink asked me.

"I don't know," I replied, "but I doubt it. He didn't say
anything until you came in, and I imagine he's trying to say
thanks for saving his life."

"Fat chance," the shrink responded. "Fat chance I'm going
to save a Nazi's life."

"How do you know he's a Nazi?" asked Strumpf, gently but
firmly. "He could be any kid drafted into the German Army."

"Sergeant Strumpf, *I* am a Jew. Any Jew can spot a Nazi
when he sees one."

Strumpf smiled. "Captain," he said, "*I* am a Jew and *I* can't
tell if this man is a Nazi."

"He's a Nazi, Strumpf. Take my word for it."

"Maybe he's a Nazi, Captain. I don't know. But to me he's
just another wounded kid who needed help."

"Strumpf," the shrink replied, his voice rising, "what kind
of fool are you that you can't see this man is a Nazi?"

Strumpf shook his head in disbelief. The G-2 officers stared
at the shrink. The German guy on the litter, understanding
only one word—"Nazi"—looked at the shrink with anger and
fear.

The shrink said, "I'm going to get an interpreter." And he
left the tent.

Strumpf was embarrassed. Turning to the G-2 officers, he
said, "I'm sorry about this; it never happened before. I don't
understand it."

The G-2 officers shrugged, and one of them, lighting a cigarette, looked over the burning match and said, "Don't worry
about it."

Moments later, the shrink came back, with the mess sergeant
in tow. Our mess sergeant did the best he could, I suppose,
with whatever they gave him to cook—although we were mostly
feeding on big cans of "C" rations. But he was pretty good at
trading off "C" rations for live chickens, when he came upon

a country hausfrau who would bargain with him. This guy spoke German like a native. Not only did he bargain for chickens and eggs and fresh vegetables, he also served as our company's semi-official translator.

It was old stuff for our mess sergeant to be dragged into the medical tent to translate. But the mess sergeant looked at the three G-2 officers, the German guy—now looking defiant—and the shrink pointing an accusing finger at the German. Well, our mess sergeant wanted no part of whatever in hell was going on, and he asked the shrink's permission to take off.

"No!" our shrink retorted. "We need you."

The mess sergeant turned his head toward the G-2 officers, his eyes pleading for help. They remained deadpan.

"Now, sergeant," our shrink said, "I want you to speak your German to this man and ask him how he has been treated and how he feels."

Obediently, the mess sergeant made the translation. The guy on the litter looked at him in surprise and muttered a reply.

"He says," the mess sergeant told our shrink, "that he has been treated good and that, while he is weak, he feels all right."

The shrink nodded. He said, "now ask him if he is aware that we gave him a transfusion."

The mess sergeant hesitated for an instant but made the translation. The wounded German shook his head up and down and muttered a reply.

"He says," the mess sergeant told our shrink, "that he knows he got a transfusion and he is grateful for it."

The shrink smiled. "All right," the shrink replied. "Now I want you to ask him if he knows that the blood we put in him is *Jewish* blood."

The mess sergeant stepped back, his mouth open and his eyes wide. "My God, sir, I can't tell him that!"

"Sergeant, I have given you an order! Tell that man we have injected him with Jewish blood. Tell him! That is an order!"

The three G-2 officers, listening to all of this with stone faces, watched the mess sergeant turn to the wounded man on the litter and pass on the word that the American captain said the man now had Jewish blood in him. A look of horror, turning to hate, appeared on the German's face, and the shrink—hands on his hips—smiled his evil smile. The G-2 officers, who presumably could understand German (they had to know German to interrogate POWs) did not change their expression. The mess sergeant, mortified, lowered his head. The rest of us were engulfed by the tension.

When the German on the litter finally said something, speaking despondently, the shrink turned on the mess sergeant and demanded, "What did he say? Tell me what he said!"

The sergeant shook his head. Visibly agitated now, our shrink leered at the mess sergeant and roared, "Tell me! Tell me, goddamn you! Tell me what he said!"

The mess sergeant looked the shrink right in the eye. And then he said, softly, with no emotion, "Captain, this man says that if it is true that you put Jewish blood in him, you should kill him because he would rather be dead."

We were clubbed into silence, every one of us, by this message of the damned. The shrink seemed to be more shocked than anyone else by the mournful message of hatred that the sergeant had delivered. Under the intent gaze of the German kid, the shrink—the muscles of his face twitching—made his way out of the medical tent with the unsteady gait of a drunken man. With a sigh, Strumpf reached up for a dark bottle ominously labeled with skull and crossbones, opened the bottle and poured stiff drinks into paper cups. The G-2 officers nodded their thanks. Strumpf worked up a smile and said, "It's our private stock—for emergencies." The G-2 officers grinned. "I think it's an emergency," the lieutenant colonel said.

Turning to the kid on the litter, our Jewish staff sergeant asked him in English if he'd like a taste of American whiskey. Not understanding the words, but understanding quite well Strumpf's gesture with the bottle, the German guy smiled. So Strumpf soaked a small sponge with the booze and gently placed the wet sponge in the German guy's mouth. That was it. That was the last night that any of us saw the bane of our existence, the psychiatrist from New York City.

CHAPTER 7

DEAD SOLDIERS
AND LIVE HEROES

IN A LOVELY LITTLE TOWN IN ALSACE we had so many
GIs brought in with shattered nerves that we didn't have
enough ambulances to move them out to Evac. Our medical unit had a busy time of it in Sarralbe. The Germans
had inflicted a great many casualties on our division, and they
had launched an artillery attack of such magnitude that we had
an extraordinary number of terrorized GIs—what the Army
euphemistically refers to as "victims of combat fatigue."

By way of making the trembling soldiers comfortable, we set
up a ward in the top floor ballroom of a mansion. The men,
under heavy sedation, lay beneath Army blankets on litters
placed side by side. It was a pitiful sight and most medics—
fearful, I suppose, that they might be next to break down—
couldn't bring themselves to look at the nerve-shattered GIs.
The only medic who accepted this situation as part of our
normal duty was my friend Eppifanio.

Eppifanio, a pensive sort of guy from Brooklyn, demonstrated an angelic kindness in his dealings with wounded men.
He was especially gentle with the victims of battle fatigue. He'd

165

go from man to man on the litters, speaking softly to each one. He'd go up and down four flights of stairs many times a day to fetch water or coffee for the shell-shocked GIs. There was a grand piano in one corner of the ballroom, and Eppie played Strauss and Beethoven to soothe the men on the litters. Eppie's music was hypnotic. One gentle guy at a grand piano did more for the nerve-shattered men than anyone else in our unit.

During one of Eppie's concerts, huge explosions sounded not far from the mansion. Big artillery shook the elegant old home. The kids were terrified. They threw off their blankets and struggled to their feet. I was terrified, too—of the effect of artillery rounds on the thirty or so shell-shocked GIs. Eppie didn't change expression and didn't miss a note. After a few moments, he looked up from the piano. Showing no sign that he saw the panic of his charges, Eppie said, "If you're wondering about that blasting, it's the Army Engineers, blowing out the ice that's been slowing up the convoys; that's all it is, so don't let it bother you." Then, with a show of indifference, Eppifanio—who knew damned well it was enemy artillery—lowered his eyes to the piano keys and resumed playing.

The enemy guns fired at us for about fifteen minutes, and then they ceased—so that our spotter planes could not get a reading on them and knock them out. When the battle-fatigue kids settled down, Eppie got up from the grand piano and suggested to me that we go have ourselves a look around this place called Sarralbe.

On the road leading downhill from the mansion, an elderly German on a bicycle went past us, turning a friendly face toward us, tipping his cap, and saying, "Guten tag." A half block or so farther down the hill another elderly civilian strenuously worked the pedals of his bicycle to get up the incline. As the two Germans on bicycles passed each other, both extended their right arms in an exchange of greeting. We were too far away to hear what they said, but not so far that we could not see they had greeted each other with the Nazi salute.

"I guess they haven't noticed that things have changed a little in the past few days," said Eppie, showing a grin. Then, sheltering himself from the breeze on the leeward side of a cylindrical kiosk, he stopped to light a cigarette. As he took a drag of his cigarette, he gestured toward a figure painted on an eight-foot-high concrete kiosk. It was a black man in a flowing black cape and large slouch hat. Below the figure, in yellow block letters, were the words *Find hort mit*. The foreboding guy in the black cape was on countless kiosks throughout Germany and occupied France.

"I don't think there's one guy in the whole goddamn Army," Eppie said, "who knows the name of those goddamn things."

"It's a kiosk," I said.

Eppie shook his head. "No," he said. "It isn't a kiosk. They *call* it a kiosk, but that's not what it is; not really."

"So what is it?"

"It's a *Litvosssoile*."

"How do you know?"

Eppie smiled. "I was writing my mother a letter about the things I have been seeing, and I started to tell her about this black guy in the slouch hat and the cape, on account of how they put this drawing everywhere, and so I got curious about what they call these things and I started asking around and everybody said, 'It's a kiosk.' Then I started asking the German guys I was carrying out to the ambulance, and they looked at me like I was crazy, although a couple of them seemed to understand what I was talking about and they told me it was a kiosk. But I knew that. What I wanted to know, for the letter I was writing my mother, was the real name of this thing."

"Well, *that* is the real name; *kiosk*," I said. "You even said a couple of Germans told you that."

Eppie shook his head. "No. Not kiosk. That didn't sound German to me. So I keep asking the German guys and finally I am carrying a German guy to the ambulance and this German guy speaks pretty good English, so I ask him. He didn't seem to get it at first, what I was driving at. Then the electric bulb goes on in his head and he says, 'Litvosssoile!' I don't know if it's true or not, but he tells me this is the only word in the German language that has three consecutive *s*'s in it."

"OK, Eppie," I said, surrendering to his superior knowledge. "But why would you write your mother a letter about this?"

"She's interested in things," he said.

"Kiosks, with black men in capes?"

"I'm not joking," Eppie replied. "My mother always is looking up little things like this. Interested in unusual things, my mother is. She's an educated woman, my mother is. So I told her that according to the dictionary this thing was invented by a German printer by the name of Joseph Litvoss and that the reason he invented it was to have a place where he could paste up his advertising—big sheets of advertising that he printed—which I think was a pretty brilliant idea. And his idea caught on, and that's why you have these kiosks with advertising on them everywhere."

"You're telling me, Eppie, that your mother's interested in methods of advertising?"

"Well," Eppie said, with a bit of a sigh, "you have to know my mother to understand. My mother is always searching for symbolic things; her idea is that this tells you a lot about other people. So I was writing her about the guy in the black cape on the Litvosssoile and the words underneath, *Find hort mit.* You know what that means?"

I shook my head.

"It means—well, it's a warning to the German people: 'Cover your ass.' 'Keep your mouth shut!' 'Beware, the enemy is listening!' *Find hort mit* means something like that. Not exactly, but that's about what the warning is."

"Did you write your mother about this?"

Eppie nodded. "Yeah, I did. And my mother wrote back about it. My mother said that if this *Find hort mit* warning is painted everywhere, along with the black man on the Litvosssoile, it's hard for my mother to swallow the story that the German people aren't all together on this war and that they don't know what the Nazis are doing. It doesn't seem logical, my mother said. It seems to my mother, and I'd have to go along with her on this, that they are all in this together."

Concluding our sight-seeing in Sarralbe, Eppie and I returned to the homes in which we were billeted. The owners of these modest homes near the mansion were compensated for putting us up. The elderly couple who owned the little house where I was quartered had one son in the French Army and a second son in the German Army—which gives you an idea of how screwed up, especially in Alsace, this war could be. There was not the slightest indication in this house of what the owner's sentiments in this war might be. No Allied designations, no swastikas, no flags, no pictures of Hitler or French patriots—nothing. A household of innocent bystanders in a great war.

We moved our medical station from the mansion in Sarralbe to a schoolhouse in Sarreguemines—about 8 miles north—as the 63rd advanced.

There Eppie and I watched from the roof of the school building as wave after wave of B-26 bombers dove a few hundred feet above us and for hours rained bombs on the nearby German industrial city of Saarbrücken, turning it into a pyre. The bombing set the school bell tolling. The bell tolled maddeningly, monotonously. The bell tolled without interruption all through the day, as heavy smoke poured up out of Saarbrücken.

Taking advantage of a little free time some days later, my friend Eppifanio and I took a look around Sarreguemines. As we wandered around the city on a lark, we were startled when we turned a corner to find ourselves facing a conference of U.S. brass. General George S. Patton was standing in the main street of Sarreguemines. The other generals, though neat, seemed grubby alongside Patton, with his spit-polished boots and shiny helmet with three stars on its front, a riding crop in his right hand, and the butts of two pearl-handled pistols showing at the top of the wide belt fitted tightly to his narrow hips. General Patch of the U.S. Seventh Army was there. And Major General Louis B. Hibbs of Patch's 63rd Division was among the commanders standing there, talking quite seriously. One well-placed shot from one of the German 88s that were sending in an occasional shell would have killed all of them, but none of them seemed interested in the enemy fire. Eppie and I saluted this covey of generals, although neither of us had mastered the skill of doing this in businesslike fashion. Only Patton, looking at us with a stern but not unfriendly gaze, bothered to acknowledge our clumsy saluting. We did an about-face and got the hell out of there.

When I told my friend Captain O'Neill about running into the brass in the middle of the main street of Sarreguemines, he said he had heard the generals would be meeting. "The story is that Patton wants to peel off a couple of his divisions and have them break through the Siegfried Line," O'Neill said. "He wants his Third Army, not Patch's Seventh, to have the honor of opening the way into Germany, but somebody bigger than he is has decided otherwise. It's supposed to be top secret, but like most top secrets, everybody seems to know about it."

"*I* don't know about it," I said.

O'Neill arched his eyebrows as he looked at me. "Really?" he said. And when I shook my head he smiled and said, "They've given the assignment to Patch, and he has given it to General Hibbs, and General Hibbs has given the job to the 254th."

"That's hard to believe," I said. Mess Kit Louie's 254th Regiment had acquired the reputation—perhaps undeservedly—of not having the skill to lace its shoes.

"Well, that's the word that came down from Division HQ," O'Neill replied. "All I know is that they'll cover the first wave with an artillery barrage. But they're sending somebody up to the gate to blow it open and tanks to pile through. That's all I know about it."

Captain O'Neill had good information. The Medical Battalion got a call early the next morning that a number of casualties were on their way to us from the front line. A couple of ambulances pulled up in a matter of minutes, and about five guys were carried in to us. They were the survivors of a nine-man strike force that had been sent to blow the gate of the Siegfried Line, a couple of miles east of Sarreguemines.

Actually, there wasn't any gate to blow. What they had to clear away was a barricade of pine logs. The logs were laid horizontally and piled on top of one another, about four logs wide and five logs high. The survivors said it looked like a roadblock of telephone poles piled five or six feet high. One of the wounded survivors told us:

"There ain't a tank in the world strong enough to bull its

way through somethin' like that. So we got sent up there in a jeep, haulin' a trailer with some of the guys and the dynamite, the detonator, and all that. They put a direct hit on us before we even got up to the barricade. The driver and the lieutenant next to him got it straight on. A couple of the other guys in the jeep got it, too. Me and the other guys you got here were in the trailer and all we got was shrapnel, but I thought, 'Oh, my God! That damn dynamite is gonna blow!' But it didn't blow and, hurt or not, we scrambled out of the jeep and hit the dirt. Them 88s were smackin' all around us, and I knew we weren't gonna get out of there. But the medics got up to us and gave us a shot of somethin', stickin' a needle into us right through our shirt, and some way they dragged us out of there."

One of the survivors died on us, right there in the classroom of the schoolhouse in Sarreguemines.

Later that morning, word came that the second wave of 254th engineers had made it to the Siegfried Line barricade and had succeeded in blowing hell out of it. The report was that tanks and columns of foot soldiers were pouring through the gap into Germany. "It sounds," Captain Nolan said, "as if this is the beginning of the end."

Before the day was out we had struck our gear and medical stuff and had loaded it into a six-by-six truck to move through the Siegfried Line. As we passed through the opening where the timber barricade had been, we could see the squat pillboxes that dotted the area—barrels of cannons protruding through the apertures facing Alsace. But there was no indication of an enemy presence, nor had there been when the first U.S. tanks and infantry went through. It struck me as odd that for the ten years or so since Hitler had defied the Western powers and constructed his own, improved Maginot Line, the French had lived in dread of this thing that was now getting from U.S. Army personnel no more than a passing glance.

Directly outside what had been the barricade of pines, the wreckage of a few U.S. Army tanks and trucks could be seen. Most of them were charred from the flames ignited by direct hits by German 88s. Moving slowly past these crippled tanks, you knew without looking that the crews of some of the tanks had been trapped inside and cooked alive; you couldn't see the bodies, but you could smell the roasted flesh.

One of the tanks, its treads hanging loose like the tail of a kite, had swung into an earthen bank on one side of the road that led into the Siegfried Line. In its skid, it had caught a milk cow amidships and had pinned the cow against the bank. It seemed to me unfortunate that the cow had wandered into a place of human combat and had gotten itself killed in this fashion. There was a picture of Marlene Dietrich in the *Stars and Stripes* a few days later showing Miss Dietrich standing at the spot where the Seventh Army had breached the Siegfried Line, and you could see the crippled tank and the poor cow behind her. In later years, when it became part of my job at NBC News to interview famous personalities, I had always hoped for a chance to interview Miss Dietrich to ask her if she remembered posing for a picture with this cow—but I never had that opportunity, so you will have to take my word for it that a cow was one of the casualties of the U.S. Seventh Army's penetration into Nazi Germany.

Virtually every day and every night, as we moved deeper into Germany, massive fleets of British and American bombers droned above us on their missions of destruction. By day, we got advance notice of the four-engine planes loaded with bombs. When strips of tinsel filled the sky, we knew as many as a thousand planes would soon be flying over us. The tinsel, dropped from high-altitude fighter planes to confuse enemy radar, draped every tree and clump of shrubbery. It looked like Christmas.

Gazing up at the incredible procession of bombers, we would speculate on the target city. As loyal Americans, with a working interest in this matter, we didn't trifle with the question of how many German civilians would perish in the raids; our concern, rather, was fixed on the matter of how many of the bombers would be shot down. An hour or so later, when the skies were filled again with big planes—returning to base after having dropped their bombs—we would try to count the bombers in each formation in an effort to determine how many had been hit by German antiaircraft fire. Later in the day, Armed Forces Radio or the BBC would provide a report on what city had been hit by the U.S. Air Force.

It was mostly through the BBC, with the backup of Armed Forces Radio, that we infantry people got news that Hitler's Germany was taking a terrible beating. Those of us who listened to the British news programs, which came on the air with four bars of Beethoven, were impressed by the accuracy of the BBC's information. But even the BBC made a mistake or two.

Pushing toward Kaiserslautern, the 63rd Division had captured thousands of German soldiers. But the BBC reported that the U.S. Third Army, under the command of the flamboyant General George S. Patton, had captured the German forces. Patton, who had a reputation for scratching up any brownie points that could redound to his credit, had claimed to have subdued the enemy troops that had been bagged by the 63rd Division of the U.S. Army. Everyone in the 63rd had been pleased that, in grabbing thousands of Germans, the 63rd had done something noteworthy. So the news report that Patton's Third Army was getting hailed for having landed our big fish did not sit well with a great number of men in the 63rd—especially with those who had made this great capture—nor, I imagine, with our commanding general, Louis B. Hibbs.

It wasn't much of a victory, if you want to know the truth. Mess Kit Louie's 254th regiment, having dynamited its way through the Siegfried Line, had moved down the road toward Kaiserslautern. The 254th met little resistance as it proceeded. Most of the German defense positions had been abandoned. On the western reaches of Kaiserslautern, a city already badly damaged by air attack and artillery, the 254th finally made contact with a sizable force of the enemy. But there was no battle; the Germans surrendered.

It is part of military dogma that every contingency has been anticipated and that you can't go wrong if you "follow the book." The problem that confronted the 254th was that there was nothing in the book about massive surrender. A force of German prisoners far larger in numbers than the total complement of the 254th had the effect of immobilizing the 254th by forcing it into the role of baby-sitter for an unmanageable number of German troops. Pinned down by this unique state of affairs, the 254th was delighted when General Patton's Third Army showed up and resolved the problem by taking charge of the 254th's prisoners. If General Patton translated this curious affair into a great victory for his Third Army, well, he was welcome to whatever pleasure he got out of it.

Patton took another prize from the 63rd: Kaiserslautern. Minor skirmishes with the retreating Germans held us up as we moved toward the city. Eventually we got there. But before the 63rd reached the city, word came that the celebrated Fourth Armored Division of Patton's Third Army, on our left flank, had torn right through Kaiserslautern. There was some disappointment among the brass of our Battalion that the Fourth Armored had plucked our prize, but I thought it was good news: the 63rd would not suffer casualties fighting its way into Kaiserslautern. Besides, when we finally got into the city, the 254th Regiment had uncovered several large, well-stocked wine cellars in the rubble—and for a few days we were awash in cognac and excellent French wines, which the Germans had taken as prizes of war and stashed away. The Fourth Armored had been in such haste to speed through Kaiserslautern that the Fourth Armored didn't even know that choice French wines were there for the taking. Such are the disappointments of the great victories of war.

Our primary interest, however, was not in turning up a cache of booze but in getting the war over and done with. The top brass may not have shared this priority. It had struck me, long before we moved into shattered Kaiserslautern, that the generals and other top-rank professionals would feel great sadness when they ran out of places to attack and Germans to kill; my view of this was that the professionals were having a glorious time. It is a peculiar way of life, I think, dedicating yourself to the business of smashing things up and killing people. Somebody has to be in command of things, I suppose, and I guess it is a weakness of character on my part that I haven't any appetite for this kind of thing. The by-products of warfare are not so attractive, if you ask me. The only thing you can say about combat is that it is better to give than to receive.

Accustomed as we were to areas of destruction, we gazed with awe on the damage that had been done to Kaiserslautern. We had seen other places more extensively damaged, but, as the first bombed-out city we had seen within Germany, Kaiserslautern was a sign to us that the defeat of Hitler's Germany was imminent, and it was utterly futile for the enemy to fight on. This was in the spring of 1945, and it was evident that Nazi Germany was finished. But the desperate resistance of the enemy went on and on.

Just south of Heidelberg, we adopted our first DP. He was a Pole, standing beside the road and waving his arms to cadge a ride, as our convoy of jeeps, trucks, and ambulances was going by. It was one of those things that just happen. We had sped by several DPs who had tried to flag us down on the road out of Heidelberg, hardly giving them a second glance. The major of our battalion was certain to raise hell if we picked up a DP, but when this smiling fellow came into view somebody said, "Let's pick him up." Somebody else rapped on the driver's shoulder, the driver pulled over, and somebody at the tailgate of our open truck reached down to the now ecstatic DP and pulled him in. There was a slipshod pile of our stuff in the back of the truck—medical chests, shelter halves, and I don't know what all—and we motioned to our DP to climb up and make himself comfortable. So there we were, driving along in a medical truck in an Army convoy, a grinning DP tearing open a box of K-rations that somebody had tossed him and sitting like a prince on our pile of stuff.

The DP, sitting high up in the back of our truck, became the center of attention in our part of the convoy. The word about our passenger managed to spread, and trucks in front of us started pulling off to the side of the road in order to get a look at our prize. Some of the guys in the other trucks shook their heads in disbelief. Strumpf and Fagg did not seem too happy about any of this; I guess they thought we were asking for trouble. But Eppifanio was delighted. Gesturing to our DP, Eppie said, "This is fabulous! You're a real celebrity." The DP, on his throne of our medical stuff, grinned back at Eppie. It was a lovely moment.

We got involved in a few situations that were not so lovely in the days that followed. Somewhere south of Heidelberg we came up against the 17th S.S. Division. If Nazi Germany was staring into the prospect of certain and total defeat, which it seemed to be, Nazi Germany nonetheless was not yet ready to unfurl the white flag of surrender. If defeat were imminent and inevitable, the 17th S.S. Division hadn't received the word. Like it or not—and we didn't—there was a lot of fight left in the 17th S.S.

We were in pursuit of a German army unit that, even at this late date, was well armed. The Germans methodically calibrated the distances from their 88s to key points that our tanks would have to pass on the road over which the Germans had fled. At intersections and naked turns in the road, our tanks were exposed to artillery attack—frequently accurate fire from the distant 88s. Everybody dove for cover when the first shells of the 88s started coming in.

A couple of German fighter planes put a few shots into some of our medical battalion vehicles when we were in convoy in Bavaria one night, and it was simply a lucky break that none of us got hit. They had us cold. Several battalions, including ours, were traveling in convoy on a narrow road, and the German pilots were sure as hell trying to hit us.

The convoy stepped up its speed as we moved down the road, our vehicle lights blacked out. An order was passed that anyone with a rifle should take a shot at the German fighters if they swung back to take another crack at us. They did swing back, and the infantry guys started banging away with their M-1 rifles. At the high speeds at which we and the planes were moving, I didn't think there was any chance of anybody hitting anything. Then, incredibly, one of our GIs got a hit on the lead plane of the two German fighters. The German plane belched fire and peeled off, engulfed in flames. Seconds later, not far from where we were—a hundred feet off the road, perhaps, and certainly not more than two hundred feet—the German fighter slammed into the ground and exploded. Almost everyone cheered. I thought that was a hell of a thing to do—to cheer when somebody is getting cooked to death. But I felt better about it when I looked up to see that the man who cheered the loudest was our mascot—the Polish DP. I guess they owed him one.

In a historic little city called Günzburg, the 17th S.S. suicidally provoked the U.S. Army into one last fight. The 63rd Infantry Division had been in pursuit of the 17th S.S. since our first contact with them. Periodically the 17th S.S. would halt in retreat, dig in, and fight back.

The 17th S.S. had managed to get across the Danube into Günzburg, leaving the higher ground on the western bank across the river to the 63rd U.S. Infantry. As dusk was falling one day in early May, 1945, two small, single-engine spotter planes came across the Danube at low altitude for a reconnaisance of the 63rd U.S. Infantry position. Soon after the German spotters returned to Günzburg, German artillery, the 88s, began firing at us.

No one in combat takes lightly the matter of the other side taking shots at him, and the German 88 was something to put fear in you. But for inexplicable reasons, the 88s, fired from inside the city of Günzburg, were off the mark. As the intermittent rounds of enemy artillery whined in from the other side of the river, the top brass of the U.S. Seventh Army were conferring on the matter of this act of defiance by the Germans. O'Neill had been summoned to the hastily assembled conference, and afterward he filled me in.

"We are going to finish them off at 0100 hours," O'Neill told me. "Every tank in this area is going to be brought in and lined up to pour their 37 millimeters at them. Every gun they can get here—the 105s and the 155s of the divisions on our flanks, anything they can find in Corps, anything that's available in other units of the Seventh Army—they've decided to bring it all in. It's going to be quite a show."

"They think this will finish off the 17th S.S.?" I asked.

O'Neill smiled. "Yeah," he said. "That's the plan. And if this doesn't do it, I don't know what will. Most of the 88s are dug in along the other side of the Danube—or so they say. If we manage to blow them out, the 17th S.S. won't have anything left to fire at us. Or so they say. Anyhow," he said, looking at his watch, "if you've got nothing else to do at 0100 hours, you might come and watch the fireworks. I'll bring the refreshments."

At 0100 hours, all hell broke loose. I was sitting in a jeep with Captain O'Neill, a bottle of Scotch between us, when the earth trembled as every gun on the line, and all the heavier stuff behind us, let go at precisely 0100 hours. At one instant before one o'clock in the morning, on this fateful day in early May, 1945, there had been hardly a sound as we sat in a jeep on the western bank of the Danube. The next instant the night came alive with horrific sound. Every gun that had been put in place for this engagement fired. Artillery shells whined overhead, and the tank guns fired again and again and again. In an instant the darkened waterfront city of Günzburg erupted in flames, and the Danube, as we looked down on it, was shimmeringly beautiful in the light of the fires.

At dawn of the day that our tanks and artillery had laid it into Günzburg, Eppie and I borrowed a jeep to take a look across the Danube. Günzburg was now in the hands of the U.S.Army. Whatever part Günzburg was to play in the final days of Nazi Germany was clearly over and done with.

We sat for a while in silence, gazing at the smoke that curled out of the waterfront ruins of the historic little city that our division had subjected to intense attack in the predawn hours of this day.

As we headed back to our company area, we were startled to encounter a seemingly endless line of bedraggled German infantrymen. I stopped the jeep at the side of the road and shut off the engine, and Eppie and I leaned back to watch.

We knew, without having to be told, that these were Germans of the 17th S.S. Division. They did not goose-step or march in military order; they slouched along, shoulder to shoulder the width of the road, row after row after row.

A solitary GI, his rifle slung on his shoulder, was leading the Germans to some POW compound at the rear of the combat zone. A step or two behind the GI was a German boy about ten years old. He was wearing Bavarian leather shorts, a sweater, and a placid look. Never faltering in his step, never looking back, and never relaxing his grip on a stick from which hung a white cloth, this little German boy marched on. The defeated troops of Nazi Germany followed.

Eppie and I sat silently in the jeep, watching the procession of Germans. At the end of this parade of the defeated was another German boy—also clad in leather shorts and a sweater, carrying a stick from which hung another square of white fabric. Two steps behind, helmet at a jaunty angle on his head, wearing torn fatigues and scuffed army boots, his rifle hanging from the strap on one shoulder, was a second GI.

"So much for the 'master race,' " said Eppie.

From Günzburg, we took a fifteen-hour convoy trip to Buchen, one of those towns that had served as a sort of county seat for the Nazi party. The Germans in Buchen were not so stupid that they didn't understand that it was all over for Nazi Germany. Their attitude toward American GIs was benign. Their young ladies displayed such instant affection toward the conquering heroes that a warning came down from Division that it would go hard with any American caught "fraternizing" with enemy ladies. It was fascinating, in view of the U.S. Army's dedication to the doctrine of political celibacy, to hear the heretical teaching of George S. Patton. More of a realist than his colleagues, Patton declared that it was perfectly moral to sleep with the German girls—as long as you didn't talk to them. Judging from the immediate upsurge in the incidence of venereal disease, the evidence was that the gospel as preached by General Patton prevailed. Although God only knows how much conversation there was under the down comforters.

I had had the quaint idea that when we finally got to our billet in Buchen everybody would be so exhausted that they would hit the sack—alone. Herbie, Strumpf and some of the others did. The only reason Tom Fagg was up all night, that first night, was that he had gulped the wine that somebody had brought in a five-gallon "jerry can" and was sick. But I thought my friend Captain Nolan was turning into one of those by-the-book medical officers when he said that we had better set up an aid station to deal with the casualties. When I raised the question, "What casualties?" Nolan said, "With the war practically over, you turn all of these guys loose in a nice, safe place like Buchen—you're going to get casualties."

Well, with the help of Eppifanio and a couple of other guys, I set up a station—fixing a litter with blankets so I would have a place to sleep. I drank some of the wine to celebrate the ending of the war, or to honor the grand experience of being in Buchen—or maybe because I found the wine that had made Fagg sick to be pretty good wine. But I didn't get any sleep that night in Buchen. Nolan, it turned out, had been right on the mark in his prediction that this was going to be a bad night.

They started coming in early, and they came in for hours. Nolan, who didn't get any sleep either, was on deck all night; he even got Strumpf out of the sack. Nolan hollered for somebody to find out where we could get some ambulance drivers and where in hell they could find a field hospital or an Evac to take these guys that we were patching up.

We had guys brought in who had smashed up jeeps and trucks while drunk. We had guys who had managed to shoot themselves. We even had a guy brought in who had suffered what seemed to be a heart attack, how he suffered it unknown. But our prize of the night was an infantry company courier who had managed to shoot himself with his carbine. This kid was obviously in pain and should have been placed on a litter. But he came in with his arms encircling the necks of two litter bearers. The kid's boots hardly touched the floor; the litter bearers sort of floated him to what we called the "work litter." He winced when they set him down. Nolan and I hurried to his side to see what his problem was; I mean we *hurried* to his side, because this kid was "family."

He was a courier assigned to Division who had made frequent, urgent trips for plasma and medical supplies for us. He was a cheerful kid who never had shown a flicker of fear of the enemy fire that might be kicking up dust near his speeding jeep. Several times, having driven through heavy enemy attack, he had walked into our medical tent with not even a mention of what he had driven through to get to us. Several times Nolan had remarked that this young courier didn't seem to know what fear was. And now here he was, in the middle of what we held to be the last night of the war, wounded.

Raising the kid's eyelids to see whether somebody had given the courier a shot of morphine, Nolan said, "What happened to you, son?"

"I'm ashamed to tell you, Captain," the kid replied in a whisper.

"OK," Nolan said. "Let's see if we can find out." Nolan rolled the kid on his stomach and with medical shears cut open the kid's blood-soaked Army pants. The kid's rear end was wet with blood. Wiping up with sterile flats, Nolan got a look at the wound. He put a hand on each side of the kid's hips and gently pressured one side and then the other. Blood gushed up as he did this.

"I don't know how it happened, son, and I don't care," Nolan said. "But what matters is—however you got this—the slug missed the bone and went through the flesh; it's what we call a through-and-through. The slug went in one side of your butt and came out the other. We'll give you a shot of something for the pain and take care of this in no time."

"Captain—" the kid whispered. "Captain—I shot myself in the ass."

Nolan laughed. "You what?"

"It was an accident," the kid went on in his whisper. "I was drinking a little tonight; I got a bottle of schnapps in my jeep, if you guys want it. But with everybody talking about the war is over and having a celebration—you should see what's going on out there—I got me some schnapps and I was having a few, you know. And it was then I got it."

"Then you got *what*?" the amused Nolan asked him.

"I'm bouncing along in my jeep, making time as always. And I got the rifle under my butt to hold it down, the same as always. I'm gunning along in the jeep, like always, and I figure, 'Oh, what the hell; I'll have me a taste of the schnapps.' So I reach under my butt for my bottle, which is down underneath me with the carbine, and I guess I hit a rut and I pretty near lose control of the jeep, and the gun fires, and it happens.

Damn, the last night of the war, a courier with a perfect record shoots himself in the goddamn ass!"

During all of this, Nolan was attending to the kid's wound. Looking up, he grinned and said to the kid, "Well, you're lucky. This isn't much of a wound, but it's good enough to get you an ambulance ride to Evac, and I'd say a good chance to be back in the States in a few days."

"God," the kid on the litter exclaimed, his butt sticking up so that Nolan could work on it. "They can't do that. A guy shoots himself in the ass and they send him home?"

"Sure," Nolan replied. "Nobody knows you shot yourself in the ass. As far as I know, you were wounded in enemy action. That's how we're going to write it up on your medical tag, and you wouldn't make me a liar, would you? You just keep your mouth shut; just say some Kraut took a shot at you. I'll give you a little bonus, too; I'll put on the tag that you're entitled to the Purple Heart."

The kid with his butt in the air was disbelieving. He said, "You're going to get *me* a Purple Heart?"

"Sure," Nolan said. "We owe you one. How many times did you make a run for us to Evac when we needed a few bottles of whole blood? A Purple Heart isn't anything, but your folks back home will be proud of you."

"You can't do that," the kid protested.

"The hell I can't," Nolan responded. "Listen, we've got a doctor in this outfit who cut his finger opening a bottle of Scotch, and one of his buddies wrote up the ticket and put this bastard in for the Purple Heart. Alongside *him*, you *are* a hero."

"But Captain—"

"Son, you're going to be a hero."

CHAPTER **8**

DACHAU

ON THE FIRST DAY OF PEACE IN EUROPE, I drove through a tranquil village that was identified on black and yellow signs as *Dachau* and then onto a good two-lane highway, lined on either side with healthy, carefully pruned trees—linden trees, I think they were—and headed eastward. I was on the road to a concentration camp. It hardly seemed possible that a place to exterminate people could exist in so peaceful a setting.

I had gotten my hands on a jeep by volunteering to make a delivery to Seventh Army. Our company clerk, a gregarious, opinionated kid named Zinck, troubled by being so near the front line, had gone outside of channels to get a transfer to Seventh Army HQ in Augsburg. The transfer came in as the fighting stopped. The CO of our medical battalion was so hot about Zinck going off on his own to get a transfer that he put a hold on providing Zinck with transportation to Augsburg. "If that Zinck is so goddamn clever about getting himself a transfer to Seventh Army," the major said, "let him find a way to get himself to Augsburg."

I volunteered for the mission of transporting Corporal Zinck to Augsburg. And I took along another GI for company.

At Seventh Army HQ, I wished Zinck luck, told him it had been nice knowing him, and, before he was up the steps, I had pulled out of there.

I found another road, more or less going eastward from Augsburg, and the jeep was tooling right along when my companion said,

"Do you mind if I ask you where in hell we are going?"

"We're going to Dachau."

"Dachau! Holy Christ, you're not going to Dachau!"

"I don't know if we can get in," I said. "They've probably got it off limits by now. But I want to see it, if I possibly can; Dachau is what this war was all about."

"I won't go in," my passenger declared. "Just the idea of it is too sickening to even think about."

"OK," I said. "Nobody is asking you to go in. You can sit outside in the jeep, and I'll see you when I get out."

Driving slowly down the tree-lined road on a warm and lovely day in May, 1945, I came upon a well-built brick building—a barracks, judging from the looks of it. The sturdy building bordered the southern fence of the concentration camp. At full staff on two flagpoles were the flag of the United States and the standard of the 45th U. S. Army Division. Two GIs, rifles on their shoulders, stood guard at the entrance.

As I slowly drove up, they read the stenciled markings on the front of the jeep that identified the vehicle as belonging to Company D, 363rd Med Bn, 63rd Inf Div. Clearly, they were wondering what in hell *we* were doing there.

"We're on an authorized mission," I said as I got close. "We were driving by, and I thought maybe we could take a look at this place."

One of the guards nodded. "You got travel orders?"

I fetched out the papers that our major had signed. The papers didn't say much, really, but they were addressed to G-1, Seventh Army, Augsburg, Germany, and they looked fearsomely official. The guard made a pretense of reading the travel order. "It looks OK," he said, "but I think you better see our first sergeant." Handing back our authorization paper, he pointed up the stairs.

As we went inside the building that had housed the S. S. who ran the Dachau concentration camp, a not-unfriendly first sergeant was passing through a corridor. "Hi. You got something for us?" he asked. "No," I replied, the travel order still in my hand. "We had to make an important delivery to Seventh Army at Augsburg and we just happened to be passing through." I handed the travel order to the sergeant. "I thought we could take a look at this place," I said.

The first sergeant pursed his lips. Then he flashed a little smile and said, "There isn't a hell of a lot to see. There was no resistance when the 43rd moved in; the Krauts got their asses out of here before we moved in. As far as I can tell, the prisoners in this camp didn't need the 43rd or anybody else to liberate them; hell, they could have walked right out once the Nazis got their tails out of here. I guess some of the inmates scrammed when they got the chance. But a lot of them stayed right here because there was nobody they could turn to and they had no place to go. Some of them are still here. You'd think they'd get out, but they're still here. My God, give me a chance to get out and I'm going. But not these people. They're like animals who've been starved and beaten and it's horrible to look at them."

"How do they eat? Where do they sleep? What do they do all day?" I asked.

The first sergeant shook his head. "I don't know, exactly. We've got guards posted at the gates but mostly it's a case of not letting somebody, some German, in with a gun to finish them off. Chow? Seventh Army comes in with K Rations and C Rations and dumps them at the gate. The stuff disappears, but I don't know how they come to get it. There's no regular mess or anything like that."

"Do your men go in there?" I asked.

"They can if they want. Some of the guards have gone far enough inside to see that the prisoners are still living in those barracks that the Nazis put up. But it stinks in there, and I guess the lice have never had it so good. You know, the guys who ran the camp really had them packed together in those barracks; cheap wooden bunk beds three high, sometimes four high, jammed together so bad there wasn't enough room between one guy and the guy up above to turn over. No blankets that I could see, only straw mattresses—thin ones—heaven for bugs. The whole place was a mess in the one I saw, and I suppose they're all like that. Somebody ought to put a match to the goddamn things, but the inmates who stuck around are still living in those places; there isn't anywhere else to live. All I know is we've got to stand guard over this goddamn place."

"So this is Dachau," my companion sighed.

"This is it," the sergeant said. "Nobody seems to know what's going to be done with the inmates. I don't have any orders. I suppose somebody will come along and try to delouse these people and give them physicals and put some clean clothes on them and haul them away to be rehabilitated. But, search me— *I* don't know what's gonna happen."

We looked around the barracks that had been occupied by the S. S. It was a better-built barracks, of more permanent construction, than those in Camp Van Dorn, Mississippi. It was built to last a long time.

With the sergeant's OK, we took off in the jeep for the western entrance to the concentration camp. There a GI guard stepped out in front of the laced metal gate. He held his rifle across his chest as I drove up. He had a look of surprise on his face at having visitors at his post. I handed over the travel order—our passport to Bavaria. As the guard, obviously puzzled, read the order, I said, "Your first sergeant told us you'd want a look at this; we just came from over there."

"Yeah, we're supposed to check everybody out. But we don't get many visitors, if you know what I mean."

The guard murmured that it looked to him that we were all right—meaning, I guess, he was pretty sure we weren't going to steal anything at the concentration camp. "You have to leave the jeep outside and walk in. I don't know what harm it would do, but they'd have my ass if I let you drive in."

"I'll stay with the jeep," my companion said.

"You don't have to stay with the jeep," the guard replied. "We'll watch the jeep."

"No, *I'm* not going in," my passenger said. "*I* don't want to look at this place. *He* does."

The guard grinned. "I'm with you," he said. "Bad enough we got to look at them skeletons in their pajamas. Bad enough we got to see them walkin' around in there. But it's full of germs and rats and dirt, and not on your life is anybody tellin' me to go in there and mix around with them inmates." And to me he said, "Are you sure you want to go in? If it's a report you got to turn in, you can make it up, maybe; you don't got to go in there."

"I understand," I said. "I appreciate it, your wanting to talk me out of it. But it's important that I see this. Especially with so many of the inmates still here. I have to see the survivors myself, and talk to them. So, nobody else wants to go with me—I'll shove off."

As the guard swung open the big wire gate and closed it when I slipped through, I was sorely tempted to back out of this walk into a concentration camp. Something inside me said I didn't have to do this, that it was foolhardy to do this. Something warned me that it was foolish to go through with this idea of taking a close, personal look at a Nazi concentration camp. I had a sense of panic for a moment, if you want the truth of it.

I was momentarily overcome by the dark thought that I was voluntarily walking into a foreboding place. I was getting into something evil that would be implanted in my mind and in my belly and in my soul. The memory of something so terrible, this experience I was getting into, was destined to be part of me for all the rest of my days.

A quarter-mile or so in front of me, the survivors of the Holocaust were gathered in clusters of ten or twelve in an open area some distance from rows and rows of wooden buildings. A warm sun shone down from a cloudless sky on the emaciated men and women huddling together to give strength of spirit to one another. With one glance backward toward the gate, I set out at a slow pace toward the inmates.

I didn't walk fast or in resolute fashion. I had a consuming desire to get close to the inmates—to see how they were dressed and what physical condition they were in—but I thought it best to make my appearance slowly. I was afraid, actually, that getting a look at someone in military uniform walking toward them, they would scatter and run. But the poor devils had long since learned that it was useless to run, that there was no place to run.

They paid no heed to me as I approached the first of the little circles. They didn't even look at me. I looked at them, but not a single man or woman in any of these groups showed the slightest interest in me. I can't remember how many circular groups there were; a half-dozen or a dozen. What I remember are the faces of the men and women who had been subjected to all manner of anguish. Reduced by starvation to nothing more than skin and bones, their meager bodies loosely covered by pajama-type uniforms, each sat on his haunches like an exhausted animal—gazing, transfixed, at a tiny fire burning in the center of the roughly formed circles.

The coarsely woven, cheap cloth uniforms seemed as lifeless as the skeletal men who wore them. The rough material out of which the uniforms had been made had gone dead from constant wear. The gray of the uniforms was a tired kind of gray. The blue striping was faded. This was the stipulated costume of those who fell victim to a self-proclaimed master race. This was the shroud.

It seemed incongruous that on a warm day, despairful people would make a tiny fire and reach out their bony hands to feel the heat. Each tiny fire in each circle looked about the same; each fire no more than five or six inches across on its longest side; each fire made up of small twigs and bits of wood and ignited God knows how. Perhaps these tiny fires awakened distant memories. I don't know what it was that made these little fires so important to burned-out human beings. All I know is that the fires seemed to be exceedingly important to the poor souls who gathered around them.

There wasn't a solitary word passed among the inmates at Dachau concentration camp that afternoon. And when I made a stab at one circle of these dehumanized creatures and then at another circle and then at the next and the next—in my futile effort to get someone to look at me and talk to me— there was not a flicker of response. They continued squatting on their haunches, mesmerized by the fire. They simply could not be persuaded or cajoled by any powers I had to even ac- knowledge that I was there. Until, at last—at the very last circle that I pleaded with—a tall, surprisingly self-possessed man got up and turned big, sad eyes on me.

In halting English, as if trying to speak in a language that he had learned a very long time ago, this tall, gaunt man said, "What is it you want to know?"

"I want to know what went on here in Dachau."

"Why do you want to know?"

"I am a journalist," I replied. "It is important that I learn what happened here in Dachau."

This tall man of skin and bones, dressed in his faded uniform, did not reply. He simply looked at me. As far as I could judge, no one else within earshot had any interest in this conversation. Not a single inmate glanced at us. We were speaking softly, the tall man and myself, yet our words came out like thunder— rumbling out of an utter silence. Finally, the tall man—his eyes still fixed on mine—said, "You come with me. I will show you Dachau Concentration Camp."

Glancing back, as we quietly walked away, it seemed unreal to me that not a single head came up and not a single inmate— out of perhaps the dozen that were squatting around the tiny fire—was following us with his eyes.

The tall man was going directly, it appeared, to one partic- ular place. A mere shadow of the big-bodied man he must have been, he seemed to glide across the barren ground. Coming to the far side of the rows of wooden, one-story barracks, a much-larger building at least two stories high came into view. Close to this large building, which was separated from the bar- racks by a wide area that military people would regard as pa- rade grounds, the tall man stopped. He gestured toward the large building with his outstretched right hand, the palm up and the fingers spread, and said, "This is where it all began, when they brought us in the railroad cars to Dachau."

Very high up on the face of the large building, in big block letters painted in black, was a message of welcome to the arriving inmates. I asked my guide what the message said. He looked at it and lowered his head. Then, with just a trace of a wry smile, he replied: "It says—how can I translate it for you?—it says to the inmates that if they do not work hard, something bad will happen to them. That is not it precisely; but that is what the words were painted there to say."

"And every inmate of Dachau saw this?"

"Oh, yes of course. The tracks of the railroad are behind this building, directly behind the fence. You will see the tracks through the bushes that are growing near the fence. When we get closer you will see how everyone was brought here." He paused, as if trying to get the chronology straight in his mind. Then he said, "Not many knew what place this was that they had taken us to. Some did. Those Jews who had lived in this part of Bavaria—they spread the word that this was Dachau. Then everyone knew what this place was, Dachau, and why it was we had been shoved into the railroad cars and taken here.

"The S.S. opened the doors of the railroad cars when the train arrived and dragged us out. Those that did not want to get out, they beat them with clubs, and the women and children were screaming; a great many of the men were screaming, also. All around this open place the S.S. were standing with guns and those little machine guns, and it was the same on the other side of the fence, where the people were being dragged out of the railroad boxcars. If someone showed resistance or defiance or said anything threatening to the S.S., they were hauled out in front of the people and clubbed.

"A great many of the women, and some of the men also, had taken sick on the train, and there was much vomiting and cries of despair. The children screamed a great deal, worse than anyone else, but no one paid heed to that—on the train or when we got here. There is an overwhelming desire—how do you say it, an instinct—to stay alive, even in the worst of conditions; everyone has that. The S.S. knew this, and they taunted us."

Perspiration was now glistening on the forehead of the tall, gaunt man. His chest heaved, and a terrible look of grief appeared in his eyes, as he matter-of-factly recounted his tale of horror. "A few were shot to death by the S.S., in view of everyone. When someone was shot and lay dying, with wounds bleeding, one of the S.S. would approach him with a Luger pistol and fire it into his head, putting an end to him. Then, one soldier or two would be summoned to take hold of the legs and haul the dead man off to the side, as if his body were the carcass of a dead wolf. Everyone watched this, and it was an unbelievable thing to see." The tall, gaunt man shook his head when he came to what seemed to be the ending of his stark recital. It appeared that he could not bring himself to tell me anything else. Then he said, "I have thought, many times in the years I have been here at Dachau, of those who were shot dead by the S.S. when we arrived here in the train. Long ago, I came to realize there was no reason to grieve for those who were shot dead by the S.S.; they were the fortunate ones."

"What happened to the others when they were dragged off the train?"

"We were marched up to this building that we stand in front of. Nearly everyone carried a sack of personal possessions; some people carried bits of jewelry and things of that kind the whole distance from their homes. They ordered us to place our sacks on the floor and disrobe. Everyone did as he was told, and we stood naked. No one was concerned about this. They took us in groups into a room with shower faucets in the ceiling and they supplied us with bars of soap and everyone had a nice cleansing. When they turned off the water, they gave each of us a towel and they handed each of us some clothing—a freshly washed uniform, such as I am dressed in—and they marched us off to our lodgings. Until we reached the housing, which was not clean and the beds placed one alongside the next, our feeling was that we were to be treated all right. After all, we had had a warm shower that revived our hopes, and some of

the people with me were talking about getting warm food—
'not tasty, perhaps,' they would say, 'but nourishing.' But we
quickly learned, being pushed into our lodgings, that it was
madness to expect that we would be treated decently."

"What happened to the clothes you had been wearing—and
the personal things people had carried all the way to Dachau?"

The tall, gaunt man shrugged. "I do not know. When we
came out after having our warm showering, the clothing we
had worn—some of the women had been wearing furs—had
been cleared away and we never saw any of these things again.
Also, the sacks of our possessions, we never saw any of those
again, and a few of the women cried that they had lost their
jewels—rings and valuable necklaces and things of that kind.
This was how it was with us when we arrived at Dachau."

The tall, gaunt man turned his back on the large building
that he had described as the reception center and started walking toward the wooden barracks. I followed. I can't hazard a
guess as to how many wooden barracks there were.

My surprisingly erect guide, in his threadbare pajama–like
clothing, walked slowly past long rows of the neatly constructed
buildings, row after row of them, with not so much as a glance
at any of them. I was at his side, filled with wonderment as to
what it was that he wanted me to see. He left me so alone with
my thoughts that I began to think he had forgotten I was there.
He didn't turn his head to look at me or the earth or the blue
sky. He gazed straight ahead as we walked along. An eerie
feeling possessed me. I was following the footsteps of a ghost.

I still found it hard to believe that so quiet and bucolic a
setting in beautiful Bavaria could have been a place of horror.
I thought back to the townspeople of the picture-postcard village that had given its name to this place. We had stopped in
the village on our way to the concentration camp, and the well-
fed villagers had been at pains to assure us they never dreamed
that such terrible things as they were now hearing about could
have gone on. It seemed highly unlikely that people living in
the village, only a couple of miles up the road from the concentration camp, could have remained ignorant of what the

Nazis were doing in this camp. It was troubling to find Dachau on such a lovely day as this to be a tranquil place.

My guide brought me back to reality. Turning toward one of the barracks, he went to a door, kicked it open, and gestured for me to step in. The stench of stale urine and decaying fecal matter and God knows what else was overwhelming. I tried to hold my breath, putting my fingers to my nostrils, as I gazed at torn straw mattresses and other debris strewn all over the floor. The wooden bunks, three bunks high, literally occupied every square foot of floor space. I was astounded at the evidence that so many people had been packed into one barracks. I wanted to count the bunks, but the odor was awful; I backed out. Looking at my guide, I said, "Typical?"

He said, "All of the housing for the inmates is the same." And then he turned and slowly resumed his walk to the western side of Dachau concentration camp, and I followed. The stink of the barracks had permeated my clothes; I dearly wanted a bath.

We came upon two small, red brick buildings and the tall, gaunt man walked into one. The cement floors were clean. The whole place was neat and orderly. On a wooden bench, alongside a wall near the entrance, were two or three piles of towels—carefully stacked and of good quality. Alongside the towels, bath-sized bars of yellow soap were stacked—many stacks, each bar resting evenly on the one below it. For the first time the tall, gaunt man gave me a questioning look; I could see he was interested in my reaction to this.

"You were brought here," my escort said, "on the promise that you were to have a shower, the second shower you had had since they brought you here in the train. Some knew better. They knew why it was that they had been brought here. Some, I suppose, were suspicious, but they had no voice about being taken here, so they hoped for the best. Some, I fear, believed that they had been brought here for a shower. I will now take you to the room where you were supposed to have your shower." Explaining that everyone shed his clothing in the room with the soap and the towels, and that each inmate was allowed a whole bar of soap, my guide took me to a low-ceilinged room. There were shower nozzles high in the ceiling. The nozzles were about fifteen inches apart, and they extended from wall to wall. There were no controls to blend hot water and cold. On all four walls—beginning at about chest height and extending up to the ceiling—there were the marks of fingernails dug deeply into the plaster. There were stains of dried blood along the fingernail marks. A great number of naked men and women and children had made a desperate effort to crawl up the walls to get out of this room.

Standing off to the side, watching me, the tall, gaunt man in the pajama suit pointed to the ceiling. "No water," he said. "Only gas."

We had asked about this in the village of Dachau. The townspeople were outraged when we asked them about Jews, and others, too, getting gassed at the Dachau concentration camp. "Oh," they had all declared, "nothing so dreadful as this occurred at Dachau; at other concentration camps, perhaps—but not Dachau."

Alongside the shower room was the crematory of Dachau. Its huge metal baskets—four or five of them side by side—received the bodies of those who had had their second shower. Outside the crematory was an open area fenced by wire. The ground was covered with gravel, and a shovel stood in a pile of gravel at one end of this pit.

The tall, gaunt man ended the tour by showing me the heavy metal baskets in the neatly swept crematorium and the graveled area outside. There, he said, special prisoners such as captured Russian officers were ordered to kneel down. An S.S. man with a Luger pistol would place the mouth of the barrel on the back of the guy's head and squeeze off a shot. "It is bloody, the coup de grace," my guide said. "And someone must come in and spread fresh gravel."

"Do you believe the Russians knew they were brought here to be executed?" I asked.

The tall, gaunt man nodded his head firmly. "The Russians could sense that they had been brought to a place of blood; you can sense a place of death." Gesturing toward the crematorium, my guide said, "And when he was dead, the Russian was dragged in there and turned to ashes."

"The Germans in the village," I said, "insist that this camp was not a place of extermination and cremation."

My guide shook his head resignedly. "Anyone who spent time here—anyone who is still alive—could tell you it is so. We saw the smoke of the burning come out of the chimneys of the crematorium; everyone could see that. We saw the smoke after inmates were marched off to have a shower, and we saw that none of them ever came back. We saw the chimney smoke, also, on the days that the S.S. killed a Russian. We heard the shots. It was always quiet, and the S.S. did not attempt to conceal it."

We stood there for a while, contemplating all this in silence. Finally, after more than two hours in Dachau, I extended my right hand to the man. With the look of a man who has found a long lost ritual, he took my hand and squeezed it hard.

I wanted to do something for the tall, gaunt man to show him I was grateful. There did not seem to be anything that I could do. It came to me that I had some money in my pockets. I had an assortment of U.S., French, and German occupation money; they paid us once a month and you accumulate this stuff when you have no chance to spend it. So, rashly I suppose, I drew out the wad of assorted bills I had in my pocket—sixty, seventy, eighty dollars, I guess—and held it out to the tall, gaunt man. He looked at the paper money as if it were something he had never seen before. Then he looked at me and said, "Thank you, no. I was once a man of means, but now I have no need for money." It appeared that he appreciated my having made the gesture. I smiled and told him I thought he was a brave man.

I looked at this ghost of a man and said, "I'm sure you have thought a great deal about all of this—the Nazis, the purges, the concentration camps. Do you have any thoughts about all this that you could share with me? Whether we have seen the end of these terrible wars and the death camps and all of that?"

The tall, gaunt man gave me a puzzled look. I felt like kicking myself for asking a stupid, convoluted question that he couldn't understand. Finally, he spoke. Not remorsefully. Not in anger. Not in bitterness. He simply looked me straight in the eyes and spoke from the depths of his soul.

"For all of the thousands of years that earth has known man," he said in a soft voice, "man has made war on other men. For all of the thousands of years that earth will continue to have man, I am sorry to say that man will make war on other men. It is something that continues. It is like the rainworm. You can crush the rainworm with your boot and it will survive. You can chop the rainworm into segments to kill the rainworm, but all of the segments will defy you; they will wriggle, each segment, and stay alive. Such it is with man's efforts to exterminate other men."

Taking a step or two closer to me, he raised the head of his emaciated body, a terribly deep look of sadness in his eyes, and he said, "The curse of human existence is not that some men hold other men captive and kill them in such a place as this. The curse is that the children of the men you kill, or their children, will stay alive to seek vengeance for what you have done. This tragic pattern is destined to continue until the end of time."

Without another word to me, he turned slowly and walked away, leaving me to find my way back to wherever it was that I came from and wherever it might be that I was going.

CHAPTER 9

I DIDN'T ASK TO BE
A STREET REPORTER

WHEN I RETURNED TO CIVILIAN LIFE IN CHICAGO, the newspapers had one thing going for them that NBC did not have—street reporters. And those reporters consistently beat the hell out of us. If you wanted to learn something about a gangster murder, or a big fire, or what in hell Mayor Edward J. Kelly was up to, you had to read the newspapers; all you could hear on radio news were brief snitches that had been pilfered out of the local newspaper accounts. Doing an interview with the mayor or the Democratic Party chairman, or the governor or U.S. senator— well, this was unthinkable in radio news.

But in the late '40s, using clumsy film recorders and then wire recorders and then tape recorders and then the picture and sound systems that came along with television, broadcast news invaded the territory controlled by the print media. I had received a couple of letters from Bill Ray when I was in France or Germany, and in one letter, Ray revealed he had an idea that it was time broadcasting stations had reporters out on the street. The practice of getting information from national and international "correspondents" had become routine in the network newsrooms. But in 1945, local radio newsmen stayed put—in their newsrooms. Local radio street reporting was unheard of, and using recorders to get the voices of those who were making the news—that was unthinkable. It is hard to believe that on-the-spot coverage, so commonplace in the present day, was not even attempted until Bill Ray got NBC-Chicago into it in 1947.

I refused to return to sportswriting when I got out of the U.S. Army. My refusal was based on money. I had written the damned sports program that was making other people rich up until the time I had gone off to the Army, but I damned well was not going back to it. Prewar NBC would have told me to take it or leave it, but I was certain postwar NBC wasn't going to sack a combat veteran. And, in fact, they gave the sportswriting to a guy from Fayetteville, Arkansas—who loved it—and they put me to work on straight news. I moonlighted a bit, writing specials and one-act radio plays and an occasional ad, but on the whole, I was doing what I wanted to do: straight news.

This is not to say my life in the NBC-Chicago newsroom was bliss. Management held firm to a few quaint practices that irritated the hell out of me. It was a network rule, for example, that if there were an airline crash, we could not mention it in our news shows until we had in hand the names of all passengers and all casualties. No kidding. At one time, this was the policy of NBC News. It was exasperating to obey a policy that precluded any mention of a breaking news story until you had a list of the people who were aboard—a list that took hours to obtain.

Management decisions brought other aggravations. In our newsroom every night was a young college graduate named Myron Wallace, who eventually hit it big as Mike Wallace. Wallace didn't really belong to us. He belonged to Marshall Field III, the grandson of the founder of the posh store on State Street. Marshall Field III, generally regarded as an expatriate, had lived in France until Nazi Germany inspired him to move out. He returned to Chicago as a born-again American. Having sizzled from a safe distance at the let's-mind-our-own-business preachments of Colonel Robert R. McCormick, the born-again isolationist who published the *Chicago Tribune*, Field took a reckless stab at going head to head with Bertie McCormick by establishing a morning newspaper called *The Chicago Sun*. Field also bought a small radio station that he set up as an all-news operation, quartering the operation in the attic of the then-thriving *Chicago Daily News*. Unfortunately, the station broadcast on so low a frequency that hardly anyone in Chicago was ever able to dial it in.

Field had laid out big money to hire a man by the name of Clifton Utley to run the radio news operation. Utley, a quasi-socialite and student of foreign affairs, had been head of a highly regarded organization of "big thinkers," the Council on Foreign Relations, for which another quasi-socialite, Adlai E. Stevenson, served as president. Utley was short of practical experience in the news business, but with Field's money he hired some good people to write the news reports that hardly anyone heard.

Failing to acquire much of an audience with their low-kilo-cycle news station, the Utley-Field combination persuaded NBC-Chicago to sell them fifteen minutes of time on the top local radio station, WMAQ. This was an unprecedented departure from NBC policy—allowing an outsider to come in with its own news broadcast. The agreement was that NBC-Chicago would have editorial approval of the Utley-Field news copy.

The young man sent over to read this news copy was Mike Wallace. Wallace worked harder rehearsing his copy than any of our staff announcers. In fact, I never worked with a more dedicated "wood-shedder"—meaning he labored in his personal rehearsal over every sentence of the copy we fed him, reading the script in his on-the-air voice and making pencil marks on the copy to remind him where he would want to emphasize something. My private opinion was that our staff announcers were apprehensive about an outsider's taking a news-reading job that would have earned our people a fee. But Wallace had the good sense to become a member of their union—the American Federation of Radio Artists. The staff announcers were not in a position to lodge a complaint about this guy Wallace. After all, NBC-Chicago was then the origination point of a vast number of soap operas, which were the mainstay of network programming; many AFRA outsiders were working on NBC's soaps.

The deal that Utley had worked out with NBC-Chicago was that the Mike Wallace newscast would be written in our newsroom, but by someone who was not on our staff. The outsider hired for this job was a highly competent newsman named Paul Courtney, who was paid the princely sum of $200-a-week. Courtney, who was then working all night as one of two men doing rewrite on the first edition of the *Chicago Evening American*, a Hearst paper, was a very good writer. He was fast in grinding out copy; he had the rare gift of interjecting good phrases that did not impede the flow of his stories; and—having worked for CBS News—he knew the special skills of writing for broadcast. He had a chronic habit of showing up late, allowing himself too little time to write the Mike Wallace show, but Wallace couldn't have asked for a more skillful writer.

Courtney was inclined to take his pleasure in lifting a few. There were times when the *American's* legendary night city editor, Harry Romanoff, would call the district police station with a request that a squad car be dispatched to Paul Courtney's apartment for the purpose of getting Romanoff's star rewrite man out of bed. Today's newspaper editors wouldn't bother to go to this extreme to get a man at his typewriter, but Romy— as everyone called him—was a newspaper editor of the old school. Romy regarded having to scheme up a way of getting a man to his typewriter as simply a part of the job of night city editor.

Paul Courtney's thirst was more of an annoyance for me, because I had to write the Mike Wallace show when Courtney didn't show up. And on the nights Courtney showed up with a silly grin on his face, I had to parcel out the wire copy to him one story at a time and indicate, with a spread of my thumb and little finger, how long the story should go. There were times when I was tempted to tell Clifton Utley, Marshall Field III, and Mike Wallace to go to hell. Mike Wallace, always at pains to be agreeable, never uttered a word of complaint about the whimsical way in which his show was put together.

Thanks to Bill Ray, our newsroom got a running report of everything transmitted by the Police Department's short wave radio to the squad cars on patrol. Ever watchful for a potential story, Bill Ray had had the engineers set up a couple of speakers that enabled us to eavesdrop on the Police Department. The police radio speakers had been installed in our newsroom before I had gone off to the Army, and having the police radio to keep us informed of what was going on in the streets of our city had given us a big advantage over CBS and other competing stations.

After the war, Bill Ray came up with another bright idea: to put a mobile unit on patrol of the city. Compared to the sophisticated mobile units that became commonplace in the broadcasting business in later years, the first one we had at NBC-Chicago wasn't much. What it was, actually, was a bulky old sedan that had been used on rare occasions to transmit "special events" by short wave.

It was a complicated business to get our first mobile unit into operation. We had, first of all, to find a studio engineer at NBC headquarters in the Merchandise Mart who was technically capable of operating the short-wave equipment in our clumsy old unit—and break him free of his other assignments to do what we called a "pickup." It wasn't enough to line up a radio engineer who was capable of "heating up" the short-wave equipment to transmit our story from the place where a fire or a shooting or something like that was to be covered. Equally important was the matter of finding another two engineers who could operate the NBC short-wave receivers on top of the Civic Opera House, several blocks from the Merchandise Mart, and feed the story on a telephone line to the master control room at the Mart to get our big story on the air.

We had no reporters. Incredible as it may seem today, the first radio "reporters" were the guys with voices trained to sing the praises of tinned soup and soap. Staff announcers, coached by one of the newsroom guys as to what to say and what questions to ask, posed as "reporters."

The whole thing was pretty primitive. The transmission didn't always work. Everything might be fine up until the moment when the staff announcer got a finger cue from the engineer operating the short-wave equipment in the rear seat area of our "mobile unit." In the prebroadcast testing, when the engineer counted off "one, two, three, four" to his colleagues at the Civic Opera House, the transmission might be good and clear. But something mysterious sometimes happened when the mobile unit engineer threw a cue to the "reporter." The staff announcer, uncomfortable and self-conscious in his role as reporter, would start gabbing away, but the engineers at the Civic wouldn't get a word of what the guy was saying. It is terribly disheartening to go to all of this trouble to "get a story" and not have it go through. God knows what happened when the short-wave transmission did not get through to our engineers at the Civic; the electronics were in perfect order an instant before we started to "send," and the equipment appeared to be working OK an instant after the attempted transmission.

Some months after having "lost" a story in transmission to the Civic, we got a letter at NBC News from some fellow who lived up in the Arctic Circle. His letter seemed to exonerate our engineers of any guilt that might have attached to them in the failure to get our story on the air. I have no idea what this guy was doing up there in the Arctic Circle or why it was that he was listening to his radio. The guy apologized for the delay there would be in our getting his letter—explaining that the mail boat made only two stops at his locality in the course of a year. But the important thing was that in his letter he summarized the details of the report we had tried to get on the air—a story about the assassination of a well-known gangster in a restaurant on Wabash Avenue, on the east side of the Chicago Loop. What this guy at the top of the world wanted to know was whether the police had found whoever it was who had committed this terrible murder. A giggling secretary had unthinkingly tossed away this letter—but I retrieved it and answered it, explaining to this fellow who lived up there with the walruses that the Chicago police more or less regarded it as futile to pursue the question of responsibility when one crime syndicate gangster murders another member of the lodge. Even as the blood still oozes out of the wounds of the guy who has been "hit," homicide detectives reconcile themselves to the virtual certainty that this is another murder to be added to the long list of unsolved cases. I don't know that the guy with the walruses appreciated the distinction I tried to make between the murder of a mobster and the murder of a banker or shop owner, but at least I gave it a try.

None of us who had a part in creating the wheel in electronic news had even a faint notion that in the space of one generation the voices and even the pictures of reporters and their stories would be bouncing off satellites in short orbit some twenty-three thousand miles out in space. Electronic news has come a long way from the time when we failed to get a short-wave transmission through the heavy metal of the elevated structure that encircles the Chicago Loop. But even in those early days when some of us at NBC-Chicago were playing Marconi roulette in this new game of trying to beat the pencil reporters with on-the-spot radio reporting, invading the area that the newspaper people regarded as their private domain, we sensed that we were the vanguard of a new news-gathering force that the print people would have to live with.

Within a year or so after going to a great deal of trouble to provide a companion of walruses, and apparently no one else, with a short-wave report on a gangster murder in downtown Chicago, we started experimenting with other methods of communications.

The first thing we tried was a rectangular box with a leather covering that housed a complicated recording device. The engineer had to lace this thing, in much the way you load a movie projector, with a ten-inch reel of 35mm film. When the engineer punched a button to activate this contraption, the sprockets of the apparatus would turn, pulling the wide film over a recording head. Somehow—optically, I guess—the voice of our "reporter" got recorded on the film.

The film seemed to resist this business of being dragged around by gears to the recording head. It hardly seemed possible that so complex a thing could record anything. However, except for the unfortunate occasions when the film got jammed in the mechanical guts of the machine, the recordings were on-the-air perfect. It would drive you wild, though, to use this machine to record a spot news story. There was no way to edit the film; the best you could hope for was that the engineers at the studio could transfer portions of the sound from the film to a glass disc and get your story on the air by way of a turntable. It was one hell of a system to rely on to broadcast a news item.

We gave up on the film recorder, as we had pretty much given up on the use of short-wave, and our on-the-street crews were reduced to feeding their stories by telephone directly to the NBC recording room. Finding an available telephone at the scene of a big fire or explosion or something like that was sometimes an insurmountable difficulty. But even if you managed to find a phone and get someone in the overworked NBC recording room to patch up your line and make a disc of whatever it was that you were calling in, you once again had the frustration of not being able to edit your story.

I was just about ready to admit to the newspaper people that I was abandoning the mad ambition to give them a run for their money, when Bill Ray came up with another gadget. With a grin, he told me, "I think we've solved the problem of covering news stories for radio, right on the spot." This time it was a wire recorder. It was a little thing, compared to the film recorder that we had given up on. The wire recorder weighed only about twenty pounds and had a handle for carrying it around. There was a place on the outside where you could plug in your microphone lead. It had a couple of dials on it that made it possible for an engineer to ride gain on you—to modulate your voice. The wire recorder looked to have some possibilities. Magnetized wire, held taut by a gathering spool, fed over the recording head smoothly and quietly. The recorded voices were a little bit raspy, even though we used top-grade microphones, but quite readable, as the engineers say. The mobility of the wire recorder made it ideal for covering on-the-scene stories; it weighed so little and was so small that you could take it anywhere.

The wire recorder was convenient for street reporting—at least, it was more convenient than anything else available. Occasionally it would get temperamental and refuse to work, or the magnetic wire would snap, and the revolving spool would shoot the wire all over the place. Hardly a day went by without technical difficulties of one kind or another. And editing a wire recording was murder.

To get an interview on the air, I'd listen over and over again to the recording, then decide precisely what I wanted to use for broadcast. The individual segments I had selected would be fed to the recording room, where the segments were recorded alternately on two glass discs. Then I'd sit down and write a script that provided the director, the studio engineer, and the turntable operator with the information needed to harmonize their efforts in getting the story on the air. Such a script included the opening and closing words of each recorded segment and the exact timing, in seconds, of each segment on the glass discs. The script often included copy to be read between recorded segments by the announcer who tried to pull the story together, this guy reading into a microphone as the turntable operator scurried to get his next "take" ready for airing. Or, if one recorded segment was to follow another immediately, the turntable guy—on cue from the director—would have to start the new segment at precisely the instant that the last words of the initial segment went on the air. In other words, part of an interview would go on the air from the disc on one turntable, and the rest of the interview would go on the air from the disc on the second turntable. If this sounds like a complicated way to broadcast a story that you got on-the-spot—well, it *was* complicated.

No sooner had we mastered the wire recorder than magnetic tape recorders pushed the wire machines onto the ash heap. Magnetic tape gave us a fidelity superior to the quality of even the best wire recordings. And it was relatively simple to edit magnetic tape. With magnetic tape you simply slice the tape, then splice the end of one segment to the pickup point of the next segment. We were always careful that there would not be a noticeable difference of modulation or background noise in the sound bite—from the point where you cut off some wordy guy to the point where you made the splice to let him go on talking. Do enough of it, and you get so you can even detect where a few bars of a symphonic recording have been redone to replace a flubbed note.

The almost frightening realization that we had embarked on a new and compelling way of covering news was underscored by the resentment and resistance of the newspapers' street reporters, who regarded the city as their turf. Some pencil reporters advised fire chiefs and politicians and police detectives that it was a waste of their time, and not altogether prudent, to let a radio guy interview them. A few of the freedom-of-the-press newspaper guys made a practice of kicking out the plug of our recorder. The guys who did this looked to their colleagues for grins of approval and generally giggled like school girls at their daring. It was a nuisance, having your recorder deliberately unplugged in the middle of an interview or the taping of your report, but it was interesting to observe how unnerved the pencil-reporters became when we arrived at the scene of a developing story and set up a radio recorder. In the earliest days of our invasion of the newspapermen's territory, they were not so unfriendly, because the print reporters could see that the guy with the mike in his hand was only an announcer who made no pretense of knowing how to cover a story. But our problems intensified when our news director wised up and started replacing the professional voices with newsroom guys who knew as much about getting a story as any print reporter.

The street reporters of the newspapers had a strong ally in their resistence. Our staff announcers groaned when they were assigned to get into the mobile unit with a newsroom guy and an engineer and go out on a story. This was unfamiliar work for the professional announcers and, at least as a group, they clearly did not like the job of pretending to be reporters. Some staff announcers would bridle when the newspaper people gave us a hard time. Customarily, though, the staff announcer would shrug and point to me or whoever was responsible for getting the story—as if to say, "Don't blame me; blame *him*." In the early days of our efforts to win a foothold for radio news in the public domain that seemingly was the private preserve of print people, I was disheartened to hear our staff announcers apologetically explaining to newspaper people that, personally, they didn't think they should be doing this—invading someone else's jurisdiction—and wouldn't be there if they had not been ordered to go out on the story. It's tough to be a pioneer cowboy when your own Indians are slyly shooting arrows at you.

In the beginning it never occurred to any of us in the newsroom that we were the ones—not the unionized staff announcers—who belonged on the air. Most of the staff guys we had to take along on stories were not very good at conducting interviews, even if we armed them with a list of questions to ask, and some of them were simply awful when it came to doing ad-lib wrap-ups. Those of us who got sent out with these trained-voice guys knew we could do a better job of reporting than the professional announcers were doing. But no one in the newsroom ever made the slightest suggestion that the day would come when we would do on-the-air reporting. That possibility was unthinkable.

It was a novelty for radio listeners to get reports from the scene. Sometimes those of us on the working side of these reports were pleased with the results. Other times the on-the-spot stuff that was getting on the air was terrible. Our professional announcers could read anything beautifully, but as the "voice" of our coverage of big fires or political scandals or gangster assassinations, these guys left a lot to be desired. They didn't know what they were talking about, and the listening public sensed it. These guys had great voices, but their credibility as "reporters" suffered, because the listeners were aware that the sweet-talking guy on the radio didn't know the significance or the background of the news story he intoned. It hardly appeared that the print media's domination of street reporting was in jeopardy.

There were only a couple of us at NBC News-Chicago who got shouldered with the burden of trying to make reporters out of professional announcers. En route to whatever it was we wanted to cover, we'd try to instruct the guy on what sort of situation we were getting into, what the possibilities were of finding someone with information who would talk with a microphone thrust in front of him, what kind of questions to ask, and how to get a wordy individual back on track when he wasn't saying anything pertinent.

When we got a tip on a big local story, we had to find a staff announcer to go to the scene. And it was tough to scrape up an announcer. The announcers with seniority shunned us. They had no interest in playing a role in this strange new thing of gathering news for broadcast—if only because it minimized their chances of getting extra money for reading commercials. A few of the newly hired announcers, who were not selected by the advertising agencies to read commercials, solicited assignments from the newsroom to be sent out on breaking stories. But what we needed, in the long-ago time when we were trying to get a big-city radio news operation functioning, was a full-time professional announcer who had some interest in and understanding of what covering a spot story was all about.

Bill Ray figured Dave Garroway, who had wangled a disc-jockey job, might be an acceptable news broadcaster, and offered him the job. Garroway gave it a good deal of thought, but he finally turned the job down—figuring, I think, that nobody would ever make big money in the news end of our business. Ray also offered the job to Hugh Downs, who seemed very much interested in what was going on in our city and the world. He was an agreeable sort of guy, his articulation was top grade, and we all thought he would fit very well into our fledgling news operation. But with his hopes fixed on attaining something of greater success, he modestly declined to become one of us. In later years, both Garroway and Downs became nationally known personalities on NBC's "Today" program. And Garroway used to tell me, "It's a good thing I didn't let you fellows make a newsman out of me—or I'd still be chasing fire engines in Chicago."

Bill Ray put in a lot of time calling around the nation, writing letters, and all of that—trying to get a lead on somebody who might make a decent news broadcaster. Ray did get a lead on some guy in New Orleans or Houston or some such place, and the next thing I knew, he was introducing me to a trim, military-postured guy who wore sunglasses with gold frames. This newcomer talked in a clipped, confident sort of way. He had a professional-announcer style of speech, granting that he was on the twangy side. But he seemed to know something about the news business. He appeared eager to get this job with NBC News-Chicago, and it impressed me that he was an experienced guy who seemed to understand this innovative thing that Bill Ray was cutting him into.

This guy's name was Bud Thorpe. As the nation's first full-time radio news reporter-announcer—at least as far as we were aware—Bud Thorpe got to be a genuine celebrity. One of the newsroom guys lined up the stories, did the research, edited the spots, and wrote the scripts, but Thorpe did a pretty acceptable job, once you filled him in on what the story was all about. However, Thorpe's career with NBC-Chicago was brief.

It was the beginning of the end for Bud Thorpe the day a high-speed Burlington Northern train, en route from Chicago to the West Coast, slammed into another Burlington train, which had inexplicably stopped at the station in Naperville—about thirty-five miles west of Chicago. One of the wire services reported that at least six persons had been killed, so we got on the phones.

In our hunger for a regular source of local news, Bill Ray had been romancing the editors of the *Evening American* with the idea of setting up a daily news program of mutual benefit. Nothing had come of these negotiations, but I knew some of the guys who worked for the *American*, and I called the city desk over there, by way of letting them know that we knew a story when we saw one. I ended up talking with a gentle-voiced city editor named Harry Reutlinger.

"I wouldn't get too excited about the train wreck," Reutlinger counseled me. "The first flash you get on something like this is always exaggerated."

"But aren't you 'sending' on the wreck?" I asked him, meaning wasn't he dispatching a reporter and a cameraman to Naperville?

Harry Reutlinger chuckled. "I've got a reporter out there. We've been trying to put together a series on shady real estate deals, and I sent one of our guys out there to check up on whether the real estate people out there are on the square. You know, the usual shot-in-the-dark stuff."

"And you've heard from your reporter? The guy called in on the train wreck?"

Reutlinger laughed and said, "Yeah. He was in a sales office near the Burlington station, and he hears the crash and runs out and takes a look and runs back into the real estate place to call the desk. According to our guy with his quick look, there were smashed-up Pullman cars and bodies all over the place. Our guy is all excited and he says, 'Jeez, there are a lot of people dead out here in this wreck—fifteen people, twenty-five people—lots of people dead.' Well, hell, by this time we've got a phone call through to the police chief out there, and the kid who's talking to the cop passes me a note telling me nobody was killed. There was no crash; one train just bumped into another one. Our guy out on the real estate story went overboard. He sees a couple of passenger trains bumping into each other and he gets hysterical, see? So I get him to give me a phone number to reach him, if the story develops into something—which it won't. If you want to call back, I'll fill you in on what comes out of it. But I don't think you want to bother with it."

I wasn't prepared to argue with the great Harry Reutlinger, but my gut feeling was that he was underplaying the possibility that this might be a big story. "Harry," I said, "I know it doesn't make any difference to you, but we're going to send our unit out there. If it amounts to something, we've got to have somebody on the scene. We're not like the newspapers—we can't recover with phone calls; we've got to be there to get recordings of eyewitnesses and all of that."

"Well, you do what you want," Reutlinger replied. "But my guess is it's not worth it."

On any list of legendery newspapermen—in Chicago or elsewhere—you'd have to include Reutlinger. He could spot a big story before anyone else. He was renowned for being able to smell a big story, but even a famous home run hitter like Babe Ruth strikes out a good deal—and Reutlinger struck out on the Naperville story.

The wire services were updating casualty figures before our mobile unit got to the scene. In due course, the AP, UP, and INS reached agreement on a death toll of fifty-eight. The number of injured was placed at "over a hundred" to "well over two hundred." By phone, we were trying to line up eyewitnesses to be interviewed when our guys finally got there; one of the interviews I managed to set up was with the reporter who had tried in vain to give his city editor a good beat over the competition on a tragedy that was developing into a national news story.

As a penalty for seeming to have more information than anyone else in the media on this wreck at Naperville, our newsroom was flooded with phone calls from Chicago-area residents who had husbands or wives or mothers or children on the Burlington trains. We had to assign two members of our meager staff to handle the urgent pleas for identification of the dead and injured. This was a new experience for us—being regarded by the listening public as a more reliable source of information than the newspapers. We didn't know a solitary thing that the newspapers did not know, and probably not nearly as much, but it was gratifying to discover that the public believed we did.

One of our men handling the calls put down his phone, looked at me, and said, "I've got a man on the line who claims he's the police chief in Naperville. I can't make any sense out of what he's shouting about—he says NBC is corrupting the Boy Scouts of America. This guy is madder than hell about something. You want to talk to him?" I punched up the line and picked up a phone.

I was pretty surprised to hear what the police chief was complaining about, but I didn't have any difficulty understanding him. He said a couple of troops of boy scouts had come to the scene to make themselves useful in an emergency. Some "announcer man" who claimed to work for NBC news, "Bud Thorn, or something like that," he told me, had pressed two boy scouts into service to run over to a liquor store to fetch him a half-pint of whiskey. Oh, my.

"He didn't do it once; he did it twice!" the police chief roared. "The second time, the man who owns the liquor store calls us up and says he knows it's a big train wreck and all of that, but he's not going to lose his license selling half-pints of whiskey to no boy scouts. What are you folks at NBC going to do about this joker who's sending boy scouts out to buy whiskey?"

I told the police chief we'd take care of our man with the booze as quickly as we could. Bill Ray was a damn sight angrier than the police chief. "The next time he calls, you tell him to get his ass in here," Ray told me. When Thorpe called in, I told him that Bill Ray wanted him to wrap it up and come back to the office. Thorpe was smart enough to figure out that we had had a beef about the boy scouts; he was at pains to explain to me that he hadn't jeopardized the boy scouts' morality or anything like that. "Hell," he protested, "I don't see anything wrong with sending them off to get a little bottle. It's like asking them to get a ham sandwich."

Our spot news coverage took a turn after the Naperville train wreck. Bud Thorpe was phased out. We went back to having to scare up a staff announcer when we wanted to go out on a story. It seemed to get a little more difficult to find a staff man who was free and willing to go out and voice a story for us. We had to pass up on-the-spot stories because we couldn't find an announcer who would accept the assignment. It was exasperating for those of us who were trying to put news shows together, but I never thought it would change life for me. Yet it did.

On St. Patrick's night, 1947, at about ten o'clock, the police radio began gabbling about something fearful having happened in a dance hall on the North Side. All we knew was that numerous squad cars and ambulances were being dispatched to such and such an address. We had in our newsroom a special kind of directory that listed the telephone numbers at every building in Chicago, block by block. It was our standard practice, when a story was breaking, to check our book and telephone homes and businesses in close proximity to the address mentioned on the police radio; it's a pretty good way to get a fast "read" on a developing story. And this is what we did on St. Patrick's night.

The average person that you reach by phone is rarely able to provide details. But if something extraordinary has occurred in a neighborhood, the chances are good that you will get confirmation of the police radio flash. It is best to be wary if the party you call gets wordy. A rather high percentage of people relish the opportunity to be a source of information, and a lot of them are inclined to build up their role by elaborating, with minimal concern for the facts, the little bit they do know about the story you are trying to pin down. But when everybody you call has some information—which had been the case, for example, when we made our first inquiries about the train wreck in Naperville—you had better get ready to roll on the story. And this is how it was on St. Patrick's night in 1947 when there was trouble at a dance hall.

I alerted the NBC engineers that we'd be going out in the mobile unit. And I quite clearly remember trying to find a staff announcer. I came up empty. And I suppose I will never forget the conversation I had with Bill Ray when I called him at home to tell him we had a pretty good story in the making—but no announcer. The reason I won't forget it is that Bill Ray said, "Why don't you go out there and do it?"

"Me?" I replied. "Are you crazy?"

"Listen," Ray said, "that dance hall sounds like a good story. We've got it in our hands. It'll be all over the front pages tomorrow. If we blow it—a good chance like this to show what we can do—we'll be kicking ourselves in the morning."

"Look, Bill," I said, "the rule is that we have to use a staff announcer—a member of AFRA. The union would scream bloody murder if I did an announcer's job. Management would raise hell—and I'd be caught in the middle."

"Don't worry about it," Ray said. "If AFRA raises hell, we'll take care of it; if there's a penalty or something, we'll pay it. I've been trying to figure out a way to get our newsmen to do the reporting on spot stories. Now a chance to do it has dropped in our laps. So go cover the dance hall story and let's see how it works out. Let's see how an honest-to-God newsman can do it."

"If you're telling me to go out on this, I'll go. But you'd better be ready for the results, because I know that I'm going to be terrible."

Bill Ray laughed cheerfully. "It won't be that bad," he said.

More or less scared to death about handling a microphone, I got into the mobile unit with an NBC engineer named Art Hjorth. Hjorth was a first-rate technician and a strong union man. He held some kind of position in the Chicago chapter of NABET, the radio engineers' union. Hjorth gratuitously expressed his opinion that Bill Ray's sending me out on an announcer's job showed very bad judgment.

"It's none of my business, maybe," Art Hjorth declared, as he drove our unit to the dance hall, "and I want you to know that I'll help in any way I can to get your story and interviews recorded. But I've got to tell you that I don't like this business of sending a nonunion guy out on a union man's assignment. It's nothing personal, you know, it's just that the company gets away with putting nonunion men on the air, the next thing you know, the company will send you guys out with your own recorders—so they won't have to pay NABET members."

I knew from previous experience with Art Hjorth that union jurisdiction was a sensitive area of discussion, and I never had much interest in it, in any case. The matter of who was entitled to operate what kind of equipment didn't concern me. So, with foreboding as to what kind of fool I would make as an announcer-reporter, I kept my mouth shut during the drive to the dance hall.

There were squad cars and ambulances and a good deal of fire department equipment in front of the two-story building that housed the dance hall. There was no odor of smoke, but a couple of the truck companies—the hook-and-ladder units—had already put a few ladders up to the windows on the second floor. The window panes were shattered. Firemen are trained, I guess, to smash up windows the first chance they get; it seems to be one of their few pleasures.

On the street level, a tavern was doing a nice business behind a neon sign. A customer who had satisfied his thirst, or who perhaps wanted to do his drinking in a quieter place, came out of the tavern and stopped to have a look at this queer vehicle— our mobile unit—with all of its antennae sticking up.

I jumped out with the mike in my hand. Counting on Hjorth to get the wire recorder operating, I startled the guy who had come out of the tavern by asking him, "Where's the dance hall?"

The guy looked at me suspiciously. Then he turned and motioned to the second floor. With a bit of a brogue and a tone of authority he said, "The dance is over; the floor caved in and that was the end of it."

"How many were hurt?"

"Oh, I wouldn't be knowin' that," he replied. "Quite a number; twenty-five or therty or so, I would say; many with cuts and some with fractures of the limbs. 'Twas a bad fall they had."

"What made the floor collapse?"

"Oh," he replied, "I wouldn't be knowin' what made the floor collapse. There were a lot of them up there dancin'; doin' the jig, I would imagine from hearin' the music of the violins and the fella with his bangin' of the spoons—my, that lad was good with the spoons!"

"You didn't see the floor collapse? You weren't there?"

My eyewitness bristled a little when I suggested he hadn't been there. "I had an excellent view of the trouble," he replied. "I was at the rail, havin' a little glass, and I heard the floor begin to creak. And then, all at one moment it seemed, the tiny tin squares in the ceilin' at the back of the tavern rip loose. The fella behind the bar looks up with great concern, watchin' the ceilin' rip open in the middle, and them that had been dancin' the jig come tumblin' down through the big hole in the ceilin'—and the man behind the bar cries out, 'God, Almighty! What in hell's name is happenin' up there?' 'Tis this fella's place, you know—the one behind the bar; the tavern, the dance hall up above and everythin'. He has cause for concern, I would say. And I would think that if this wasn't St. Paddy's night, he would shutter his place until he could make repairs. If you will excuse me now, I'll be movin' on to attend to my private matters." And with a tip of his hat, he moved away.

I asked Hjorth, "Did you get it?"

Hjorth nodded. "You were lucky," he said, "to find a guy who saw what happened and could talk that good."

I nodded and said he could close up the wire recorder, we were going back to the newsroom.

"Wait a minute!" he replied. "I don't mean to be telling you your business, but you haven't got it wrapped up yet—who was running the dance, how bad those people got hurt, and all."

"They'll have that information in the newsroom," I explained. "We need something more, we can get on the phone and get it."

So he shrugged and closed up the equipment and we headed back to the Merchandise Mart, Art Hjorth mumbling the whole time that we should be sticking around to wrap up the story. But I had learned something important that night about covering spot news for radio. You don't need to get the complete story at the scene; all you need is a good sound bite that touches the heart of the story. You can pick up the details later.

I learned something else that night. I had dreaded handling the microphone. But driving back to the Mart that night, I realized it doesn't take any special talent to do this kind of thing. All you have to know is how to ask questions. If you find somebody who is willing to talk and knows what he's talking about, it's a cinch to get an acceptable recorded piece. The only thing you've got to be careful about is that when you put a question to somebody, you give him a chance to answer it. To my last day, I guess, it will annoy the hell out of me to hear a radio or TV reporter break in on somebody who is willing to tell him something. It is hard to keep your mouth shut when the person you are talking to says something that offends you or, in your opinion, gets careless with the truth. But the listener, or the viewer, is not particularly interested in what a reporter has to say; the star of the piece, even though he might be saying something outrageous, is the party you happen to be interviewing. Having sense enough to remain silent when somebody is trying to give you information is, I think, essential.

The day after the dance hall piece was broadcast, Jules Herbuveaux, the program manager of NBC-Chicago, presented me with the glass disc. With a grin on his face, he said that now that I was launched on a new career I might want to keep my first air piece. I had no intention of entering a new career. As Herbuveaux was known for his sense of humor, I figured he was working a little joke. But I took the disc, and later I made a practice of listening to it whenever I'd done a piece that I thought was pretty good. I got better at doing this street reporting as time went on, but I used to play that first piece by way of reminding myself that I had been a rank amateur when I got into this news-on-the-spot business. It's good for your soul, I think, when you start attaining a degree of success, to remember how terrible you were at the beginning. As clumsy as NBC-Chicago's innovative street reporting might have been, the listeners' response was immediate and gratifying. As Bill Ray had anticipated, hearing reports from the scene of a news story was far more compelling than reading newspaper accounts of what had happened. The frightened voice of a thief who has just been shot by a policeman, or the helpless grief of a woman who has just seen her lover killed by assassins, or the arrogant bravado of a public official who has just been convicted of accepting bribes—man, there is simply nothing a newspaper can do to come even close to having the impact of radio—or television.

CHAPTER 10

THE PLAY PEN OF
REUTLINGER'S RATS

THE GUYS WHO WORKED FOR THE NEWSPAPERS didn't much like us, of course. Some of the print reporters who were friends of mine struggled for a long time to put aside their disdain for radio news. I attempted to persuade a couple of these guys that radio news was simply a quicker way of telling the big story. My personal opinion was that the newspaper guys had a fearful premonition that this was the beginning of a reporting system so fast that the newspapers wouldn't be able to compete. There was, among the pencil reporters, a great deal of resentment against this new thing—radio news—that threatened them.

Following my adventure of covering the St. Patrick's night dance hall story in 1947, there was less anxiety in the newsroom about finding an AFRA staff announcer to send out in the mobile unit. I became the handy substitute who would be sent into the game when a professional announcer was not available. And when I was sent out on a seemingly complicated story with a staff announcer, it became not-unusual to have the AFRA guy hand me the mike and say, "Why don't you do it?" The staff announcers weren't collecting any fees for street work, and my recollection is that most of them were more than willing to let me do the ad-libbing and reporting. However it came about, and I was as surprised as anyone else, it got to be commonplace for my untrained voice to be heard on the news broadcasts. The guys in top management thought this was just great, this business of NBC-Chicago going out to get its own news. And Bill Ray seemed to think it was at least the beginning of his dream to have news guys do on-the-spot reporting.

We got a little fan mail on this spot news stuff, though nobody in broadcasting is greatly impressed, as far as I could ever see, by audience fan mail; it's the negative mail, the beefs about this and that, which seems to make an impression on people in radio and television—especially management.

It was evident to the few of us who were involved in the tedious work of getting a crew together and going to the scene of a news story—getting the stuff recorded, going back to the Merchandise Mart to transfer recorded segments from magnetic wire to glass discs, and painstakingly typing out a script to tie up the whole thing in one package for broadcast—that, even though we were in a primitive stage, we were into something new that would get a great deal better and endure.

I was not eager to be sent out on these assignments. I was not comfortable doing on-the-air reporting. It would have been unthinkable, of course, that I would qualify as a staff announcer; my phrasing was awful and I had the flat vocal qualities of a Chicago native, with little prospect that I would show any improvement. I was so poorly qualified to be a professional announcer that I was certain from the beginning that I would never make it in this line of work; and I didn't even try to develop a style that would get me by. But "how you sounded" was less important to Bill Ray than having credentials as an experienced street reporter, so I found myself being eased into a job I did not covet when old Bud Thorpe was eased out.

The radio critics at the Chicago newspapers didn't know what to make of me when I started doing spot news stories on a regular basis. They took little shots at me for the nonprofessional quality of my voice. The sum of their criticism was that nobody who sounded like me should be going on the air every day. But the other side of it was that I seemed to know what I was doing in covering the top news stories, and sometimes the critics would quote in their columns excerpts from my recorded interviews. *Variety*, which was regarded as the bible of show business, seemed to think that what I was doing, this street reporting on a daily basis, might be the beginning of something new in the radio news business; the guys who wrote for *Variety* didn't take offense at the lack of polish in my voice— and I was relieved that *Variety* didn't take any shots at how I sounded.

Often, I was tempted to chuck the whole thing. I was not attracted by the opportunity of carving out a new kind of live-lihood as a radio street reporter. A number of people in the business, including the well-paid staff announcers, were kind enough to tell me that working with a microphone was where the money was going to be. But I was doing pretty well, fi-nancially, as it was—getting fees for writing half-hour radio plays, knocking out one-minute radio commercials when a small ad agency got caught in a bind, and working a good bit of overtime. Bill Ray did make my air work more agreeable by adding broadcasting fees to my paycheck. On infrequent oc-casions, when I managed to get a recorded piece on an ex-traordinary story of some kind, the "News of the World" guys at NBC-New York would take it and I would get an extra fifty dollars for a minute-and-a-half report. Fifty dollars doesn't seem like much of a stipend for doing a piece on the network news show with the largest audience, but it was a nice chunk of money at a time when AFRA staff annoucers were getting seventy-five-a-week base pay, and only a couple of our guys in the newsroom, myself among them, were paid the princely sum of fifty-a-week. By dangling an extra hundred a week under my nose, Bill Ray helped me overcome the reluctance I had about becoming what is called an "air person."

I had always been reasonably good as a pencil reporter in getting eyewitnesses to tell me what they had seen, or getting information out of someone I managed to get on the telephone, or persuading people to tell me anything they happened to know about whatever it was I was asking about. Predictably, whatever ability I had to get people to tell me what they knew stayed with me when I got into the business of on-the-spot radio reporting. Getting information out of people didn't trouble me; even as a kid reporter, I had always been comfortable doing this—no matter the power or eminence of the person that I was trying to get to talk to me. However, the more frequently I showed up in the mobile unit at the scene of a breaking story, the more distasteful were my relationships with the newspaper reporters. A few of my old friends among the print reporters made a point of avoiding conversation with me.

The better known I became as the reporter with a microphone who might put somebody's voice on the air, for all of his friends and admirers to hear, the easier it became to woo sources away from the pencil reporters—which was one of the reasons, I am certain, that most of the newspaper guys came to have a personal dislike for me. Without my doing much to bring it about, people in the news were eager to tell me what they knew. A microphone had a magical effect in breaking down shyness and inhibitions. The more of this stuff that we got on the air, the easier it became to persuade otherwise reluctant individuals to talk to me. With the choice of telling a guy with a microphone what they knew or talking to a reporter with a pencil, a high percentage of men and women preferred to talk to me. The newspaper guys resented this, of course, and some of them didn't conceal their desire to put me out of the on-the-spot news business.

At the beginning of on-the-street radio reporting, one customary ploy of the newspaper guys was to sidle up to the microphone as I was interviewing someone and mouth some profanity or vulgarity. These vocal intrusions irritated the hell out of me—especially when the pencil reporter with the loud mouth was taking notes on something new about a story that I had wormed out of the person I was interviewing. The aggravating thing about this was that the pencil reporter was getting the benefit of information that I could not use on the air because of the reporter's cursing or vulgarity.

One of the first things I discovered in this new game was that you lose a great deal of the flavor and spontaneity of an interview if you are forced to get someone who is not accustomed to being interviewed to repeat something he has already told you; the guy you are talking to might understand why it is that you are asking him a question he has already answered—he can see for himself that the recording equipment has momentarily conked out, for example—but he loses his spark when he repeats what he has already told you. So it was pretty tough when a pencil reporter intentionally interjected something unprintable into a good interview.

Bill Ray merely sighed when I complained to him that I was being plagued by newspaper guys who were bent on lousing up my recordings. He knew it was rough, trying to operate as a radio street man, but he didn't seem to have an easy solution for my problem. So I worked out some answers of my own. Occasionally, when one of the pencil reporters cut in unexpectedly on one of my interviews with a relevant question, I not only put his voice on the air, I identified him and his newspaper in the script I wrote to embrace the interview. The pencil reporters acquired a more friendly attitude toward me, when, on occasion, I made an effort to interview *them* and get *their* voices on the air. And when I got better information on a shooting or something than they had been able to scrape up, I let them know what I had been able to find out. My generosity was based on my awareness that we would have the stuff on the air hours before their reports could be read in the newspaper.

When I put a newspaper reporter's voice on the air, the guys in his city room often said something agreeable to him about the significance of the question he had asked or how good he had sounded. The pencil reporter, visibly pleased, would tell me, "Hey, how about paying me for doing your work?"—or some such pleasantry. Well, I decided, if the guys at the newspapers are starting to get interested in the spot news we were broadcasting—maybe I could switch it around and permanently solve the problem of pencil reporters' nosing into my interviews.

NBC News didn't have a strong enough stomach to let me get away with putting one of the offending print reporters on the air with the strong language he had used in butting into one of my interviews. But I edited the recordings, and I selected the stuff that went on the air. I would be held accountable for anything offensive that I allowed to get on the air, but I was unfettered in making a judgment of what recorded segments got broadcast. So, in my evil planning, I chose to let the pencil reporters know that potential embarrassment attached to their practice of messing around with my interviews.

We had four major newspapers publishing in Chicago in those days—the *Tribune*, the *Sun-Times*, the *Daily News*, and the *Evening American*. Confident that if my strategy worked on one reporter they would all get the message, I waited for my chance. It was a reporter from the free-soul Hearst paper, the *Evening American*, who walked into the trap. This fellow, who subsequently got to be a friend of mine when his paper sponsored my on-the-spot news program and I started working out of its city room, spoke "dese and dem"—his pronunciation was strictly Chicagoese. I hadn't had him in mind particularly when I set out to free myself of pencil-reporter harassment. But he deliberately butted in one day as I was interviewing a homicide detective named Leon Sweitzer. When I sat down to edit the interview, I decided that Buddy McHugh was the target I had been looking for.

McHugh hadn't said anything offensive when he moved in on my conversation with Sweitzer. But he wasn't too bright and was by nature pretty boorish. He whined a little when he asked questions. His grammar was atrocious. He was a newspaperman of high reputation, but he couldn't write a lick—some rewrite man put together the pieces that wound up on the front page with McHugh's by-line. But Buddy McHugh was a tiger when it came to digging into somebody who had information that he wanted. He had "the nerve of a burglar," as the saying went, in moving in on a story. So it was very much in character for him to have moved in on me when I was trying to get some information out of a guy from the Detective Bureau.

I really liked this old pro, and I felt some regret about using him as my sacrificial lamb, though he would have been the last reporter in the city to beef about what I had done to him; in a similar situation, I think, he gladly would have done the same thing to me. But, to be candid about it, I was pleased that I had picked on a big-reputation guy rather than some kid reporter. I had to put a spike into a well-known guy to make the point that I was sick of having pencil reporters lousing up my act. I brought it off, I think, and what I did contributed a little something toward getting myself and the radio reporters who followed me a degree of respectability and the freedom to do a tough job without our colleagues in print fouling things up.

What I did to this guy, by way of warning him and the other pencil reporters that they had better be careful about what they said into our microphone, was to make a fool of him on the evening news of our fifty-thousand-watt station. I didn't fiddle with what he had said, in breaking in on Sweitzer and me. I didn't transpose his remarks to make him sound silly. I merely lifted complete segments of what this guy had said to Sweitzer—including his opening, an ingratiating plea that Sweitzer certainly would want to cooperate with the *Evening American*. The editors of the *Evening American* must have found our report mortifying. Their star reporter sounded like a whimpering idiot.

Every phone in the newsroom seemed to be ringing when I walked in from the studio after putting this garbage on the air. The listeners demanded to know why we would foist the mumbo jumbo of this so-called newspaper reporter on them. Bill Ray looked at me quizzically when I came back into the newsroom. He said, "Was that the best you could get out of your recording on that story?" I guess I kind of smiled and replied, "I thought it was time we dropped a little valentine on the pencil reporters." Bill Ray smiled and said, "Yes, it was all love and kisses—and I hope the newspapers got the message."

One of our guys, clutching a phone, looked at me and said, "Harry Reutlinger of the *American* wants to talk to you." I went to my desk, punched up the line, and picked up a phone. A little to my surprise, Harry was chuckling. "I thought I'd call to ask if you people are going to hire our reporter," he

said. "He sounded so great on the radio, I'm worried you people will take him away from us."

"Your guy's one hell of a reporter, Harry," I said, "but I
don't think he's quite what we're looking for. He has sort of
a quaint way of expressing himself, you know."

Reutlinger laughed. "Listen," he said, "I didn't call to complain; I called you because I know the newspaper guys have
been rough on you, and I'm calling to tell you I think you've
straightened them out. I don't think you'll have any more trouble."

When I thanked him for calling, Harry Reutlinger said,
"They're all right, the street reporters. It's just they're afraid
you're starting to beat their ass on good stories—and it's true.
The newspapers have got in the habit—especially around this
place—of trying to cover breaking stories on the telephone.
Crissakes, you can't do a job covering a city like this on the
telephone! We get a tip on something, the photo desk sends
out a photographer right now and he hops right on it; I give
the tip to one of my guys, the guy reaches for the telephone.
God Almighty! What in hell is happening to the newspaper
business?"

Without having done a blessed thing to bring it about, and
having had no voice in the matter, I got into a close professional
relationship with Harry Reutlinger. It began, I think—and I
wasn't too pleased to be caught up in this—about the time that
one of the weekly news magazines, *Time* or *Newsweek*, I don't
remember which, went overboard with a long, praise-loaded
piece on the "Front Page" characters in Harry Reutlinger's
city room. "Reutlinger's Rats" was the caption the newsmag-
azine put on the piece. Everyone in the other Chicago city
rooms chuckled, because it was common knowledge in our
business that Harry ran a wild place. He had reporters working
for him who were bold and sometimes outrageous in scratching
up the information they would call in to some disdainful guy
doing rewrite. I wasn't too attracted by the notion of spending
a lot of time with guys like this. But I didn't have much choice;
the *Evening American* had decided to put up some money to
sponsor our on-the-spot radio program, stipulating that I was

to work out of the city room, and I either went along with this arrangement or let somebody else take over as Chicago's first radio street reporter.

Not in the slightest way, in the five years or so that I worked out of the *Evening American* city room, was anyone over there unpleasant or disagreeable. I made an effort to be unobtrusive, believing that a number of the guys in the city room regarded me as an outsider who would never quite qualify as "one of us." I showed up every morning about eight o'clock and took a seat at a rim of the city desk—listening to everything that was called in. The reporters who were out on their beats at City Hall or the Criminal Courts Building or Police Head-quarters called in to let Reutlinger know what they had. Reutlinger then turned them over to somebody on rewrite.

I sat at the city desk, alert to a potentially good story that would lend itself to radio. Sometimes, when I was trying to make up my mind about going out on a story, Reutlinger would gently suggest that whatever it was that was breaking looked to him to be "a pretty good piece"; if I had a sensible reason for not wanting to go out on the story, or if it seemed to me we couldn't use the stuff on radio because it was too compli-cated or lascivious or grisly, Harry would just nod and not question my judgment.

You don't get to know everything that is going on in your city if you sit around the city desk of a major newspaper; you lose out on a lot of the nuances, and you don't get to know anything much about the personalities of the people who are the center of attention. Guys who work around a city desk fall victim to the delusion that, having their fingers on the pulse of all that is making news, they are endowed with omniscience when it comes to having intimate knowledge of what is hap-pening in their city. But a great deal of the flavor of what the street reporter encounters evaporates in transmission to the city editor, to the rewrite man, and to the copy desk before it comes out in the sterilized form that the average bloke reads in his newspaper. For no other reason than this, news coverage on radio and television has an impact that the print people can never hope to match.

By no means can it be argued that, as a breed, electronics reporters are superior to print media reporters. But, urged on by the opportunity to win renown as radio and television "personalities," not to mention the enormously better pay, the best of the electronics reporters are every bit as capable as their newspaper counterparts and—in some instances—a lot better. It requires a new kind of skill to make the transition from pencil reporting to television and radio reporting, but it is relatively easy to learn how to speak without swallowing your words, how to present your information comprehensibly, and how to avoid inverted sentences, parenthetical phrases, and other grammatical constructions that make it difficult for the listener or the viewer to understand what in hell you are talking about. But ever-increasing numbers of print media people have been able to make the change—and the bonus of this transition is that radio and television personalize reports in a way that is beyond the capability of the print media.

If you interview a verbose old politician like the late Everett McKinley Dirksen, which I did on numerous occasions, there is no way you can preserve his grandiloquence if you reduce the sugary loveliness of his words to the confines of quotation marks on the printed page. If you interview someone like the jowly Richard J. Daley, longtime mayor of Chicago, which I did on numerous occasions, you lose a lot in the printed translation when you quote him as expressing his indignation over somebody's innuendo—when his pronunciation of the word invariably was "induendo."

Newspapers are restricted by the time-honored practice of cleaning up the grammar of elected officials, sports celebrities, visiting movie stars, policemen, preachers, and gangsters. The scrubwoman quoted in the newspaper seems to have as much command of the English language as her Majesty, the Queen. The print people drain the individuality, if not the life, out of the quotes of those in the news. What you get in the printed quotation might be essentially what the person being quoted meant to say. But the printed quotes are limp, compared to the unedited voice of the guy who did the talking.

I had frequent discussions about this with Reutlinger when

things were quiet in the *Evening American* city room and we sat around shooting the breeze. Harry, who was what you would call an "old-school" newspaperman, contended that the rewrite men and the copy desk had to straighten out the quotes or the story they were doctoring wouldn't be worth putting in the paper. "My God," Harry used to say, "you print what somebody actually said at a fire or explosion or anything like that—like a scandal at City Hall or something—the readers won't understand what the goddamn guy is talking about. My God, you limit us to using the actual quotes, I gotta fire most of my reporters. When they call in, half the time you don't know what the goddamn guys are trying to say. Yeah, the rewrite man cleans up the quotes, and the guys on the copy desk make sure whoever buys the paper can understand what the hell it says. We can't go to press with quotes that indicate the guy being quoted doesn't know what in hell he's talking about."

"I know how the desk people clean up the guy's language, Harry," I said. "All I am saying is that radio reporting does it better. We let the listener hear the guy's voice—bad grammar and all."

"You don't use the swearing or the dirty words; you edit that out," Harry argued. "You don't use any rough words, or the preachers and the holier-than-thous would be right on your tail."

I don't recall that I ever argued beyond that with Harry Reutlinger, the fabled city editor of the *Evening American*. It fascinated me that a knowledgeable print media man of his reputation seemed to think it was important to make a case for the newspaper practices in handling copy. It didn't trouble him that a bunch of guys in a city room were deciding what was fit to be read. But, many times in conversations like this, I got a feeling that Reutlinger was voicing a deep-seated fear that, somehow, the development of radio street reporting might prove to be a threat to the newspapers. I don't know that he actually had this apprehension, but it seemed pretty obvious to me that as electronic reporting got better, the print people were going to be confronted by tough competition. It grieved me, actually, that the newspapers were becoming sloppy and lazy in doing what they should have been doing best—covering the news.

Harry Reutlinger had what they call a "phone man" seated opposite him on the *Evening American* city desk; except for Harry's private line, which rarely lit up, every call to the desk was picked up by the phone man—a guy named Myron something-or-other. Reutlinger appeared to be sublimely indifferent toward the seemingly endless flow of telephone calls that came to the city desk; I guess he had been in the business for so long that he assumed that the call would be brought to his attention in due course, if it amounted to anything. The calls that came in were more important to me, because I had the problem of trying to decide where I could go with the mobile unit to record a piece for broadcast; I eavesdropped on nearly every call that came in, which meant I had some idea of every story that was breaking before the city editor did. I spent a great many hours eavesdropping at the *Evening American* city desk. I didn't have the problem, that Reutlinger and his guys had, of staying on top of everything that was making news in Chicago; all I had to do was make a judgment on what could be an interesting spot for radio and hope that the engineer who was assigned to me would be waiting in the mobile unit and had not wandered away to have a sandwich or run an errand for his wife or something like that.

When I decided to "go" on a story, I would contact the engineer by calling him up on the mobile phone. Bill Ray had read a little story in the *New York Times* about Mother Bell's invention of this thing, and, somehow or other, he made an agreement with the public relations people of Illinois Bell to install one in our mobile unit as soon as it became available. I think we got the first one in the nation—or in our part of the nation, at least. Fixed in place under the dashboard of our unit, it looked like any other phone—except that a green light came on when somebody was calling in. You had to press down a little lever on the phone to activate the channel when you wanted to talk. Driving along in traffic, I'd yak away on the mobile telephone, and other motorists—catching a glimpse of me talking into the phone—would look at me incredulously. A guy in a station wagon on the telephone? My, God!

All too soon, alas—somebody always moves in on every good thing that comes along—having a phone in your car became a status symbol. Mother Bell must have been delighted that numbers of people were willing to shell out good money to get one of these things, but using the mobile phone, especially when you had to depend on it for getting information, got to be exasperating. The trouble was that everybody who got a mobile phone was on the same channel. So, hoping to make a quick call to NBC News, the *Evening American* city desk, or the fire commissioner or someone—there was somebody on the damned line.

The mobile phone proved valuable only for certain kinds of people. Gangsters and professional bookmakers shunned the thing as an invention of the devil, because anything that was said on the mobile phone line could be heard by anyone else who picked up the phone in his car. It was strictly conversation on the party line. Anyone who had a phone was free to listen in. Sometimes when I was anxious to get a call through, I would monitor somebody's conversation in hope of being able to place my call as soon as the guy hung up. Generally you wouldn't hear anything interesting; the canning companies put mobile phones in the cars of their produce buyers, for example, in order that the guy doing a round of the farms could inform his office of prevailing prices on cabbages and soybeans. Every once in a while some well-heeled guy would call his girlfriend and drool a sickening spiel of "kootchy-coo" into the mouthpiece of his phone—apparently too stupid to know, this guy, that anyone with a mobile phone might be listening. Mostly what you heard when the channel was busy was meaningless. The popularity of this thing ruined it.

In the first days of having a mobile phone in our unit, the guys at the *Evening American* were amazed by the thing. Reutlinger sent a feature writer down to our mobile unit, which we customarily parked along the curb at Wacker and Madison, in front of the Hearst building. The writer placed a call to Reutlinger and got the conversation all screwed up because he couldn't remember to depress the button on the phone to open up the channel. The feature story on this remarkable innovation in the NBC mobile unit pleased Harry Reutlinger, because the newspaper got several letters from readers who wanted to know how they could order one of these things from the telephone company. Sitting at the city desk, Harry read the letters aloud to the city room, and then he threw them in a waste basket.

The guys in Reutlinger's city room were indifferent to the outside world, including readers, politicians, big wheels in business, and even the managing editor and other newspaper executives. As far as I could judge it, these fellows seemed to think fate had tossed them into a shabby kind of work, and hardly a one of them appeared to have any delusions about being in an exciting or romantic business. Some of them—especially the best writers—would speak dolefully about having wound up working for a Hearst paper. The tone of their voices suggested that somewhere along the road they had lost their professional souls. I used to wonder, sometimes, if Bill Ray had any understanding of this bizarre place he had put me into.

I spent a lot of time sitting on the edge of one of the six desks in the rewrite section of the city room. The *American* had some first-rate writers—Elgar Brown, a reformed drinker who was the best of the lot; Basil Talbott, who had once been a song-and-dance man in vaudeville and often said he wished to God he still were; and Copeland Berg, an artist of considerable talent, who thought it humiliating that a great painter like himself had been forced by penury to pound out what he called "crap." They were pretty interesting guys that I used to sit around and talk with. In one way or another, these Hearst paper rewrite men shared a quiet disdain for the human race—especially for the successful people who have the queer notion that they are better than everyone else. Maybe it damaged my vision of life to associate with guys like this, but that association gave me a perspective on such curiosities as what gets into a newspaper, a perspective I could not have acquired in any other way.

The *Evening American* scratched around shamelessly for anything its arch-rival, the *Chicago Daily News*, did not have. The editor and publisher of the *Evening American* burdened Reutlinger with all manner of "inside story" features. They put a series of true confessions of a remorseful abortionist on him. Reutlinger had to find space for a phony series that had the title, "I was a Willing Victim of the Crime Syndicate." The *American* did a series one time that had some such headline as "Confessions of a Girl for Hire." The guys on rewrite got stuck with the thankless job of writing this drivel, having nothing to go on, generally, except for a few vague notes on a conversation some nut had had over the telephone with the managing editor or somebody like that. The ME, or publisher, or whoever, had the strange idea that this nonsense would give the *American* a few points over the *Daily News* in the continual circulation war.

I used to read this garbage that was passed off as "human interest" stories. I was the only one in the city room who read this junk, I guess. But I knew the rewrite guys who agonized over this stuff, and it fascinated me to see how they were making out in their Perils-of-Pauline stories. I was utterly captivated, for example, by the daily installments of "Confessions of a Girl for Hire." I had no lascivious interest in the misadventures of this poor maiden from the farm country who landed in the big city; the daily installments were pretty short on the details of her difficulties. But the care and feeding of this poor girl for hire had been placed upon my old friend Copeland Berg, the artist, and it pleased me to stand alongside his desk as this slovenly, obese, irreverent man pounded his typewriter, muttering curses on Reutlinger, the managing editor, and all who had had a part in forcing him to turn out such drivel. Even Elgar Brown, who was customarily indifferent to the not-infrequent outbursts of guys in the city room, would stop typing and gaze at Copeland Berg with admiration when Berg was having a tantrum. A couple of times while he was working on "The Hired Girl" series, Copeland had uttered prayerlike pleas that city editor Reutlinger would roast in hell until the end of time—"and thirty days extra." But it didn't seem to matter to Reutlinger that Berg was in a rage. Harry's desk was only a few steps away from the rewrite men, and he couldn't avoid hearing the curses that Berg was pouring down on him, but Harry calmly puffed on his Havana cigar and waited for a copy boy to come to the desk with Berg's new episode of "The Girl for Hire." I think it annoyed the hell out of Berg that Reutlinger would not respond to his ranting.

One day, near the end of Copeland Berg's ordeal—his patience at the breaking point, I guess—he stood up and shook his fist at Reutlinger. Casually, Harry turned his head around and looked benignly at his rewrite man, who appeared about to explode. In a gentle voice, Harry said, "Is something wrong, Cope?"

Copeland Berg almost choked. "Is there something 'wrong,' Harry?" he shouted. "Listen to our city editor!" he declared, waving an arm to invite the attention of everyone in the city room. "We are working for a family newspaper that panders to everything that is evil in society. God Almighty in heaven!" he roared, in pretty dramatic language for a man who treasured his reputation as an agnostic, "We slave away, manufacturing drool, for a so-called newspaper that has not the decency to let the whores have a little peace of mind, and our city editor wants to know, 'Is something wrong?'" Reutlinger chuckled. "When you finish that last piece, Cope," he said, "I'd like to see it." Glowering, Copeland Berg sat down at his typewriter to close off the last installment of the "Hired Girl" series with the sentimental moralizing he knew the editors demanded.

Not a solitary one of the six rewrite men escaped having to struggle through distasteful assignments. The publisher employed the news pages to further his practice of cultivating favor with the Democratic Party officials who ran Chicago. The guy who ran the advertising department had no shame about asking the editors to work up a complimentary story about some dubious character who was buying ad space for his used car business or something like that. On a regular basis, one of the front office guys came up with some whacky idea for a series. Having to grind out bilge was a cross the *Evening American* rewrite men had to bear.

When a couple of high-ranking police officers—a lieutenant named Drury and a captain named Connolly—got suspended for refusing to testify before the Cook County grand jury about some shameful thing, the front office of the *Evening American* raced to the rescue. Drury and Connolly became "reporters." No one ever explained why it was that the *Evening American* decided to defend the good name of these two police officers by putting their by-lines on the front page. The gossip among police reporters was that neither of these cops had much virtue worth defending. However it was that the *Evening American* got into the battle of repairing the reputations of the two cops, the guys on rewrite got stuck with dreaming up the front-page stories that carried the by-lines of these two guys.

In the normal course of producing copy in a newspaper, the rewrite man does what his job designation implies: he takes information from a street reporter and tries to translate the facts into stories that eventually get set in type in the composing room. At the *Evening American*, in my time, one particular guy would write a circulation-building series—such as the one Copeland wrote about the country girl who sold her virtue in the city. For some reason, it didn't work that way in the Drury-Connolly series that somebody in the front office visited upon the city room—to the chagrin of just about everyone in the place. Perhaps aware that it would be onerous to place responsibility for churning out this junk on a solitary rewrite man, Harry Reutlinger divvied it up among all six of his guys. One guy would grind out one episode of this ridiculous series on crime and corruption, and somebody else would have to dream up something new the next day, and so on. The continuity of the story line of this fictionalized exposé got a little sticky, day by day, when the rewrite man who had the burden of doing it today couldn't figure out what in hell it was that the rewrite man who wrote it yesterday had been trying to say and had to guess at what the story line of the Drury-Connolly disclosures was now supposed to be.

Some of Reutlinger's rewrite men didn't seem to be troubled by the lack of consistency in the seemingly endless reports of Lieutenant Drury's and Captain Connolly's imaginary struggle with Syndicate gangsters and other bad guys; I guess the rewrite men who didn't seem to care figured their readers

wouldn't notice that the brave police officers, who were described in today's installment as coming out of a two-flat on
the South Side holding service revolvers on four black policy
kings, had been portrayed in the closing lines of the previous
day's installment as racing fearlessly into a high-rise on the
North Side in pursuit of two Mafia hitmen. A few of Reutlinger's rewrite men—Basil Talbott, for one—weren't very tolerant about screwing up the facts, even fictional ones. If you
gave Gus Talbott a clipping from yesterday's paper that had
Drury and Connolly chasing two mobsters into a big building
in one section of the city, you had better not ask him to believe
that Drury and Connolly emerged from a small building in
another section of the city, holding guns on four black guys.

I wandered over to Gus Talbott's desk one day when it was
his turn to do the Drury-Connolly piece, and I found Gus in
serious conversation with the two coppers. Gus had the clip
from the previous day's paper in his hand and was waving it
at our heroes. With a look of concern, his eyes searching the
faces of Drury and Connolly for an explanation, Gus was saying, "This stuff we ran yesterday contradicts the pitch we were
making last week, when I wrote a piece about how smart you
guys are. My God, where did this stuff about you guys arresting
four policy kings come from?"

Drury and Connolly exchanged worried glances, as if trying
to decide which one of them was going to take the rap for the
fractured facts that had crept into their adventure story on the
previous day. Then they stared at Gus Talbott, apparently unable to answer his question. Gus looked at them with disgust
and said, "Listen, if I'm going to get this straightened out, I've
got to know where these four policy kings came from. They
weren't even mentioned until yesterday, and now whoever
wrote this"—and he waved the clipping—"has you arresting
these policy guys. My, God," Gus declared, "we've got a pretty
sloppy operation around here, but Reutlinger will be on my
ass if I don't get this straightened out." Waving an arm at the
other rewrite men, Gus asked, "Maybe it'll help if I talk to the
guy who wrote this yesterday. Who wrote this stuff of yours
yesterday and worked in that bullshit about you guys arresting

some policy kings? Surely you remember who it was that wrote this stuff yesterday!"

Lieutenant Drury and Captain Connolly exchanged troubled glances. Almost inaudibly, they whispered to each other. Then Connolly spoke up. Pointing a finger at Drury, Connolly said, "Yesterday? *He* done it." Drury, a contrite look on his face, nodded to signify his plea of guilty.

Turning toward me, Gus Talbott sighed and said, "This is a crazy place, but would you believe we've now got a disbarred police lieutenant who claims to be his own ghostwriter?" Drury and Connolly looked uncomfortable, apparently regretting that they had tried to pass off the con that Drury was writing their stuff. Gazing sadly at the two ex-cops, Talbott said, "If somebody asks you what you are doing for a living, now that you have lost your jobs on the Police Department, you just say you are working now at the only daily newspaper in the world where the left hand doesn't know what the left hand is doing."

CHAPTER 11

TELEVISION
STEALS THE SHOW

EARLY TELEVISION PROVED TO BE A SOCIAL BOON. The fortunate family who owned a set became accustomed to unexpected visits from friends and neighbors who dropped in to have a look at this new thing. And saloons in the cities where TV stations went into operation found it necessary to have a television set installed, because their clientele would go elsewhere to drink beer and quaff bourbon and ginger ale if a place didn't have TV; having a television set that presented a good picture was more important to a tavern's survival than the quality of the brew it served. When we got a phone call at the studios in those early days, the compliment or complaint almost always came from some guy who had been having some drinks at a bar as he watched TV.

"Watching" the news on television began, as far as we were concerned in fashioning our first TV news shows, in the early autumn of 1948, when NBC's owned-and-operated station in Chicago—WMAQ Radio—inaugurated a television station with the call letters WNBQ. A meager number of householders in Chicago, only a few thousand, splurged on the purchase of a television set. The best of these new things reputedly was an RCA model with a whopping ten-inch screen. Bill Ray, our news director, and Jules Herbuveaux, who was destined to be our general manager, worked out a thirty-minute format that included ten minutes of news, followed by five minutes of weather report, followed by five minutes of a gal named Dorsey Connors demonstrating the use that a housewife could make of wire coathangers, followed by ten minutes of sports.

Nobody "on camera" was really very good in the beginning, as I recall, though everybody tried to work up an acceptable style for this new medium. There were no teleprompters; the commercial announcers were forced to memorize their spiels, and some of them ended up as gibbering idiots when they couldn't remember their lines. There was precious little news film available, and we had to resort to eight-by-ten glossy prints and hastily prepared graphics. The radio engineers, who also were learning a new trade, pushed their bulky cameras around to an easel on which the pictures had been placed and worked feverishly to get the glossy or the graphic in focus before the control room switched to them and put this picture of theirs on the air. It got pretty hilarious at times, and everybody agreed that television was a good way to get ulcers. A lot of the people involved in all this were convinced that televised news would never amount to anything.

Herbuveaux, who had been an orchestra leader back in the 1920s, created what came to be known as the "Chicago School of Television." The Chicago School was hailed by critics everywhere as the most skillful television programming in the nation—although the reason that NBC-Chicago got this reputation was that it was so short of studio space that our guys had to dream up all manner of tricks and innovations to get our shows on the tube.

I don't recall that the few of us who had a hand in producing this stuff took any particular pride in what we were doing; every once in a while, when we got on the air with a first-rate piece, we would be pleased with the drama and the impact of our report—but the broadcasting business, like a shark, has an insatiable appetite. There is no opportunity in the radio or television news business to lean back and take a bow when you have done a report of obvious quality; in radio and television news, the best reporters have no time to admire themselves. As they voice the last sentence, the good reporters are haunted by the painful wonderment of what report of comparable public interest they can possibly come up with tomorrow.

The advertising agencies shunned TV in its earliest years; there was not much of an audience out there. Very few people were willing to spend several hundred dollars on a receiver that presented a "ghosty" picture most of the time. There was prestige in owning one, but early television didn't offer much worth looking at. As the pioneer TV stations and the networks struggled to develop the technique of using this new means of communication effectively, the ad people—though unimpressed by the "numbers" they were getting from the rating companies on the discouragingly few viewers—began trying to work out a technique for packaging their commercials. Everybody seemed to be talking about the tremendous impact that television would make. But in the first couple of years, television looked to those of us who were in it from the beginning as an unproven thing.

In television's first year, NBC News pushed me into covering politics. I was not too enchanted by this pressure to start chasing politicians, along with the fire engines and the squad cars, but 1948 was a big election year, and somebody had to do it.

At our place, WNBQ, our star newsman on the evening news program was Clifton Utley, who had been hired by NBC when Marshall Field III abandoned the radio business. A condensation of my political interviews for radio was used on Utley's TV show. Sometimes Utley put me on his television show. He would interview me as to what the candidates had revealed to me, what my personal opinion of the candidates might be, and stuff like that. I guess I was pleased to be treated as the in-house expert on political affairs, but I never expressed any personal opinions to Clifton Utley during these TV appearances—because I have always been pretty well fixed in my judgment that, except for rare situations in which a reporter's personal assessment of something is essential to his story, it is of no consequence what he, personally, happens to think about somebody or something; the basic intention of an interview is to get the guy you are talking to to say what *he* thinks.

No individual in radio or television can lay claim to having discovered a new way of reporting news. The most that any of us can claim, I think, is that some of us have been able to figure out effective methods of getting our information on the air. The primary requirement of a reporter is to get the news—and there is no essential difference, in doing this, between the guy who is working in the electronics media and the guy who is working in print. There are, of course, other considerations: the reporter who goes on radio has to have a speaking style that is understandable and doesn't grate on the listeners, and the reporter on television has to make a reasonably decent appearance. But if you reduce the requirements of good reporting to the basic of turning up interesting bits of news, the radio-TV guys and the newspaper-news magazine guys are working the same side of the street. You simply cannot do a responsible job of covering news if you are short on contacts. And not having any contacts in the area of politics was the most disturbing aspect of being nudged into this particular tent.

Oh, I knew who all the "name" guys were—Ed Kelly, the mayor, Democratic County Chairman Jake Arvey, Governor Green, Senator Brooks. I had met all of these guys in one way or another, but an occasional, isolated interview with the big men in politics is not the same as getting to know them. And I was woefully unschooled in the matter of knowing what made each of these guys tick. When I first wandered into the green field where such well-known political writers as George Tagge of the *Tribune*, John Dreiske of the *Sun-Times*, and Charlie Cleveland of the *Chicago Daily News* were feeding, all three of these guys seemed to regard me, coming into their pasture with an engineer and a radio recorder, as having a social disease that might be contagious. It was pretty tough in so unfriendly a climate to establish myself as having any credentials to be in their company. I guess that when they checked me out with the street reporters of their newspapers, which I am pretty sure they did, they got the message that I wasn't all that bad to get on with. But, not detecting the odor of printer's ink when they got near me, none of these guys displayed any interest in having anything to do with me.

The newspaper political writers proved to be more civilized than their colleagues in expressing their disdain for me, but I had to deal with the old problem of newspaper guys' resenting an invasion of their territory by a broadcast guy. There was now the need for resolution of my new difficulties with the guys who covered politics.

A couple of solutions surfaced to pacify the political writers' aversion to me. For one thing, NBC-New York came up with a weekly panel show called "Meet the Press." Nothing quite like it had appeared on television, and the viewers became attached to watching it. After all, a fellow who had invested in a television set got to watch reporters play hard ball with some big wheel in government. Such papers as the *New York Times* treated the questions and answers that came up on this innovative discussion program as important stuff that was entitled to full coverage.

"Meet the Press" had been on the air for only about a month, an instant success, when Bill Ray launched a Sunday panel show just like it on NBC-Chicago. Having come into broadcasting from a newspaper, Ray called his program "City Desk." The format was exactly the same as "Meet the Press": three or four knowledgeable guys who worked for the daily papers engaged in verbal duels with major politicians and people of consequence in Chicago's business community.

To beef up his program with guys who might know what was going on in our city and state and might be capable of asking intelligent questions, Bill Ray invited the newspapers' political writers to sit on the panel. As a sort of second thought, he invited me to be a panelist, as well, and somehow or other I became a regular on the panel every week for many years; it meant breaking into my weekend to go down to the NBC studios every Sunday to take part in this thing—but being on "City Desk" got to be a status symbol, with invitations to be on the program eagerly sought after, and it was an agreeable way to pick up a $50 fee.

Well, with a carrot like this dangling under the noses of the political writers, and with me on the panel every week as if I were part of the franchise—and with the newspaper guy's having become aware that their editors were developing an interest in what was being talked about on this "City Desk" show—a little bit of respectability rubbed off on me. This was one thing that helped erase the political writers' objection to having me butt in on their beat.

The other thing that helped me was that guys like the mayor and the governor and our two U.S. senators and the big wheels of commerce and the arts came to regard me as a special kind of reporter, and I had remarkable success in getting them, in the course of my daily interviewing, to give me information they wouldn't even mention to the newspaper guys. If this suggests that they felt more comfortable being interviewed for radio and television, or that they trusted me more than they trusted the newspaper guys—well, I guess that had something to do with their willingness to talk to me. But however it was that, on a rather steady basis, I was getting information from politicians that they withheld from the political writers, I got into the practice of passing on to the newspaper guys at least a little bit of the information that the guy I interviewed had given me, but not them. Why not? There was nothing to be gained by keeping it from them; after all, I was going to put this stuff on the air in a short time—so it wasn't confidential. Besides, I hate to see somebody like a political writer walk away from a big wheel in politics with information that was all screwed up, subjecting him to criticism from the bosses at his newspaper for coming up with a story with facts out of harmony with reports in the rival papers. It was no skin off my nose, as the saying goes, if I took the trouble to straighten out a reporter before he wrote his story. And two important advantages accrued to me from letting the political editors know what the big pol had said to me. Most of the political writers began passing on information to me; even when they were motivated by a desire to let me know that they were more informed than myself, I was always grateful to hear what their version of something might be. Even more importantly, the more success I had in getting politicians to get lippy, the closer I got to having equal status with the newspaper guys—especially when I was willing to share whatever "exclusive" stuff I had squeezed out of the pol I had been talking to. I was not unmindful, of course, that it enhanced the public's conception that you get it straight when you hear the big shot say it on radio, if—hours after the broadcast of my recording—there was confirmation in the newspapers of whatever startling thing I had reported.

Even when Bill Ray started his "City Desk" program and invited the political writers to sit in on the panel, these guys didn't warm up to the idea of accepting me as an equal. I don't think it was until they started quoting in their post-"City Desk" stories the answers that politicians had given to my questions that I detected the first faint signs that maybe—just maybe—I was one broadcast news guy who didn't have to take off his shoes and count on his toes.

In 1948, Jacob M. Arvey, chairman of the Cook County Democrats, had slated a political unknown, Adlai E. Stevenson II, for governor and a political maverick, Paul H. Douglas, for senator. Arvey was a tough, smart, gracious man who, in his time, exerted much greater influence on the flow of political tides than anyone ever gave him credit for.

Whatever it was that inspired the Democrats to run Stevenson against Governor Pete Green and Douglas against Senator Curly Brooks, the consensus of knowledgeable people was that Arvey had come up with a ticket that was bass-ackwards. Not only the political writers, but the seasoned politicians in both major parties, thought that Arvey had blown his chances for upset victories by slating Stevenson for governor and Douglas for senator. Most people figured that Adlai and Paul were fated to go down the chute with President Truman in November. The Chicago newspapers were pretty well agreed that it was refreshing, but futile, for Arvey to have chosen two non-Organization candidates like Douglas and Stevenson for the top of his party ticket. The prevailing opinion of everyone in the news business was that, faced with what appeared to be the impossible assignment of trying to unseat two formidable Republicans, Arvey was attempting to salvage what he could out of a losing situation by slating two class candidates for high office. Better to lose with a pair of highly respected men than to lose with a couple of cigar-smoking old war-horses of the Democratic Party; this was thought to be Arvey's rationale. My personal judgment of the Douglas and Stevenson chances was that they didn't have a prayer.

Having come to prominence as alderman of a Chicago ward—the 24th—where the practice on election day was more a matter of weighing votes than counting them, Arvey was making a surprising effort as party chairman to attain respectability for the Democrats of Chicago. The previous year, when "the boys" became resolute in the matter of dumping Ed Kelly, Arvey had picked Martin Kennelly for mayor. And his decision to present two more clean-looking guys, Douglas and Stevenson, looked like more of the same. The Democratic ward bosses had reservations about Arvey's slating two more "clean" guys; but the ward bosses—many of whom had served in the City Council with Arvey in the good old days when a crap game frequently ensued in the back room of the council chambers—had worked out an accommodation with Mayor Kennelly, finding him agreeable in the matter of not infringing upon their perquisites. So, if it was to be Arvey's ploy to keep the ward healers in power while dressing them up in a cloak of respectability, they were not about to argue with his decision to run Douglas and Stevenson against Brooks and Green. What the hell? As the old Democratic bosses said, there wasn't anybody among the "regulars" who wanted to run for jobs they couldn't win. Except for a guy who wanted to draw a little attention to himself, or a guy who figured that some of his campaign contributions would spill into his pockets, professional politicians are not eager to be candidates in an election they cannot win.

I wondered if ward bosses Paddy Bauler and Charley Weber would make an effort to get out a big vote for Douglas—or whether they disliked him so much that they would "stiff" him, which is Chicagoese for putting him down on election day; they did that in some Organization wards, you know. Bauler and

Weber had made life miserable for Paul Douglas when Douglas was in the City Council. In a gross display of incorrigibility, Bauler had mortified his friends in the council—and the thick-skinned Mayor Kelly, who was presiding—with an embarrassing parting shot at Douglas on Paul's last day as alderman. What had happened was that Mayor Kelly, who could not abide the sight of Alderman Douglas, interrupted the proceedings to speak in his clumsy way in praise of Douglas. The Organization aldermen, which included just about everybody, were astounded at hearing Kelly pay tribute to his most articulate critic. But they dutifully broke into applause and voiced their admiration when the mayor disclosed that Alderman Douglas, although about fifty years of age, had enlisted in the U.S. Marines and was going off, as a private, to fight the Japanese.

The Organization aldermen struggled to their feet and waved to the presiding officer for permission to add their compliments to their courageous colleague, Alderman Douglas. The only man on the floor who exhibited distaste for what was going on was Bauler of the 43rd, who sat scowling. Finally, in a lull—as Douglas got up, waved a hand in thanks for the lavish things that had been said about him, and walked slowly off the floor—Paddy Bauler scrambled to his feet, glared at the departing Douglas, and shouted, "Good riddance to bad rubbish!" There isn't much that offends the membership of the Chicago City Council, but the Organization guys were aghast at Paddy's farewell shot at the scholarly Paul Douglas. Mayor Kelly looked daggers at Bauler. But Paddy just grinned at his audacity. Later, when questioned about his tasteless remark, Paddy Bauler merely shrugged and said, "He ain't one o' us; he ain't no good."

In the fall of 1948 there weren't many of us who thought Douglas had a chance of winning, much less winning big. Surprisingly, Paddy Bauler kept telling me, "Douglas is gonna beat dat guy, big." Paddy threw a big beer bash in his place on North Avenue, declaring, in a speech shouted to his precinct captains as Douglas listened with a mystified smile, "De senator here is gonna be one o' de greatest dere is, when we get 'im elected t' de Senate. I was in de City Council wit' 'im and,

lemme tell ya, he's a stand-up guy, all de way. Ya want somebody who's real good when it comes t' talk, lemme tell ya dis
fella can talk. Ya want somebody wit' brains, dere ain't nobody
who got more brains. He's at de top o' our ticket, dis fella, and
I want ya should get 'im a big vote. Ya guys don't work at it
t' get 'im a big vote, I don't want ya hangin' around here wastin'
my time, askin' for favors and dat. So, let's hear it for our
candidate and our friend, our next U.S. Senator!" and Paddy
Bauler's precinct captains cheered. And Paul Douglas won. It
wouldn't have been for Douglas that Paddy turned out a vote.
It would have been Bauler's anxiety to demonstrate to Arvey
"and de fellas downtown" that he was able to deliver his ward
in a tough election. It was sort of amusing, though, to watch
Paddy Bauler climb into bed with a philosophical enemy like
Paul Douglas. That's politics.

If there was anything to be learned from the surprising results of the 1948 election, it is that you never, ever, can be
certain who is going to get elected. I spent election night, 1948,
doing two things I had never done before. I spent half my time
on the street, covering the election headquarters of Paul H.
Douglas at 188 West Randolph Street and the headquarters
of Adlai E. Stevenson at 7 South Dearborn Street, on the other
side of the Loop. The other part of my time was used up racing
back to NBC in the Merchandise Mart, where Clifton Utley
interrogated me as to what I had to report on what was going
on at the Douglas and Stevenson headquarters. As WNBQ's
"political reporter" on this first televised election, I was "covered" on the other two top candidates. Republican stalwarts
Governor Green and Senator Brooks were so confident of easy
reelection that we had filmed their victory statements the previous day.

Everything worked out pretty well in our coverage of the
1948 elections. We had attempted some of this election night
coverage on radio in the past, but this was our first try on
television, and I think the reason it came off pretty well was
that all of us who had a part in the planning had agreed from
the beginning that we would be sparing in the use of props
and gimmicks, that we would try to keep our visuals to a min-

imum. Our advance thinking was that our responsibility would be to give frequent reports on the vote count, that our modest number of viewers would be served best if we kept sidebar stuff—such as the information I picked up at the Douglas and Stevenson headquarters—to the bare bones.

That night, NBC-Chicago was an island. The electronic techniques for coast-to-coast television broadcast had been worked out. Sound and picture were transmitted on what we called "the cable." But television had been operating only a few months, prior to the November 1948 election, and the coaxial cable out of New York went only as far west as Cleveland, Ohio. Cleveland was getting a live feed from New York, but it wasn't available to us in Chicago. It was frustrating to know that NBC-New York and NBC-Washington were sending late-breaking stuff on the national election, while NBC-Chicago was left pretty much out of it. But that's how it was on election night in November 1948.

There was some kind of transmission facility between Cleveland and Chicago. New York had sent Bill Ray to Cleveland to handle the coverage there, and somehow, late election night, Bill Ray managed to get national stuff to us on the cable going west out of Cleveland.

It seems a long time ago, 1948, and measured against all that has happened since then, I guess it was. Yet, it was only nine years before the Russians had the world shaking in its boots by putting something that was called "Sputnik" into orbit around the earth. In 1948 we had no facilities to bring a picture of Governor Thomas E. Dewey out of New York or President Harry S. Truman out of Washington—and now we take it for granted that, if there is an astronaut walking about the surface of the moon, we can watch him walk and hear whatever it is that he says. At least in the matter of having transmission to and from distant places, we have come a long way.

We had hired top-grade newsreel cameramen, soundmen and lightmen by late summer 1948. And we had developed a system to process 35mm news film in an astonishing eighteen minutes and get it onto a television projector in about thirty minutes. When, on election night in 1948, I made my calls on the jubilant headquarters of Douglas and Stevenson, one of the news crews would snap into action, ready to roll and record. The newspaper guys didn't try to mess with the newsreel crews; in the twenty years or so that they had been shooting film for the newsreels that played in movie houses across the nation, these guys had become as tough as cameramen come. And they were good at what they did.

When I checked into Stevenson's headquarters on election night, 1948, to do a short interview with him on his response to the astoundingly good showing he was making in the early vote count, it was disappointing to learn that Stevenson was not there; he had gone out, a couple of hours earlier, his press secretary told me, to have dinner. My God!—I thought—a guy is running uphill for governor, and he takes time out to go have dinner? So, I went down to the lobby of 7 South Dearborn to wait for him. My film crew followed. We were the only ones in the lobby.

The early returns had provided a solid clue that Stevenson and Douglas were on the verge of an unbelievable upset; even if this first indication did not hold up, I wanted a film bit of Adlai Stevenson's response to the possibility that he would beat Governor Green. The film crew was on its feet instantly, when Stevenson, his wife, Ellen Borden Stevenson, and two of his young sons came through the revolving door. The crew went into action as I hurried to talk to the candidate.

As the Stevensons got into the elevator, making small talk about what a nice meal they had had, my crew and I got in with them. Adlai was quite pleasant. Cheerfully, but with the manner of a man who felt an obligation to make conversation, Stevenson looked at me and said, "How is the count going in the race for governor? Do you have any word? Is it going well?"

I stared at him in disbelief. A man spends weeks of his life—months!—campaigning in a seemingly hopeless effort to get elected governor, and he doesn't know, two or three hours after the polls have closed, that he is doing incredibly well in the early tabulations? My God! What kind of politician is this? "You don't know," I said, "that Arvey is running up a big vote for you here in Chicago and that you are running well ahead of Governor Green in the early returns of the important counties downstate?"

"Really?" he replied. "Oh, that's splendid!" But the look in his eyes told me that he didn't believe me.

"How is Paul Douglas doing?" he asked me. Stevenson merely nodded when I told him that Douglas appeared to be leading Curly Brooks by about the same margin that Stevenson had built up over Green.

"This is quite astounding," Stevenson said, "What is your analysis of it?"

I shook my head. "I don't know," I replied. "Everyone was certain that you and Douglas didn't have a chance against those two Republicans, but the voters of Illinois apparently didn't get the word."

"Have you heard how Truman is doing?" Stevenson asked politely.

"I've been away from the newsroom for more than an hour," I replied, "and I don't know, actually, how any of you are holding up. But the last I heard about Truman was that he was trailing Dewey in a lot of states. The *Tribune* is on the street with a first-edition headline that says flat-out that Dewey has beaten Truman. I don't know what the *Trib* is basing this on; the *Trib* must have something to back up a headline like that, but I haven't seen anything else that says that Dewey has been elected."

"The public opinion polls all agreed that Tom Dewey would be elected president," Stevenson said. "That was so, wasn't it?"

"Yeah, that was so," I replied, "But you never know. All the polls here in Illinois had you and Douglas down as dead losers, and it doesn't seem to be working out that way."

"Poor Truman," Stevenson purred. "He was an unlikely man to become president. He has been a brash president, but he has served honorably, and it saddens me if he is fated to lose."

The elevator stopped at the Stevenson headquarters' floor. As the elevator doors opened, the crowd of Adlai's camp followers shouted joyfully and surged toward him. Stevenson looked at me and said, "Are you coming in?" I shook my head and said I had to be going. It was hard to be heard, I guess, with all of the shouting. But I stood in the opened door of the elevator and watched as the crowd engulfed Adlai, and then— having seen enough—I punched the button for the lobby floor.

It was a different kind of crowd that I had seen thirty minutes earlier at the Paul Douglas headquarters. At Stevenson's the men had all been wearing their suit jackets and holding cups of coffee. At the Douglas headquarters the scene was more raucous. The men were pared down to their shirt sleeves, with ties askew; even Paul Douglas was marching around his well-wishers without a jacket. The only one I remember who was wearing a jacket was a joyful young man named Sidney Yates, a personal friend of Paul Douglas. Yates didn't appear to quite believe that he had won election to Congress, and none of us had the slightest notion that he was destined to spend most of his life as a member of the House of Representatives. In his enthusiasm, Sid Yates pounded me on the shoulders and shouted, over and over, "We did it! Would you believe it? We did it!" Just about everyone in the place seemed to be holding a paper cup with bourbon and water in it.

Smiling broadly, a happy Paul Douglas made his way through the crowd toward me. He was waving his right arm in a gesture of triumph; his left arm, badly shot up by the Japanese during a U.S. Marine invasion of an island in the Pacific during World War II, hung limply at his side. I had interviewed Douglas several times during his campaign against Senator Brooks, and even though I had developed a personal admiration for this tough, gaunt man that Paddy Bauler called "de perfesser," I guess I had been negative in my broadcasts about his chances of getting elected. I had a hunch that he was going to stick it to me a little as he pushed his way toward me that victorious election night in November 1948. He did.

Putting his good arm around me and looking up to get attention from the crowd, he shouted good-humoredly, "I want you all to give applause to our friend here, who broadcast all those reports that the Democrats didn't have a chance of defeating Pete Green and Curly Brooks!" Everyone cheered; well, just about everyone cheered. A couple of fellows—Sid Yates being one of them—looked a little embarrassed. Yates came over to me, and, with Douglas holding his good arm around me and listening, Yates said, "Paul doesn't mean any offense, you know. We're all just carried away with the joy of victory." Douglas looked at me soberly and said, "I didn't intend any offense, old friend." I smiled at that and said that he hadn't offended me. "You *did* broadcast reports several times," Douglas went on, "in which it appeared to me that you were clearly stating that I could not win."

Once again carried away by the ecstasy of victory, Douglas exclaimed, "You didn't think I could win, did you?"

He seemed to be waiting for some kind of admission from me, so I looked at him and softly said, "Paul, nobody thought you could win." The newly elected U. S. Senator smiled and patted me on the shoulder. "Forgive me," he said. "You are completely honest and accurate about it; unfortunately, no one thought I was going to win."

Being dead wrong every once in a while sort of goes with the territory. As Harry Reutlinger once told me when I was moaning about having goofed up a story about the mayor or somebody, "You spend your time walking around the swamp to earn a living, you're bound to get bit in the ass by an alligator every once in a while."

12

EVERYBODY GOES WHEN THE WAGON COMES

I N THE YEARS I WANDERED AROUND THE CITY in the mobile unit—listening to the police radio, talking to the office on the mobile phone, explaining to my engineer that, if I were rich, I could find some kind of honorable work to do—I answered more calls that came in on the police radio than any cop in the city. I would automatically ask the engineer who was driving the unit to "go in on that" if the police radio screeched "robbery in progress," or "shots being fired," or "policeman needs help." Even when we were on our way to another assignment, a promising report on the police radio would divert us from our original intention; if we had started out to keep a date with somebody in City Hall or the Criminal Courts Building or with a movie star or a U.S. senator who had pearls of wisdom to toss at our microphone, my judgment was that this stuff could wait. It didn't have the immediacy of a policeman shooting it out with a stickup man.

We were headed south on the Outer Drive to keep a date with some big-name professor at the University of Chicago one morning—it was always someone like this that I scratched up to interview when things were dull—when the police radio informed us that a "man with a gun" was holding up a tavern on 47th Street. My engineer that day was Don Fitch, a highly capable technician who found great pleasure in being assigned to work with me. Fitch, noting the tavern was close by, asked if I wanted to go in on the robber with a gun. Well, why not?

Fitch was right on my heels, lugging his equipment, when I walked into the tavern. What I saw was not what I had expected. What I saw was a big, burly guy in work clothes and a knitted cap on his head. He was seated at the bar with a beer and a shot in front of him. There was no one else in sight; no other customers, no bartender, no policeman, no man with a gun—nobody. The man with the shot and the beer was built like a guy who could wrestle a bear. He took a glance at me in the back-bar mirror and went back to his drinks.

"Listen," I said to the guy, "the police radio reported, less than a minute ago, that this place was held up."

Looking down at his drinks, the man matter-of-factly replied, "Yeah."

"The holdup guy have a gun?"

"Yeah."

"Were any shots fired?"

"No."

"Why isn't there somebody behind the bar? Where is the bartender?"

The man turned and studied me. "Ya want a drink? Ya want a drink, I'll get it for ya. I ask dis kid what comes in and does da holdup, did he want a drink. He wants a beer and I go get it for him. I put da beer in front of him, and he comes out of his pocket wit' a gun and says he don't want no beer—all he wants is money."

"So what did you say?"

"I tells him dere ain't no money; only a couple a dollars. I tells him da fella what runs da place done gone off to da bank wit da money. I tells dis fella wit' da gun he can look in da register for hisself, he don't believe it about dere ain't no money. So he goes behind da bar and has a look and he grabs what's in dere and out da door he goes. Seems like he goes out and you comes in. Dat's all I know."

It wasn't much, to be sure. But Fitch had hastily set up the recorder, and when he handed me the mike I figured, oh, what the hell—why not? So I told the big burly guy I had to interview him. The man didn't seem to object, and we were well into the big fellow's account of his problem with the stickup man when a couple of squads of dicks came in, the first two with revolvers in hand. I didn't know them, but they seemed to know me and what I was doing, and they kept a respectful distance, listening as I wrapped up the piece with the guy at the bar.

Almost always when you are doing something like this, even when you are making a recording that you're pretty certain will never get on the air, you throw in a last question in hope of getting an interesting reply. So, to wind up this useless interview about the tavern stickup, I looked this big, burly guy straight in the eye and said, "When this fellow pulled the gun on you, were you scared?

The man looked at me as if I were stupid and replied, "Scared? It scared da shit outta me!"

The coppers who had been monitoring this interview cried out in protest and scolded the big, burly guy, telling him, "This is for radio! You can't use words like that on the radio!" Well, the man looked remorseful and mumbled some words I took to be an apology. "Don't worry about it," I said. "We can erase it as easily as we can record it." Then, by way of giving him a chance to feel better, I told him we would go over the last part again.

You try to invent some new questions when you have to repeat an interview; even a highly educated guy at the University of Chicago will get to think of himself as an actor who must remember his lines if you go over the same ground with him a second time. It protects the spontaneity if you change the questions. But I sort of liked the go-away line I had used the first time. So, once again, I gave the guy a straight-in-the-eye look and said:

"When this fellow pulled the gun on you, were you scared?"

The big guy looked at me as if I had led him into a trap. He glared at me defiantly. The coppers who were standing around us showed their anxiety as they waited for the man to answer my question.

The big guy's chest heaved. He shook his head in a show of great sadness and said: "Scared—dis guy puts a gun on me? It scared da shit outta me!"

The coppers groaned. Fitch, hearing this on his "cans"—the earpieces—looked as if this were the worst recording he had ever done. The big, burly guy was glancing around as if wondering what everyone seemed to be upset about. I shook the guy's hand and said, "You are all right, and I want to thank you for talking to me. You're what I'd call a great witness."

We didn't have many such problems in all of the years that I was out on the street, cutting tape and making film clips for NBC-Chicago. It happened every once in a while, though, that we got "sound" that would have offended the listeners or the viewers and we had to scrub it. The cuts made for great conversation among the newspeople and the engineers back at the Mart. The engineers saved the cuts and spliced them onto a reel, taking it out to play it when they wanted some laughs. I wasn't partial to having this reel of cuts kicking around; I was afraid it would accidentally get on the air one day, and then there would be hell to pay.

In the course of earning my living as a radio-TV street reporter, I got into quite a number of gun stories; it sort of goes with the territory I was working. You hear something about a shooting in progress, and you go; right now, you go. Getting there too quickly can get you closer to the gunfire than you have to be or should be, but if covering this sort of thing is part of your trade as a newsman, you sometimes do get too close to the shooting. It happened to me a couple of times and it deeply depressed me to see someone killed. Some of the coppers I knew used to tell me you get used to it after a while. But I had seen a great many young men die in World War II, and I'd have to say I never got used to it.

Dan Hozak, the engineer, and I went hightailing it out of the Mart one afternoon when we got a police radio flash that a cop had just been shot to death on the lower level of State and Wacker. Police squads poured in from all directions, and the North Loop area was a garden of screaming sirens and speeding squad cars when we drove out of the Mart. There were policemen all over Wacker Drive—some in uniform and a great many in soft clothes with stars pinned on their jackets. They were shouting and cursing at the traffic, waving their arms in some wild effort to direct the traffic. But none of the motorists could figure out what in hell these crazy policemen were ordering them to do. It was bedlam.

As Hozak stopped the mobile unit on the wrong side of the street, at the intersection of Wacker and Orleans—not knowing where in hell he was supposed to go—one of the policemen raced over to us and, calling me by name, shouted: "He went over the bridge! They've got him pinned down across the river— you've got to go over the bridge!"

Well, that would be the Lake Street bridge—more than a half-mile from where somebody was supposed to have killed a cop. It didn't figure that a guy who had shot a cop would be running around like this, going over the Lake Street bridge with a gun in his hand. I detected no signs of a police chase. But the guy who had done the shooting had to have fled some- where, so I told Hozak to go over the bridge. It is terribly frustrating to be this close to the scene of an important story and not know what in hell you are looking for or where in hell you should look.

The puzzle started to fit together when Hozak got our unit over the bridge. A half-dozen squad cars, a couple of them with doors open, were parked in haphazard fashion near the truck entrance of the freight section of the North Western Railroad station. There were two uniformed policemen at the truck entrance, and one of them hollered at us: "You can't go in there!" But the other cop, who recognized me, said, "He can if he wants to!" So Hozak gunned the mobile unit and in we went.

Nothing seemed to be moving. There were a great number of trailer-trucks in and near the freight dock, but the drivers had cleared out. Periodically we could hear shots fired from hand guns; not in the rat-a-tat-tat style that you see in the movies, but in the short bursts that are characteristic of combat. I jumped out of the unit and hurried into the bowels of the railroad station where the shooting seemed to be. Taking cover behind a thick cement pillar, I had a close-up view of the battleground. I waved to Hozak to bring in the recording equipment, and he picked up the two suitcaselike leather containers in which our stuff was packed and set up our recorder on a protected corner of the dock. Hozak plugged in the mike and gave me a sign that he was ready to go when I was. Someone unfamiliar with recording spot stories would say, I suppose, that it doesn't make sense to cut a news tape when you don't know what in hell it is that you are covering. But it isn't often that a radio or TV reporter gets within audible range of a shoot-out, and all I can say on that score is that you had better "make the sound" while you can—even if you don't know what all the shooting is about—because not even the friendliest cop you know is going to shoot the guy a second time just to please you.

I had done enough "one chance" recording, as a radio-TV reporter, to know that afternoon in the freight area of the railroad station that I had to record this shooting and the occasional frightened cries right now, even though I didn't know who was shooting at whom or why. So I got over to the spot where Hozak could hand me the mike, and I started talking. You don't have to worry about sounding dramatic when your mike is picking up the sound of guns being fired; the sound of the shots overriding your voice will be dramatic enough. All you have to be careful about is that you don't say something into the mike that will sound asinine when the shooting is over and you play back the tape to check on what it was you said and what the "quality" of your voice was when you made the recording; you don't want to go to all this trouble and end up scrubbing the tape because it sounds ridiculous.

Well, I would do a little bit of talking into the mike, race back to my observation point to check on how the gun battle was getting on, race back to the recorder to put something more on the tape, and run back to the spot where I could see what was going on. Taking pity on me for all this hustling back and forth, or possibly eager to get a look at what was going on, Hozak picked up the bulky recording equipment, put the mike into his jacket pocket, and came over to my observation point.

From what I could see, the quarry had dashed into a small office in a far corner of the loading dock floor to escape from the detectives who were pursuing him. The detectives who had taken cover at various places in front of the office, most of them sprawled out on the floor and all of them with service revolvers in hand, were cautioning each other to stay out of the line of fire. The guy in the office occasionally cracked open the door and fired a few shots. I gathered from what the detectives were stage-whispering to each other that there was no way the guy they were after could get out, except through the door. But it looked to me like a Mexican standoff. The guy in the office gave no sign that he would try to make a run for it, and the detectives showed no interest in "hitting the door"— going in to shoot it out with him.

Off to the side of the loading dock, a detective of slight build suddenly slipped into the area, his gun in hand. With the cunning of a smart rat, this detective—his attention fixed on the closed office door—cautiously worked his way in. The half-dozen detectives staked out within range of the office were transfixed by the sight of their colleague moving in to take charge. They stood at protected places, watching the dick move into the open space before the office door. If the guy who was hiding opened the door and fired, the detective would be shot to death. The tension was almost unbearable. Then, almost at the closed office door, the detective took four or five fast steps and leaped behind a large, wooden box ten or twelve feet in front of the office door.

"Hey!" he hollered, looking toward someone out of my line of sight, over in the area whence he had sneaked out, "Skid me the short one!"

Almost instantly, a sawed-off shotgun slid across the worn, wooden floor. The detective reached out for it and gave it a quick inspection. He stood up, pointed the barrel of the shotgun at the door, and called out: "Hey, you in the office! I don't know what your beef is, but I want you to throw out your gun and come out!"

Nothing happened. No one said a word. It was terrifying. Then, ever so slowly, the office door opened and a young man in blue jeans and a sport shirt—a pistol in his right hand—stood in the doorway and stared at the detective with a shotgun in his hands.

Keeping his eyes on the guy in the doorway, the detective, in as sweet a voice as you can imagine, said, "Throw it in. Throw it in or I'll kill you."

The response of the guy in the doorway was to squeeze off a shot of his pistol. The shot was off the mark and tore a line on top of the wooden crate alongside the detective. Instantly, the detective fired the shotgun, the double-o round pellets tearing into the fugitive's face. Blood bursting out of him, the man pitched forward and fell onto the floor like a sack of grain. The detective, the shotgun cradled in his arms, walked up to the bleeding body and passively inspected it. Then, with just a little bit of a sigh, but showing not a flicker of pleasure or remorse—there had been a job to do and he had done it, that's all—he turned away. A couple of the dicks who had been close enough to see the last scene of this big-city tragedy cried, "All clear! All clear!" The crisis had now passed, and the call was picked up and relayed all the way back to the coppers on duty outside the railroad freight building.

It was our practice, when we were working with audio recording, to "keep the pot open"—which meant that we would have wild sound that I could talk over, giving my piece both drama and authenticity. When we checked on the tape, playing it back while we were still set up on the freight dock, I was pleased that the mike had clearly picked up the cries of "All clear!" It was the only part of this adventure that pleased me.

I guess I will always be appalled by the sight of a human being getting "blown away," as the Bureau detectives say. It always bore down heavily upon me and gave me a feeling of guilt about the kind of work I was in, when my day was finished and I drove home to have dinner with my wife and children.

The shoot-out in the freight area of the North Western Railroad station had been especially painful, because the slightly built detective who killed the guy who shot the cop was a friend of mine—a great cop named Emil Smiklas, pronounced "smykils" who worked out of Robbery at the Bureau.

Hoodlums feared Smiklas, and a great many policemen feared him, too, because he had shot and killed six or seven dangerous characters at one time or another, and he was unjustly regarded as a cop eager to settle problems with his gun. I knew a few policemen who sought out the opportunity to blow somebody away, and I had seen infantry men in combat who seemed to enjoy killing. But Emil Smiklas wasn't like that. He was a soft-spoken, decent family man who didn't drink or gamble or chase girls in his off-duty hours.

When we had checked our tape and Hozak started packing our gear to move out, I walked over to Emil. The area was now filling up with officious-looking guys in uniform—the brass from Police Headquarters. A party of political people strode in, and two of them vomited when they spotted the body. Smiklas was standing off by himself, as if everyone were afraid to talk to him. Catching sight of me, Emil smiled and stepped toward me.

"By God," he said, "I should have known that on something like this you'd be here."

"Emil," I said, shaking his hand, "how are you?"

He shrugged. "I'm all right," he replied matter-of-factly. "I'd like to get out of here, but one of the chiefs said the mayor is on his way over and I have to stay. Can you imagine that—the mayor? Those goddamn politicians—they go anywhere to get their pictures in the paper."

"The whole city must be buzzing about this shooting," I said.

"Yeah, I suppose," Smiklas replied. "A guy shoots a cop and there's a big chase and now this windup. People seem to get interested in something like that. You want to see the body?"

I shook my head. I was close enough. We were standing only a few feet from the spot where the dead man lay, the serum of his blood already turning gelatinous.

In his soft voice, the trace of a wry smile on his lips, Emil said, "The son of a bitch wanted to kill me. I tried to give him a break; I took a chance and gave him time to throw the gun in. And what does this joker do for me? The son of a bitch takes a shot at me and wants to kill me. He didn't leave me any choice. Can you imagine that? You got a shotgun pointed at a guy and all he's got is a .32, and the crazy son of a bitch wants to shoot it out with you. Sometimes I just can't figure these guys out."

I told Smiklas I had to get moving, and he said OK, he would give me a call and let me buy him lunch some day. And, feeling drained, Hozak and I went back to the mobile unit and headed for the Merchandise Mart.

It had taken me a long time to cultivate the trust of any of the soft-clothes guys who worked out of the dreary South State Street building called "the Bureau." As a radio street reporter, and the only one around for a long while, I had been regarded as strictly an outsider by just about every detective in the place.

Bureau dicks had a special understanding with a couple of police reporters. The cop or his unit would get a nice mention in the reporter's newspaper, in return for inside information. But on the whole, the Bureau dicks were wary of reporters assigned to cover what was also called "the Building." The soft-clothes guys had been privately advised by newspaper reporters that it would not be "smart" to cut me in on anything, and in my early ventures into the Bureau, the dicks had clammed up or gotten evasive when I asked questions. It was a tough place for a radio reporter to get a story, the Detective Bureau.

The most fearful place for a reporter, print or radio, to get a story was the unit that we all referred to as "the fourth floor." This was the Homicide Unit, and the coppers there didn't like having outsiders come in or wander around in the unclean hallway outside. In their zeal to encourage a murder suspect to provide an admission of how it was that he had killed some-one—his wife or uncle or a bill collector from Commonwealth Edison—it was more or less standard practice to bend the sus-pect over a chair and whack him with a short piece of rubber hose. It effectively jogs the memory of a murder suspect, judg-ing from the remarkable record that Homicide had in clearing up murder cases. It also hurts like hell to have a guy flail away at you with his rubber hose—and it isn't any consolation that the hose doesn't leave bruises. On the not-infrequent occasions that the homicide dicks used their powers of persuasion on a suspect they were convinced had murdered somebody and only needed encouragement to admit it, it was standard practice to keep their place off limits. But the wild cries sounded through a good part of the building; there was no mystery about what was going on on the fourth floor when the dicks were "working on a confession." The homicide guys regretted all that hollering and cursing and screaming. The homicide guys, a bit self-conscious over the frightening racket that occurred when they "worked" on a suspect, would have preferred to carry on their business privately. But the shame of creating an uproar in the course of seeking a confession was simply a cross the homicide guys had to bear.

The most skillful interrogator of them all was a detective named Leon Sweitzer, who was referred to in a bittersweet way as "Whispers." Occasionally, a suspect led into Homicide was an Outfit guy—customarily picked up quietly by Sweitzer, who had negotiated the Outfit guy's surrender with Syndicate lawyers, under an agreement that the suspect would not be roughed up when they got him to the fourth floor.

Sweitzer was a well-dressed, handsome man who displayed no fear of any living thing. Sweitzer was born with the gift of laughter—or, more correctly, wry disdain—and a sense that the world is mad. We established over the years a high and trusting regard for each other. The blending of our chemistry was right, I guess. He never asked me for a favor or a nice mention in my reports, nor did he burden me with sad stories about the terrible work he was in. At times I did stories that impugned Homicide's virtue or cast a cloud on someone Sweitzer happened to admire in the world of policemen, politicians, or celebrities—though he admired few people. Sweitzer simply accepted this as something I had to do—or felt like doing. Even if I spilled a little dirt on Homicide that would reflect back on him, possibly embarrassing him, it didn't seem to alter the regard we had developed for each other. He was a very special guy, this Leon Sweitzer. Best cop that ever was.

I hardly expect that Mother Church will ever get around to canonizing him. He lived in a small apartment with his quite elderly widowed mother, who went off to Mass every morning and despaired of her son's disinterest in going to church, even for a wedding. Sweitzer was a stranger to sexual morality, having the appetites of a mink and the secretive methods of a mink in fulfilling them. He had two sisters who were BVM nuns of high postion in that order, and I suppose they prayed constantly for him, although I saw no sign that this had any effect on him. He believed in the institution of marriage. He believed in it so much that he got married five times. A man who didn't have much faith in anything, he entered into matrimony on *his* terms, and each bride-to-be had to assure him that she understood the terms: the marriage would last for precisely two years. On the second anniversary Leon Sweitzer packed his bags and got out. Explaining this unusual custom to me one time, Sweitzer said that marriage is supposed to be a contract, and he limited himself to a two-year term because he didn't think the relationship could get any better after that, and it might get worse.

Sweitzer got me into many stories that contributed a great deal to any reputation I got as a reporter who had insights into what was really going on. How could a reporter not get to know a lot about his city if he were constantly getting leads and inside information from a smart copper who had an accurate dossier on every politician and big criminal in the city? If he didn't lead me directly into a big news story, I could trust his background information and his assessment of a story I had turned up on my own. Over the course of many years, he told me a great deal about gangsters and the so-called respectable people whom Sweitzer knew to be in league with the Syndicate.

Breaking his personal rule of never revealing anything about himself, he quite casually told me the details of some incredible things he had been mixed up in. He quit the Police Department once, to go into the Prohibition speakeasy business with a Jewish guy named Lyon. They opened Chicago's most exclusive nightclub, The Little Club, on North State Street. Gentlemen were required to wear "white tie and tails" to Sweitzer's club. But he had to go back to being a policeman again when the federals clobbered the place and put a padlock on it.

I'd take him to lunch every once in a while. He liked to go to the Cape Cod Room of the Drake Hotel, unashamedly pushing the check at me when it was time to leave. I'd take him to dinner—he used to like a place called "Fritzel's," at State and Lake, which we thought was the best place in Chicago—but that was about all I ever got stuck with in trying to do a little something for Sweitzer. It wasn't that Sweitzer couldn't afford to pay the check. And it wasn't that he was an ungenerous man. He seemed to think it was good for my soul to pay the tab.

Many times I had seen him dig into his pocket to buy a warm meal for a suspect he had been hollering at. When the Little Sisters of the Poor made their periodic rounds of the police building, I had seen Sweitzer hand them "a half a hundred" or a "C note"—which is pretty good alms collecting, when a Little Sister is putting out her hand to a policeman. What I mean is that money didn't mean anything to Leon Sweitzer. His uncle, who had been county treasurer, had bequeathed $250,000 to Leon—this would be like leaving him a couple of million now—and Sweitzer had sailed off to Europe with a chorus girl, first class on the S. S. Berengaria, and spent it all on a grand holiday.

As a uniformed policemen assigned to a district, his sensibilities were offended when other coppers put the arm on errant motorists for a five or a ten, or shook down a saloon keeper for twenty or thirty to ignore the dispensing of drinks after the legal closing hour. Petty graft was distasteful to Sweitzer. But he cheerfully took the money when a mobster, a policy king, or a crime lawyer peeled off a thousand dollars or two thousand. When I asked Sweitzer one time how he rationalized the taking of a big payoff, when coppers who solicited small bribes infuriated him, Sweitzer said, "It makes you look cheap, if you're always on the make for a quick ten or twenty; the guy who has to hand it over doesn't think much of you for taking it. If you take a thousand or something like that from an Outfit guy or his lawyer, he thinks you're all right and that you have a little class. You run into the guy in a restaurant later, and chances are he'll send over some wine and holler, 'Salute!' A guy who drops a thousand and then sees you having a meal in a restaurant will stop at your table on his way out and smile at you and ask how everything is going. The guy in the restaurant that sends over the wine knows as well as you do that you didn't have anything on him when you were threatening to pull him in; the guy knows he was going to 'walk' as soon as you booked him. But he thinks you're nothing if you take a twenty dollar bill to give him a pass, when you could have had a thousand just for the asking."

Sweitzer always seemed to be walking around with a good deal of money in his pockets. I would imagine that over the years that I knew him he shook down the hoods and their lawyers for a considerable sum. But his practice was to distribute this cash generously among other dicks in Homicide. His regular beneficiaries were the guys who worked with him on what were called "the big murders." But he would quietly place large amounts of money in the hands of anyone in the unit that he discovered to be "short"—a Homicide guy with a sick kid or a wife having another baby or something like that; if Sweitzer learned that one of the men in the unit was really hurting, and he made it a point to know everything about everybody, he would instantly provide whatever help he could give—without a word. It was obvious to me, spending so many hours up there in Homicide, that the sizable amounts that Sweitzer was shaking down from the Syndicate guys and their lawyers were funding his largess. Everybody in the unit seemed to understand where the cash was coming from, but nobody ever asked any questions.

In the table of organization, Leon Sweitzer was just another name on the homicide personnel sheet. He was listed as nothing more than a detective, one step above patrolman. There were three sergeants in Homicide, and a Lieutenant named John Golden was in charge of the unit. But there wasn't a man in the place, including the commanding officer, who didn't understand that Sweitzer was running the show. When the crime lawyers had reason to telephone Homicide—to arrange for the surrender of a guy wanted for questioning—they would discuss the arrangements with Sweitzer and nobody else. A couple of the sergeants were displeased that such power had been vested in Sweitzer. The people "downtown," in the Police Commissioner's Office, were uncomfortable with the nonmilitary command of Homicide, where a detective was running the show. And Sweitzer's candor in ridiculing the big shots from downtown, or district commanders who impeded the investigation of a big murder by voicing ludicrous theories, didn't enhance his standing with the brass. The only superior who appeared to take no exception to Sweitzer's taking charge of things was Lieutenant Golden, who was getting credit for the remarkable record that Homicide was running up in solving its murders. "Old Whispers," Lieutenant Golden would say when someone up above would question his insistence on keeping Sweitzer in Homicide, "is in a class by himself." But even Golden began to wonder about that, I think, when Chicago's major policy king was assassinated near his home on South Michigan Avenue.

The men in Homicide were not surprised when the call came in that Teddy Roe had been hit. A gunman had stepped out from behind a billboard near Teddy's home and blasted him away with a shotgun. The Crime Syndicate had been moving in on the lucrative numbers racket, and the most knowledgeable guys in Homicide figured that Teddy's number had gone up, as their saying went, when they got information that Teddy Roe had said no when the Outfit tried to take over his highly profitable operation. The few Homicide guys who knew that Teddy was resisting the Syndicate had anticipated that the Syndicate would blow him away. Sweitzer figured it was simply a matter of days before Teddy Roe was executed. Sweitzer, who knew the policy king better than anyone else, told me: "They will hit him, but he doesn't care; Teddy is dying of cancer."

When Teddy got hit, the mayor and the police commissioner and I don't know who else were mortified once again by another nationally reported murder on a Chicago boulevard.

"There must be an end to this!" the mayor declared. The four major newspapers then printing in Chicago splashed a good deal of front-page ink around, venting their indignation. A South Side mortuary patched up the bullet-shattered body of Teddy Roe to make him presentable. Sweitzer put a squad car on watch outside the funeral parlor to see who showed up to mourn for Roe. A long line of poor black people lined up outside the mortuary and slowly walked up the steps to get a last look at the man who had fleeced them out of their nickels and dimes across the years. And the next morning, amid a good deal of extravagant preaching, Teddy Roe's casket was placed in a hearse, and a long cortege set off for the cemetery.

I had gone out near the church for a look at Teddy's farewell to this vale of tears. Then, with the casket in the hearse, we took off in the mobile unit to hunt up a story for our evening report. Covering funerals was not my game. I don't remember where we went for a story that day. What I remember is that it was getting close to the time of day when I should be getting back to the Mart to do the editing, put my script together, and get my show on the air when I got a call on the mobile phone. It was Sweitzer, and this surprised me because he hardly ever called me in the mobile unit. His voice didn't sound urgent. He sounded remarkably cheerful, and he said he was glad that he had found me, because he had something remarkable to show me that no other reporter knew about. He said it was very important that I get over to Homicide right away. I told him I couldn't go, that I was heading back to the Mart, and that I was getting a little tight on time. His response was that, while he couldn't tell me on the phone what it was that he wanted to show me, he didn't think there would be another chance like this, and he really wanted me to drop in for a couple of minutes. Checking my watch and deciding that, well, I could spare a few minutes, I told Sweitzer I was on my way.

Just inside the corridor at Homicide, in those days, were two benches side by side against a wall. Seated passively on these benches were six very well-dressed black guys, in black raw-silk suits, white shirts with expensive-looking ties, new shoes, and white silk socks with black clocks woven into them. Sweitzer stood proudly off to the side and, standing with feet apart as if he were about to throw a punch at somebody, waved an arm at the six black guys as if showing me his prize. Then he looked at me, as if awaiting words of congratulations.

I was aghast. I was shocked. "Lee," I exploded, "you arrested Teddy Roe's pallbearers!"

"No, no," Sweitzer replied sweetly. "These gentlemen are not under arrest. These gentlemen were associated with the late Mr. Teddy Roe in the policy wheel business. It is possible, you know," he went on, speaking openly as if the six unhappy-looking guys in the black silk suits couldn't understand English, "that some of these gentlemen have information about the business problems the late Teddy Roe had been having with the Outfit. It is possible that, if we refresh their memories, those who know something will be glad to cooperate. And this is what we have a Homicide Unit for—to solve murders."

The six guys on the benches gazed at Sweitzer venomously. I was stunned. Sweitzer grinned, turned, and walked into a private office. I followed him in, and he closed the door.

"I don't know what you're upset about," he said defensively, as he leaned back in a chair. "The mayor is hollering that we've got to do something about these big murders. The newspapers, those phony bastards, are screaming about blood on the streets. So who is going to complain about our trying to solve a big murder?"

Lieutenant Golden, who had slipped into the room and had taken a seat alongside me, nudged me in the ribs. "Don't make Whispers feel bad about his big pinch," he said, smiling wryly. "He's only tryin' to do his duty, you know."

Sweitzer whirled on his unit commander and demanded, "You're beefing because I picked up Teddy Roe's pallbearers?"

"Oh, I didn't mean to hurt your feelins, Sweitzer," the lieutenant replied. "It's only that it's a little unusual to arrest pallbearers before they even have a chance to place our friend Teddy in the grave."

"You're wrong, John," Sweitzer instantly replied. "I didn't break in on Teddy's burial. We laid off until they carried him to the grave. Why, hell, we let them get back into the limo and drive off. My God, they had to be half a mile out of the main gate—a quarter of a mile, anyway—before we closed in and curbed them."

"You didn't have to bring 'em all in," Lieutenant Golden argued. "One or two of 'em, maybe; that's about all you had to nail, if you were lookin' for somebody who might be able to tell us somethin'."

Sweitzer frowned. "Pick up just one or two of them, Lieutenant? That would be breaking my old tried-and-true rule. *Everybody* goes when the wagon comes. That's the only fair way to do it."

Golden stared at Sweitzer. "You think that's the way to do it, do you? Everybody goes on a sweep?"

"You bet your sweet ass, Lieutenant," Sweitzer replied. "That's the trouble with this world, John. There's a shortage of equalizers. Why should anybody get out of something, just because you don't happen to know who the 'wrong' guys are?"

Lieutenant Golden sighed. "I'm afraid, Lee," he said, softening his voice by way of pacifying his top cop, "I'm afraid we're gonna get some beefs about the pallbearers."

Sweitzer smiled. "I've already had one, John. Teddy Roe's wife called up and complained. I think you know that every once in a while Teddy would call me up because he wanted to make a little drop to me. You know, we had him in here that other time the Outfit tried to put a shot in him, and I let him go because we knew he wasn't the one who fired back and killed the hit man. You remember, it was that sergeant out in 'Five,' who used to ride alongside Teddy as bodyguard. You remember, the hit car pulls up alongside Teddy and the young punk takes a bead on Teddy with a .45 that he pokes through the open window, and the guy from 'Five,' with a .38 in his lap, squeezes one off and gets a lucky shot that burns a line across Teddy's new coat and right between the eyes of the Dago with the .45."

Lieutenant Golden nodded solemnly. "Yeah, Sweitzer, I remember all about it. Yeah, I remember. You were on the street with a couple of our guys, and you moved right in and all you found was Teddy Roe sittin' quietly at the wheel of his car, waitin' for somebody to show up and start askin' him questions, and the hit man with his head hangin' out the window. Yeah, sure, I remember all about it—but what in hell has it got to do with you gettin' a call from Teddy's wife?"

"Well," Sweitzer said. "I brought Teddy Roe in here that night, and I liked the guy, and I told him that I would try to help him out if he would level with me and tell me who it was on the seat alongside him who had put the shot into the hit man. So we go into an office, and Teddy tells me it was his heavy man, the copper out of 'Five,' who fired the lucky shot. Teddy tells me the guy from 'Five' says he has to get out of there, because it wouldn't do for a policeman to get caught mixed up in something like that. So Teddy says he tells the copper to clear out and that he will sit there and answer the questions. So a couple of minutes later, not being but a couple of blocks away, I pull up, and I bring Teddy in here. And when he levels with me about what happened, I give him a pass. Next morning, I have to take him out to the West Side, on account of the killing, and some young punk in the State's Attorney's Office is hollering that he's going to charge Teddy Roe with murder, and I say to this state's attorney, 'Are you out of your goddamned mind or something, wanting to hold him for murder when he didn't murder anybody?' And that was about all there was to it, the time when the Outfit sent a hit man to get Teddy Roe and didn't score."

"And that's when he started makin' drops to you?" asked Lieutenant Golden.

"Yeah," Sweitzer replied, "I guess he thought he owed me something, and he would give me a call. It was Teddy's wife who would give me the envelope. She has a beauty parlor—a front for something. But I would take a run out there, and she would hand me the envelope and tell me that she appreciated what I had done for Teddy. Then, this afternoon, she calls up and she is as mad as a son of a bitch about me picking up the pallbearers."

Golden looked momentarily anxious. "You think she's goin' Downtown with this beef?"

Sweitzer shook his head. "Naw," he said, "She doesn't trust

anybody downtown. She doesn't even trust *me*. She told me it was 'mean' to deny her dear departed husband a decent burial. She said, 'This is a dreadful thing for you to do, when you have been accepting our hospitality.' Honest to God, that's what she called the drops—'hospitality.' "

In all seriousness, Sweitzer looked at Golden and me and said, "They have a lot of unusual expressions, the colored— but either one of you ever hear anybody call it 'hospitality' when they put a couple of big ones in your pocket?"

Well, having kicked around for a while with Sweitzer, I never got comfortable with the open manner in which he talked about graft and fixes and other offshoots of police work that a reasonable policeman shouldn't be talking about in front of a reporter, but I got so I could tell when he was telling the truth and when he was saying something merely for the pleasure he got out of its shock value. I was certain, on that afternoon in a private office in Homicide, that he was telling Lieutenant Golden and me exactly what Mrs. Teddy Roe had told him on the telephone. To my last day, every time I hear the word *hospitality*, it will mean that somewhere there is an envelope with some big bills inside that Teddy Roe has put aside for a friend.

I asked Sweitzer one time about this reckless habit he had of discussing Police Department secrets when I was sitting there. Didn't he think it was terribly unwise to speak so casually of such intimate matters as who was making a drop and who was getting it? Sweitzer laughed and said, "It's part of your education. I'm the teacher, and you are my star pupil."

"Well, that's great," I replied, "but how do you know I won't put inside stuff like this on the air and destroy you?"

Sweitzer smiled. "I never put the brake on you. Not one time have I ever told you, 'Don't use this, don't mention that.' You want to put something I have told you in one of your broadcasts, you go right ahead. I will be the first one to congratulate you. But if you think back on some of the things I have told you that you were tempted to do a story on—well, I imagine that you put down the temptation because you realized that I had held out a little on you and you didn't have all the information you would need to do the story you were thinking of doing."

"I did a long piece on the air about you arresting Teddy Roe's pallbearers," I said.

Sweitzer laughed. "I really enjoyed hearing that one," he said. "The newspaper people assigned to the Building raised hell with me about that, wanting to know why I gave you the inside track. I had to tell them I didn't give you a tip on that; I told them you just happened to walk in when we had picked up the policy-wheel guys for questioning and nobody in Homicide could do anything about it once you had seen these colored gentlemen in silk suits. I said to that girl reporter from the *Tribune*, 'What did you want me to do—say these guys were Santa Claus and his helpers, who just happened to be sitting there waiting for a bus?' It caused some heat, you using the story about the pallbearers; one of the papers—the *Tribune*, I think—took a whack at us in an editorial. They said it was disgraceful that Homicide didn't have the decency to let Mr. Roe die in peace. But you had enough to go on then, and I wouldn't give you an argument over using that."

"You'd give me an argument if I used something else?" I asked.

Sweitzer frowned. "Like I say," he replied, "we've given you information about this and that, but we're not crazy. We're not loading up the gun and handing it to you so you can shoot us down. Anyhow, I'm not worried about you going to dirty us up. You dirty us up bad on something and we will take care of it by getting a dozen guys to deny it—to swear you don't know what you're talking about. Besides, you dirty us up and the next thing you know every unit in the Building has shut off the spigot and you'll die of thirst before you get a drop of information out of anybody."

CHAPTER **13**

STRANGE MATES
IN THE POLITICAL BED

SORT OF LIKE A GOOD-LOOKING DOLL who divorces the
man she really loves to "improve" herself by marrying
some guy who is rich or social or famous—even when
she doesn't think much of the new husband—it was with
some feeling of regret that I weaned myself away from Homicide and moved into politics. For a mere observer, politics is
sort of like the remark that Winston Churchill is supposed to
have made about sausage: the more you know about how it is
put together, the less appetizing it becomes.

In covering political campaigns, I have always been more
comfortable with the working stiffs of an organization than
with the so-called "legitimate" people who live in the best suburbs and the city's upper-crust neighborhoods and who get
involved in politics as a sort of lark. They act as if the campaign
of some snob who graduated from Princeton and wears Brooks
Brothers suits is a holy cause. The more civilized people who
get into politics preach this idea that the enormity of modern-
day problems demands the attention of the well-educated and
well-heeled who once shunned politics as a grubby business.

The working stiffs of a ward organization are not encumbered by the weighty thoughts that seem to bear down on the better element; the guy who is striving to "do good" in his precinct—never forgetting that his job on the garbage truck or in the sewer department depends upon how well he "carries"—has a somewhat different perspective from the North Shore stockbroker who grudgingly attends a political rally because he feels a civic obligation to "get involved."

Even when the working stiff and the well-to-do suburbanite have the same political affiliation, one guy invariably is ill at ease in the company of the other. There is a difference in their priorities. The broker is almost exclusively concerned with getting a "quality" candidate. The payroller who works a precinct for a benefactor like Charley Weber—one of the last of Chicago's saloonkeeper politicians—concentrates on getting a vote for Charley's candidate, with hardly a thought as to whether Charley's man is qualified for the job. When the Brooks Brothers crowd succeeds in nominating a candidate they approve of, a ward boss like Weber has to go with whomever the Organization put on the ticket. And except in a most unusual situation, the ward boss will do the best he can for anybody the Organization nominates.

Political theoreticians who delve into an analysis of the Democratic Machine of Chicago sometimes get misled, I think, by the sheer simplicity of it. There is nothing satanic about the Chicago Machine—not any more satanic than a lot of other things, really—and there is nothing mysterious about the consistency of the results it has produced. The basis of its success has always been the Machine's dedication to a policy of doing little favors for the people. If a humble householder is getting the runaround from City Hall, when he complains about a crew from the Department of Streets and Sanitation smashing up his curbing, a ward committeeman who learns of this will instantly raise hell with "somebody Downtown" and get the curb fixed. The widow who is struggling to make ends meet will get a food basket delivered from the ward office. When somebody is known to vote straight Democratic and is in desperate need of a job, an alderman with good connections "at The Hall" will make a serious effort to do something about it. If there is an election coming up, it is not by chance that the son of an alderman like Paddy Bauler will be found out on the sidewalk—putting a couple of half dollars in the palms of registered voters who are "down on their luck"; when he shakes hands with them he quietly remarks that he certainly hopes they remember to show up at their precinct polling place on election day. And so it goes. Is it all calculated to get ordinary folks to vote Democratic on election day? Of course it is. Who should these people vote for—the Republicans?

It was sort of a ritual with me, the afternoon prior to election day, to pay a social call on Alderman Charles H. Weber. Sitting there in his ward office, watching Charley, you could get quite an education on how a man like this gets ready to carry his ward. Charley had a trusted aide named Eddie Meyers, for example, who had the task of putting a little money in the hands of every precinct captain in Charley's ward. Eddie's regular employment, obtained by Alderman Weber, was to sort out a couple of hundred decent citizens who had been directed to show up for jury duty. It was a politically valuable job that Eddie had; he could get you out of jury duty, if he wanted to. But his election-time job in Weber's organization was to hand out the precinct captain's money.

Prior to election day, Eddie Meyers would walk into Charley Weber's office with a funereal look on his face and say: "Joe's out dere; he wants two hunnert."

The translation of this was that a precinct captain named Joe something-or-other had come in for the cash he needed to spread among his prospective voters—five to this one and ten to that one and maybe twenty to somebody with a goodly number of registered voters in his house. Charley Weber, without even bothering to look at Eddie Meyers, would matter-of-factly reply, "Give 'im four hundred." And, with not even a nod of assent, Eddie would go out to give Joe four hundred.

Sometimes the precinct captain would ask for a hundred and fifty—and Charley would tell Eddie to hand over three. If Eddie said the guy outside was asking for three hundred, Charley would automatically order Eddie to give him six. Charley explained to me, "It's the only way there is to give ya a chance to get the job done."

"I don't get it," I said. "Eddie says a guy needs two and you tell Eddie to give him four—the guy needs three and you tell Eddie to give him six."

"It's the only way there is to make sure the guy gets his vote in," Charley explained, spreading his hands in a gesture of helplessness. "The guy asks for two and he knows that's what he needs—a ten spot here and a twenty somewheres else. *We* know that's what he needs; from past experience, we know. But ya give a guy two and ya know he's gonna snitch and put the first hundred in his pocket and have only a hundred left to drop a little here and there to people in his precinct. So, he wants two, I tell Eddie to give 'im four; that way, he puts two hundred in his pocket and he's got two hundred left that he needs to work his precinct."

It was standard procedure in Charley Weber's ward in the 1950s for the precinct captains to show up in the ward organization room at the back of his German restaurant-saloon a day or two before election day to give Charley an accurate report on what his "count" would be when the ballots ultimately were cast and tabulated. Each precinct's estimate was written in white chalk on what they called "the board." The board was a large blackboard on which the hundred or so precincts were listed, along with the exact number of registered voters in the precinct and the precinct captain's report of what his vote count would be on election day. It was obligatory for a ward boss like Weber to notify "Downtown" what the election night vote count would be, so the Machine bosses knew in advance where the Democratic ticket was having trouble and where it might be advisable to send in some reinforcements of Machine people to work on reluctant voters.

A Chicago ward boss who knows his business will do extraordinary things to get a vote. The way they figure it, every vote cast against you translates into *two* votes—one to equalize the vote that goes against you and the second to put you "a vote up." Even when a registered voter makes it clear he would rather be dead than vote Democratic, the Organization never

lets up in its effort to convert this voter to the true faith. I was
in Charley's office one afternoon, for example, when he picked
up a phone to take a complaint from a woman well known as
a die-hard Republican. Graciously, and with a great show of
humility, Weber was the soul of sympathy and regret. After
this woman had finished pounding her indignation into his ear,
Weber promised that he, Alderman Weber, would personally
resolve her problem.

When he hung up the phone Charley looked at me with
sadness and said, "That woman's lived in the ward for more
than twenty years and she's Republican. It ain't so bad she
votes against us every time—she is always blabbin' that the
Democrats are crooks and should be arrested or somethin' like
that. Now she's got a dead rat in the alley, behind her house—
and she don't call no Republican to come over and take care
of her dead rat; she calls the Alderman."

"So what are you going to do, Charley?"

"What can I do?" he replied. "I got to go over there, like I
said, and pick up her rat and find a good garbage can with a
top on it and, well, take care of it."

"With one phone call," I said, "you could get somebody to
do this."

Charley Weber looked at me in amazement. "You crazy?"
he said. "It's a good chance, dealin' with the rat. This woman'll
be peekin' out the kitchen window and see the alderman drive
up in his Cadillac and get out and pick up her dead rat and
drive away with it. She'll tell everybody. Come election day,
maybe my takin' the rat will learn her to keep her mouth shut
about us and maybe even give us a vote for a change. It's a
good chance to win 'er over, this old bitch." And out he went
to do what his political instincts told him he had to do.

In the post-World War II period of my life, I lived in an
apartment complex on North Sedgwick Street, in an area that
came to be known as Old Town. Gus Talbott of the *American*
lived there, also, and we used to walk up to Alderman Mathias
P. Bauler's North Avenue saloon every once in a while to have
a couple of drinks and observe the crazies who were Paddy's
precinct captains. There is an old saying that nothing of much

good ever comes out of a saloon, and I guess there is a little truth in that. Sipping on the bourbon and water one night, Gus came up with the attractive idea that we should collaborate in the writing of a play.

Gus Talbott displayed a nice touch for writing dramatic stuff while we were trying to put our three-act play together. We had no disputes over what should be retained in the manuscript and what should be cut, and we were in accord on the method to be followed in developing our dominating theme. It was our intention to portray the depths of Machine politics in a city like Chicago.

Our story line centered on the struggle of a comely, cleaner-than-snow young woman pursuing election as "Miss Sanitation of Chicago." Our heroine was to be the loving daughter of a big German who ran a saloon and a bookie joint on North Orleans Street. Our virtuous young lady was to be sort of a Joan of Arc of the city garbage collectors, and the dramatic crisis of our play would center on the crass refusal of the Democratic Machine to accept the garbage men's candidate for Miss Sanitation. Even yet, it seems to me that Gus Talbott and I had the essential ingredients for a true-to-life Chicago play, and, while we had no dreams of getting up there with Moliere or Eugene O'Neill, it is too bad that Gus and I didn't stick with it and finish it up.

I still remember how Gus and I planned to bring down the third-act curtain; my memory is that in the final scene, our girl—who had been tossing down drinks in her old man's saloon, along with everybody else—announced that she had run off with one of the garbage men and gotten married and was going to have a baby that she hoped would vote straight Republican. Her old man, infuriated, would then take a punch at the bridegroom and all hell would break loose. Then a guy who looked like Paddy Bauler would walk onstage and holler curses at everybody in the place, taking a poke at some of the guys who wanted to quiet him down. In our play, the Paddy Bauler character would holler at the pregnant bride to stop sobbing. He would pat our heroine on her bottom and console her saying, "It don't mean nothin', kid, not gettin' elected Miss

Sanitation. 'Dere ain't no money in it. Alls you get outta it is maybe your picture in de paper and people in de grocery store pointin' at ya. Ya stick wit' me and forget about dem Republicans and I'll get you made a schoolteacher or somethin' like dat where dere's a little somethin' in it for ya.'' Our heroine, wiping her eyes and smiling now, would race to the alderman's side and embrace him. Grinning, our Bauler character would shout, "Now dat's more like it! Let's ever' body go t' de bar and have some drinks. And don't let nobody ferget: Losin' ain't nothin' t' cry about. It don't mean nothin'—losin' an election. It only counts for somethin' when your guy who gets beat is runnin' for mayor or pope or somethin' like that." According to the way in which Gus Talbott and I had blocked out our play, everybody onstage would cheer when the Bauler character finished his speech about the mayor and the pope, and that would bring on the final curtain.

If you put me under oath, I couldn't tell you why it was that Gus Talbott and I lost our interest in trying to write a wonderful play for what is quaintly referred to as the "legitimate theater." We drank a little bit more than we wrote, I guess, as we gathered in the after-dinner hours to sit around in his place or mine blocking out the three acts of our drama. We actually went to the trouble of writing the first act. We spent so much time at Paddy Bauler's place on North Avenue—soaking up atmosphere for our play and getting a little soaked ourselves—that Paddy, who had an aversion to newsmen, started acting civil toward us and even gave us one on the house every now and then.

One night, in Paddy Bauler's place on North Avenue—when Gus and I were doing some pleasurable research for our play— I persuaded Paddy to recount the details of the great tragedy that had been visited upon his pal, Mayor Cermak. Tony Cermak had been shot in 1933 by an assassin in a waterfront political rally for President-elect Roosevelt. It was always a matter of some fascination to me that—to his dying day—Alderman Mathias P. Bauler blamed himself for getting his pal, Tony Cermak, shot and all that followed thereafter in the politics of sweet Chicago.

As Paddy told Gus Talbott: "I had dis here place in Florida, an' I was down dere mindin' my own business when who pops up but Tony Cermak. Well, it's in all de papers dat Roos'velt's in town on a little vacation an' dat he is havin' a meetin' wit' all de people at de lakefront park. So I figure dat Cermak's come down to say hello or somethin' t' dis new pres'dent. An' it surprises me when Cermak says no, he ain't goin' t' no meetin' wit' Roos'velt. Cermak never had much t' say 'bout Roos'velt—'cept for a lotta dirty words dat he calls 'im, as fellas do when dey don't like somebody. So, I says t' myself dat dis is one hell of a t'ing—de mayor of an important city like Chicaga not goin' over t' say hello t' de new pres'dent. Dese are hard times dat I'm talkin' 'bout an' de mayor of a big city, wit' not enough money t' run t'ings—he had better be nice t' somebody who maybe can help 'im out. A pres'dent can't help ya outta a jam in hard times, ya ain't findin' nobody else what can give ya de dough-re-mi. I try tellin' Cermak, but he won't listen.

"All Cermak says, when I try t' tell 'im it's important t' make up wit' dis Roos'velt an', whatever de trouble is, t' let bygones be bygones, all Cermak says is, 'Oh screw 'im; he ain't our kind, Roos'velt. I ain't doin' no business wit' 'im. So I got hot 'bout it. So I puts de eye on Cermak, down dere in my place at Florida, an' I lays it right on de table wit' 'im.'"

Gus Talbott looked at Paddy and said, "You put what on the table with Cermak, Alderman?"

Bauler shot a look of disbelief at Gus—as if to say, "My God, ain't you listenin'?" And then, directing himself to Gus, Paddy said: "I says t' 'im, 'aw right, ya don't want nothin' t' do wit' 'im, dis Roos'velt. I ain't sayin' ya gotta marry 'im. What I'm sayin' is dat, like 'im or not, dis Roos'velt's de dog wit' de big nuts an', ya wanna keep Chicaga runnin', ya better make up wit' 'im.' "

Gus Talbott said, "You told Cermak he had to make peace with Roosevelt? You told the mayor of Chicago to work things out with a president?"

"Ya bet your sweet ass I told 'im," Paddy replied.

"You were only alderman of the 43rd Ward and you told

the mayor of Chicago he had to deal with Roosevelt?" asked Gus.

Paddy Bauler nodded. "Listen," he said, "we went back a long way wit' Tony Cermak, Charley Weber 'n' me; we went t' Europe wit' 'im a few times—Germany, Bohemia, and places like dat. In style, we went—on de best boats, in de first class, an' we always had de best dat money could buy. When Tony Cermak gets inta de fight wit' Brennan and de Irish crowd for control o' de Organization, Charley and me stood wit' 'im. He decides t' run for mayor, Charley 'n' me got 'im de big vote he needed t' beat Big Bill. We was real pals, me, Charley Weber, 'n Cermak. We was wit' 'im all de way, me 'n' Weber. So now he's de mayor 'n' Chicaga's in trouble, ya tink I shouldn't tell 'im he's makin' a mistake, not makin' up wit' Roos'velt—who can help 'im outta his trouble? You ask Charley Weber, you t'ink I'm lyin' to ya; Weber wasn't dere, in Florida, but he knows—on account dat is how it was. Weber will tell ya, on account I called 'im on de telephone right after I got de word."

"What word?" asked Gus.

"When Cermak got shot," Paddy replied. "I told Charley Weber on de telephone, it was my own goddamn fault—our pal gettin' shot. Ya ask Weber; he'll tell ya."

Gus Talbott took a sip of his drink. Then, looking at Alderman Bauler, he said, "You blame yourself for Cermak's getting shot?"

Glumly, Paddy bobbed his head. "Listen," he said, "my pal ain't goin' over dere till I tells 'im dere ain't no cash in de kitty t' pay schoolteachers. I tell 'im, on account o' dese hard times, dey are payin' off de teachers wit'—whadyacallit?—scrip is what dey call it. Dey are payin' off teachers wit' IOU'S. I'm runnin' my place an' dese teachers come in, askin' will I cash scrip. Like hell, I'll cash scrip; give 'em sixty cents on de dollar maybe, is de teacher a reg'lar customer what comes in for a few drinks or somethin'—everybody wit' a place in dese days havin' t' operate wit' one eye on de front door, on account dis is during Prohibition. But, like I tries t' tell Cermak, ya gotta pay dem teachers or ya ain't gonna have no schools open. Ya load up some woman wit' all her kids, on account dere's no school for dem t' go to, dere ain't no better way t' lose a vote. I tell Cermak, 'Ya do what ya want, but if I was ya I'd hustle over dere to dis Roos'velt an' tell 'im what bad shape we're in and genuflect or kiss his ass or whatever ya gotta do t' get 'im on your side—whatever ya gotta do wit' a pres'dent. However ya gotta do it, talk 'im outta some goddamn money." Paddy Bauler shook his head in sad remembrance.

"How was I supposed t' know some crazy son of a bitch would put a shot in 'im? I was t' blame for it; so wit' Cermak outta de way, back in comes Pat Nash an' Ed Kelly an' Kelly's de new mayor. An' wit' de Outfit guys gettin' shot up all de time an' de high-class crowd hollerin' 'bout gamblin' an' a wide-open town an' all o' dat, Kelly gets pushed out an' now it's Jake Arvey runnin' everthin' an' who does Arvey give us for mayor? Fartin' Martin Kennelly, dat's who. An' what're we gettin' for senator an' governor? Dis guy Paul Douglas an' dat other one—Stevenson, who don't even live in Chicaga because Chicaga ain't ritzy 'nough for 'im. It ain't like de old days, when we had reg'lar fellas runnin' for de big jobs."

The "nonregular" who so offended Paddy Bauler, Senator Paul H. Douglas, was too much a man of principle ever to attain the heights of influence that ought to have come with seniority in the august body in which he served; he was woefully incapable of compromise, which appears to be an essential in acquiring power in the U. S. Senate. Getting a little something for yourself is more or less the standard benefit of devoting one's time and energies to politics. Douglas was a rare political bird. He was as dollar-honest a politician as I have ever come upon—and, ironically, was handicapped in his efforts to get things accomplished because of it. Holding membership in the U. S. Senate is no small thing. But, like the pigs in George Orwell's *Animal Farm*, some senators are "more equal" than others. The utterly honest Douglas, in his third term in the Senate, was visibly offended when Robert Kennedy's first act as U.S. Attorney General was to indict two of Paul's friends from Gary, Indiana—Mayor George Chacharis and Lake County Prosecutor Metro Holavochka—for federal income tax fraud.

Paul's friends wound up in federal prison in Milan, Michigan. Indignantly, the senator told me one day, "George said that Bobby got a line on them in the early days of Jack Kennedy's campaign for president, when he and Metro gave Bobby an envelope containing a contribution to Jack's campaign, which was then very hard-pressed for money." Senator Douglas went on to relate that Bobby had thanked them warmly for the contribution, and Chacharis and Holavochka said they were delighted to help out a little. The next thing they knew, the Gary, Indiana, contributors were the first two guys indicted by the Kennedy Administration. When I asked Senator Douglas if he knew what had been in the envelope given to Bobby, Douglas said, "Chacharis told me it was cash. And Chacharis told me he thought this was a dirty thing for Bobby to do; to take their money and then indict them for having had it." Did Douglas know how much money was in the envelope? "I couldn't swear to it," the senator replied, "but Chacharis told me it was fifty thousand dollars, and my judgment would be that he was telling me the truth, because he and Holavochka were honorable fellows about things like that."

I don't believe I ever met a more honorable man in politics than Paul Douglas. Not even his bitterest political enemies dared impugn Paul's integrity. Douglas proudly proclaimed his allegiance to the Democratic party, holding it to be the protector of the common man. But the fact is that his fellow Democrats often found his fierce and forgiving loyalty to his friends to be naive and somewhat trying.

I had had some polite difficulty with the "ritzy" Stevenson during the 1948 campaign; he was one of those notables who likes to have the situation spelled out for him before he's interviewed. Early in the campaign, I had walked into his headquarters to interview him on film for NBC-New York. He had known I was coming over, but he surprised me when he emerged from behind the closed door of a room I took to be his private office and politely inquired what I intended to ask him. I can't recall another occasion when someone asked me in advance to specify what my questions would be. I found Stevenson's insistence upon this unacceptable. I didn't want to blow the in-

terview—but I gave my crew a sign to stop setting up until I
worked this thing out.

Seated at a little table, a sort of reception table with a telephone on it, and impassively taking everything in, was a fellow
I had gone to school with—an outgoing man named Mike Howlett. Even as a student at St. Mel's on the West Side, the gregarious Howlett had a consuming interest in politics. I had lost
track of him, though I knew that Jake Arvey had taken a liking
to him. The last I had heard about Mike was that he was office
manager of the Chicago Park District. Mike certainly was not
Adlai Stevenson's type, and it mystified me to find Howlett at
a desk in Stevenson's headquarters. But I hadn't had a chance
to ask Mike about it; the candidate for governor had emerged
from his private office before we could get into the question
of what in hell Mike Howlett was doing there.

I got into negotiations with Stevenson about this interview.
I didn't budge from my position that it simply was not possible
to lay out my questions for his approval in advance. Even if
you want to, you can only tell someone what your opening
question will be; you can't specify what you're going to ask
next until you hear the response to the first question. With
Mike Howlett sitting there with a faint look of amusement on
his face, we worked out a vague understanding on the general
topics I expected to explore. And the next thing I knew, Stevenson scurried back into his private office and closed the door
behind him.

I looked at Howlett and said, "What the hell is he walking
out on me for?"

"He's working out the answers to your questions," Howlett
said.

"How can he do that when he hasn't heard the questions?"

Mike shrugged. "Let me tell you," he said, "this is a new
kind of politician, this Stevenson. It doesn't matter what you
ask him—he'll be ready with his answers. I know it sounds crazy,
but he's a bright guy and he'll work it out some way to make
himself look good."

There were a few things I had in mind to ask Stevenson:
How does a socialite like Stevenson fit in to the Democratic

Machine of Chicago? What kind of accommodation does a cultivated fellow like Stevenson make with earthy "regular" Democrats like Paddy Bauler? Is there really a place for a top-drawer man like Stevenson in the grubby business of politics? Stevenson was a little startled, I guess, to get questions that had no pertinence to the handwritten answers he had hastily prepared, but it didn't disturb him that my questions didn't seem to lead into the replies he had prepared himself to give me. He was glib and articulate in his spontaneous answers and—when I closed off the interview—he appeared to be pleased with himself.

Apparently, I had been squeezed into a busy schedule. The camera crew and engineer had hardly started breaking down their equipment when Stevenson, pulling on a topcoat, dashed out to keep what he said was an important appointment. I walked over to talk to Howlett.

"I'm sort of surprised to find you here, Mike," I said.

He smiled and said, "Arvey sent me over here."

"What's your job?"

"If you want the truth—and you're not going to quote me," Mike replied, "Arvey told me not to let our candidate for governor pick up any checks."

"What?"

"Our man, Adlai Stevenson, is very careful with his money. Campaigning downstate, they stop into a place for a cup of coffee or a piece of pie—all of the newspaper guys, a half-dozen of 'em or so, follow him in, naturally, and sit down at the counter with Stevenson to have a sandwich and a cup of coffee. Then, when the girl comes with the checks—Arvey tells me—Stevenson takes his own check, leaves a dime on the counter, and walks out. It's bad enough a fellow looking for votes leaves a dime for the waitress. But here is the Democratic Party candidate for governor making the reporters who are covering his campaign pay for their own coffee. Arvey hears about it, raises hell, and sends me over here to travel with Adlai. The order he gives me is, 'Don't let him pick up any checks.' He is an unusual guy, this Stevenson."

Stevenson, having been fed to the sharks as a presidential

candidate in 1952, surprised a lot of us when he was willing—
if not eager—to try it again in 1956 and even held out hope
for nomination in 1960. Professional Democrats—the veteran
party bosses, the old pros—more or less regarded Stevenson as
a country bumpkin who had been trimmed out of his pocket
money on the midway of the county fair and had some stupid
daydream that he would have better luck the next time he
went up against the carnival man's wheel.

I came to know Richard J. Daley pretty well when he was
Governor Stevenson's State Revenue Director. Daley was a
Chicago Machine Democrat, but Adlai Stevenson was fond of
his hardworking, capable aide. Built on the plump side and
always neatly dressed, Daley was self-effacing to the point of
looking shy. He appeared always to be striving to make a good
impression, especially when he was dealing with people he regarded as having status in society or business or—in the early
days of his rise to power—the media.

Early in his reign as mayor, Daley strove to be recognized
as a smart, honorable, highly capable mayor, but the so-called
"better element"—the fashionable people of Chicago, the "Gold
Coasters"—regarded Daley disdainfully as a boorish, Back of
the Yards Democratic politician whose election as mayor had
been a humiliation to the city. The business and industry crowd
made guarded efforts to patch things up with this jowly, clumsy-
speaking fellow who had cunningly maneuvered himself into
political control of the city. But the upper-crust folks found it
painful to work things out with Daley. And his Bridgeport
neighborhood tradition of putting up one's dukes in response
to criticism made him difficult to get along with.

Three years into Daley's first term as mayor, John S. Knight,
the owner and publisher of the *Chicago Daily News*, made a
gesture of peace toward Daley: Knight went off with Daley,
media guys, big wheelers and dealers of Chicago's business
community, and a few other Chicago notables to do some civic
bragging before their counterparts in then-prospering Detroit.
Everything went beautifully—until the big shots of the two cities gathered in an exclusive Detroit club for a lavish spread.
After a grand luncheon, with good wines, there was an ex-

change of complimentary speaches. Being a prestigious Chicago resident, John Knight had agreed to make the formal introduction of Mayor Daley. And it was this introductory speech, alas, that touched off the fireworks.

A public speaker of considerable experience, Publisher Knight gently conceded that the "leading" newspapers of Chicago—his *Daily News* included; the rival Hearst paper, the *Evening American*, excluded—had strongly opposed mayoral candidate Daley. "We had grave doubts," Knight said, "that Richard J. Daley could provide Chicago with the 'dynamic leadership' that he promised in his campaign against Mayor Martin H. Kennelly. We doubted his abilities. We doubted the city would be served if Daley defeated Kennelly." Most of the Chicago delegation grinned, because Knight was telling the story straight. Daley sat glumly, looking out into space, in the manner of a man who doesn't want to hear any more of this. Daley scowled—even as John Knight slid into a graceful transition, praising the early accomplishments of Mayor Daley, and parenthetically confessing that the important elements of Chicago had seriously underestimated the administrative skill of Dick Daley. Knight praised Daley for the commercial rebirth the city was experiencing with Daley as mayor, and Knight graciously introduced the guest of honor.

Still scowling, Daley bounced to his feet. He jumped out of his chair at the speakers' table with the swagger of a prizefighter determined to throw a few hard punches of his own. The luncheon guests could sense that something had gone awry. Daley sneered at John Knight, Daley's voice took on the ominous tough-guy intonations that can only be described as "pure Bridgeport," and Chicago's mayor said:

"It's easy to criticize. Anybody can criticize. But, lemme tell ya—in Detroit or any other place—we don't have to take any back seat to anyone. You want us to apologize for somethin'? Why don't you tell us what these things are, on your mind. There is somethin' we are supposed to be ashamed of? God knows we're not perfect in Chicago. Nobody says we're perfect. Everybody makes mistakes. Nobody is perfect. But it's a great city, Chicago. Chicago, it's the greatest city—and don't say I'm tryin' to take anything away from Detroit and the other places where the mayor is tryin' to do a good job. Anybody can criticize, and it don't bother us, from Chicago. We're proud of the record of doin' what we are doin' and no other city can say that—not even here in Detroit."

A pall settled over the intercity luncheon as Daley spoke. A few of Mayor Daley's pals, who had come along on this trip, were painstakingly nodding toward the mayor in agreement. Some of the other guests looked as if they couldn't believe what Daley was saying, the harshness of his voice adding belligerent emphasis to his words. As if oblivious to the effect his little talk was having on the guests at this exclusive little gathering, Mayor Daley turned to John S. Knight and, wagging a finger at him, said:

"You were against us, when it was Kennelly we were runnin' against. Now you are comin' around, to make up. Well, that's fine. You give fair credit for what we are doin' with the great city of Chicago, the transportation and the new buildin' and the plans for the expressways and everything else; we don't hold any grudges. You stand with us and the newspaper is not attackin' us, when we are accomplishin' everything; we will let you endorse me when I run for my second term. We are a great city, Chicago. We don't hold any grudges." And then, with the publisher of the *Chicago Daily News* gazing at him in disbelief, Daley sat down.

I don't recall that any of this was ever printed in the Chicago papers. They all had people there, and they all heard Daley's extraordinary speech. All of the newspapers ran a front-page report of the visit to Detroit. But not even the *Chicago Daily News* carried the fascinating details of Daley's little speech. That's one of the beefs I have always had about newspapers; when they run an interesting story, they often don't print the best parts. But I must admit that at this mark in time—in the late 1950s, when radio and television news reporting was merely crawling along, not yet having the skill or courage to stand up and take a position on controversial matters—I glossed over the matter of Daley's display of temper in my radio report of the visit to Detroit.

I suppose that Daley thought I would report his outburst and stand behind him, taking his side. Prior to the Democrats' crude treatment in dumping Martin Kennelly, slating Daley as the party candidate and forcing Kennelly into a primary fight, I had been pretty partial to Daley. I don't suppose, thinking back on it, that Daley ever trusted anyone in the news business; he got along quite well with a few of us who happened to like him, personally, but I don't think his friendly relationship with any of us in the news business was deeply rooted. Prior to his having put the skids under Jake Arvey and having taken over control of the Chicago Democrats—his springboard to take over as mayor—I had more or less enjoyed interviewing him and being in his company.

I had been at Comiskey Park with Daley a couple of times. I was invited, in his early days as mayor, on a rather frequent basis—but I would beg off because Comiskey Park was far distant from where I lived, I wasn't all that enthralled by the Chicago White Sox, and I discovered that it was futile to think of having a conversation with a man who was absorbed in every pitch, every swing of the bat, and all of that. Besides, you are rather conspicuously "wit' da mare," as the Back of the Yards people say, when you are sitting with him in his box along the third base line, and I didn't think this was a prudent place for me to be. Have a cup of coffee or something with the mayor at a political convention or some such thing as that? Oh, sure—and glad to be with him. Being his frequent guest at the baseball game? Well, maybe I exaggerated the possibility of "compromise" in something like that—but begging off this kind of invitation was more or less how I thought I should play my game.

Early in his administration, I became impressed with Daley's consummate skill in running city government. For openers—and it always surprised me that hardly anyone in Chicago took note of this—Daley had retained virtually all of the people that Kennelly had selected to run his budget, his Police Department, the city's multimillion-dollar water system, and other key jobs in city government. Daley's response to me when I asked him about this—telling him I had expected he would dump all the Kennelly guys and replace them with his own pals—was that Kennelly had been a smart businessman who had selected the best people he could find. "If I don't catch them double-crossin' me, why should I change?"

Even though I thought that Martin Kennelly had been given what Chicago people call "a raw deal," I wanted Daley to be recognized by the look-down-their-nose set as a good, decent mayor. Several times, when I was about to interview him about election matters of one kind or another, I tried to caution him that the word "precinct" is not pronounced "pree-sint." Daley always looked surprised and giggled when I said this; I suppose that if you have heard ward organization people say "preesint" all of your life, it is amusing to hear somebody trying to pronounce the familiar word in some other way.

When Daley became mayor, I interviewed him at Midway Airport—"Busiest airport in the world," everybody said—when it was opening up to international flights; Mayor Daley went out there to dedicate a new U.S. Customs office that the Kennelly Administration had negotiated. Not wanting to do a short civic-duty piece like this twice, I cautioned Daley—in advance of the interview—that it would be well to remember that there were a number of big cities in the world that were well into the business of handling overseas traffic and that it wouldn't sound too good if Chicago, late into this new game, did too much bragging. He thanked me for the reminder and was careful not to say anything foolish during the interview. Rather graciously, he said something about Chicago's being pleased to have airport facilities available for travelers from distant lands. He looked at me for approval of this, and I nodded. But then he said, his voice taking on the Bridgeport flavoring, "And the openin' of this here facility of the U.S. Customs is proof that Chicago is tryin' to be the most hospitial city in the world." I lowered the mike and shook my head.

"What's the matter?" Daley said, surprised that I was cutting him off.

"There is no such word," I replied.

Daley looked at me perplexed. "No such word as what?"

"No such word as *hospitial*. You just said that Chicago is the most 'hospitial' city in the world—and there is no such word."

Daley looked at me with astonishment. He said, "Isn't there?"

In the course of his years as mayor of Chicago, Daley had dealings with kings and queens who popped in for a visit. I have no idea what manner of verbal invention he dropped on any of these regal people—but I used to wonder about it when the red carpet was laid for these royal personages and Daley marched up to greet them.

Daley got over his appearance of self-consciousness in dealing with visiting royalty across the years, getting quite skilled, actually, in raising his glass to them at official luncheons and dinners. I didn't get to too many of these affairs; as time wore on and the gulf widened between Daley and me, I didn't get invited most of the time. When I got invited and showed up and got within speaking distance of our mayor, he was warmly hospitable—to use the word that I guess he was trying to come up with during our interview at Midway Airport. But when I was present and close enough to study Daley, it always seemed to me that deep within him was a regret that he wasn't sitting in his box at Comiskey Park, watching the White Sox play a night game.

As wise old Alderman Charles Weber observed to me, in the early stages of the campaign to gather up convention votes for Jack Kennedy, "Them Kennedy people don't mean nothin' to me; them, I can do without. But, lemme tell ya, they catch on pretty fast." They did, too.

Dick Daley was too well schooled in Chicago politics not to have been aware that there was deep-seated resistance to his efforts to whip up enthusiasm for the nomination and election of Jack Kennedy; you don't stay boss of the Chicago Machine if you do not sense the vibrations of the guys in your organization. But Daley was one of those ultimate realists, which is what you have to be if you are a political boss, and so long as his organization people got out a big vote for his candidates, it didn't concern Daley if the organization guys disliked the candidates they were turning out the big vote for. Besides, Dick Daley, the guy from the Back of the Yards, was positively enchanted by the upper-crust Kennedys.

There seems to be precious little evidence that the pedigree of a candidate for president of the United States has any bearing on how well he will do with the voters. It must have been apparent to Daley that Joe Kennedy, patriarch of the clan, didn't know much about how you work a precinct or ward. Joe Kennedy had been feasting too high on the hog, as the saying went, to understand the painstaking way in which you keep your voters in line. Nonetheless, as Hy Raskin, former vice-chairman of the Democratic National Committee and a prime mover in the Kennedy election effort, told me one time, "The mayor is in awe of the Old Man. And I'll bet you never heard that—Daley being in awe of anybody."

Me, I was not so enchanted with the Kennedys. Jack Kennedy was handsome, well-tailored, and wore British shoes. But, in several one-on-one interviews I had with him in the early months of his struggle for the Democratic nomination, I didn't detect anything in him to commend his election to the presidency. Jack Kennedy was an affable, gracious man. He was articulate and had a smile that would fetch nods of approval from old nuns. But he was notably not forthcoming in voicing his views on controversial issues; Senator Kennedy was cordially unresponsive.

It seems to be characteristic of presidential candidates that they scrupulously avoid taking a position on controversial questions, in fear of turning a bloc of voters against them; special interest groups are ever ready to sound a protest if a candidate says something to offend their noble cause. I can't recall an instance when I ever had a sense of accomplishment when I did an interview with somebody who was running for president. Guys who are running for president uniformly appear to be pleased and eager to be interviewed off the cuff when they see a radio or TV guy set up to cut a little piece with them—and anxious to get it over and done with as soon as you begin. Maybe there are some guys in the broadcasting business who have a gift for interviewing presidential hopefuls, but it always pains me when I see one of these things on television, and I can't recall an instance when I looked enviously at the thing and privately wished that *I* had been able to do that. Nobody, as far as I know, is any good at it.

In the late '50s, Senator John F. Kennedy frequently visited Chicago. He always seemed to fly into Midway on the same flight, on a United Airlines DC-6 out of Washington National, arriving at Midway at about two o'clock in the afternoon. In United's scheme of things, this particular flight was always assigned Gate 1, which was the gate at the most easterly part of the terminal. It was my practice to meet Senator Kennedy's flight. I always waited until the athletic-looking senator came down the ramp before I gave the sign to the technicians to set up our stuff; there is no point in putting the technical people to the bother of unpacking their gear until you know for certain the man you are waiting for is on the plane. I would approach Senator Kennedy and ask him if he had time for a few questions. Invariably he would say sure and ask how long it would take to get ready. I would tell him it would be a few minutes, and he would say that he wanted to have something to eat. He would head for a drugstore in the terminal to have a cup of coffee and a bite of something—sauntering back in a few minutes, as he had promised to do. I never figured out why Kennedy always wanted something to eat; he rode first class and he could have eaten during the flight—but when I asked a United stewardess about this one time, she told me he spent the two hours or so reading papers he carried in a small briefcase and shook her off when asked if there were anything she could serve him. I got the notion, once, that he didn't really want to eat at the counter in the drugstore—that all he wanted to do was shake a few hands. As Senator Dirksen used to say, you can make speeches and run your commercials on television "until the cows come home," but there is nothing that takes the place of "pressing the flesh" when you are looking for votes. But, surprisingly, Kennedy didn't even glance at anyone, much less try to shake hands at the drugstore counter. I remember mentioning to Senator Dirksen one time that I had peeked in on Kennedy at the drugstore once, curious as to what in hell he was up to, and that he had shown no desire to "press the flesh." Dirksen's reply to this had been, "Well, you know, Jack is a very nice fella, but he is awfully shy, you know."

It got to be sort of a nuisance, going out to Midway to interview young Senator Kennedy. I wasn't getting anything much out of him, though I made an effort to find something in the tape or the film that I could put on the air. I never managed to get him to say anything that I found to be of much interest. I couldn't get him to say anything of consequence about the racial problems that were bubbling in the Deep South. I asked him what, as president, he might do to counter the ominous threat of the Russian Sputnik that had been sent into orbit. Well, if he had any thoughts about such problems, he wasn't about to tell me. He was nice enough once to tell me that I asked good questions, but he was reticent about answering them.

His lack of response didn't really surprise me; once you get people of Irish ancestry to talk, you have the devil's own time trying to shut them up—but until they really get comfortable with you, I have found, people with Irish blood in them are reluctant to tell you anything. Even when you give an Irishman a chance to say something that might do him some good, my experience has been that he is resistant to talking. Mayor Daley had this practice of avoidance and evasiveness, and police captains of Irish ancestry take shelter in the same way. The only Irishman of importance that I ever found to be completely confident and outgoing was Sean Lemass, an Irish prime minister I interviewed in Dublin. Sean Lemass quite candidly expressed his disapproval of U.S. involvement in the Viet Nam War and shocked his own staff when he revealed during the interview that he and his counterpart in the six northern counties had been secretly conferring, striving to work out a solution to the religious and economic differences the two men believed were certain to create bloodshed if something weren't done about it. The prime minister's candor was a most uncommon case of an Irishman's being totally honest and above board; there he was, in a conference room outside his office, revealing an astounding secret, not known even by his staff, to an interloper from American television whom he had never seen before. But, being of Irish ancestry myself, I shipped the stuff to NBC by air courier as quickly as I could—without giving the Irish press a chance to hear the tape and use Lemass' disclosure to pacify the anger in both the northern and southern counties. I don't know what good it might have done, but I have always felt I let Sean Lemass down by not leaking his top-secret story about the desperate effort to work out an under-standing that might bring peace and save lives; why in hell had Lemass told me the inside story on this, if he hadn't figured I would leak it?

I can say with certainty that young Jack Kennedy never tested me with confidential information. The closest we ever came to confidentiality didn't concern anything he told me—but, rather, something I told him. I had gone out to Midway one afternoon to do another of those vacuous interviews, and I thought the senator seemed to sigh when he came down the ramp and spotted me. He didn't wave hello and say he'd be right back and strike out for the lunch counter in the drugstore this time; no, he marched right over to me and said,

"Could I ask you how you knew I would be on this flight?"

"You always come in on this flight," I replied.

"I don't come to Chicago on a regular schedule," he said. "Only every other week or so and not always on the same day of the week. Until about three hours ago, nobody knew I was coming to Chicago, because I had no plan to make the trip; something unexpected has brought me here. When the plane was coming down, the question crossed my mind as to whether you would be here. I come down the ramp, and there you are. I find this mysterious."

"You must have figured it out by now," I said.

"No," Senator Kennedy said, shaking his head. "Are you free to tell me?"

I thought about that for a couple of seconds, deciding—well, why not?

"It's a girl who calls to tell me," I said. "A secretary, I imag-ine—but I don't know whose. At first, the girl who makes the call used to ask if it would be possible to interview Senator Kennedy, if he were coming to Chicago. Lately, she just says that I might like to know the senator is arriving at Midway on the early-afternoon United flight from Washington. Some-times I come out, and sometimes it doesn't fit in and I skip it."

Senator Kennedy nodded. Then he said, "Do you get anything out of it? I mean, is it worth the trouble?"

That is a tough question to deal with when the fellow who is asking it has his thoughts on getting elected president. But, I figured he asked it—so I would answer. "Not really, Senator. I don't expect you or any other candidate for president to say anything important in a brief airport interview—with me or anybody else. I've been doing this because somebody apparently wants you to think the Kennedy people here in Chicago are really on their toes."

Senator Kennedy flashed his boyish smile. Then he said, "Would you mind very much if we knocked it off, these interviews at the airport?"

"Somebody ought to tell those people at the Merchandise Mart that we're calling off the dog and pony show," I said, smiling back.

"Starting right now?" asked Kennedy.

"Sure," I said, "starting right now."

He stuck out his hand, we shook hands, and he said, "I owe you one." He walked away. We packed our gear and got out of there. And I never got called again.

I had an unexpected little confrontation one time with Joe Kennedy. He showed up, to my surprise, at a fund-raiser for the Catholic Interracial Council of Chicago. It was a big affair with cocktails and a buffet supper in the Imperial Suites at the top of the Conrad Hilton and a show afterwards at the Civic Opera House. Joe Kennedy had flown out from New York on Sunday afternoon in black tie. It seemed to please him that he was the only guest at the fund-raiser in formal attire—but, when I mentioned this later to Mike Howlett, Mike shrugged and said, "Well, that's the Kennedys for you; they make up their own rules."

Old Man Kennedy had found it to be politically expedient to be present for the Interracial Council's fund-raiser; R. Sargent Shriver, who was married to Joe's daughter, Eunice, was president of the Interracial Council. Mayor Daley didn't show, nor did anybody show up to represent him. Hailing from the Bridgeport area, where a black family was likely to get burned out if it had the audacity to move into this white enclave, Daley blithely avoided racial issues. Whatever Joe Kennedy's attitude on racial justice might have been, he had a son he wanted to put into the White House—and he was smart enough to know that a black vote is as good as a white one when it comes to electing a president.

Everybody fawned over Joe Kennedy at the cocktail party that preceded the buffet. Standing off to the side, I was fascinated to watch the multimillionaire's efforts to look delighted to be in the company of folks, both white and black, so dedicated to their cause. Then, abruptly, Kennedy appeared to have caught sight of someone on the other side of the room, my side of the room, and, without so much as a word of farewell to the admirers crowded around him, he pushed off.

I thought for a moment that maybe the mayor had come in. But when I looked around to see who it might be that Old Man Kennedy wanted to talk to, I didn't spot anybody important. So it was kind of a shock when Kennedy walked up to me. He was smiling, in a defiant sort of way, but he had the confident look of a dog who has treed the fox. He didn't waste any words on pleasantries; arching his eyebrows, he said,

"I understand you think that Jack can't get nominated and that he can't get elected when he gets the nomination."

I smiled at Kennedy. "Where did you hear that?" I asked.

"Never mind who told me," Old Man Kennedy said. "I have good information on you."

I had a pretty good idea who Joe Kennedy's "source" was. I had made a few negative comments to Old Joe's new associate, Hy Raskin. Raskin had cut his eyeteeth in Chicago politics before working on Stevenson's presidential campaign of 1952 as the right-hand man of Stephen A. Mitchell, the Chicago lawyer who managed the campaign. Raskin moved to the Democratic National Committee with Mitchell, and in the late '50s Old Man Kennedy snapped Raskin up. In a readout to Old Joe on the sentiments of media people in Chicago, it would figure that Raskin might have mentioned me. I had no quarrel with Raskin's telling the Old Man about this; there was nothing "privileged" about what I had said to Hy, and that was his job, to pass on any crumbs of information that he came upon. But my feeling was that Old Man Kennedy was making a big deal out of nothing.

"What difference does it make, Mr. Kennedy," I said, "if I don't happen to think that your son the senator can make it?"

"You are on television every day," Old Joe replied. "It is damaging to a candidate, if there is somebody on television telling the public that Jack isn't qualified to serve as president."

"I don't believe I ever said that on television, Mr. Kennedy."

"Well, that is what you think. If you think it, you'll say it," he countered.

Somebody took Old Man Kennedy by the arm and led him away to meet someone important. As he turned away, he said something about seeing me later. I wasn't sorry to see him go.

The crowd was directed from the bars in the suite at the south end of the top floor of the Conrad Hilton to the buffet tables in the twin suite at the northern end. My wife and I obediently joined the buffet line, but somebody came up to us, took our plates away, and said Old Man Kennedy wanted us at his table. Kennedy got table service. None of this nonsense about standing in a buffet line—no thank you, not for Joe Kennedy. It startled me that a man who had come out from New York, apparently to show what a regular fellow he was, would be so thoughtless as to assume he was entitled to special privilege.

There were about twelve of us at Mr. Kennedy's table. Among the guests were John H. Johnson, the publisher of the magazine, *Ebony*, and his wife; George E. Johnson, who was making big money in cosmetics, and his wife; and a couple of entertainers, Keely Smith and Louis Prima, who had flown in from Hollywood at Old Man Kennedy's request, to headline the Civic Opera House show that was to be the big money maker of this Catholic Interracial Council benefit.

It was kind of mortifying to be seated there, with Old Man Kennedy putting on his act as a scintillating host, while important politicians and well-heeled captains of industry walked past us from the chow line—trying to balance plates and cups and saucers as they looked for a place to sit down. I remember thinking, as Old Man Kennedy burdened us with his pointless anecdotes, that this may be how it's done in Boston, but it doesn't play very well in Chicago. I regretted that Mayor Daley wasn't there. I wondered if Daley would have joined the buffet line, by way of giving Old Joe a lesson in maintaining humility before the voters.

I suppose there is a need for a better class of people to get into the unwashed business of politics. I don't know. But given a choice, I would rather eat hot dogs and quaff beer with precinct captains in a saloon than spend an evening in some fancy spot with well-mannered people who delicately scoop up a little of the cheese dip and wash it down with white wine.

14

THE FELLOW UPSTAIRS CAN GUN YOU DOWN

I RECEIVED A TELEGRAM OF CONDOLENCE one day in the late '50s. It read: "Only Capone kills like this." Friends at NBC-New York, hearing that I had been bounced from the ten o'clock news, borrowed the famous quotation attributed to one of the first policemen to go in on the St. Valentine's Day massacre—a copper reported to have cried, "Only Capone!" when he found seven bullet-ripped bodies sprawled out on the floor of a garage on North Clark Street. A great many people at NBC-Chicago also expressed resentment over what a new management had done to me, though I was never certain as to whether they grieved over my getting booted off a good spot or they feared they might be next.

Apart from being arbitrarily cut off from about two-thirds of my income, and apart from the embarrassment of getting kicked out of a job I thought I had been handling pretty well, it bothered me greatly that the new management was totally indifferent to the matter of owing a guy decent treatment because of his past service. The management more or less was saying, "What have you done for us lately?"

My friend Jack Chancellor thought I was going to quit. *He* had come to me once in the Chicago newsroom, livid with rage over some offense, declaring that he was walking out of NBC News and would never come back. "Well," I had replied, "you do what you want to do, but I think you will be making a serious mistake if you quit. You've got a good reason to be boiling, Chancellor," I said—and he did—"but you don't want to get mad; you want to get even." As I told Chancellor, when the dice are rolling against you, you have to stay in the crap game to have any chance of pulling out of it. I had not expected, when I was giving Jack Chancellor gratuitous counsel about the wisdom of staying in the crap game, that I would have to confront the same question. In 1958, I was sorely tempted to say "the hell with it" and get out.

Here's what happened: In the early '50s, I went on the "Today Show," hosted by my old pal Dave Garroway. Four times each morning, I cut in on the network show with five minutes of local news. And I spent the remainder of my day out on the street getting spots for radio and television. I had been at this for about eight years, doing radio and TV reports on all manner of things and all kinds of people—interviewing captains of industry and Skid Row bums and just about every kind of character in between—when my assignment suddenly changed. In the mid-1950s, I was taken off the daily spot-news forays in the mobile unit.

NBC-Chicago's star news personality, Clifton Utley, suffered a stroke, and I was assigned to take Utley's place as anchorman on the ten o'clock news. I guess I was more or less the logical choice to take his place, because I regularly sat in for him when he was ill or went on vacation or ran off somewhere to make a speech. Assuming that Clifton Utley would soon be back, I tried to maintain his format; the substitute for a star like Utley, I thought, was like a fellow who takes over your apartment for a short time—it is untoward for him to start moving the furniture around. I didn't feel free to start rearranging things until it became clear that Utley wouldn't be coming back to the ten o'clock news. Then I figured I had better get my own act together, if I were going to survive as the new anchorman.

I liked the job, because it paid a lot more money than I had been getting. But I wasn't comfortable. Utley's reputation was built on his interest in national and international news; whatever reputation I had was based on knowledge of Chicago—crime, politics, big business, the racetracks, meat packers, bums, and so on. The CBS station had been beating our tail in the ratings, and, if my assignment was to close the gap, NBC's chances were not too promising. It was pretty chancy, I think, to replace a man who specialized in national and international affairs with a guy whose area of interest had been limited to state government, City Hall, movie stars, pigeon-chasers, fire engines, and gangster murders. The irony was that Chicago is a pigeon-chasing city—and the local stuff that I was comfortable with started producing an improvement in our ratings.

I continued going out to tape interviews with people in the news—something Utley had done only in the rarest of circumstances. Utley seemed to think that if there were someone of importance to be interviewed, some lackey should do it. Utley would clip out whatever part of the interview he might want to put on the air. I didn't happen to subscribe to this business of letting someone else do an important interview, but every man to his own poison, as the saying is. I did report national and international stories in considerable depth. But airline pilots were starting to report sightings of what came to be known as "flying saucers," and, like a Hearst editor, I went heavy on such things—even though I suspected the ailing Clifton Utley would have scoffed at these reports as stuff and nonsense. What I guess the experts would call the "thrust" of the NBC-Chicago news program changed from what might appeal to readers of the *New York Times* to what might attract those more inclined to read the *Daily Racing Form*. Our ratings did start to go up, and everybody at NBC-Chicago seemed to be pleased. Give us some time, I thought, and we'd outstrip CBS.

It surprised some people that the ten o'clock news started to move up in the ratings when I was put on it. I wasn't all that good, to be honest about it. But Chicago has always been sort of a "cops and robbers" town, much more interested in its own affairs than in anything that happens elsewhere, and I came closer than Utley did to catering to this provincial appetite. But good ratings are holy writ in the broadcasting business, and, if it had been a surprise that I had been placed in Utley's spot, it startled a lot more people when a new management came in and unceremoniously dumped me out.

In his wisdom, Robert E. Kintner, the president of NBC News, sent us a new general manager intent on saving money by cutting down on paper clips, copy paper, and the highly paid people who were going on the air. I was dropped down the chute in 1958 by the new management people sent out to Chicago to fatten up profits.

The new general manager's petty economies might not have bothered me, my view being that the man in charge of the candy store can do what he wants. The new guy's standing with the big bosses depended on the financial balance sheet. But I got a steady flow of telephone calls from listeners who seemed to trust me with inside tips on scams that the sanctimonious big shots in politics and business were getting away with. So, when our new general manager bought himself an expensive apartment in the Drake Tower, an exclusive Lake Shore Drive building, the men who were doing the decorating and putting in expensive carpeting called to tell me that NBC was paying for their work—in trade-offs for commercial time on the air. This wasn't the first time I had heard about these trade-offs, but it annoyed the hell out of me when I learned that a general manager who could get nasty with a secretery for "wasting" paper clips had no qualms about ripping off the company to save himself the costs of enjoying the good life. It annoyed the hell out of me when our greedy general manager whined that I was getting paid too much money for the ratings that I was producing.

At a much later time, when I was having lunch with Bob Kintner at a posh place in Washington, DC, he apologized for his "mistake" in sending to Chicago the "stupid" general manager who had canned me. I told Kintner it was one of the occupational hazards in the broadcasting business; after all, by the time of our lunch, the NBC board of directors had fired Kintner. But, at least for the record, let me say that I remember telling Kintner that, apart from the decision to take me off the ten o'clock news, which I would still regard as a legitimate management decision, the guy he had sent us had been a rare bird—in that he qualified, in my opinion, as a one hundred ten percent son of a bitch, as the precinct captains would say.

It had offended me that Kintner's general manager didn't have the guts or the decency to tell me, personally, that he wanted to put somebody else in my spot. Kintner's man didn't show any class in the matter of cutting me down. He sent an embarrassed underling to break the news to me—along about four-thirty one Friday afternoon, while I was busy preparing for the news show. The embarrassed junior-level executive told me I wouldn't be doing the ten o'clock news that night—that the bosses had decided someone else should take over the show. It didn't surprise me that I was being sacked; the new general manager, eager to make a good showing by cutting the payroll, was firing people in wholesale numbers—at a time when NBC-Chicago was grinding out multimillion-dollar profits. The mortified-looking guy from the business office told me: "They said I should tell you that you will be paid out on your contract, for the four weeks or whatever it is, but that somebody else will be doing the show tonight." I thanked him for bringing me the notice; it wasn't *his* doing, and it was established practice for the networks to fire people without warning. I suppose that broadcasting executives are no different from any other executives in dropping the boom on employees they decide to get rid of. This seems to be part of the American tradition that helps make this nation great.

I had expected that the next advisory would be to clean out my desk, pick up my severance check, and get the hell out of the place. But this didn't happen. I couldn't figure out why it didn't happen; if I had been the boss who sacked someone and didn't bother to tell him why, I think I would have told him to clear out, right then and there. But the new manager didn't do this; all he did was put a big gash in my income and nudge me into limbo. Minutes after being told that I had been fired, another underling of Kintner's new general manager walked into the newsroom with the surprising word that I hadn't been fired, after all. It is a screwy business, the broadcasting business.

For reasons that were not explained to me, the new message was that I wasn't getting kicked out of NBC—just off the ten o'clock news. They were just reassigning me to other shows and putting me back on the street again in the mobile unit. I was still on the weekly "City Desk" panel, getting paid twice what the newspaper guys who were brought in were getting, but the new deal provided that they would double my fee for continuing on that. And the new general manager's man talked vaguely about my making more money for half-hour documentaries and other specials. It sounded pretty good, even though I suspected that the new general manager might be covering himself from any protests NBC might get for arbitrarily taking me off the ten o'clock news. I figured that throwing me a bone to give him an alibi was a stopgap measure. I didn't think it was much of a bone when I added it up and found that the bottom line reflected a two-thirds cut in my compensation. It seemed pretty obvious to me that my number was up, but I said I would think about this offer and let him know. I didn't know where I would go or what I would do, but I was pretty sure that I wasn't going to be working for this general manager that Kintner had visited upon NBC-Chicago.

Considerable heat was generated by the decision to take me off the ten o'clock news show. U.S. senators, City Hall pols, and indignant viewers raised a stink about these NBC carpetbaggers coming in and putting the axe to me. NBC's executives would have been better off if they had kicked me out and been done with it. Why they didn't do this, I will never know.

Word spreads pretty fast when somebody who has been on the air gets fired. Only minutes after being told that I was off the ten o'clock news, I got a phone call from the general manager of a rival network station who invited me to lunch and made it clear that he wouldn't mind having me do the ten o'clock news at his place. You wonder, at a time like this, whether you are being lured by a worse devil than the one you know. Harry Reutlinger of the *Chicago American* called to ask if I wanted a job. Some of the street reporters at the other radio and TV stations, which had started to play catch-up with us, were relieved to hear that I was being neutralized by my management; it wasn't that I was all that much better than the guys who worked for the other stations—it was that I had been at it for so long that I had more moxie and better contacts. It is tough to compete with someone who has better connections than you have. Some of the news people in Chicago told me that I had been insulted by the dumb bastards in NBC's management. Some of my friends on the papers advised me to quit. Never had there been in Chicago broadcasting so much of a fuss over something so little. I was pleased that so many viewers and big wheels were hollering about my being taken off my cushy spot. But my judgment was that I had better stick around and stay on the payroll until the smoke cleared and I could get a look at my situation.

I like to think that I had paid my dues at NBC News. They owed me a decent shake, and I don't believe they gave it to me. I think a lot of people who knew me thought that I was going to light the fuses of a few skyrockets and quit. The guys who had demoted me weren't asking me to stay, of course. I think they expected—and hoped—that I would quit and not be a lingering nuisance to them. But I practiced the prudence I had preached to Chancellor. I reluctantly decided to stay in the crap game for a while. It is not especially pleasant to stay on the payroll of somebody who doesn't want you. For the first time in years I didn't have any deadlines staring me in the face—and you get weary sitting at your desk with the papers and an ever-present cup of black coffee.

Alex Dreier, an NBC-Chicago newsman, had a high regard for the new general manager and had helped him get settled in our city and get into some clubs and all of that. But Dreier seemed to be as distressed as everyone else who learned that the general manager had dropped his bomb on me. Alex Dreier, a garrulous guy and a smart operator, had counseled me to make an effort to get along with the new general manager— something I was not inclined to do, not liking the look of the self-centered new boss. But even Dreier was startled when the new guy axed me, and Alex wanted me to let him plead my cause for retention as the ten o'clock man. But I didn't want anyone to plead my cause; especially someone on cordial terms with the enemy.

Not too long after offering to go to bat for me, Dreier self-consciously disclosed that the new general manager had just asked him to take my spot as anchorman. Well, I thought Alex was a pretty good choice and I told him so. Alex said that I had a wrong opinion of the new man and that I would come to like him when the new general manager had had the time to implement some of the great ideas he had. I don't remember what response I made to that. All I remember is that Alex Dreier cooled off in his warm admiration for the general manager, had a noisy argument some months later with his erst-while bosom buddy, stalked out of NBC-Chicago, and went directly to ABC to anchor the ten o'clock news there. This guy that Kintner sent out did a lot of damage.

Bill Ray, who would have been my candidate for the guy who could get along with anybody, seemed to be having a really bad time with the new bosses. We liked to think, and not without reason, that Bill had put together the most professional radio-TV news operation in Chicago, but this didn't make the slightest impression on the new boss; he didn't care what kind of newsroom he had. All that concerned him was "How much does it cost?" I found it sort of entertaining to have Ray come storming into my office after a command appearance on the executive floor, cursing the new general manager as "that dumb bastard!" I could see that Bill Ray was closer to quitting than I was.

We were both pretty sure we weren't long for NBC. We talked a good deal about buying some local no-account radio station that we thought we could build into Chicago's premier source of news. There were a couple of small stations on the market, but we were disheartened to find that they were priced beyond our reach; we knew that with our track records we could get funding—but we didn't want any part of that. We thought it would be great to start our own station, but we knew without even searching it out that the Federal Communications Commission had long since allocated every possible spot on the dial. So we had a search made of the availability of a "directional antenna" in the area around Chicago, and—miracle of miracles—we found one. It would take a little extra money to erect three or four antennae to carry our signal into Chicago and keep it from encroaching on the wave length alloted to an existing station, but we made a deal with some people in Wheeling, who seemed to be delighted at the idea of our having a transmitter on their property. And it looked as if we were going to get our chance to show NBC and all the other stations in Chicago how to handle the news. The same as so many dreams, it didn't come true.

There were three or four other applicants for the open spot on the dial—a couple of license-seekers in Michigan, somebody in Indiana, and somebody just over the state line in Wisconsin. They had all done the spadework and had paid for feasibility studies and engineering reports and all of that; if you seek a broadcasting license from the FCC, you had damned well cover all the bases. Bill Ray and I had the documentation carefully prepared, we had good personal credentials, and we hired a Washington, DC, attorney who was not only exceedingly knowledgeable about license requirements—having spent a great number of years as an NBC lawyer—but a dear guy and a personal friend of ours. Bill and I figured that if there is any justice in the world we were a cinch to get this license. We didn't get it.

We hadn't had a chance of getting the license, we later discovered, because our friend, the brilliant lawyer, forgot to file our application with the FCC. Something like this is enough to make you blow your top, but when we found out about it, Bill Ray and I smiled sadly and shook our heads. There wasn't anything we could do about our tediously prepared and expensive license application that hadn't been filed, because the deadline was past—and our brilliant Washington attorney was dead. Our friend, the attorney, had gone bananas over the pressure of his work, stopped his car on a bridge over the Potomac while on his way to the office one morning, run to the rail, and jumped in. I have had some big winners in my lifetime, and I can't complain about getting shortchanged. But

I have had some big losers, also, and the tragic end of the dream to get rich in the broadcasting business was one of them.

It is strange how one bastard on the management side can foul up an organization, but the new boss had a talent for it. Several key people at NBC-Chicago had quit. Then Bill Ray asked me to come into his office and shocked me with the news that he had just quit. I couldn't believe this; there wasn't a news director in the nation, in my opinion, who could hold a candle to Bill Ray. But it seemed that Bill had been having a running dispute with Kintner's general manager, that he resented having this new man project himself into news department decisions, that he had told the new general manager it was just plain stupid to take me off the ten o'clock news, and that, by God, he wasn't going to take it anymore and he had quit. "No!" I said. But Bill Ray said, "Oh, yes." And there we were without a news director.

Bill Ray, eager to find any escape hatch out of NBC, had bought a radio station in Ames, Iowa. I asked him, "Why Ames, Iowa?"

"Well," he replied, "that's where Iowa State University is located. This station hasn't been programming right for its audience, and I think I can make something out of it. You want to come in as partner?"

"Ames, Iowa?" I replied. "No, thanks."

So Bill Ray cleared out of NBC-Chicago, and I settled down to see what was going to happen to me.

Bill Ray had a good deal of success in giving Ames, Iowa, a respectable radio station. Ames appeared to be a desirable place to set up a quality operation. But operating his own station aggravated Bill Ray more than it pleased him. It was not long before he sold out and got out of there. We had a president then named John F. Kennedy, and he had a young Chicago lawyer of considerable skill—Newton Minow—as chairman of the Federal Communications Commission. Newt Minow was a friend of mine. He was likewise a friend of Paul H. Douglas, the senior senator of the state of Illinois. So, putting things together as people do, Bill Ray was hired to work for the FCC. In a short time Bill was made chief of the complaints division, which I always thought was a promotion that had a touch of poetic justice about it, the complaints division being the place where all the beefs that listeners and viewers filed against me ended up.

The only New York NBC guy that I seemed to hit it off with was Bob Kintner, the boss of NBC News. Kintner treated me quite as austerely as he treated everybody else in NBC News. He was a smart, cold, tough bastard who knew what he wanted— and God help you if you didn't deliver it. I don't remember when it was that I got to know Bob Kintner, but I came to know him pretty well, and we got along nicely even though he was regarded as being tough as hell and hard on the help. You would think that a guy in NBC News-Chicago who was on good terms with the man in charge of the whole show would be in fine shape. It didn't seem to work out that way, though he did stand by me a couple of times when everybody else in NBC News was avoiding me as if I had a contagious disease. When, years later, NBC and I did part company, Kintner sent me a long, personal letter, telling me it grieved him that I had quit. For, eventually, I did get my belly full of another of NBC-Chicago's general managers and walked out—but if you want to know about that, check the Chicago newspapers for the fall of 1974; it was the one time *I* was front page news. Even after I had left NBC, going to work for WGN-TV, the *Chicago Tribune* operation, Kintner had me out to his Georgetown house in Washington, DC, and took me to lunch at a couple of fancy places. The reason I belabor the warm relationship I had with Robert E. Kintner is that it was he who pushed me into doing something new in the news-broadcasting business: writing daily commentaries. If, in 1958, someone had told me that two years later I would be going on the air every night with my personal opinions of what was right and what was wrong with this world and that I would do this for 20 years, I would have told the guy he was nuts. But that is what happened.

The new generation of radio and television newspeople might equate all of this with an analysis of tactics employed in the Peloponnesian War, for all I know. But I'd like to think that some of the things we did in the formative years of electronic news reporting had something to do with providing a foundation for what is being done in the present day. Considering the common practice of television stations across the land having a fellow sit at a desk and scold his viewers about the caprices of their politicians and lecture them on what is wrong in Washington and the world—well, maybe it serves a purpose to set forth one man's version of the beginnings.

It was a brilliant, compassionate guy named Bob Lemon—nudged along by Kintner—who got me into the commentary business. The pleasure of chasing fire engines or going to a big murder in one of the homicide squad cars or badgering the mayor had gone out of me. Going back to street reporting, after being kicked out of my job on the ten o'clock news, I didn't seem to have any heart for the old stuff I used to do. I kidded myself that I was as interested in things as I had ever been, but this wasn't true. I assured myself that I was as skillful an interviewer as I had ever been and that my copy was as sharp as I had ever been able to turn it out—and I'm afraid that this wasn't quite true. I was unhappy with the management, and I was ready to chuck the whole thing. And then Bob Lemon came in and started talking about my doing what he called "personal opinion pieces."

Lemon had come to Chicago as the right-hand man of the general manager who plagued us. Lemon was as fiercely loyal to his benefactor as a first assistant could be. But Lemon was so different from the guy he served that those of us with a working interest in this affair suspected that these two new bosses were working a slick con on us: the top guy being mean and stupid as hell and the other guy, Lemon, playing the role of "nice guy." Lemon smiled boyishly and was quite agreeable and had good programming ideas. If you had to talk to the top guy, you were wary of anything he said, and it was a relief to get away from him; if you had to go to Lemon's office, you found him to be pleasant and reasonable and good company. When Bill Ray walked out and a news director named Frank Jordan was shipped in from New York, a lot of us had reservations in the matter of how much trust we could put in Lemon. In retrospect, I would have to confess that we were as unfair in our judgment of Bob Lemon as the abominable general manager was in his judgment of us. So I had instant doubts about Lemon when he asked me to come into Frank Jordan's office and made his surprising pitch about my going on the air with my personal opinions.

What knocked me off guard, I guess, when Lemon called me in to talk about this personal editorializing, was Lemon's opening statement that something had been bothering him for a long time and he wanted to get it off his chest. What, I wondered, is this guy talking about? Well, what he was talking about—or so he went on to say—was a serious mistake he and his boss had made when they were sent out to take over NBC-Chicago. I don't remember exactly how he put it, but I do remember that Lemon said they had "underestimated" me and, in closing his apology or explanation of a dead deed or whatever it was, he said, "We shafted you."

I couldn't believe the guy had said this. Lemon went on to say something else, but I was so stunned at hearing his apology, or whatever it was, that I have no remembrance of what else he said. All I remember is that I looked at him and said, "I appreciate your saying this, Bob, but it's water under the bridge. You didn't shaft me; I think you shafted yourself." Bob Lemon twirled the cigar in his mouth and nodded. And then he got into the matter of my doing fifteen minutes of editorializing on radio every day. I was kind of a reluctant bridegroom on this; it simply did not figure that the new general manager, who hadn't had enough confidence in me to keep me on the ten o'clock news, would trust me to go on the air every day, voicing my own opinions.

"I thank you for the offer," I told Bob Lemon, "but I'm afraid it won't work. It sounds to me as if you are looking for a 'house man' to express the management's view of things. And it wouldn't work out. I just couldn't do that."

"I don't think you understand what I'm talking about," Lemon replied. "I'm not suggesting that you submit your copy for approval to me or the man upstairs or Jordan or anyone else. There won't be any limitations on you. All I am saying is that we think it's time for broadcasters to start taking a position on things—and you just happen to be the man we think should be doing this. So, how would you feel about it?"

Well, there was not the slightest sign that Lemon was dealing me cards off the bottom of the deck, but I had a deep suspicion that, somehow, I was being set up. "I'll think about it," I said.

It is pretty exciting when somebody offers you a chance to do something that no one has ever tried before. But I couldn't believe that this invitation to editorialize was on the level. Keeping my own counsel, not wanting to talk even to Jordan about Lemon's proposal, I did indeed give a lot of thought to it. Finally, I decided it would be an innovative thing to do; there was nobody at NBC-New York—or anywhere else in broadcasting that I was aware of—who was allowed to pop off every day with his personal opinion of things. Maybe it was some kind of trap to get rid of me; I didn't know about that. All I knew was that, hazardous or not, I was being asked to try something that nobody in broadcasting had ever tried before— and while the chances were that I would fall on my face, giving the general manager and Lemon just cause to get rid of me, I wasn't going anywhere in the broadcasting business if I said no. And that is how, with reservations, I got into the commentary business.

It was mid-year 1959 when I started voicing my personal opinions every day on the Chicago NBC radio station. I think my colleagues thought it was a pipe, sitting in a private office, pounding out my thoughts on the big happenings and the inconsequential things of the day. But I found it exhausting work. For one thing, with the audience's limited attention span in mind, I had to break up my copy into four segments—which was like having to do editorials every day on four distinct subjects. The total copy count on every day's program ran to well over two thousand words. Fifteen minutes is a lot of time on radio.

At the end of each day, I anguished over how I could possibly think of four new things to talk about tomorrow. At first I worried about getting phone calls of complaint from listeners who would say I didn't know what in hell I was talking about, but both at the beginning and over the years that I did commentaries, it was rare that some irate listener called to tell me off.

If it weren't for the physical and mental labor that this thing entailed, it would have been a gratifying kind of work. The ratings were good. The station was getting a lot of mail. The Chicago newspapers took to taking notice of what I was putting on the air—although, generally, their "recovery" stories would take a little shot at me. The sales department thought I was great, because they found it easy to sell the commercial time in our program. Bob Lemon and that general manager of ours were pleased by the public reaction to this stuff I was doing, though I never was able to subdue the doubts I had about the general manager's sincerity when he said something nice to me. A couple of the other network radio stations made a stab at having somebody do what I was doing, but they never seemed to bring it off. Kintner sent a reporter from the New York station to Chicago to study my methods, and I tried to be helpful—but when he went back, after having watched me for a couple of weeks, something got lost in the transition; his opinionating didn't score with the audience when he tried it in New York. I don't know whose idea it had been to put me on the air with this editorializing; it hadn't been *my* idea. I didn't invent this commentary business; I just did it. I suppose it was simply somebody's lucky shot; somebody had dreamed up this way of giving radio a little transfusion and it worked.

Along about December of 1959, the Great Kintner came out to Chicago, and I was sitting with him and the general manager and probably Bob Lemon in one of the executive offices, discussing this editorializing that I was doing. Kintner didn't bother with any questions about whether I liked what I was doing or whether the general manager liked it. Obviously, *he* liked it and, by God, he was running NBC News, wasn't he? Well, for a moment or two I was thinking that he was going to be running it without me. Kintner, believe it or not, had come out to Chicago with the crazy notion of putting me on TV! The general manager looked for a moment as if he just couldn't believe what Kintner was saying, but he recovered to work up a smile of agreement and said that Kintner certainly had a brilliant idea. The other management people who were present echoed this approval. I guess I just sat there, reacting as if Kintner had just told me that my dog had died.

Kintner turned his attention to me. "You don't like it?" he asked, accusingly. "I offer you the chance of a lifetime and you don't like it?"

"I don't think that what I do on radio belongs on television," I replied.

"Why not?" demanded Kintner. "Same audience. Same kind of people. Same desire to get the inside story of what's going on—"

"It's not television," I said. "No film, no graphics, no props— just me at a desk, reading stuff that I've written. The radio listeners can use their imaginations to provide a pictorial back-drop for what they're hearing me say. All the television audience can do is watch me stumble around trying to read whatever it is I've got written on the copy I hold in my hands."

Kintner grumbled his displeasure at my response. The general manager, frowning at me, said, "It's a mistake to overlook the intelligence of the television audience." Old Kintner gave him a displeased look that more or less conveyed the impression that the general manager must be nuts, if he believed this stuff he was saying about the "intelligence" of the TV audience. I thought Kintner was going to nail our general manager to the wall for that one. But, instead, Kintner directed his attention to me and said, "Do you have any other reservations about doing your comments on television?"

I could hear the general manager sucking in his breath when I said, "Yeah, I do. I suppose there will be some money in this for me—going on television every night—although I notice no-body has mentioned it. But I think it's too risky to put a guy like me, who doesn't have too many restraints when it comes to saying what he thinks, on a sensitive medium like television."

Our general manager chortled. "Oh," he said, "we'll put plenty of restraints on you when you're on television. The company has millions of dollars at stake in television, and we're not going to take a chance on losing sponsors—or our license."

"That's exactly what I'm talking about," I said. "I agree

with you; with all that money at stake, why should NBC take a chance with somebody like me?"

Kintner was turning purple. He shook a finger at the general manager, who now looked uncomfortable, and said: "If you're talking about censorship or making cuts in his analyses that you don't happen to like, you're not going to do a goddamn thing. I don't intend that we put someone on the air to speak the viewpoint of NBC; all we want is a reasonably reliable and well-informed man to appear on television and state his personal opinions. No censorship! No editing!"

Boy, I wondered, does Kintner appreciate what he is saying?

Pointing at me, the general manager hesitantly said, "His expertise is in local and state affairs, and I think there should be an understanding that this should be his area of commenting."

"I'll buy that," Kintner said.

"I'm not saying that we will read his material and give it our approval," the general manager said. "All I'm saying is that everyone should understand, going into this, that he'll have to keep his opinions down to things that happen here in the Chicago area or have a connection to our 'listening area.' "

Kintner nodded and, turning to me, he said, "Can you live with that?"

"I think so," I said. The opinion pieces that I had been doing on radio for months were pretty much localized, and it appeared to me that doing it on television would simply be more of the same. Unfortunately, I was wrong.

I started the television commentaries in January of 1960, on the Monday of the New Year's weekend. There was not much available to editorialize about, and I was really scratching my head for an idea. Discovering from long stories on the news wires that the traffic death toll for the holiday weekend was running higher even than the dire forecast of the National Safety Council, which was headquartered in Chicago, I decided to express disapproval of the shocking statistics of motoring Americans' killing themselves. I did not anticipate that the general manager would take exception to a dull, public service piece like this. I was wrong. He did.

The general manager charged up to me in the hallway or the men's room or some such place and, in offended tones, said: "On the television commentary about the traffic death totals, I thought we had an agreement that you would limit yourself to *local* matters."

"Well, I did. The holiday death toll forecast is put out by the Safety Council, right here in Chicago. The whole point of the piece I did centers on the council's indignation over the death toll's running well over the figure that the council had predicted. Every newspaper in the country will carry the National Safety Council story, under a Chicago dateline."

"That part of your comments is all right," the general manager said, "but I don't consider your report about that French writer getting killed in a car near Paris a 'local' event. No harm done, I'm sure, but I wouldn't want to see you make a practice of using outside information, when the agreement is that you will concentrate your editorials on Chicago events." And with a warning shake of his head, our general manager strode away.

I was aghast. Maybe he had a valid beef; I don't know. But it seemed to me he was nitpicking, by way of letting me know that Big Brother was watching me. What I had done, by way of getting myself into the shocking report of the highway death toll on the New Year's weekend, was start out with the details of how Albert Camus, the French existentialist, had been killed when the car he was driving went off the road and hit a tree on a highway south of Paris. What I was trying to do was make the point that nobody was exempt from the possibility of getting killed in an auto accident—the high and the mighty, including famous writers like Camus, being in as much danger as any no-account. It depressed me that on the very first day of my televised editorializing, our general manager would carp at me for leading my piece with a reference to the unfortunate demise of Albert Camus. My God, I thought, if the guy in charge of things was going to raise hell with me about something like that, what kind of second-guessing had I let myself in for?

My fears were unfounded. I don't recall that ever again did our general manager quibble with me over anything that I said in my commentaries. I don't know whether Lemon or Kintner or somebody advised him to cool it in dealing with me, but he apparently decided to refrain from criticism even when I did a commentary that upset him because it scorched someone in the business or social set with whom he was eager to ingratiate himself. Our general manager was going to the Lyric Opera every Monday night in season, liking it or not, because that is when the wheelers and dealers attend. You could count on it that he would mention it if he got invited to have dinner at the Casino, the snobbish little place that has been socially exclusive since the days when meat packers and retailers were the elite of Chicago. However indifferent he was toward the NBC employees under his command, our general manager was grossly eager to identify with those who ran in the "best" circles.

I am not beefing about our general manager's wanting to mix with the upper crust. Some of the nicest people you would care to know go to the Lyric Opera on Monday evenings, sitting in the same seats season after season, and belong to the Casino set. And I think it helped me, as I made my independent path into the TV commentary business, to have our general manager attempting to carve out a little place for himself in what might loosely be called "Chicago society"—because it came to be sort of fashionable for those folks to listen to what I was saying on television, to talk about it, and to say complimentary things about me when I happened to take an editorial position they agreed with. General managers of radio and TV operations, as a breed, are gratified to hear nice things said by influential people about the opinion makers the general managers are putting on the air.

From the standpoint of getting the job done, 1960 was as good a year, I guess, as I ever had—which is gratifying for a fellow who suspects that his top boss, the general manager, is itching to sack him. I simply could not shake my suspicion that the general manager wanted me out. However it came about that the general manager did not boot me out as he cavalierly fired other guys, it was lucky for me—because election year 1960 turned out to be a rather successful year for me. Keeping

me on the air turned out to be fortunate for NBC News, also—
if having a guy around who is lucky enough to come up with
an exclusive national story or two is the measurement of
whether a network is outperforming the competition.

In the early '60s, NBC-New York sent us another news director. The new guy, whose name was Angus William Corley,
was a big-bodied man with a placid disposition. On his first
day, he called me into his office and gently interrogated me
for a couple of hours, asking me about Mayor Daley and other
well-known politicians, about who was really important in the
power structure of Chicago, about my opinion of the ability
of individuals on the newsroom staff, and about a lot of other
things, including the matter of good places to eat. I figured
that Corley was deceptively agreeable, and I was wary of him.
Having had a bad couple of years with the station manager
New York had dumped on us, I was gun-shy of anyone New
York sent out to be in charge of anything, and I kept a frigid
distance from this fellow, Corley. He was a nice enough guy,
and I was startled by the casual way in which he was spending
NBC's money on beefing up the staff and improving our facilities; it amazed me that he got away with this, while a penny-
pinching general manager sat upstairs. But my thinking was
that getting rid of me was high up on the list of things that
New York had told him to do, and I wasn't inclined to be
friendly to the executioner. I was wrong.

Corley asked me into his office one day, made a point of
closing the door, and said, "I am sure you know this, but Kintner and McAndrew hold you in high regard."

I didn't say anything. What in hell do you say when your
news director tells you something like that? Kintner, of course,
was the big cheese of NBC, and Bill McAndrew—with whom
I had become friends in the long ago, when he was condensing
wire copy for the great Earl Godwin—was vice-president of
NBC News. Yeah, sure, these two guys knew me—but they
hadn't come riding to my rescue when our general manager
shot me out of the saddle.

"When I was coming out here from New York," Corley went
on, in a quiet voice, "Kintner and McAndrew told me to watch

my step with you. I don't know whether they are your close friends, but I have been doing my best to get along with you. I was on the phone with McAndrew this morning, and he asked how I was getting along with you. I told him there hadn't been anything disagreeable, but I was beginning to think that you thought I had a communicable disease. McAndrew simply laughed and said, 'Oh, you two will work it out.' But, frankly, it disturbs me, and I would appreciate it if you would tell me what's the matter. Have I offended you in some way, do you simply dislike me, or what?"

I guess I smiled at that. "It's nothing personal, Corley," I replied. "All it is is that I think I have worn out my welcome, and I don't see much point in hanging around here. I've been talking to some people about going somewhere else. There is one outfit that has made me an offer that sounds pretty good. So, I will be out of your hair pretty soon. I should have cleared out when Bill Ray quit, but I thought I had better look around first. Maybe the devil I've got is better than the devil I'll get; these network-owned and -operated places are all the same, I guess: general managers scared to death that the New York bosses might bounce them and consequently being miserable to the help and all of that. But I've had it up to here with NBC, to be honest with you. It's like being married to a shrew— no way can you please her. So, I figure the hell with it; I'll get out. I'll give you my resignation right now, if you want."

I didn't know whether Bill Corley was a good actor or what, but he seemed to be genuinely shocked. "My God," he said. "You can't walk out on us! I've got plans. There's a lot I think you should be doing—more documentaries, some one-on-one interviews in Washington, some special assignments overseas."

Well, I figured this was what is regarded as a con, but it is nonetheless kind of flattering to have somebody put you on like this. So I told Corley that I would hold off jumping off the bus for a while, if he were serious about scratching up some stuff that the competition wouldn't have. I wasn't very sanguine about Corley's chances of getting his grand ideas on the road; working for a boss who seemed bent on squeezing every silver dollar until the eagle screamed, it did not seem likely that

Corley would get an OK to spend sizable sums of money, simply in hope of boosting our ratings. But I underestimated Bill Corley's powers of persuasion.

With nobody raising an eyebrow, I went to more places than I cared to go—traveling first class all the way, using up money on cars and crews and expensive dinners for people as if the cost of these junkets didn't concern me (which it didn't). Corley sent me to London and Lisbon and Dublin and Rome and I don't remember where else. Sometimes it would be for what we called "hit-and-run" interviews, or commentary pieces; sometimes it would be for extended periods of filming and interviewing—a week in Dublin two or three times, a month in Rome on one occasion, and so on. We would have a courier take the cans of film to an airport as fast as we shot it, sometimes bribing the pilot to carry it back to Chicago, where one of our couriers would pick it up and speed it to the Merchandise Mart for developing and editing. Corley got his money's worth.

When the Poles were getting up steam to commemorate the Polish Millenium, Corley went overboard. Motivated by Chicago's being the world's second-largest community of Poles—second only to Warsaw—Corley even hired a secretary named Lucyna Migala to translate the Polish language newspapers for me, by way of backgrounding me for covering the celebration. It grieved Corley when not even the press officer of the Russian Embassy in Washington—for whom Corley had done some professional favors—could come up with a visa for me, the Communists being particular as to what kind of reporters they allow into Poland. By way of putting the Soviets on notice that he was not a man to be put down, Corley directed me to cover the Millenium ceremonies in Rome—which I did. There Pope Paul VI celebrated a Mass of jubilation. Poles who had gathered from all over the world were jam-packed into St. Peter's Basilica for the Mass. And in Monte Cassino, Italy, where a shocking number of Poles had been killed in their sole military victory of World War II, a solemn Mass was held in memory of the Polish soldiers buried there in neat graves marked with a cross or a star of David.

I always got great pleasure out of running into an NBC guy

that I knew and spending a couple of hours with him, gossiping over drinks or dinner in some distant place. As a reporter, you feel part of a small community, when—in Hong Kong, Tokyo, Stockholm, or somewhere—you run into old friends you haven't seen in a long time. The bonus, invariably, in meeting up with a foreign bureau guy, is that the "local," as we referred to him, always knows the very best place to eat. I encountered Jack Fern, for example, one time when I was in Hong Kong. I knew Fern from way back, when he had worked with us at NBC-Chicago, before moving on to NBC-New York, and afterwards, God knows, everywhere. Jack was running NBC's Hong Kong bureau—not so much to get the news there as to take charge of the stuff coming in by air from Tokyo and Saigon. Fern "put it on the bird," which meant transmitting it to New York on satellite.

Fern took me to a place that he declared "serves the best Peking duck in Hong Kong—and that means the best in the world." Although he appeared to be on the best of terms with the restaurant owner, Fern said something authoritatively in Chinese to the proprietor, who nodded his head in reply. Seeing that I was mystified by this ritual, Fern explained: "I told him I want the duck carved at our table. They're cute, the Chinese; they steal a little of the duck and put it aside for something else, if you let them cut it up in the kitchen." There was a sign, with gold-leaf Chinese lettering on a neatly cut square of plastic firmly fixed on one wall. An English translation was in block letters at the bottom of the sign. I guess I was sort of hypnotized by this sign, because it said: "Don't Spit on the Floor!"

I'd have to say that Corley moved me around a little bit. And, by way of justifying Corley's extravagance—and by way of doing a little showboating of my own, I guess—I made an extra effort to put together, in addition to the assigned stuff, a half-hour documentary every once in a while. I had some good times; I would have to admit that. Mostly, it was exhausting work, but I guess I had a little fun in this job I had.

15

THE BITTER SWEETNESS
OF GETTING A BIG STORY

IN JULY 1960 I checked into a fleabag hotel in Los Angeles. I didn't want to stay there, but I was assigned to cover the Illinois delegation to the Democratic National Convention, and with genuine regret I declined an invitation to move out to a better place. When Richard J. Daley and his family arrived in Los Angeles, in a private railroad car that had been hooked onto the Santa Fe Chief, he was shocked by the hotel assigned to the Illinois delegation by the "host committee." Daley wouldn't even set foot in the dump. I didn't much blame him. Daley, of course, had to have more elegant accommodations than this, and he drove off, with his family, to a luxury hotel, leaving the rest of us to make out with bad beds, slovenly housekeeping, cockroaches, and other inconveniences as well as we could.

It mystified a lot of us that the Democratic National Committee would give the back of its hand to Illinois by assigning its delegation a third-rate hotel. I asked a good friend of mine, a doll of a guy named James A. Ronan, for an explanation. Ronan had accepted a crummy room in this place, even though his wife, Peg, was with him, for the same reason that I had accepted mine: he had to. As state chairman of the Illinois Democrats, he had to be available. Jim Ronan smiled in response to my question. "Butler's revenge, I guess," he said. "Butler doesn't like Daley, and he doesn't like Kennedy."

I had heard that Paul Butler, of South Bend, Indiana—who had become national chairman of the Democratic party when Steve Mitchell quit—was having some kind of feud with Daley. I hadn't believed the story; national chairmen don't play mean little tricks such as giving a fleabag hotel to the convention delegates of a guy like Daley. Mitchell, a Chicagoan, had had something to do with Butler's getting to be named chairman— and Steve was "in good shape," as they say, with Daley.

"Yeah," Ronan said, "it's unusual. But I'm not going to worry about it. Butler's going to be gone, no matter who gets nominated. The candidate will bring in his own chairman, just as Adlai did in '52 with Mitchell."

"Who is going to be nominated, Jim?"

Ronan shrugged. "My guess is it's going to be Kennedy. He's got the votes, I think. Johnson let Kennedy get too far in front of him. Johnson's people are talking now, in the private conferences, about stopping Kennedy. But I don't think they've got a chance. There's a fight going on in the conferences. But I don't think Johnson can do anything. I've been telling them, but I hope you won't put this on the air, that we should patch things up and not have a fight in the party. It's going to be tough enough to beat Nixon in November, without having a fight among ourselves. But it doesn't seem to matter what I say."

"What about Stevenson, Jim?" I asked.

Ronan shrugged. "It's like Johnson," he replied. "Adlai waited too long. You want to get nominated, you've got to get started early and never let up. Adlai layed back like he was going to be handed the nomination on a platter; it doesn't work that way. At least I don't think it does, and I've been coming to these conventions for a long time."

I thought I would try something else. "Listen, Jim," I said, "the word we're getting from Chicago is that there's some kind of a movement going on back there to flood all you Illinois delegates with telegrams, urging you to vote for Stevenson. Is there any truth in it?"

Jim Ronan grinned. "Yeah," he said, "they're bringing in Stevenson telegrams by the boat load. I had to talk to the manager of Western Union to work out a system for handling them."

"That many?" I asked.

Ronan chuckled. "You want to know something? They were bringing up so many Adlai telegrams that we could hardly get to the bathroom. A kid brings up a luggage cart loaded with bundles of telegrams—maybe a hundred in each bundle. Adlai telegrams are all over the place, piled up everywhere."

"You're kidding," I said.

"No, it's no joke," Ronan replied. "I'm paying for a room now just to put these things in a room somebody wouldn't take, wanting to go to a better place. We've got bundles of Adlai telegrams on the floor, on the dresser, on the bed—we've got them everyplace; I'll give you the key and you can go up and look for yourself. Maybe you ought to go look; you'll never see anything like this again."

"How do they sort them out—the Western Union people? How do they take out the telegrams for Stevenson and let the other telegrams come through?"

"Beats me," Ronan replied. "I told the Western Union man what our problem was, and he said he would take care of it. So far, he seems to be doing fine. The important telegrams to me seem to be getting delivered OK. I don't care how they do it, so long as they keep doing it."

"What do the Stevenson telegrams say?" I asked him.

Ronan shook his head. "I don't know; nobody reads them. I read the first three or four of them, and they said the people of Illinois were demanding that the delegation support our native son, Adlai Stevenson. Then the boy starts coming up to my room with a whole cart full of these things. So I phoned Western Union and tell this fellow that I get to talk to that he has got to do something about this. He said he would take care of it—and he has."

I shook my head. "It's an old dodge, isn't it, people sending telegrams to influence somebody's opinion?"

Ronan smiled. "Well, I imagine Western Union is making a few dollars out of it. It makes the person that sends the telegram feel good I guess—doing a little something for Adlai."

"What'll you do with thousands of telegrams, Jim?"

"Oh, I don't know," he said. "I guess I'll just let them pile up in that room—and when the convention's over, I'll call for a boy and give him twenty dollars to haul them out of there and get rid of them."

When I parted from Jim Ronan, I called an old pal of mine named Rex Goad, at NBC convention headquarters, and asked him if he wanted to hear something funny. Rex, an old pro of NBC News, with a great deal of experience at running the desk at a convention newsroom, found the story about Adlai's telegrams hilarious. He asked me to come right over and do a piece on it for the network. The network with the best sidebar stuff like this seemed to get the best ratings. I thought the people back in Illinois would be mad as hell when they heard what was happening to their telegrams, but my recollection is that not too many people hollered about it. One of the great mysteries of life, I guess, is that you never know when somebody—even with a reasonable cause for lodging a complaint—is going to holler and when he isn't.

At the 1960 nominating convention in Los Angeles, despite the tidal wave of pro-Stevenson telegrams from his devotees in the Chicago area, I don't recall talking to anyone who seriously believed that Adlai had any chance of being nominated a third time. Adlai was scurrying around some of the hotels where delegates from such big states as New York were settled. His old-guard friends like Mrs. Franklin D. Roosevelt and Governor Herbert Lehman of New York seemed to be trying to work up enthusiasm for him; I went over to the hotel where the New York delegates were quartered, when a report got out that Mrs. Roosevelt was mounting a big rally for Adlai. A ballroom was crowded with his admirers, and I found myself pushed into the speakers' table, looking down on Adlai, who was seated there. Recognizing me, Stevenson appeared embarrassed to have someone who knew him catch him reading a ridiculous statement that his fight was "not over yet." Like hell it wasn't; his chances for getting the nomination once again were so remote that you could safely bet the grocery money it wasn't going to happen.

On his occasional visitations to the troops, driving up in a black limousine driven by a Los Angeles policeman, Mayor Daley never mentioned Stevenson. Daley was having enough problems without getting involved in the possibility of Adlai's getting the nomination. The Downstate people in the Illinois delegation were devoid of enthusiasm for Senator Kennedy. Two of the "heaviest" Downstate guys were Paul Powell, the canny old pro who was fated to get caught posthumously, ten years later, with a cache of $800,000 in the closet of his Springfield, Illinois, hotel room; and Scott Lucas, the former majority leader of the U.S. Senate whom the F.B.I. observed paying visits to the posh suburban home of Tony Accardo, the Syndicate gangster chief. Powell and Lucas were attempting to scratch up some delegates for Senator Stuart Symington of Missouri. Guys like Powell and Lucas didn't give a damn about Symington; all that Symington had going for him as far as Powell and Lucas were concerned was that he was their pal Harry Truman's man. The fact was that the Downstaters had such intense dislike for John F. Kennedy that Lucas and Powell took pleasure in letting Daley know that under no circumstances were they going to vote for the nomination of Jack Kennedy. They never did, either. Even after Kennedy was nominated, Powell and Lucas spurned Daley's plea that they change their votes for Symington so that Daley could announce that the Illinois delegation stood unanimously with John F. Kennedy. Early in the convention, I had wondered whether Lucas and Powell and their crowd might foul up Daley's nest a little by swinging their votes to Adlai Stevenson. But the Downstaters didn't like him, either. Daley was with the Downstate guys on this. Daley's undisguised rejection of his onetime benefactor was a little shocking.

Stevenson didn't come into the convention hall, as I recall, until the night that the chair called for the nomination of presidential candidates. Somebody got up to nominate Kennedy, the great senator from the great state of Massachusetts, and somebody did likewise for Lyndon Johnson, the great senator from the great state of Texas. The delegates who favored these nominations cheered and marched around in traditional idiotic displays. Somewhere in the midst of all this nonsense, Adlai Stevenson had his moment of adulation and glory.

Illinois and Texas were located across the center aisle from each other. Texas guys like Sam Houston Johnson, Lyndon's brother, occasionally stood to holler insults at the Mayor Daley crowd. Texas and Illinois had been assigned seats at the extreme rear of the hall, Chairman Paul Butler having thought of everything by way of giving the back of his hand to the Kennedy and Johnson adherents. The inconspicuous way for a late arrival like Adlai Stevenson to take his seat in the Illinois delegation would have been for him to come into the hall through a rear door. But he didn't do that; he came in through a VIP entrance under the platform, at the very front of the convention hall. Stevenson grabbed hands and looked ecstatic. Daley scowled in disapproval. Stevenson made his triumphant march to the Illinois delegation and took his seat beside delegation chairman Daley. Looking as if he were about to boil, Daley didn't greet Adlai and sat dourly, staring straight ahead.

Whoever it was who had occupied the seat alongside Daley—Jim Ronan or Jake Arvey—had vacated it for Stevenson; Ronan and Arvey weren't going to get caught up in a family quarrel. With a frozen smile, and perhaps sensing that Daley was not pleased to have had him show up, Adlai tried to stir up a little conversation between himself and the delegates who were seated near him. Nobody responded. None of the delegates dared offend Daley by showing cordiality to Stevenson. I remember wondering if the network television cameras were picking this up—wondering what in hell the TV audience would be thinking as Daley gave an obviously cold shoulder to Stevenson. But the

networks didn't stay on this very long—because the rear doors
of the convention hall suddenly burst open, and a great mob
of people carrying "Stevenson for President" banners poured
in and staged an electrifying demonstration. Adlai climbed up
on his chair, as did a great many delegates throughout the
convention floor, and waved joyfully as the invaders, mostly
young people, shouted his praises. Daley, sitting stoically, didn't
even look up.

The Stevenson camp would never have been able to pull this
off without the approval of national chairman Butler. But if it
were true that Butler was anti-Kennedy and anxious to shut
him out of the nomination, Butler had waited too long; Kennedy had it.

The outburst for Adlai was cunningly contrived, and a great
many of the delegates believed that the seemingly warm demonstration had been a spontaneous expression of the convention's will to nominate Stevenson for president a third time.
At the very least, the Kennedy people feared that the unexpected show of affection for Adlai would result in a sizable
sympathy vote for him on the roll call and that Lyndon Johnson, his pledged delegates holding fast, might somehow sneak
in to exploit this surprise weakness in the Kennedy count and
run off with the prize which had seemed safely in Jack's pocket.
Old Man Kennedy was holed up with Hy Raskin in a palatial
home that had been the residence of Marion Davies, a silent-
film star who had been saved by Joe Kennedy's cunning from
bankruptcy in the cataclysmic stock market crash. Old Man
Kennedy sat cursing as he and Raskin, in dismay, witnessed on
television this frightening ploy to steal the nomination for Adlai. As Raskin told me over breakfast back in Chicago about a
week later, "We hadn't figured that Stevenson would be smart
enough to think up a trick like this, but it was the goddamned-
est thing I had ever seen at a convention. Sitting there in Marion Davies' house, watching those people going crazy for Stevenson, I told the Old Man, 'We better watch out; Adlai's
people are trying to steal the baby.' "

Raskin telephoned his orders, and Bobby Kennedy and Sarge
Shriver hit the convention floor to reassure the delegates who

were pledged to Jack that the situation was in control. Bobby hurried over to the Illinois standard, where Mayor Daley was seated with three telephones in front of him and Adlai Stevenson beside him. The mayor waved Bobby away in a gesture that said Illinois would hold firm, but that Bobby had better work on other delegations who might be wavering.

I hadn't seen anything this dramatic at a presidential nominating convention since 1932, when—sitting in our family's box at the Chicago Stadium—I had watched a brilliant politician named James A. Farley put down a revolt against Franklin D. Roosevelt, who had fought hard to secure the Democratic nomination to run against Republican President Herbert Hoover. A California Senator named William Gibbs McAdoo, seated alongside us with his mother-in-law, Mrs. Woodrow Wilson, had jumped over the railing of their box and onto the convention floor, grimly saying, "I'll settle those bastards from Texas, with their John Nance Garner." The flash powder of the still photographers exploded all around us, filling the air with small clouds of white smoke, as Senator McAdoo strode off to the platform to declare that the California delegation was going to cast its votes for Roosevelt.

It didn't take any melodramatics at Los Angeles to save Jack Kennedy; the roll call brought forth an occasional gasp as some delegates switched from Kennedy to Johnson—the Texans cheering and the Kennedy people, who seemed to hate Lyndon, groaning. But the nomination went to Kennedy, and the convention hall thundered with the customary paroxyms of joy before the last states had been called. John Fitzgerald Kennedy—put down by his detractors as a "mackeral snapper," that is, a Roman Catholic—was acknowledged by his own people to be facing an uphill fight to get elected president, but he was on his way.

Presidential nominations are almost always anticlimactic. Most of the time the choice of a nominee has been made before the delegates are gathered in convention. Almost always, after the chair has intoned the outcome of the balloting—which everyone knows without having somebody affirm it—an empty feeling pervades the convention. The delegates begin thinking about packing their bags and making arrangements to get back home. The media people customarily take a little pleasure in telling each other what a great job they did on the coverage— a custom which I think reflects their relief that they got through the damned thing without lousing it up too badly. But naming the guy who is to run for president seems to diminish everyone's excitement. There were only two presidential nominating conventions that I had ever seen where something astonishing occurred after the candidate had been nominated.

Delegates to the Democratic convention in Chicago in 1932 had been electrified, after they had chosen F.D.R., by the announcement that their candidate was going to fly out from New York the next morning to accept the nomination. Not many people, only the most daring, were making flights like this in 1932, and the American public thought it incredible that the man everyone expected to be elected president would be so bold as to do this. I was offended that nobody else in my family was eager to make the trip to the Chicago Stadium to see Roosevelt and hear what he might be planning to get the nation out of the Depression. I went to the Stadium on streetcars. A twenty-year-old, I thought this would be a great chance I would never have again, no matter how long I lived. I was the only member of my family who sat in the box to observe this historic event.

Our box was directly across from the convention platform, with a grand view of what was going on. Consequently, I was utterly dismayed—as I think a great many of the delegates were—when the handsome and smiling Roosevelt was wheeled up in his cripple's chair and introduced to the convention as the next president of the United States. F.D.R., bubbling with grand phrases and confidence, had an instant, magnetic effect on the convention. I found it utterly amazing, that the delegates so warmly embraced a man who could not even stand up—as he sounded a convincing oratorical promise that he would lead the nation back to the high road of good times. Well, that was one time when I was more deeply moved by an event that followed the nomination of a presidential candidate than I had been by anything leading up to the selection of this candidate. The second time I had an experience like this was in Los Angeles, in 1960, when an announcement was made to the delegates that John F. Kennedy was en route to the convention hall to address them.

Kennedy's acceptance speech didn't have the impact that Roosevelt's had had almost thirty years before. It was pretty dramatic, though, to stand in the shadow of the convention platform, my credentials hanging on a string around my neck, looking up at this youthful, handsome man, who alternately smiled and looked serious and brave as he declared, "We are going to win!" My private opinion was that he wasn't going to win, but I thought it was a great speech and beautifully delivered. I was a little weary of listening to politicians make speeches by this time, however, and I wandered back to the Illinois delegation before Kennedy had finished with his. Jim Ronan, seated near Daley—who was enrapt—got up when I approached and asked me if I had had dinner. He invited me to join him and his wife when the convention adjourned. When the applause for Kennedy subsided, the chairman finally hit the gavel and my wife and I joined the Ronans to have a leisurely meal. As far as I could see, the fireworks were over. It turned out that I hadn't been able to see far enough.

It was after three in the morning, when the four of us got back to our fleabag hotel. Our ladies went directly upstairs to our rooms. Jim Ronan and I lingered in the deserted lobby for a few minutes. A mousy little night clerk came out from behind the reservation desk and, studying the two of us, turned to Jim and said, "Excuse me, but are you Mr. Ronan from Illinois?" When Jim acknowledged that he was, the night clerk said he had an important telegram for Ronan and handed it over. Ronan had received numerous hand-delivered telegrams since he had arranged to have the "Stevenson for President" wires sidetracked, and he was disinterested in ripping open the envelope containing this one. But he smiled when he read it and then handed it over to me to read.

The telegram was from Bobby Kennedy, and it was notification of a top-level meeting to be held at eight A.M. in a conference room in the Kennedy headquarters hotel. The telegram didn't "request" Ronan's presence at this meeting; it directed him to be there. The last sentence of Bobby's telegram had made Ronan smile. The last sentence said: "Be sure to bring Mayor Daley with you."

"Orders from on high," Ronan remarked, as I handed the telegram back to him. Then he said, "I imagine this is supposed to be a secret meeting about who Jack wants for vice-president; maybe Adlai. But I'll meet you here in the lobby when I come back and fill you in on what goes on over there." Then he said good night and went to the elevator. I don't recall that this made much impression on me. What did I care who Jack wanted for a running mate?

The lobby of the fleabag hotel was crowded with network people and columnists and wire service guys when, at about eleven o'clock that morning, the white car assigned to Ronan pulled up at the entrance and Ronan got out and came in. So much for high-level secrets at political conventions.

"What had gone on at the secret meeting in Kennedy's hotel?" the media people wanted to know. Had they decided who was going to be Jack Kennedy's running mate? There were a lot of questions in the same vein. Jim Ronan was cordial and low-key, as always. Apologetically, he said that he couldn't really say anything, because there had been simply a general discussion of how the Kennedy campaign was to be put together. "God Almighty," one of the media reporters declared, "you must have decided on who the candidate for vice-president is going to be! God Almighty, you've got to nominate him this afternoon!" But Jim Ronan simply shook his head and said, "I just don't know what they are going to do about that. All I can tell you is that they didn't come close to naming somebody for the number two spot—and I was in the room the whole time."

Most of the media people looked to be a little petulant, discovering that Ronan of Illinois wouldn't tell them anything or didn't know anything that he could tell them, and hurried away to write their pieces or scratch around for something better to report. Ronan looked at me and said, "You have been offering to buy me a cup of coffee all week—and you haven't done it yet. Looks like the convention will be over and I won't get the coffee." I grinned at him and asked him where he wanted to go. With a shrug, he gestured to the tiny coffee shop of the fleabag hotel and we walked into the not-so-sanitary-looking coffee shop, sat down at the marbletop counter, and asked the waitress for coffee. I was pleased that none of my colleagues had followed us.

Jim Ronan seemed to be wrapped up in his private thoughts as we sat there, sipping the terrible coffee. I didn't say anything. And I didn't say anything when a cockroach appeared on the marble counter in front of us to reconnoiter. Or when Ronan idly picked up a fork and poked gently at the cockroach. Finally Ronan said, "It was the damndest meeting I ever saw. Everybody who amounted to anything was there. Only one who didn't show, I guess, was Sam Rayburn, but a guy who said he was "Mr. Sam's man" was there—a Texan, with boots. Bobby was running the meeting and he was talking a lot, but all of us were looking at each other—wondering—because Bobby was talking a lot but not saying anything; nothing about picking a vice-president or Kennedy's plans to go around the country on the campaign. Finally the guy from Texas, the one with the boots, stood up and wagged a finger at Bobby and said: 'Before this meetin' gets down the road any, I got a message you-all are gettin' from Mister Sam.' Well, we all start gaping at this guy from Texas who claims to be speaking for Rayburn, and everybody is wondering what he's up to. And then he says it and all hell breaks loose."

Looking perplexed as he thought about hell breaking loose at Bobby's big meeting, Jim Ronan sighed, picked up his fork, and went back to the game of annoying our cockroach. He was acting as if he thought I knew all about what had transpired at Bobby's big meeting. Not having the faintest idea what it was that Ronan was trying to tell me, I said, "Jim, what was it the Texas guy with the boots said that caused all the excitement?"

Ronan shook his head in the manner of a man who finds it hard to believe what he has heard someone say. "What the guy said was that Mr. Sam wanted it clearly understood that under no circumstances could Kennedy have Lyndon Johnson for his running mate. The guy said that Mr. Sam wanted everybody to understand that it was very important for the Democratic party—and Texas—that Lyndon stay in his job as majority leader of the Senate. He no sooner gets these words out than all hell breaks loose at Bobby's meeting—some of the guys getting up and hollering who in hell does Lyndon think he is, that he can call the shots? Some of the guys were mad as hell at the idea that Kennedy or anybody else wanted Johnson for vice-president. The Texas people are shouting that Mr. Sam is adamant about it and some of the other Southerners are hollering that they will stand with Mr. Sam on this. Some guys are shouting a question about where in hell did Rayburn ever get an idea that Jack wanted Lyndon. Bobby is standing up there at the podium, looking frantic and pounding his fist on the table and shouting for the meeting to come to order. It was the wildest meeting I've ever been mixed up in."

"What did Daley say?"

Ronan smiled. "Daley didn't say anything. He didn't take anybody's side. He just sat there, in the chair alongside of me, looking like an altar boy. When Bobby finally gets a little control and hollers that the meeting is adjourned and hurries out a side door, Daley jumps up and scampers out of there. He didn't say a word to anybody. Not even to me. He just cleared out. So I followed him out and came back here."

The two of us sat there at the counter with our coffee, neither one of us saying anything. I suppose, each in his own way, we were wondering how in hell Jack was going to run a campaign for president when he couldn't even get his ticket together. I don't know how long we sat there; not long, I guess. But Ronan's cockroach had vanished and the coffee had gotten too cold to drink and a bellhop who seemed to know Jim came into the coffee shop, went directly to Ronan, and said he was wanted on the public telephone in the lobby. Saying he would be right back, Jim went out to take the call. I stayed at the counter, wondering what those media people who had crowded around Ronan would do with this story—if Jim had spilled it to them. In a short time Ronan came back. He had a look of disbelief on his face, and he did not sit down. "That was Bobby," he told me. Looking at his watch, Ronan said, "They're having another meeting—at one o'clock. So I had better get moving; I'm lucky I've got that car they've given me out in front."

"What's up?" I said.

Jim shook his head. "I don't know," he replied. "I imagine they've worked something out on vice-president. Hell, the convention reconvenes in three hours. If you stick around, I'll fill you in on what happens at the meeting, when I get back." And he hurried out, leaving me to tip the waitress and pay the check.

I went to the lobby, now pretty well deserted. I thought I would be in for a long wait. I went to the desk and checked for messages. There was only one: a terse note from my friend Rex Goad, who was running the NBC desk. Goad said they were desperate for any clue I could come up with on who Kennedy was picking for vice-president. His note didn't say that this was now the big story; hell, he knew I was aware of that. The problem was that nobody in the media, including myself, had a clue. I telephoned Goad from the lobby, and shortly after I'd hung up, Jim Ronan walked in. He came directly to me and said, "Have you got a minute?" He beckoned me to follow him to one corner of the lobby, and we leaned against the wall. "It's not even one-thirty," he said. "We've got a little time before we have to go to the hall."

I nodded and waited for him to say whatever in hell he was going to tell me.

"You're not going to believe this," Jim Ronan said. "After what I told you less than an hour ago, and that was the straight stuff, you're not going to believe it. Jack has picked Lyndon for vice-president."

I didn't say anything. I just stared at Ronan as if he had gone crazy. Ronan ignored my look of incredulity.

"Bobby calls the meeting to order and, in control of himself now, he says we have to attend to the 'grave' business of selecting a running mate for Senator Kennedy. Same people in the room who had been there this morning—except that Sam Rayburn and Adlai come in, Sam holding Adlai by the arm. Looking at this, I figure, 'Well, it's going to be Adlai.' Adlai is sitting there, alongside of Mr. Sam, and Adlai has got a big smile on his face, and he's nodding friendly hellos to all the fellows around the room; it sure looks to me like it's going to be Adlai. And then a side door opens up, and in comes Jack with Lyndon. Jack's got his arm around Lyndon, and they're both wearing big smiles and—well, that's the Democratic ticket."

The big hotel that was serving as convention headquarters for the networks and wire services was only three blocks from our fleabag, and a cab got me right over there. On this short ride, I pondered what I would be able to do with the big story— now that I had it. I hoped that Rex Goad would be at the NBC desk when I got there, because he was a newsman of uncommonly good judgment—with the guts to use an unconfirmed story of importance, if he had faith in the guy who brought it in. Encountering a number of newspeople and delegates as I hurried to the elevators, it seemed that everyone was speculating on the question of who the Democratic candidate for vice-president would be. I wasn't getting into any of that.

Rex Goad got up from his desk and walked directly to me when I came into the NBC newsroom. Guys like Rex Goad seem to have a special gift for sensing when one of their reporters shows up with a big story; I don't know how they know it. When he got close to me, nobody else near us, he looked at me inquisitively—but said nothing.

"You won't believe it, Rex," I said quietly, "but Kennedy has picked Johnson."

Rex stared at me and said, "You got it firm?"

I nodded.

"*Jesus!*" he exploded. "Johnson? Johnson!"

"After what happened at the meeting this morning, I know it's hard to believe," I conceded.

"Can we name your source? On the air? Can we use his name?"

I shook my head. "I don't think so, Rex. He gave me the story, knowing I'd use it. But this is a marvelous guy, and I wouldn't take a chance of getting him into trouble for leaking it."

"I can't make the decision on this," Rex said. "It's too big for me; I'll have to buck it upstairs. I'd go with it in a minute on your word. But if I go with it, they'll start crawling out of it, the first beef they get that this NBC exclusive is nothing but a wild stab in the dark. I'm sorry, but it'd be my ass. Even if we beat the hell out of everybody with it—and if I had to bet on it, I would bet you're dead sure you've got this locked up—they would really be on my ass. I've got to buck it up to somebody bigger than I am; maybe they'll tell me to go with it, I don't know. But Kintner is upstairs, and you know our top guys are scared to death of Kintner; my guess is that they won't take a chance on having him blow his top by using an unconfirmed story. Sit down and relax; I'll try, That's all I can do."

Goad took off for an executive suite somewhere. I felt rotten. You get them the story they're dying for, and now they're afraid to use it. Such is broadcasting in the big city, I guess. Rex was back sooner than I expected. He looked angry. "They put the monkey on *my* back," he said. " 'Take it up to Bob Kintner,' they said. 'He'll have to make the decision on this one.' So now I'm going up to see Kintner—and I won't be surprised if he's in one of his bad moods and throws me out the window." And Rex went out again, looking miserable.

He was back in a few minutes—exultant. "Kintner says 'Go!' " he shouted. Then Rex told me to sit down and write as much as I could about Lyndon Johnson's being the nominee. I went to a typewriter and knocked it out as fast as I could. When we had the story on the air, a number of NBC guys raced into the newsroom, most of them shocked by this "exclusive" NBC report, and one of the big-name personalities thunderously protested that we were engaging in "outrageous journalism" of the worst kind.

When the protests quieted down for a moment I had a chance to talk to Rex Goad. "What did Kintner say," I asked, "when you told him?"

Rex looked at me and replied, "Is Kintner a personal friend of yours?"

I shook my head. "He knows me," I said. "That's all. What'd he say when you told him it was Johnson for vice-president?"

"He wanted to know how we got it," Rex replied. "He wanted to know who got it. So I told him."

"So what did he say to that?"

"Well, he surprised me," Rex replied. "I thought he would blow his stack—you know how he does. But he just looked at me, calm as can be, and he said, 'Don't stand there like a goddamned fool. We got a big story. Get the goddamned thing on the air.' So I got the hell out of there and came down and put it on the air. And now we've got more than two hours to sweat it out, with every son of a bitch in Los Angeles denying it. You really got one that's got everything stunk up." He was brooding.

"You're overlooking something, Rex," I replied. "I didn't call you about a vice-president; you were the one who called around, hoping for one of us to come up with the story on the vice-president. I stumble into it, and now you don't like it."

Rex Goad glared at me. Then he said, "Sorry"—which is as close as I had ever heard him get to making an apology. "It's a hell of a story."

A lot of my NBC colleagues didn't think so. The AP and UP teletypes soon were yammering away with snide little reports of the "rumor" without attribution that NBC was spreading around the nation on radio and television. I was shunned by a lot of guys I knew; they avoided me as if I had been found with some horrible disease and they didn't want to get too close to me. So I got out of there and went back to the fleabag hotel.

I ran into Jim Ronan in the lobby of the fleabag. He smiled and said, "Are you getting a little heat on the Lyndon story?" I nodded and said yeah, I was getting a little heat.

"Are you going out to the hall for the grand finale?"

"Yeah, Jim," I replied. "I am."

"You want to ride out there with me? I've got a nice white car outside, with a driver."

I said yeah, I would appreciate that. Ronan said we had better get going; he said it was just about four and they'd probably try to keep on schedule for a change, because the delegates wanted to pack up and go home.

It was about one minute to four. Ronan and I made a little

small talk. Neither of us made any reference to the vice-presidential nomination that would shortly wind up the convention. When our car pulled away from the crummy hotel, Ronan casually tapped the back of the seat in front of us, and when his driver looked back, Ronan matter-of-factly said, "Son, is there a radio in this car?"

"Yes, sir," the young man replied. "What station do you want?"

"Oh, any one of the big ones will do," Jim said. "One of the network stations would be just fine." And the kid punched it up.

I was only mildly interested in this exchange. It occurred to me, I guess, that there was something on the hourly news that Jim wanted to hear. The network had cut out for a station break. The local announcer gave his station's call letters and read a commercial about used cars or something, before sending his station back to the network. I was completely unprepared for what I heard next.

What I heard next was the distinctive, Bostonese voice of John F. Kennedy. The young senator said, "I am pleased to inform you that I have asked Senator Lyndon B. Johnson of Texas to be my running mate, as vice-president, and that Senator Johnson has accepted."

The driver of our car gasped. Ronan told him he could turn off the radio now. Looking at me, with a little smile on his face, Ronan said, "Do you feel a little better now?"

I nodded. "Yeah, I do," I said. "I really do."

As far as I was concerned, the confirmation by Kennedy that Johnson would be his candidate for vice-president was what the broadcasting people refer to as a "wrap": the task is done.

It takes a little luck, if you are going to make it in the news business, to be in the right place at the right time. It takes a little skill, I think, to figure out what the meaning of it is when you see something. And you get involved sometimes in a situation that places your job and your professional reputation in jeopardy; it takes a weight off your mind when things turn out all right.

16

ALL YOU DO IS
ASK GOOD QUESTIONS

N
OBODY HANDS YOU A BOUQUET OF ROSES or wants
to introduce you to his mother or anything like that,
if you come up with a national "beat" on an important story. A couple of people will take the trouble to say something nice to you if you manage, somehow, to
come up with an exclusive that makes your crowd look good.
It happened to me a few times over the years. Hell, if covering
the news is what you do all your life, the mathematical odds
are that you will get a few of your own every now and then.
But radio and television newsmen are far too concerned about
lining up something for the next program to waste any time
paying compliments to a guy who got a big story that is over
and done with.

At the University of Chicago one day, a professor, who had
a weakness for listening to the stuff I was putting on the air
every day, remarked that he had decided I was a modern Ren-
aissance man. The engineer who was with me laughed when
he heard the professor say this at the end of our interview. I
thought at the time that the professor was gently giving me

the needle. But later I got to thinking that maybe he was right. If the professor meant that I was dabbling in this and that and then something else, never settling down to become expert at anything, well, yeah, that was what I did for a living. It was interesting work, I would have to admit. And, as news jobs go, the pay was good.

As a street reporter, I knew I had to keep the spotlight moving around to keep the listeners and viewers interested in my daily reports of what was happening in our city. You had better change the characters and the scenery if you want an audience to keep watching your play. I rarely knew in the morning what I would be putting on the air at the end of the day. It was only moderately gratifying when somebody in the radio or television audience complimented me on the wide variety of the stuff I was putting on the air; it struck me as ironic that the people who took the time to say something nice to me had no understanding of the problem that confronted me when I set out in the mobile unit every morning: finding a story worth reporting. Some days I got pretty desperate, as the hours passed and I didn't have anything worth putting on the air. It could give you gastric trouble, if you let it—starting out "cold" every day. But it more or less keeps you out of the saloons, as the saying goes.

In my efforts to scratch up a story, I had a little contest one time with a fabulous, bushy-browed block of a man named John L. Lewis. The head of the United Mine Workers of America, he had sort of spit at the White House and called the miners out on strike. John Chancellor, who went on to fame and fortune in NBC News, would remember—because the 1949-50 coal miners' strike had something to do with opening the door that got him into the broadcasting business.

The big money people and the government people, who get terribly upset when a labor union guy orders a national walkout that disturbs the economy, were mad as hell at old John L. Lewis. His strike had an immediate effect on the production of steel, the building of homes and automobiles and refrigerators, and I don't know what else. The newspapers were coming down hard on Old John, and even the liberals, who tend to squeal a lot when it is their pig that is getting stuck, were quoted as saying *"This* time, John L. Lewis has gone too far!" I didn't have much of a personal opinion about the national coal strike. I thought that going down into the bowels of the earth to dig coal was a rotten way to earn your living—and I didn't hear of any La Salle Street financiers walking out of lunch at their private clubs to go off to the mines and dig coal. But, judging from the bad press John L. Lewis was getting, his strike seemed to be the most disheartening blow the nation had suffered since World War II.

I don't know why John L. Lewis came to Chicago to set up his battle line. There were some big steel mills on the south side of our city and even bigger ones in the Gary, Indiana, area, but this wasn't the biggest steel-producing center of the nation. Anyhow, Big John—with about fifty of his district and union local bosses—settled into a hotel on Michigan Avenue, directly north of the Tribune Tower, and reporters tried vainly to get him to talk to us. The trouble was that John L. Lewis thought he was being treated shabbily by the press—and, privately, I thought so too. He wasn't about to waste his time on any of us. We could get into the hotel ballroom where he met with his executive committee. His worried-looking subordinates sat on metal funeral-parlor chairs on one side of the room, while the great John L. Lewis stood imperiously off to the side, scowling at the world with gray-green eyes.

A couple of the assignment guys at NBC-New York had been on my tail to get an interview with Lewis, but I struck out every time I tried to get him. I couldn't get near him; nobody could. To placate the guys in New York, I did what we call a "think piece" on the uncommunicative John L. Lewis, and they ran it on the network "News of the World" program. I stuck it to Big John, I guess, and the guys in New York seemed happy to get this piece about the great negotiator who was too self-centered to negotiate. I didn't think much of this spot I had on the network, but John L. Lewis heard it—or heard about it—and boiled over. The UMW public relations people raised hell with me the next morning, telling me that "the chief" had roared that the NBC story had been "insolent and insulting."

"I'm sorry he felt that way," I said. "But what does he expect when he stands up there looking like Caesar and won't talk to us?"

"The chief," they told me, "feels that you newspeople refuse to give the public his side of the story."

"How are we supposed to give his side of the story?" I asked, "when he's afraid to talk to us?"

"Mr. Lewis afraid to talk to you?" one of the PR guys exploded. "Mr. Lewis isn't afraid of you, or the mine owners, or the President, or anyone else!"

"He acts like he's afraid," I said. "If he wants the public to hear his side of the story, why won't he talk?"

This PR guy glared at me and then marched over to the Great Man, who had been watching us but was not close enough to hear us. It seemed pretty obvious to me that the PR fellow and his "chief" were discussing what I had said, because Lewis would take a steady look at me every now and then. Finally the PR guy came back and informed me that if NBC was all that interested in getting John L. Lewis to state his case, he was ready. I gave the eye to my engineer—I guess it was Hozak—to set up the recorder, and I walked over to talk to Lewis. Introducing myself to the resolute-looking UMW chief, I said, "Mr. Lewis, for this interview, would you like to stand, or would you prefer to sit?"

The Great John L. looked at me as if I had asked a profound question. Then, in stentorian tones, he replied; "I shall stand. The Good Lord gave me a large diaphragm, and I intend to use it."

I had a rather long interview with Lewis, but, as far as I was concerned, he didn't say anything memorable. The NBC people in New York were jubilant when we put all this stuff on the line to them, and they got a lot of mileage out of it. But if the Good Lord had given John L. Lewis words of wisdom to pass on to me, I guess I wasn't bright enough to be impressed by whatever it was that I got him to say. However, I felt pretty good about getting a man who would not talk to talk.

About John Chancellor's getting to NBC as an offshoot of the big miners' strike—well, he was a young reporter at the time, working for the morning tabloid, the *Chicago Sun-Times*. I would see him every once in a while, at a murder or a fire or something like that. Unlike most of the other young newspaper reporters I'd see at the scene of breaking stories, he didn't seem to have gotten the word that—as a mere radio-TV guy—I was to be shunned. He was quite an agreeable young man and he had considerable interest in how I went about doing these spot news recordings. He'd ask the engineer and myself a lot of questions as to how the stuff was getting recorded, how the stuff was edited, how the scripts were written, and all of that. I got the impression that this Jack Chancellor had an idea that radio-TV reporting might develop into something, in due course. And it was on this agreeable basis that we got to know each other.

I came upon him one morning during the big coal miners' strike, out on a street in the black ghetto on the South Side of Chicago. One of the newspapers had run a story about the suffering the strike was inflicting on poor people, and we had gone out there to see if we could make a few recordings with folks who had no coal to burn in the stoves in their tenement flats. There were quite a few pencil reporters and a couple of photographers wandering around out there by the time we arrived, but I could tell by the hangdog look of them that they hadn't found anything much. I couldn't find anything, either— and we were about to pull out of there when this kid, Jack Chancellor, came over and said he had talked to a guy who might sound good on radio. This guy that Chancellor had found was a black hustler who had a small quantity of soft coal in a wagon. He was in the business of going slowly up and down the streets of the ghetto, a half-dead old nag pulling the wagon, hawking his coal at fifty cents a bushel. Chancellor said he thought I might get something interesting out of the black hustler, if I talked to him. And Chancellor led me over to the guy with the wagon, telling him, "Here's a man from the radio who wants to talk to you." Chancellor stood off to the side, with the look of a successful entrepreneur who has put a good act together, as I talked to this black guy about his coal. And

Chancellor has such a good memory that he probably would remember this—if someone wanted to ask him about it.

It wasn't the greatest radio interview that anybody ever did or anything like that. All I was after was a little clip of somebody telling me of the misery that the striking coal miners were inflicting upon poor folks. The black guy with the coal was pretty loquacious. He gave me the heartbreaking story of how, with coal in short supply, he had had to boost the price of his coal from fifty cents to seventy-five cents a bushel. It grieved him, he said, to be peddling his coal at so outlandish a price as this, but, "A man gotta git his money outten it, he go 'round peddlin' coal. De woman she lean out de winder an' she say, 'How much t'day, de coal?' an' I calls out sevety-fi, an' she holler back, 'Lord-a-mercy! How can a body what ain't no money buy coal, you is astin' so much?' I tells her, 'Woman, deys strikin'; deys pushin' up de price; I ain't gettin' nuffin extra outten it; is Mr. John L. Lewis what's gettin' sumpfin outten it.' "

The coal-wagon man told of a little experience he had had with a woman who had called down to him from a tenement window for a bushel of his coal. Filling up his bushel with the coal and huffing and puffing his way up an interior staircase to deliver the coal, he made a sad discovery.

"I gits dere wif de coal an' I puts down de bushel at de stove an' dis here woman ain't got no money. I says t' her, 'Mama, it ain't right, you puttin' me t' de work o' totin up a bushel o' coal, you ain't got no money!' She say, 'I kin make do wif dis here lil' bit o' coal dust I got'—a box what's got black dirt. I runs ma fingers in dis box and it ain't no coal dust—is dirt. I says, 'Almighty Lord, woman, you cain't burn dirt in no stove. Ain't nobody gonna burn dirt in no stove!' "

"So you had to tote your bushel of coal down the stairs to the wagon again?"

The coal-wagon man shook his head. "Nah, I dumps it out in de box wif de dirt an' I tells her is cold up here in her place and maybe she better keep de coal. She say, 'I ain't got no money!' I say, 'Yeah, I heard all 'bout dat. You pays me when you get de check from de welfare or wins de Pol'cy or sumpfin.'

I don't get nuffin outten it an' I hopes Mr. John L. Lewis roasts wif de devil fo' doin' dis t' poh folks.''

Yeah, we ran that on our spot news radio show. I suppose the well-heeled Gold Coast people got a smile out of it. Chancellor seemed to think this stuff was great. I guess I had gotten to be pretty good at getting little stories of the city out of unlikely people; but, hell, you ought to get good at something, if you do it every day. Bill Ray thought the story about the ghetto woman burning dirt was terrific, so I told him about Jack Chancellor's setting it up for me. Ray asked, "You think we could use him over here?" and I said I thought it would be a good idea. Ray told me to keep it in mind; he said he would like to talk to this kid sometime. I said yeah, sure, I'd remember.

It was only a couple of weeks later, as I recall, that I came upon Chancellor on the Wells Street bridge—leaning on the rail and looking down at the murky Chicago River. I asked him how he was and he smiled and said he was fine—except that his city editor, a guy named Karen Walsh, had just told Chancellor and a few other young reporters that, because of budget considerations, they were being laid off. "So you're out of a job?" I said. Chancellor nodded. "Well," I said, "I don't know whether I can help out any, but give me a call at the newsroom in about an hour and I'll see if Bill Ray has a spot for you."

Well, when I got back to the office, I told Ray about Chancellor's getting fired. We kicked it around for a while, and finally, with a little bit of a sigh—because he really didn't have a spot open and the business manager of NBC-Chicago would raise hell if he hired anybody—Bill Ray told me to set up a date with Chancellor to talk about a job. And that is how John Chancellor joined NBC News.

I interviewed a lot of famous people over the years, and I can't say I ever was carried away with the joy of it. To be honest, I'd have to say that some important people were not enchanted with me, either. Quite often, I got phone calls from members of the "upper crust" who were involved in some supposedly worthy cause, asking if I could interview some na-

tional or international celebrity who was coming to Chicago—
almost always for a high-figure fee—to be the star attraction
at a fundraiser. Sometimes I was interested and made a date,
sometimes I wasn't and didn't. I had no guidelines, really;
whether I said yes or no depended on how I felt at the moment.
I can't remember that I ever passed up an interview and later
regretted it; but I could compile a pretty interesting list of big-
name individuals that I did talk to and wound up wishing that
I hadn't.

I shouldn't be taking a postmortem shot at a grand old gal
like Eleanor Roosevelt, but she would be pretty high up on my
list. Mrs. Roosevelt had come to Chicago to plug what was then
a poor-people institution, Roosevelt College. The school was
being put together on two or three floors of a grand old place,
once internationally renowned, that had been the Auditorium
Hotel. I didn't understand, save for her well-established interest in low-income folks, what it was that prompted Mrs. Roosevelt to fly to Chicago to lend her prestige to this new place
of higher education; my recollection is that she was a personal
friend of Marshall Field III, one of Roosevelt College's founding fathers.

Anyhow, an interview with Eleanor Roosevelt would be a
change of pace. As I recall, Harold Ickes—the Winnetka socialite who had gobbled flaming swords for the Roosevelt Administration was among the dignitaries present. I think I interviewed Ickes, but he was such an insufferable, opinionated
bore, I wasn't putting *him* on the air. Anyhow, I was with the
high and the mighty on this occasion. They gathered around
and listened, gazing at me as if I were second cook in the help's
kitchen, as I interviewed Eleanor Roosevelt. I had a few other
experiences like this over the years, and it isn't very pleasant.
But you take 'em where you can get 'em in the news business,
so, ignoring this unfriendly sea of dead-fish faces, I had picked
up the mike and gotten into the interview with Mrs. Roosevelt.

Few of the famous men and women that I interrogated ever
impressed me as being genuinely special. Frankly, though, it
was with a degree of personal excitement that I had gone over
with an engineer and our gear to talk to Eleanor Roosevelt. I

regarded her as a bright and classy woman who had suffered with remarkable equanimity all that her critics hurled at her. She had been subjected to abusive criticism and had endured it, I believed, with grace and dignity. I didn't agree with some of the far-out theses that she expounded, but my opinion was that here was a woman of real class. I had been excited about interviewing her.

To my painful regret, the interview didn't turn out too well. Oh, it was good enough; I asked the questions and she gave articulate answers. But it just didn't hang together, somehow.

A peculiar thing about interviewing the high and the mighty is that they are subject to having a bad day, the same as anyone else. Whether it is fatigue or lack of interest or whatever, the interview simply does not go very well because the chemistry is somehow sour. I don't know what it is, and maybe I should know, having done so many of these things—mostly with success, but sometimes with dismal results. But I don't know. All I know is that, almost from the beginning of an interview with someone like Mrs. Roosevelt, you get this gut feeling that, for some mysterious reason, it isn't working. Both parties seem to get this feeling. And the worst part is that both parties then get sensitive about inconsequential matters and you get into nitpicking and the whole thrust of the interview starts to unravel. That's how it was when I fumbled the interview with Eleanor Roosevelt that afternoon in Chicago. It still perplexes me that I can't decide what it was that made me do so poorly in the one-on-one with Mrs. Roosevelt. Maybe bad vibrations were bouncing off the circle of do-gooders that surrounded us and stared at me with distaste. Anyhow, it didn't work out well. And while I salvaged something out of this interview and used it on the air, I lost all interest in interviewing Eleanor Roosevelt. On her not infrequent stopovers in Chicago thereafter, I declined all invitations to interview her again—using any kind of lame excuse to get out of it, even when one of NBC's big wheels pressured me to cut tape or film with the lady.

I suppose that a reporter with less provincial attitudes would have suppressed his own feelings about interviewing someone he didn't hit it off with. But I had this prejudice against attempting a second interview with anyone I had struck out with the first time. The Chicago Council on Foreign Relations laid out a handsome chunk of cash, for example, to bring in Clement Attlee for a talk. As part of the promotion for Attlee's appearance in Chicago, the council was eager to line up interviews for him. I was really eager to talk with this man who had surprisingly taken over as British prime minister, when the grateful British people voted Winston Churchill out of power immediately following the ending of World War II. I had been in London at the time, and I had read a good deal about Attlee, in part because it mystified me that the British would reject the fellow who had saved their bacon. I had never met Clement Attlee, of course, and I just wasn't ready for him when I walked in to interview him in a hotel suite in Chicago.

Clement Attlee was not a fashionable man. He was dumpy, with an untrimmed mustache. In baggy clothes and with a pipe in his mouth, he sat as far back as he could get in his leather chair, as if wanting to put as much distance as possible between us. He had a guarded look, and I thought, oh, boy, it's going to be tough to get anything out of this old bird. It was.

He was patient when my engineer pinned a mike on the worn sweater under his jacket. But when I asked him a few insipid questions, by way of giving the engineer a chance to hear how he sounded and get a "level" on his voice, his responses were so much mush that even I couldn't make out what in hell he was saying. He mumbled, by reason of the bowl pipe that he kept smoking, and never altered the wary look he gave. I tried to get him to say something interesting about postwar Britain, and I didn't get much out of him. The Council on Foreign Relations people professed to be delighted with this interview, but I wasn't. Attlee was hard to read and antagonistic from start to finish. I was glad to get away from the boor. And when he came back to Chicago and I was asked to interview him again, I said, "No thanks."

It might have struck some listeners and viewers as a little extraordinary, when my subjects would move from Everett M. Dirksen, the Republican Party leader of the U.S. Senate, to Joe Fink, the "Bird Man"—but that was pretty much my way of bouncing the ball around. I don't know how I turned up Joe Fink; I think I came upon an advertisement for his "Roost No More" services in the Yellow Pages. Anyhow, I looked him up and he proved to be loquacious, so every once in a while I would go out and have a little talk with Joe Fink. "Roost No More" was a yellow gook that Joe's people would spread around, for a fee, on the ledges of houses and commercial buildings plagued by pigeons. His gook would give the hot foot to any pigeon with the bad judgment to step on it. Theoretically, the gook inspired the pigeons to clear out and find a more hospitable home. I never found out whether the stuff worked; all I can remember is that this yellow mush looked so ugly that I figured Joe Fink's clientele would be better off keeping the pigeons. My interviews brought Joe Fink national attention. The *Christian Science Monitor* and the *New York Times* did stories about him—when he got hired to spread his gook on the trees of Pennsylvania Avenue, in Washington, DC, to rid the capital of starlings that might otherwise make a nuisance of themselves at General Eisenhower's 1952 inauguration as president. That was Joe Fink's grandest moment, I guess. NBC-New York called to ask if we had anything on Joe Fink, NBC-New York figuring that it was important news if the *New York Times* had it, and our guys in New York were joyful when I sent them some audio tape and film of the guy.

NBC-New York was not all that pleased about some of the other things I put on the air. I was always quite curious about the judgments the guys at NBC-New York would make about the pieces NBC-Chicago pitched to them. A throwaway story on a local man who was going to protect a new president from getting dropped on by starlings in flight might set our colleagues in New York to jumping with glee. But the assignment guys in New York thought it a little tedious when we pitched them my offbeat story about Lucille Ball laughing her way through the tale of a burglar breaking into her hotel suite and stealing her jewels.

Alfred Hitchcock came to Chicago one time and got to chortling so hard with me that he couldn't talk. Our conversation had settled on the matter of his audiences' reaction of near-shock to the scary stuff he put on the screen. Hitchcock said he could not account for this queer behavior, and then roared with laughter. Having managed to knock the great and genuinely likable Hitchcock off guard, I called New York. The guys in New York didn't think this was amusing; the guys in New York made a painful effort to be polite about my offering an unusual piece on Hitchcock, but I could picture them holding their noses, and I was sorry I had called.

New York did not hit the bait when I took a chance and offered a little interview with Humphrey Bogart. The Ambassador East had a grand public relations gal named Lucia Perrigo, and when a Hollywood star she really liked was in need of some publicity, she would ask me to do her a favor and do a piece. Knowing that she wouldn't ask if it weren't important to her, I would almost always agree to interview her star. That's how I did a radio recording with Bogart.

We had had a busy day, as I recall—a big fire or an execution or something like that—and I was eager to get back to the Merchandise Mart because there was a good deal of editing to be done, to get this stuff ready for broadcast. I was about to call Lucia Perrigo on the mobile phone to tell her I couldn't make it. That would have been all right with her; she had been a newspaper woman of considerable experience and she understood these things. But we were breaking in a new engineer— a highly competent man named Bill Easely—and he was looking forward to our interview with Humphrey Bogart. I figured, what the hell—we'll do it.

Bogart and I hit it off well. When I expressed surprise that an actor of his stature would be out hustling for a movie, he told me straight out, "I've got my own dough in this one and everybody's waitin' for me to fall on my can, so I appreciate you givin' it a plug." His wife, Lauren Bacall, was stretched out on a chaise lounge, sipping a drink that Bogart had handed to her. "All I got up here is Scotch," Bogart said, "but if you want somethin' else—or a sandwich or somethin'—I can get room service to hustle it up for you." I told him thanks, but I was in a tight spot for time—and I would have to do the interview and run. So he said OK and we set up.

It was our practice to have an engineer with experience spend a couple of days with a new engineer, to teach him the ropes. The engineer who was breaking in the new man was Louie Heiden. I got to thinking of working a little joke on Bogart, and I asked Heiden if he had a good-sized wrench in his tool kit. When he said yeah, he did, I told him to hold it during the Bogart interview and to watch for a sign of what to do with it. He looked at me as if I were daffy, and maybe I was, but he said OK, he'd be alert for a signal.

Lauren Bacall appeared pleased with the movie plugs Bogie was getting in. My thinking was that he seemed to be a nice guy who wanted a little boost, so why not let him have it? At the end of the interview, and Bogart sensed that it had gone pretty well, he looked at me and said, "Is there anything else you want to talk about?"

"Just one thing more," I said. "I'd like to close off this thing on the air with you giving me your famous line about Louie."

Bacall came up on one elbow to get a better read on how Bogie was going to handle this, but Bogart was plainly mystified. "My famous line to Louie?" he asked, looking to me for help on this one. Then he chuckled and said, "Oh, yeah. Sure! Louie!" Screwing up his face and giving me a grim look, he went into character and spoke the menacing words, "OK, Louie, drop the gun!"

As Bogart spoke the line, I gave a nod to Louie Heiden, and he dropped the big wrench into his toolbox. A look of panic flashed across Bogart's face at the clang of the heavy wrench. I thought he was going to jump out of his shoes. I felt like a fool, having worked this gag on Bogart—but Lauren Bacall seemed to think it was as funny a thing as she had ever seen. Bacall laughed so hard that she spilled her drink and rolled off the chaise lounge. Louie Heiden had a "don't blame me!" look on his face. And Bogart grinned self-consciously.

I think Bogart really enjoyed this little episode. He said he did. He wanted me to come back for dinner—and when I told him I couldn't make it, he warmly invited me to look him up the next time I was in Hollywood and we would "splash a few drinks around." But I never crossed paths with him again.

Judging from the phone calls and mail that came in when I ran this thing, the Chicago audience seemed to think my interview with Bogart was great. After all, at this time Humphrey Bogart was at the height of his career, and people at parties would get a little tanked up and tell their pals to drop the gun. But the piece on Bogart had dropped dead, as the saying is, when I pitched it to my colleagues in New York. I managed, somehow, to figure out a lot of things in the 35 years I worked for NBC, but I can't say I ever figured out the news judgment of my colleagues in New York. Almost all of them came from places like St. Paul, Minnesota, but something seems to happen to midwestern boys when they maneuver themselves into the big-money jobs in New York. I never could stay on the same wavelength with my colleagues in New York.

In Ireland one time, I had made arrangements with the Department of External Affairs—the Irish state department, headquartered in the old Guinness mansion on St. Stephen's Green, in Dublin—to cut some film about the terrible day when the British executed a dozen Irish patriots by way of settling a religious war. In 1916 the Irish Free Staters had taken to guns to press their demands. They had holed up in public buildings like the Dublin Post Office, which still carries the marks of British rifle shots. The British had caught up with the leaders of the Irish revolutionaries in a lonely area outside the city and had calmly shot them down. I knew this site held a special place in the sad memories of the Irish. To honor the men killed by the British soldiers who quelled the Easter Rising, a monument had been erected.

In what I thought was as poignant an interview as I had ever done, I discussed the Easter Rising with a soft-spoken historian at the impressive memorial to the brave men who died for "The Cause."

"It was here that the patriots were slain," the professor said. "It is believed that an informer, with the greed of Judas Iscariot, led these good men into British hands. It is peaceable here now, but is was not so on Easter Sunday, 1916. The British soldiers were barracked nearby. And it is here that the Irish Free Staters were rounded up. They were beaten and interrogated. But they stood firm, every last man of them. The British got no information out of those men. And Ireland's patriots were dragged to this spot and slain."

A carved stone marker was at each grave. Irish women, with black shawls on their heads, knelt at the graves, devoutly praying, beseeching God to be kind to the souls of the dearly departed. It was a memorable thing to see.

"The men who gave their lives for Ireland are not forgotten, as you can see," the professor observed. "I say thank God we have the decency to remember what others long dead have done for us."

"There is a certain sanctity about this place," I said.

"Yes," the professor replied. "But it was not always so. The graves so nicely placed, each with its own marker, inspire those who come here to feel that the men who perished in the Easter Rising comfortably await the final day—when, our belief is, all men will rise again for judgment. But the truth of the matter is that on the day of the executions, the British lined up the patriots on the lip of a trench and gunned them down. The bodies tumbled into the trench—all in a pile—and the British spread large quantities of lye upon the corpses; so much, I would say, for any belief the British have in the divine plan that all men are destined to rise again."

If I don't have to make a case for the substantive quality of the stuff I put on the air over the years, there is evidence to support a claim that at least there was a lot of it. In a reckless departure from its policy of selectivity in gathering up memorabilia, the Chicago Historical Society once carted away about thirty-five linear feet of my scripts, plus videotape and audio tape and film interviews that I had put on the air at one time or another; this assortment includes interviews with Carl Sandburg, Nathan Leopold, Roger-the-Terrible Touhy, Senator Paul H. Douglas and Senator Everett M. Dirksen, pro football stars, princes of the Church, and Joe Fink, the "Bird Man." It's all "on deposit" over there at the Chicago Historical Society. "On deposit" is legalese for making the point that I never *gave* this stuff to the Historical Society; it is supposed to be over there on "loan"—although I have often wondered what the people in charge of the place would say if I backed up a truck and wanted it all back.

There is a collector in the Chicago area that I hear about every once in a while who is said to own a huge stack of discs of the radio shows I did over the years. How this guy came into possession of all of the glass recordings, I do not know. They had been stored away at NBC-Chicago until some wise man in an executive office decided these things were taking up space and should be junked. Radio-TV executives have a special gift for dreaming up valuable ideas like this. The stacks of records were offered to me, when NBC Chicago cleaned house, but I wasn't all that interested in them either. Occasionally, someone will tell me that there is a fellow who has my stuff who is willing to sell it back to me, and I can't say that I find this an attractive opportunity.

In recent years I've gotten to wondering how I managed to get away with the variety of subject matter that I put on the air every night. But even a big-city bartender, who probably thought he had heard every story that could be told, might have smiled at hearing my story of the high-roller from Texas—the gambling oil man who had made so much quick money that he built the extravagant Shamrock Hotel in Houston. He came up to Chicago with his entourage of butt-kissers to buy the grand champion steer of the International Live Stock Show and got stuck with having to pay an extra eight thousand dollars for his steer, because we had run out of tape. A friendly auctioneer kept the bidding alive—to give us time to change reels before he cried, "Going once, going twice—I have sold it!" I subsequently interviewed the Texan with the big white Stetson during a hectic cab ride to the airport. In response to the Texas guy's expression of wonderment that he had gotten trimmed out of an extra eight thousand, I confessed. It made him mad as hell to hear why it cost him an extra eight thousand. I had a gift for making people mad.

CHAPTER 17

THE GUYS WHO PRODUCED THE BOMB

F ROM THAT UTTERLY ASTOUNDING DAY in August of 1945, when, as a GI in London, I witnessed the wild, drunken joy of a million people jammed into Piccadilly Circus and another million at Leicester Square— the lot of them in exultation at the news that the Americans had brought an end to World War II by pasting the Japanese with an atomic bomb—I had been haunted by a desire to know a little something of how so fantastic a weapon as this had been conceived and built. Maybe the day will never come when man, in his craving to play God, will obliterate life from this planet. But even on that day in London, when mobs indulged in maddened celebration at the news that the best brains on earth had achieved the ultimate means of fouling forevermore the human nest, even then it seemed to me that man was fated to be obsessed for all time, or whatever time might be left, with the dread that the fate of all living things was dependent now on someone, somewhere, whose fingers were within reach of a button that might activate the chain of events that would lead to total destruction. From the very beginning I wanted to know something about the source of this macabre stuff.

In the course of going to the University of Chicago's Institute for Nuclear Studies—which is what I periodically did for NBC News in the late '40s and '50s—it struck me that the scientists who had contributed to the creation of the atomic bomb were weighted with sadness over what their genius had produced. They clutched at a straw of hope, it seemed to me, that somehow the nations of the earth would find a way to control this terrible thing.

I had misgivings about these assignments to interview the big thinkers. Sometimes I'd get quizzical looks when I got back to the newsroom with the tape or film. Those who knew my limitations—close friends and members of my family—were aghast that someone of such meager background as I could be so bold as to go one-on-one with someone who had had a role in producing the ultimate weapon. There is really nothing spectacular about a reporter's interviewing a big thinker, in science or business or anything else; all it takes, actually, is a bit of homework on whatever it is you want the big thinker to talk about and knowing how to ask questions that provoke interesting answers. Getting somebody to give you information, having the ability to get it out of him, is all you need to survive in the news business.

But I frequently found it terribly depressing to interview atomic scientists. The depressing part, I think, was the sense of foreboding of many of these guys when I got around to asking what the future might be for a world that had to deal with this utterly destructive thing they had managed to put together. It seemed to me that many of these atomic scientists deeply regretted that they had played a part in the creation of so terrible a thing as The Bomb.

I very much liked these guys. Not for an instant did I ever forget that on the scale of scientific knowledge, I did not belong in their company. Yet, sitting around having coffee with them when the interviews were over, it was shockingly evident that while they knew how to make a bomb, they had some unsophisticated notions about such things as reporting and politics. It is a little startling to discover that a scientist of renown can be a dolt outside his own area of inquiry. It was always hard for me to adjust to the fact that an ability to manipulate the atom does not necessarily translate into wisdom about life.

The inner corps of physicists gathered by Enrico Fermi in 1942 to work on the ultrasecret project at the University of Chicago were worldly innocents. I didn't learn about their practice of moving about the campus with no security until I got to know some of the scientists, three years after their bombs had been dropped from U.S. Air Force planes on two cities of Emperor Hirohito's Japan. And even at that late date I was appalled that such precious geniuses as these had been allowed to roam freely on the grounds of a big city university.

It was the practice of Fermi's group, which worked behind locked doors in the bowels of the university's football stadium, to gather for lunch each day in the second floor dining room of a place called the Quadrangle Club. There was nothing unique about faculty in the same discipline gathering together for lunch at the Quadrangle Club. The romance language people ate together; the art historians, the literature people, and so on, had long been in the practice of eating lunch together at the Quadrangle Club. But it struck me as chancy for Fermi's big thinkers to have done this, considering the enormity of the project these guys were working on. When they broke for lunch they generally walked down the sidewalk as a group from the football field to the Quadrangle Club, two city blocks to the south. When they finished their lunch they returned as a group to the stark offices at the football field. The Roosevelt White House must have been aghast when word got through that Fermi's people were walking around recklessly. Lunch at the Quadrangle Club was the rule, and the big thinkers were an open target for mass assassination. When somebody mentioned this to me, sometime in 1948, I could not believe that Fermi would have permitted this midday socializing; the risks of his scientists' being wiped out in one attack were too great. I could not believe Fermi's big thinkers could have been so naive as to walk around en masse, on a regular basis, with no security people to protect them.

William Morgenstern, the erudite and proficient public relations director of the University of Chicago, confirmed what

I had heard about Fermi's boys' walking to the Quadrangle Club every day for lunch and walking back to their ground-level offices at Amos Alonzo Stagg Field when they put down their knives and forks.

"I almost had a heart attack twice a day," Morgenstern told me, "when they walked out of Stagg Field to go to the Quadrangle for lunch and when they walked back after they had eaten."

"Didn't they realize that a single German agent armed with a single hand grenade could do them all in?"

"I tried to warn Fermi," Morgenstern replied, "but he just smiled and said not to worry about it. So, I worried about it—twice a day."

My friend Bill Morgenstern, a special kind of man who zealously guarded his independence, had been a reluctant recruit in the Enrico Fermi operation. When Robert Maynard Hutchins, then U of C president, broke the news that, in addition to his other duties, Morgenstern would now have to handle public relations for Fermi's group, Morgenstern had asked a question: "Who's going to fill me in on what Fermi and his scientists are up to?"

Years later, when we were having a drink at his Hyde Park home, Morgenstern told me, "Hutchins replied, 'No one is going to tell you anything about what Fermi is working on.' "

Morgenstern told Hutchins this was the damnedest thing he'd ever heard of. " 'They want me to handle public relations on a project they don't trust me to know about? It's unthinkable.'

"Hutchins indicated they wouldn't even tell *him* what it was they were working on," Morgenstern recalled. "Hutchins said he had deduced that the project was designed to create an explosive force, nuclear in nature, of a type the world had never known. 'It's all very hush,' Hutchins told me, 'but the press might get inquisitive about so many prominent physicists showing up here. Consequently,' Hutchins said, 'someone in Washington seems to think it necessary to have someone like you available to keep information out of the newspapers.'

"Well," Morgenstern went on "I told Hutchins that some

of the science writers who spend a lot of time out here were already aware that something was going on at the University of Chicago. I told him it would be almost impossible to keep such a project out of the newspapers. I turned down the assignment."

"So," I said, taking a sip of Morgenstern's booze, "How did it happen that you ended up with the job of handling public relations for The Bomb?"

"I wasn't back at my office very long," Morgenstern replied, "before I got a message to go see Fermi. When I got to Fermi there were a couple of men with him, and I explained that you can't even try to keep something secret unless you know what it is you're supposed to be protecting. They didn't dispute that, and I think it was Fermi who said that if I would take this thankless job, they'd tell me enough to know how to handle the press. So I accepted the assignment, and they gave me somewhat of a briefing. That's how I got into it. My God, what an assignment! I couldn't even tell my wife. You know Dottie—she figured it out for herself; but we never talked about it."

There was one last question I put to Fermi's public relations man.

"Did any of the science writers ever come close to breaking the story of what was going on?"

"Only once," Morgenstern replied. "One day Roy Gibbons, the *Trib's* science writer, came to see me. He called for an appointment to see me, which was unusual, and when he arrived he made a point of closing my office door when he came in—and you know I hardly ever work behind a closed door. And then he told me that he had made a list of the renowned physicists who were working behind locked doors at Stagg Field. He looked me in the eye and said, 'What would be your reaction if I told you I've figured this thing out?'

" 'And what is it, Roy,' I said, 'that you think you have figured out?' He said, 'Bill, listen: These men are working on the atom; with their scientific backgrounds, all of them hiding out at Stagg Field, it's apparent to me that they're working on some kind of explosive device. So I'm asking you: What's your reaction if I tell you I'm putting together a story on this? I haven't got it all, of course; but I've got enough, with my own conjecture, to do a pretty startling piece about all of this. So I'm asking you: Now that I've told you this, and I haven't told another soul—not my editors or anybody—are you going to tell me to forget it or go with it?' "

Recounting this story to me, Bill Morgenstern sighed deeply at the recollection of a terrible moment in his life. Morgenstern looked at me and said, "I had known it would happen. It was certain that one of the science writers would eventually figure out what was going on out here. So there it was confronting me: a friend of mine about to break the story we were keeping from everybody! How do you handle a situation like that?"

"I don't know," I confessed, "but Gibbons didn't run the story until after Hiroshima, and even then it was an international exclusive. How did you manage it?"

"Well, it was tough," Morgenstern replied. "While Roy was sitting in my office I even considered calling security at Stagg Field to come and arrest him. My God! I couldn't let anybody leave my office to print a story like that! My God! The next thing you know, the Nazis would be planting bombs at the University of Chicago to blow us up!"

"So, what did you do?" I asked.

"Well, I looked at him, and I said, 'Roy, not ever in my life have I told a reporter not to print a story; even when I know the reporter is wrong, I would never do anything like that. I'm not going to suggest that you forget about this story. If you run it, you run it. But, I have some thoughts about a hypothetical situation similar to this, if you'd care to hear it.' And he said, yeah, he'd like to hear about the hypothetical situation.

"Well," Morgenstern went on, "I gave Roy Gibbons what I recall was a 'meaningful' look, and I said: 'Roy, if some smart fellow like you stumbled on a story that world-renowned physicists were working on a secret project that might involve the mightiest explosion ever to occur in this universe—and if, having this information, this fellow was foolish enough to write the story for his newspaper, giving him the biggest exclusive of his life—do you know what would happen to this fellow, Roy? He would vanish. Neither his family nor his newspaper would know what had happened to him or where he had gone or whether anyone would ever see him again.' "

"How did Gibbons react to your hypothetical story?" I asked.

Morgenstern smiled. "My recollection is," he said, "that when I finished, Roy stood up and looked at me and said, 'I think I've got the message, Bill. It troubles me, but thanks a lot.' And then he left; I seem to remember he said he was going to see if he could scratch a story out of Leo Szilard. It was widely known that Szilard was on campus and other reporters had interviewed him. So I didn't see any real harm in that. I don't recall whether Roy actually did a story on Szilard. All I know is that Roy Gibbons decided it would be a mistake to speculate about Fermi's project—and that was what I was concerned about."

Leo Szilard was one of the truly lovable nuclear scientists at the University of Chicago. He was a teddy-bear sort of guy. Some of his colleagues at the Institute for Nuclear Studies privately pinned on Szilard the sobriquet "Leo the Lizard," which I always thought an odd name for one of the great minds on earth. My recollection is that I only interviewed him once. I came out of it wondering what it was that Leo the Lizard was trying to tell me. But from the deference his colleagues showed him, it was evident he held a place of very great esteem in nuclear science.

Every time I walked past the open door of Szilard's office he was simply sitting there, gazing at a plastered wall. There were no pictures or charts or any of the customary decorations of academia that you expect to find on the office walls of a big thinker. There was rarely a paper on his desk and no sign of a big slide rule of the kind that Harold Urey always fiddled with. I used to wonder, "If this Szilard is so damned brilliant, what's he doing there looking at a wall?"

I asked Samuel Allison, director of the Institute for Nuclear Studies, about Szilard and his wall. But Allison, brilliant in his own right, simply smiled in reply. He could have talked, because World War II was several years behind us by the time NBC started sending me out to interview the big thinkers; The Bomb had long since been dropped on Hiroshima and Nagasaki. What I mean is, there was no reason that someone shouldn't tell me why in hell it was that Leo Szilard seemed to spend his days looking at a wall. But no one ever explained it.

I asked Bill Morgenstern about it one day when we were sitting in his office drinking coffee out of paper cups. I said, "What in hell are you paying him for, this Szilard?"

Morgenstern gave me a dour look. He took a sip of coffee. And he said, "We pay him to think."

Nobody ever told me what it was that Leo the Lizard was paid to think about; they left me to figure it out as well as I could. I was never able to figure it out. I came to suspect that Leo the Lizard spent a lot of time brooding. He had wonderment in his eyes, as he sat there in his tiny office looking at the wall. He had the look of a man pondering the frightening question of what accounting he and his colleagues might have to make for the creation of a weapon that placed all living things on earth in jeopardy.

I was in the mobile unit with Dan Hozak, cruising along the Outer Drive one morning, when the networks broke into their radio soap operas to break the White House flash that the Russians had achieved atomic parity with the United States. I didn't hear the bulletin from Washington; we punched up the radio receiver in the mobile unit only for the regularly scheduled news shows. But the mobile phone lit up as we were driving along the lakefront on this lovely morning, and I was surprised that it was our boss, Bill Ray, who was calling. His voice was urgent. He wanted to know our location, and when I told him, he directed me to go as quickly as possible to the University of Chicago.

"What's up?" I asked.

"The network wants reaction from the U of C people about Truman's announcement on the Russians."

"Bill," I said, "I don't know what in hell you're talking about."

I could hear his exasperated groan over the telephone. "My, God!" he exploded. "Don't you monitor the network? The White House has announced that the Russians have set off a couple of atomic bombs in some remote part of Russia!"

"No kidding," I said.

"It happened only yesterday, according to the White House," Bill Ray went on. "The network wants some reaction from the nuclear scientists at the U of C. And the network wants it as quickly as we can give it to them. Get moving!"

I cradled the phone and told Hozak about the Russians and their bombs. Hozak didn't know where in hell we were going to do this live broadcast, and neither did I, but we sped toward the university. By the time we reached the turnoff at the Museum of Science and Industry, at 57th Street, Bill Ray had called back to give us a location for the live broadcast and a few scraps of information: Bill Morgenstern was trying to run down a couple of the atomic scientists and get them over to the site to be interviewed, and the NBC guys in New York were ready to cut into the scheduled programming and take our feed as quickly as we could give it to them. Nobody seemed to know how long a piece I would have to give them, although Bill Ray thought it might run "five minutes or longer." There was not likely to be any way I could hear what New York was saying, but Hozak would be patched up to New York control and I could take hand cues from him. The preeminent radio panel show of those times was the "University of Chicago Round Table." The nationally broadcast NBC program went on the air, live, every Sunday from a makeshift studio in a university building on Ellis Avenue. This was where they had told us to go to do our Russian-doomsday report.

Bill Morgenstern had lined up four of the Fermi wizards to talk to us about the Russians' now having The Bomb. Hozak was at the remote controls, to feed sound into master control at the Merchandise Mart, where the Chicago engineers would patch into New York. I had time only to explain to the atomic scientists that I didn't know how long we would be on the air, that this whole thing was going to be ad lib from start to finish, and that I would interview them one at a time. Hozak dropped a finger toward me, and we went on the air. I started with Dr. Urey and went on to Samuel Allison and the other scientists. Morgenstern handed me bio cards on each one, giving me a chance to let the network audience know a little something about the background of each man. Not knowing how much time I would have on the network, I quickly went from one scientist to the next—wanting to get all four on the air before I got a sign from Hozak to wrap this thing up. I don't remember how long the network stuck with us—fifteen minutes or twenty or maybe longer.

About 10 minutes into the show I looked at Hozak, expecting a signal to close it off, but he touched an index finger to a thumb, holding up his hand by way of letting me know I was doing all right. So I went back to Harold Urey. Assuming that the Russians were as secretive as we had been, and that they had tested their bombs in as isolated a place as we had tested ours, how could Washington have learned so quickly what the Russians had done?

"With the modern methods of detection," Urey replied, "There is absolutely no question of the accuracy of the White House report. We never knew, understandably, when the Soviet Union would attain the capability to do what we have done. It surprises us greatly that they have so quickly attained this ability. But for a long period of time—for a much longer period of time than one year—we have maintained in the northernmost islands of Japan a bank of the most sensitive detection instruments. It is quite simple a matter, given Japan's proximity to the Soviet Union, to make constant analysis of the elements that are carried eastward on prevailing winds. There is not the slightest doubt to be entertained of our ability to monitor the experiments of scientists in the nuclear discipline in the Soviet Union. In turn, it is equally safe to assume that the Russian community of science has created and put into place instruments to provide accurate data on what we are accomplishing. These data, taken from the atmosphere, are a thoroughly dependable indicator."

When I got the cut cue from Hozak, I judged from the confident manner in which Hozak stood up and said, "*That* was all right," that we had given the network a pretty good piece. The atomic scientists were smiling and looked pleased. Even my friend Morgenstern came over and shook my hand and murmured something that I took to be a compliment. It intrigued me that momentarily, at least, the nuclear physicists seemed free of the tense look of guilt that I had come to regard as a sort of curse that had settled on them in retribution for what they had contributed to the creation of mankind's most awesome weapon. The look of guilt was evident in their eyes on my subsequent assignments to the Institute, but it was never again so painful a look—now that the Russians had The Bomb.

The western world had reason to be grateful, albeit in a grudging way, I thought, that the Fermi crowd had been the first to do the seemingly impossible. It was fearsome news that the Russians had achieved nuclear equality with us—profoundly disturbing that there were now *two* world powers in possession of the ultimate weapon. But you didn't have to be especially bright to understand that, grave as this might be, the free people of the western world were a damned sight better off than they would have been if Russia had been the first to possess the bomb that carried the power to compel the submission of all other nations on earth.

Some of the scientists had seemed to brood a great deal over their part in creating The Bomb. In private conversations with me, Harold Urey, the heavy-water man, several times had expressed guilt over what he and his colleagues had done. But their feeling of guilt lifted, I think, when it appeared to at least some sectors of the western world that Russia would now be pointing an atomic gun at every other nation on Earth, if the Manhattan Project hadn't beaten Russia to the draw.

In my not infrequent visits to the University of Chicago's Institute for Nuclear Studies, I was always pleased when my assignment was to interview Samuel Allison. He was such a decent man, so pleasant to talk to and knowledgeable about many things. This agreeable man, with his solid-citizen look, was in charge of this institute where the scientists who had squeezed a bomb out of an atom were pursuing further nuclear possibilities.

When Chancellor Hutchins, speaking at the dedication of a new building for the nuclear scientists, took some subtle shots at his university's having played so important a role in an achievement that "qualified the survival" of all living things on this planet, Allison grinned. The other nuclear scientists seated on the platform of dignitaries were deadpanned or wore frowns of disapproval at Hutchins' apparent desire to wash his hands of any responsibility for The Bomb. But Allison sat there and smiled, looking as if he were enjoying it.

Occasionally, when I had been sent out to fumble through an interview with one of the big thinkers, Allison would cadge a ride back downtown with us. He was good company, though he sometimes perplexed us with questions such as, "If this automobile is traveling at sixty miles an hour, what is the speed of the tires at the very top?" Allison would tell us that if the tires are at dead stop when they make contact with the road, the speed, of the tires at the top would have to be twice the car's speed, or one hundred twenty miles per hour. Hozak liked to argue with Allison about the accuracy of his conclusions, but I didn't have any interest in such questions as how fast the opposite sides of a tire might move. My line of inquiry to Allison was directed to other matters.

"Were you surprised?" I asked him the day it was disclosed that the Russians had attained atomic explosive capability. Soberly, he replied:

"There are no long-life secrets in science. Trying to maintain secrecy of production of The Bomb is rather like trying to control a drop of mercury on the glass top of a table; sooner or later, it will get away from you. It is simply impossible for one nation to maintain a monopoly on scientific discovery."

"So what you're saying, Dr. Allison," I said, "is that it's only a matter of time before we use The Bomb against the Russians, or they use the bombs against us, or we use the bombs against each other."

"Well, it might come down to that, but this possibility isn't the matter of highest priority," he said. "It isn't exclusively the Soviet Union that is going to share this weapon with us. In due course the scientists of other major powers will display a capability to produce atomic weapons. But I don't regard this eventuality as a matter of first concern to us. Save for the possibility that one of the major powers will get reckless, the odds, I would think, are pretty highly stacked against any of the major powers' indulging in nuclear warfare. The chance of nuclear warfare is always present, of course, and it is a very real threat. No one knows when a foolhardy government, ours or another, will make The Bomb available to the banana republics—which can't be counted on to show restraint or prudence. But even in this event, the world is not without hope of escaping nuclear war."

"The parameters you talk about—many nations, large and small, having a nuclear bomb capability—that doesn't sound very hopeful to me, Dr. Allison," I said.

"No," he replied, "It isn't pleasant, the likelihood of every nation of any consequence having The Bomb. But the primary consideration is not simply a matter of having the scientific capability to manufacture The Bomb. The control factor for this or any other weapon rests on the question of deliverability. If, say, our government were committed to dropping nuclear bombs on the Russians—or it were their intention to drop them on us—the immediate problem is delivering the bombs to the target. A stockpile of atomic bombs is worthless, unless you have the capability to transport them enormous distances extremely quickly. As yet, no nation has this capability."

"Which nation," I asked, "is closest to achieving this capability?"

He shrugged. "I don't know," he said. "I suspect the Russians are closer than we are. Rocket propulsion has been under study in Russia for half a century. The best literature on rocket propulsion—at least until the Germans involved themselves in this science in the early years of the recent war—was published in Russia about 1924. They've been working on rocket propulsion for a long time, the Russians. So I think it is reasonable to assume they are far ahead of us in the field."

"Do you expect we'll try to catch up, Dr. Allison?"

"Oh, yes, of course. It used to be that mobility—the capability of advancing your forces on the field of battle—was the decisive factor in warfare. Then it became a matter of victory falling to the force that had the superior weaponry. In our life span victory has rested largely on a combination of mobility and air-attack power. And now we are entering the age of rocketry. The great expanse of space above us will become the battleground. When a nuclear explosive can be attached in some way to a rocket—and it will not be especially difficult to contrive this—then nations will have reached the ultimate, I would think, in making war."

"In your projection, sir," I said, "does the achievement of this ability to transport atomic bombs by rocket spell the end of what you might call 'conventional' warfare?"

"No, I am not so rash as to suggest such a thing," Allison replied. "My personal opinion, rather far removed from scientific considerations, is that nations and the people who govern them take delight in waging war; I know nothing about the political sciences, and this is simply my personal opinion. But, measuring the possibilities as objectively as I am able, it appears to me that there will always be what you call 'conventional' warfare—although I can't for the life of me distinguish a basic difference between atomic war and 'conventional' war. Both are directed to the same end, namely, the destruction of people and their cities. The Bomb simply does it more quickly and efficiently."

"Does it bother you atomic scientists," I asked, "that some segments of the public are expressing indignation over what you have done?"

The physicist smiled a sad little smile. He studied me. Then he said, "When you were in the Infantry, did it trouble you that young men were firing rifles and artillery at the Germans, with the intention of killing them? I think not. You were brought into the Army and schooled in the best methods of killing Germans, and you were transported to Europe to do what you had been trained to do. I'm reasonably sure that most of you were too preoccupied to dwell on the morality of what you were trained to do. In much the same way, really—although some of my colleagues would be offended to hear me say this— the most able physicists of the free world were recruited and put to the patriotic task of producing an atomic bomb before Nazi Germany succeeded in doing so. If you and millions of young people like you were brought into service to put down the enemy, this is likewise true of the scientists who were summoned to work with Fermi on the task of creating atomic weapons. Essentially, in my judgment, we—the military man and the scientist—were striving for the same goal. In no sense do I mean to denigrate the ordeal that men in the Infantry or any other branch of the military had to endure; you provided us with the time we had to have to accomplish, in our barren quarters at Stagg Field and the austere, monastic setting at Los Alamos, the task that had been set for us. I am grateful to all of you for whatever sacrifices you made to give us the time to do what had to be done."

"But what about the growing sense of public outrage over this frightening thing that now confronts the world?" I asked.

Allison nodded. "Yes, 'The Doomsday Bomb.' You are aware, I know, that at the university we publish the *Bulletin of the Atomic Scientists*. The bulletin makes no effort to screen the potential consequences of The Bomb. Indeed, the time clock that appears on each issue of the bulletin implies that we are ticking toward the day of disaster. The thrust of the bulletin often seems to be, 'Repent, Brother, before it is too late.' But, with The Bomb in our hands—and now in Russia's hands—I do not expect governments to repent. Do you?"

Allison had been one of the four scientist-governors of Los Alamos, New Mexico, where the nuclear physicists put the finishing touches on their creation. He was on hand when the first bomb was gingerly transported to a desert wasteland at Alamogordo, about two hundred miles south of Los Alamos. In a control center ten thousand yards from a hundred-foot tower where the test bomb named "Fat Man" was in place above the sagebrush and scampering lizards, Allison had calmly counted down to ignition.

I asked Allison one time about those moments in the control shelter, giving the count by radio at five-minute intervals to General Leslie R. Groves, the Army's man in charge; J. Robert Oppenheimer, the director of Los Alamos; and all the men tensely waiting in other shelters for the instant of decision. Had Allison been sure this thing would work?

"Well, no," he replied, "You couldn't be certain. I *thought* it would work; there was no scientific reason that I could conceive why it would not work. Nobody knew precisely what reaction we might be precipitating. But on the scale of probability, my expectation was that it would work."

"This was a uranium bomb?"

Allison shook his head. "No. This was plutonium. We had a uranium bomb, but at the time of the Alamogordo experiment, the uranium bomb—with its less-complex criteria for activation—was already being prepared for transport to a bomber base in the Pacific. This proved to be the first one of the two to be dropped from high-altitude planes on Japan. We were exceedingly confident of the reliability of the uranium bomb. We were limited in the Alamogordo test to exploding the plutonium bomb, because, of the three we had succeded in creating, we considered it to be the least reliable.

"Upper authority, whoever that might have been, was anxious to employ only the weapons of greatest certainty on Japan. This left us with 'Fat Man' for the test at Alamogordo."

"That has always intrigued me, Dr. Allison," I said, "nuclear physicists referring to the first atomic bomb as 'Fat Man.' "

He looked at me quizzically, giving me the impression that he thought I was pretty dumb. "That was the shape of it," he explained. "The plutonium bomb required a much more complicated activating procedure than the uranium bomb. The more we theorized on the means of activating the plutonium bomb, the more complex—and bulky, you would say—became the components of activation. So we ended up, to answer your question, with an obese kind of bomb. The bomb at Alamogordo, I dare say, had a belly five feet across."

And so it was that my conversations went with the men who had had a part in the creation of the fearsome thing that seems destined until the end of time to threaten the survival on earth of all living things. It was sort of incongruous for a reporter who had spent his day interviewing atomic scientists to end the day with dinner at a steak house like Gene & Georgetti's, shooting the breeze with somebody like Joey Glimco at an adjoining table. But that is what I often did. I had no reservations, moral or otherwise, about talking to Mob-connected people; they won't bother a reporter who tells things straight and doesn't have his hand out for their money or their favors. It didn't trouble me to have a little conversation with some syndicate man. On the contrary, some of those I knew were fascinating. And at least gangsters do not toy with weapons of universal obliteration. The thing that stuck in my mind, from my dealings with the atomic scientists, was Allison's almost casual remark that the ability to deliver your bomb to any spot on earth was the key to a nation's gaining world domination. Consequently, it was terribly depressing to get off the elevator at the 19th floor of the Merchandise Mart one night—Friday, October 4, 1957—and find a newswriter standing there with the news that the Russians had put something called "Sputnik" into orbit. Well, here we go, I thought. Mankind was at the threshold of the biggest crap game of all time.

I was anchoring the ten o'clock news at that time, and I had written some of the script—stuff that we figured would "hold"— before I went out for dinner. The first thing I did when I returned to my desk was to dump the copy I had written. But I had a problem: I didn't have enough information on the Russian thing to fill up the program. Moscow Radio was doing a little bragging, and that helped. Somebody found a recent *Life* magazine that carried somebody's conception of what an earth satellite would look like—a basketball-shaped thing with appendages—and we had some slides made. Then we got word that an RCA listening post on the East Coast had gotten a "fix" on Sputnik and that RCA was reporting that the satellite was encircling the globe every ninety-six minutes and that it was transmitting a constant beeping sound. Various "experts" were interviewed, but all of their comments seemed to be meaningless—what we called "garbage." When I went on the air, I filled the television screen with the blown-up drawing of *Life's* "satellite"—doing voice-over with every bit of information I had been able to scrape up on this thing. A couple of times during our news program, with full screen on the blowup, I simply shut up and went for a solid minute with the scary beeping of Sputnik. It was frightening, and telephone calls of protest loaded our lines in the newsroom. Without having intended to do so, I had touched a nerve of terror in many viewers. It was a tough night.

It had always seemed to me that the day would never come when mere humans could provoke the Master of the House into coming on stage, the ring of keys on His arm, to speak the words, "It is closing time, gentlemen." But now, who knows?

CHAPTER **18**

ONLY AS GOOD
AS YOUR SOURCE

O VER THE YEARS, some of the best information I ever got came from waiters and captains and bartenders. It has always mystified me that politicians and business executives can be so stupid as to discuss confidential matters with a waiter present. Do they think the waiter is so absorbed in putting the plates in front of them that the guy doesn't pay attention to what they are talking about? There should be a class at the Harvard School of Business to teach the movers-and-shakers-in-training that waiters and bartenders are acutely aware of everything that is said. A captain who worked in the Merchants & Manufacturers Club, for example, used to give me a confidential report on the noteworthy conversations he overheard. My friend the captain filled me in on all that Dick Daley and Joe Kennedy talked about when they met for lunch in a private office at the Merchandise Mart. You never know, in the news business, who's going to volunteer information.

At some point in my career, NBC-Chicago decided that what I needed was a secretary. My mail was getting pretty heavy, and my phones were always ringing—to the annoyance of my colleagues in the newsroom. So they put me in a private office—to get me out of the way, I think—and they gave me a wise, knowledgeable young gal named Valetta Press to put some order in my life. Val seemed to have a notion that she was getting an inside view of things and, while my recollection is that she never learned shorthand or any of the other basic skills of a secretary, she had good judgment. She knew which phone calls should be passed on to me and what the fundamental import of a possible story might be. If a radio-TV newsman had to have somebody around to look over his shoulder, Val Press was as good as they come.

Val caught on quickly that some of my best leads came in phone calls from a rather large number of "sources." Her favorite, I guess, was a guy with a tired, raspy voice who called on a frequent basis with bits of information about the crime Syndicate, politicians, and high-living businesspeople who didn't quite measure up to their pose of respectability, judging from the inside stuff the guy tersely passed on to me. This caller, whose voice Val recognized instantly, did not leave messages, never identified himself, and would not give Val a crumb of information, if I were out. I think his refusal to provide even a tiny clue as to what it was he wanted to talk to me about annoyed the hell out of Val Press. She took to referring to him as "the Spook" and, in running down the names of people who had called when I was out on a story or at lunch or somewhere, she would put him first on her list, telling me, the moment I came into the office, "the Spook called." It irritated Val that I wouldn't tell her who the Spook was. When I finally confessed to her that I didn't know, she didn't believe me.

The tips the Spook gave me were invaluable. He never once gave me bad information. This guy had an amazing amount of information—trivial and important—about what was going on in the Rush Street area. If the Syndicate guys were having a meeting in the private bar of a great restaurant they operated—a place called the Imperial House—he knew who was there, where they had parked their cars, how long they had been in conference, and who said what to whom. The guy seemed to have the entire Rush Street area of Chicago "wired." Alongside the Imperial House—in a three-story apartment building at 64 East Walton—a well-educated dame named Kay Jarrett operated a call house that she referred to as an "escort service." Kay Jarrett, who bestowed her affection on two nicely groomed lap dogs, had a practice of taking these creatures out for an airing on a set schedule a couple of times a day, my informant told me. And I remember that when I asked my friend Leon Sweitzer about this he said he would send over one of the homicide cars to "sit" on it. Sweitzer called in a few days, laughingly telling me that wherever I got it, by God, it was true! Leon added that he was glad I had called it to his attention, because he had always suspected that Kay Jarrett, at heart, was a highly civilized woman.

Every once in a while, I'd work a parenthetical reference into my copy about Kay Jarrett. Val would get wide-eyed when Jarrett called to beef about some "insensitive" or "derogatory" remark I had made about her on the air. It didn't happen very often that Kay Jarrett would be offended to the point of wanting to complain to me. But when it happened, Val would beam a big smile and say, "Kay Jarrett! Now *that* is exciting." I always found this fascinating: the governor might call, or Senator Everett McKinley Dirksen, or George Halas, or somebody like that, but they didn't impress Val. I get a phone call from one of the most celebrated madams of the western world, and that, in Val's view, was something special.

In the nature of my trade, I have done my share of stories that cut the legs off public figures discovered not to be the paragons they profess to be. A good reporter can do a lot of damage to the reputation of someone in the public eye; you can dig up humiliating information about anyone, if you know how to dig. But even when you make an effort to go after someone and you hit pay dirt, there is a pretty definite line—or so I believe—beyond which your story must not go. It can be startling or bitterly amusing to discover something shameful about a prominent person or his family. It was incredibly interesting, for example, to discover that one gangster, whose very name was enough to instill terror, lived in dread of a shrew he had had the bad judgment to marry. But when I found this out I didn't see any point in reporting it. It makes a newsman look cheap, I think, if he takes a personal shot at somebody. And sometimes there are better reasons for not blabbing everything you know.

I had a pretty good story once that I kept to myself. It had to do with a fastidious gangster of considerable renown who, some years previously, had dug his way into a manure pile to hide from detectives who had spotted him walking around the "old neighborhood" and wanted to grab him for questioning. I was not witness to this beautifully tailored hoodlum's taking cover under manure, but I got the story from a quite reliable source. An old-country woman inexplicably blurted out the information to me while I was interviewing her about something else. The name of the fashionable gangster had popped up in our interview, and she volunteered the story of how, from her back porch, she watched this gangster dive into the manure pile. It could be argued that she wasn't a good source and that she probably made it up, but you develop acute and accurate judgment as to who is telling the truth and who is lying, when you spend years interviewing people. And I had no reservations about believing what she had told me. The story delighted me, but I reluctantly gave it a pass, because I suspected that subjecting him to derision would invite reprisal from the gangster boss.

I wasn't worried about myself. It was a reliable rule of life with the Outfit guys that it was easier to suffer in silence when the media reported uncomplimentary things about them. Hardly ever, no matter what brutal act was attributed to them, did they peep. It was virtually certain that they weren't going to rough me up for putting out a story that made fun of a syndicate boss who wormed his way under manure. Unless a newsman is secretly taking payoffs from the Mob, or using their girls or enjoying other pleasures such as complimentary holidays at glamorous resorts owned and operated by the Outfit— and I always made it a practice to decline gratuities, from anybody—the rule was that nobody would lay hands on a news guy. I could have used the manure story and come out of it, as the expression says, smelling like a rose. But I was seriously concerned about the possibility that the mobster would search out my source and beat up the old-country woman who had been my informant.

Civilized people might find it distasteful to have someone suggest that the heavyweights who worked for the Mob might punch out a helpless woman and do it without a qualm. But the whole system of organized crime is structured on the old-country precept that everyone keeps his mouth shut—about everything. Somebody is gunned down in an open street of the area that was known as "The Valley," the assassination occurs within view of dozens of householders seated in chairs on their tiny front porches, and the police can't find a solitary person who saw anything. Witnesses go inside and lock the door and remain unavailable to policemen sent in to investigate. If it happens that a policeman starts asking questions, the suitable response is a blank look and a polite denial of having seen anything untoward occur on the street.

The so-called decent element of Chicago and its environs didn't seem to understand that the code of silence was a condition of survival among the struggling immigrants who lived in the Valley. The decent element had a sense of foreboding about this neighborhood of poor Italians. The decent folks were appalled by the not-infrequent front-page reports of Italian mobsters shooting each other to death with shotguns and machine guns in the streets of their neighborhood. The decent element didn't understand the valley. But I did.

As a kid, although I lived in a safe, quiet, and "decent" neighborhood on the far western reaches of the city, I went into the Valley by streetcar every Saturday morning for years. It was no place for a kid of Irish ancestry to be walking around, and I was acutely aware that I was scrutinized from the moment I stepped off the Taylor Street car at the Ogden Avenue stop until I stepped back onto it, on my journey home. Some of the young Italian kids would scowl at me, but none ever talked to me. A woman, sweeping the front porch of her little frame house, might stare at me. A Mustache Pete, coming home, perhaps, from his job downtown as a street sweeper, might look me over. But on my earliest Saturday trips into the Italian ghetto it became evident to me that I had been granted safe passage and it would go hard with any young tough who laid hands on me.

I don't think many of the people in the ghetto knew what my name was; nor did they care. What they all knew was that I was the altar bread boy. Every Saturday, I brought a little box of communion wafers to San Callisto Church. San Callisto's was too poor to support a group of nuns, so the ghetto parish was dependent on help from the outside. And that's where I came in. I went to the convent in my neighborhood every Saturday morning to pick up a little package of altar breads that had been prepared by the BVMs of my parish. I brought the wafers the women and young girls of San Callisto parish would receive at morning Masses throughout the ensuing week. Beginning at a tender age, Italian males do not have much interest in attending Mass. Most of them are content to show up at church when someone they know is getting married or buried or when a child is being baptized. But Italian men are zealous in protecting anything that pertains to the church where their womenfolk pray.

I hadn't always enjoyed the chore of having to give up a couple of hours every Saturday to deliver the altar breads to San Callisto's. There were Saturdays when I had to forgo doing something I dearly wanted to do, having to make this lengthy trip on three streetcar lines to the ghetto. But it happened that the feisty little priest who was pastor of San Callisto's, and who was fluent in Italian and most of the Sicilian dialects, was my mother's younger brother. My father and my uncles provided money and clothing and I don't know what all to help keep little San Callisto's alive. Even in hard times they somehow managed to come up with whatever was needed. So, even though I was just a little kid, not even in my teens, and even though my chums taunted me occasionally—sneering that I had to give up the baseball game "to take communion to the Dagos"—I never could bring myself to rebel against having to make the Saturday trip to San Callisto's. My mother would never have asked me to do this, if she had had any other way of getting the altar breads down there; it was only on the rarest of occasions that my mother ever asked anyone to do anything for her. My mother was a totally unselfish woman who eagerly and graciously did anything she could do for anyone. Sometimes, when she was giving me the coins for the streetcars, she would ask if it bothered me a great deal to perform this errand for her. But I always said no, because I knew she wouldn't be asking me to do it if there were any other way of getting the little package down to San Callisto's. And I revered my mother. My father, who was a thoroughly righteous man, would have put his foot down against my making the trip to the Italian ghetto—if he had had any clue as to what I was seeing down there. My mother would have brought a quick stop to it also, if she had known. It would have saddened me, though, to stop my Saturday trips to the Valley. I had slowly developed an affection for these poor Italians—and a funny thing about it is that I came to be known as a kid who was "all right."

On the Saturday afternoons of my childhood, I sat on a little chair on the front porch of the San Callisto rectory alongside my tiny uncle in his black cassock. I was identified, I think, as "belonging there." The men who tipped their caps as they shuffled by and the women of San Callisto parish came to know me as the Irish kid who had a reason to be there. This was helpful in my getting safely down the sidewalk from Taylor Street, where I got off the street car, to De Kalb, where the church was located.

Most of the poor Italians who had settled in the Valley—an expanse of grubby flat land on the southwestern reaches of downtown Chicago—"cooked" a little alky in the basements of their homes, sometimes for themselves but mostly for sale at modest prices to the gangs that were forming to peddle bootleg hooch in this period of Prohibition. Cases of grapes were available for purchase at all the grocery stores on Taylor Street. The neighborhood folk would buy the grapes, carry them home, and grind them up—skins, twigs, and all—in a wooden barrel where this mash would ferment in a couple of weeks. Most of the householders who "cooked" wine would get a little impatient with the fermentation process, and they would drain off a glass of what they called "grappa" from a spigot on the lower part of the barrel to "see how the batch is turning out." The grappa was a clear liquid, and quite warm, with an alcoholic content of about 30 percent. It would light up a smile of approval on the vintner's face. Gang members would make the rounds of the homes that were producing alcohol for them, pay off the entrepeneurs for their trouble, and cart away the alky in shiny one-gallon tins; I saw a lot of this going on. I had no disapproval of this common practice of making wine in defiance of Prohibition, but the acrid odor of mash that hung over the entire area was unpleasant. However, the permeating odor of fermenting grapes was not the worst aspect of my weekly trips to the Valley. Every once in a while, sitting there on the front step with my uncle, I would have a much worse experience.

It was only with a sense of daring that a few of the better neighborhood people would drive into the Italian ghetto for a meal at one of the popular restaurants on Taylor Street. Somewhere in the course of conversations about what a violent place the ghetto was, the decent folks must have heard that not even the district policemen felt safe in the valley. One story was that the coppers, making rounds in the two-seater black Fords that served as the first squad cars, could not leave a vehicle unattended in an alley for fear that the young toughs of the neighborhood would steal the wheels and the tires. It was well understood throughout all of Chicago that this enclave of immigrant Italians was a very tough place.

In those days when I was hardly more than a child, the traditional beat cop, who walked his territory, was being phased out. The Police Department was beginning to get mobile. Two-seater "flivvers" had been purchased for every police district in the city. The most select of the plainclothes guys in the Detective Bureau toured around in big yellow convertible Cadillacs. The hoods (pronounced in Chicago as a contraction of hoodlum, and not to designate someone, as the misguided seem to think, who walks around with a bag on his head) had genuine fear of the dicks in the yellow Cadillacs, because they had a reputation for shooting you first and asking the questions later.

There was a distinctive, frightening wail to the sirens that were standard equipment on the yellow Cadillacs from Downtown. Sitting there on the porch with my uncle, we would stop talking and look up when we heard the siren of a Bureau Cadillac. It would really scare me.

I was sitting on the porch with my uncle late one summer afternoon when we heard that terrible sound. We looked up to see a Bureau Cadillac coming toward us from the north, in high-speed chase of an expensive black sedan. A short distance from us with the bureau car on the tail of the sedan, the guy in the sedan tried to turn into a nearby alley and didn't make it. He piled into a tree. He rolled out of the car, and we could see he had a gun in his hand. He started to fire at the dicks, and the Bureau guys, guns in hand, jumped out of their Cadillac and poured shots at their suspect. They kept firing at him, even when he keeled over and lost his grip on the gun. This was a terrible thing for a kid to witness, and for a long time afterward, I had nightmares about it.

My uncle raced into the rectory and raced out again and down the steps. Clutching a stole and a little leather box that I knew contained the holy oils and holy water of extreme unction, he ran to administer the last rites to the dying man. I ran after him. I was at my uncle's side when he knelt down, the stole now around his neck, and began the prayers for the dying. The Bureau detectives backed away, and I could see their suspect had sustained numerous gunshot wounds. He had been hit in the head and chest. The man was sprawled out on the barren ground. But his eyes were open—I was a long time forgetting the sight of the anger in his eyes—and he was screaming in pain. He was cursing in his agony and pleading for a drink of water. One of the neighborhood women in the small, impassive crowd that had gathered hurried into her house and came out with a pitcher of tap water. My uncle reached out a hand to support the man's head as he greedily drank the water. He drank all of it, as if he were pouring it into a hole. Then his head fell back and he was dead. One of the Bureau detectives looked at my uncle and said, "He was no good, Father. He's better off dead—and so are the rest of us." Never having seen anything like this, I was transfixed with sadness. The worst part of it, I thought, was that this man had died cursing. I felt real bad that, dying with curses, he had lost his immortal soul.

I have never put much stock in the notion that you always get some benefit when you do something nice for someone. But I would have to say I have been greatly rewarded as a result of having given up Saturdays to hand-carry the altar breads to San Callisto's. Over the years, there were countless times when politicians and gangsters and others who had lived in the ghetto breached the code of silence and gave me information—kindnesses in belated thanks for services I had performed as a kid. The woman who told me about the fashionable gangster's taking cover in the manure pile remembered me from the long-ago days when I brought the altar breads to San Callisto's. The fashionable mobster who took shelter under manure, by the way, had been a ghetto kid when I was making my trips there. He had been a member of an incorrigible gang of young Italians, junior Mafiosi known as "the 42 Gang."

It might have been that the people of the Valley got to trusting me because I picked up a little bit of the *umberta* myself, over the years—learning when it was safe to disclose something and when you might get beaten up or killed, if you talked too much. I hardly think it would have placed me in any danger, if I had used a radio report about the mobster's taking cover in the manure pile. It was only remotely possible that the Outfit would consider my using a story like this to be a capital crime. And it wasn't only my fear that the hoodlums would retaliate against the woman who gave me the story, though I was pretty sure they could have tracked her down. The man who had hidden in the manure, gross hoodlum that he was, had tried to raise his three daughters as respectable women. He was alert to the kind of company they were keeping and made certain that they dressed properly. He returned home at a specific hour to have dinner with his daughters every evening, and he made an effort to comport himself before them as a decent man. I gave a pass on the manure story, I think, because I made the judgment that the daughters should not be mortified by something their gangster father had done. Maybe it was a mistake—

not using a good story that nobody else had. But that's what I did—and the irony of this was it was all in vain, because their doting father subsequently was assassinated, and the media people had a field day describing what a vicious guy their papa had been.

It was one of this guy's trusted triggermen, apparently, who had whipped out the gun, killing him in the basement of his own house, in one of the suburbs. It was a typical gangster "hit." It seems to happen every once in a while that someone who is close to an intended victim gets the contract to bump the guy off. So the educated guess in the matter of who carried out the execution in this particular case was that someone of position in the Outfit, someone trusted by the manure man, had pulled out a German Luger and pumped a few shots into him at close range.

The detectives I knew in Homicide gave me my first clue as to how the Mob boss had been knocked off. It was pretty much routine practice in Homicide for the soft-clothes guys to discuss the unusual aspects of a murder—going over the details, play by play. They told me the Mob boss had been bumped off by someone he knew. An ashtray on the table in the basement kitchen, where the guy who got killed had been heating up some Italian sausage, was half-filled with cigarette butts—and the guy who was murdered didn't smoke cigarettes. One of the detectives made a matter-of-fact statement that the crime lab had "dusted" the cigarettes for prints, but no one in Homicide expected the crime lab to come up with anything.

I used to smile sometimes when I read an account in one of the newspapers of how the investigation of a lurid murder was making good progress. Especially did I smile when the story said, as a story often did: "The police dragnet is out for key suspects and the Chief of Detectives has disclosed to this newspaper that the arrest of a known killer is near." I guess when you earn your living covering Police Headquarters your city editor is on your tail to come up with a lead like this. But people who read newspapers don't believe this stuff, do they?

Traveling around is one way of making unexpected contact with a guy who has the answer to something that you might have been wondering about for a long time. This happened to me, for example, when I got on a plane at the Dublin airport—en route home after having interviewed Sean Lemass, the Irish prime minister. I was boarding an Aer Lingus flight to New York, thinking that Bill Corley, who had been eager to get some stuff to appeal to the large Irish population in Chicago, ought to be satisfied. Physically, and mentally too, I was pretty beat out, and I was hoping to sleep on the plane that was taking me home. It didn't turn out that way.

The stewardess took me to my seat. Lugging an attaché case with NBC identification on it, I found a man who looked vaguely familiar already belted into the window seat. He scrutinized me, and when the stewardess went back to her station, he smiled and stuck out his hand and called me by name. Shaking hands with him, and not being too pleased at the prospect of sitting next to a guy who looked as if he were going to talk all across the Atlantic, I said, "You've got me. I think I should know who you are, but I can't place you."

"I'm Mac Kilduff," he said. "Chancellor, who's a good friend of mine, told me you were over here on assignment, and I've been looking for you—to buy you a drink or dinner. Who would think I'd wind up sitting next to you on the plane home?"

"Small world," I replied—but it puzzled me that Chancellor knew I was in Ireland. Chancellor had been NBC's White House man, but he was on leave, running The Voice of America. I had no idea how Chancellor knew I was on assignment in Ireland.

Kilduff had gone to work for Pierre Salinger, the press secretary when Kennedy was president and had stayed on with Johnson—one of the few who did—when Kennedy was assassinated. In the course of our conversation during the long flight I mentioned that I had been surprised that he stayed on at the White House when Johnson took over. He hesitated a moment when I brought it up. Then, with a shrug, he replied.

"I was the first one to call Johnson 'Mr. President,' " he said. "Salinger had gone off to the Far East on some kind of a junket, and I had gone to Dallas with Kennedy. When Kennedy got shot and the Secret Service went racing off to the hospital, I was right with them. The emergency room was bedlam, with frantic doctors and nurses running around. I could see that Kennedy's wounds were serious, and it didn't take genius to see that nobody could do anything for him. Finally, the doctors eased away from the body, and one of the doctors nodded to a priest who was standing there. Everybody knew that Kennedy was dead, and the priest moved in for the last rites.

"It was traumatic. It all happened so fast. But then I thought, 'Where is Johnson? Where in the hell is Johnson!' Somebody had to tell him what had happened. One of the Secret Service men told me that Johnson and Lady Bird were in a little room somewhere, down the hall. So I raced off to see if there was anything urgent that he might want me to do. I didn't feel like doing anything for anybody, now that our world had come to an end. But it was my job, you understand, and I had to do it.

"The door was closed on one of the little rooms, and I figured Johnson must be in there. There was no guard on the door, no Secret Service agent. So I knocked on the door and opened it and walked in. Johnson and Lady Bird, both of them looking frightened, were sitting in straight-backed chairs. They looked at me, and I took a couple of steps toward them and said, 'Mr. President, President Kennedy is dead.' That was the first he knew of what had happened."

Visibly moved at the recollection of a terrible experience in his life, Mac Kilduff took a gulp of the drink he had in his hand. I studied him as he took another gulp and then, gently, I said, "How did Johnson take it—this discovery that he was president?"

Kilduff sighed. "He was terrified. He jumped out of his chair and stared at me. Then, he said: 'Get me out of here! Get me back on the plane before they can kill *me*, too!' So I went out and hollered for the Secret Service and we climbed into some cars and the Secret Service raced us off to Love Field, where we got aboard Air Force One and took off for Washington. And I guess you know all the rest."

You get to hear a lot of things as you move around. The anti-Vietnam War movement had its most infamous hour in Chicago in 1968. I never claimed to have more information about it than anyone else. But it was my business to try to read the early signs of things—and it was in the early '60s that I became cognizant of trouble in the making. Kennedy was president, and people were smiling about the rebirth of the fanciful place called "Camelot."

One of the earliest signs that we were getting into something serious in Southeast Asia came to me in Acapulco, Mexico. Over the years I frequently flew down there for a few days—to recharge the batteries, as the saying goes, and to play backgammon with Frank Brandstetter, who had built Las Brisas and ran the elite resort.

Brandy was a knowledgeable man. He had been a colonel in Military Intelligence with a combat corps in World War II. As a New York hotelman, he had been landlord to J. Edgar Hoover of the FBI. Before building Las Brisas in Acapulco, he had been executive manager of the Havana Hilton. He had stood up to Castro's roughnecks and gotten all Americans safely out of Cuba when Castro pulled off his coup. He had been host to the high and the mighty—to presidents of the United States, to Tito of Yugoslavia, presidents of Mexico, ambassadors, movie stars, and all manner of celebrities. When Lyndon Johnson was president, he repaired to Las Brisas for sun and rest. When Johnson's alcoholic brother, Sam Houston, was in need of a place to bake out—my friend Brandy took care of him. Discovering, at an early date in the space program, that the astronauts were in need of a boost in morale, Brandstetter set up an R & R program so these guys could take a week or two to unwind before returning to the Cape for the final stage of preparation for the scary adventure of being shot up into orbit. It was pretty interesting to sit around at Las Brisas, having a drink with a couple of guys, and two weeks later watch live television of these guys float-walking on the rock-covered surface of the moon. And when the North Vietnamese began releasing American POWs, Brandy expanded his unofficial R & R program to give the men who had suffered years of imprisonment in Southeast Asia the chance to restore peace to their souls and become reacquainted with their wives. As any of the astronauts or former POWs could tell you, Brandy was a most generous and hospitable friend. The government owes a medal to my friend, Brandstetter, for all that he did.

It was kind of interesting to be at Las Brisas one time and discover that Secretary of State Henry Kissinger, who seemed to have vanished—leading to a great deal of media speculation as to where in hell he had gone—was housed in a casa Brandy had provided. Brandy didn't have to mention that it wouldn't be helpful if I got on the phone and blew the secret. I had a good relationship with Brandy. I went back a goodly number of years with Frank Brandstetter, had ridden with him in his four-wheel-drive jeep into the mountain jungle where he eventually built the luxurious homes and chapel and huge white cross that towers over Acapulco Bay. Brandy and I understand each other and respect each other and would do just about anything for one another. He is, simply, my good friend.

I used to feel guilty, sometimes, when I was picking up fascinating bits of information in my not-infrequent holidays in Acapulco, about sitting on extraordinary stories. According to the purists, who really don't understand the news business, a reporter has some kind of sacred obligation to get the story out—with nothing more than a dusting of regret if somebody gets hurt by premature disclosures. Maybe the tell-all guys are right; I don't know about that. But I knew a Jewish bookmaker one time who said he loved to bet on the horses—but he considered it sacrilegious to do so. When I asked him about this, the bookmaker told me that you won't win anything but trouble if you mix business and pleasure. And I think there's a lot of wisdom in the bookmaker's philosophy. I have always thought you should be careful not to violate a confidence.

In the early '60s, Brandy was standing a group of us to dinner one evening at Las Brisas' private club, La Concha, on Acapulco Bay. The guy sitting next to me at dinner kept yawning. When he saw me observing this, he confided that he was beat out—exhausted. He didn't look exhausted to me, but I tried to be polite and said he had come to the right place for a rest. He informed me that he was an Army general, in Ordinance. Whispering, as if he thought he could trust me to keep a secret, he said he had just come back from committing a billion dollar's worth of armor to the Vietnamese.

I couldn't believe it. A billion dollars worth of stuff as casually as that? I told him I thought you could buy the whole country for a billion dollars. Oh, he said, our friends over there needed everything—tanks, guns, trucks, everything. In the manner of a man who is impressed with his own importance, this general who had never laid eyes on me before whispered that he knew I would understand that this information was top secret.

We were sitting at a table on Acapulco Bay sipping French wine. Brandstetter directed a couple of young Mexicans in swimming trunks to jump into the bay and fetch our dinner. The young men emerged from the ocean waters grinning, with live lobsters in each hand. Guests who had not witnessed this drill were startled to see the divers hand over their lobsters to a waiting chef, and dive in to get more. It delighted Brandy when his guests, unaware that a cage of these creatures sat on the ocean floor, were incredulous at this display of the Pacific's bounty.

I had always enjoyed the show, but this night I stood up and, saying thanks to Brandy and goodnight to all the others, I got out of there. It was harmless fun to be an insider on Brandy's little trick with the lobsters, but terribly disturbing to learn that an impressive amount of U.S. taxpayer money was being spent surreptitiously on military hardware in Southeast Asia. I had never figured out how the military mind works. But I had been around long enough to know that when military guys beef up for a war it is a good bet that they are going to fight that war. So it was with a sense of dread that I got into a jeep and drove up the hill to spend a troubled night in beautiful Acapulco.

CHAPTER **19**

BROTHER MARTIN
CARRIES HIS CROSS

KEEPING ONE'S DISTANCE FROM THE BLACK MAN—
who was then called Negro, or worse—was a white
America fundamental when I was out on the streets
in search of radio and television news in the late
'40s and '50s. For almost a decade after World War II, white
supremacy was as taken for granted in Chicago as in Selma,
Alabama. If there is something valid in the notion that you
can judge a people by the songs they sing, it is likewise true
that you can get an insight into the prevailing prejudices of a
community by reading its newspapers. On a day-by-day basis,
the newspapers didn't show much interest in anything, good
or bad, that was happening in the black ghetto. When I began
spending time in the black ghetto, picking up what I judged
to be important stories—although the daily newspapers didn't
seem to think so—one of the radio-TV critics lamented in his

column one day that I had once displayed a nice touch, but it had gotten away from me.

In the mid-'50s I made the Narcotics Court of Cook County—the first court of its kind in the nation, everyone said—a regular port of call. The editors of the *Evening American* were aghast when I started doing stories on narcotic addiction. Chicago liked to boast about its freewheeling, uninhibited journalism. The newspapers traditionally imposed few restraints on what was fit to be printed. But the newspapers were reluctant to get into the growing narcotics problem. If you check back on the newspapers of this period, you will discover that only in extraordinary circumstances was mention made of so unspeakable a thing as narcotics addiction. It was, the newspapers reasoned, a problem of the black ghetto. But if newspaper reporters had spent some time at Narcotics Court, as I did, they would have learned that even in the '50s the unmentionable, narcotics addiction, was moving into lily-white neighborhoods of the city and suburbs. It was because the newspapers wouldn't touch it that I got into the narcotics reports.

I had done a ten-part series of half-hour radio shows on juvenile delinquents. We called the series "They Talked to a Stranger," because the social workers and others who regarded themselves as experts in the academic studies of juvenile crime had uniformly insisted that the juvenile criminals would never talk candidly to anyone they didn't know. I managed, somehow, to have twenty young men bare their souls to me in recorded interviews generally lasting two or three hours. In trying to pare all of this tape down to ten thirty-minute segments, I used only half the interviews, scrubbing the other ten. I limited myself to ten boys—only two of them black—because I would have only ten half-hours on the air, and, while there was grief and impact in every one of the interviews, I had wound up with duplicate case histories: two kids who had shot and killed policemen, two kids who had been so active as burglars that their individual takes went well into six figures, two arsonists, and so on. Devoting a half-hour of air time to one kid, who specialized in one crime, was more compelling—or so I thought. It made for pretty strong stuff in the broadcast series, and I wound up doing a book on it for St. Martin's Press, so you can check up on what kind of stuff I did, if you care to judge for yourself.

The "Stranger" series elicited such response from the radio audience that the bosses at NBC-Chicago wanted me to gather up and expand the spot pieces I had been doing on narcotic addicts. I didn't want to do a series on narcotics. The subject made me ill. But I finally agreed to put together three half-hours of this sickening stuff, and my bosses were delighted. I wasn't. When they pressured me to come up with a title for this series, so the NBC promotion department could place newspaper advertising and all of that—well, I gave it the title, "The Black Mark." The title of the series was based, of course, on the inevitable contusions on the arms of heroin addicts. The subdermal hemorrhaging that occurs where the needle has been inserted by the poor unfortunate hooked on heroin is a more telling sign of addiction than the sweet-sour odor of the perspiration that dampens the addict's face and body.

I put together three heart-wrenching and shocking half-hour programs largely based on at-the-moment-of-injection interviews with despairful addicts. I had managed to find men and women to interview, merely by tracking down the poor creatures who had been busted by the narcotics unit. Some were pushers, surreptitiously merchandising "flats"—their word for the little packets of "stuff." Almost all of the pushers were hooked themselves and dealt in street-corner sales to support their own habits. Some were petty thieves caught in a stickup or something like that, desperate for cash to hand over to "the man" to pay for the fix their bodies trembled for. Some were men who had spent time in the federal penitentiary at Lexington, Kentucky, falling back into old ways after having suffered the agonies of getting "cured." Some were black girls who worked in a cathouse on South State Street, not far from Police Headquarters. I had quite a cast to choose from when I was doing stories the newspapers wouldn't touch.

Some editors of the *Chicago Evening American*, the sponsor of my spot-news radio shows, were appalled by "The Black Mark." The radio and TV critics at the newspapers had given me nice notices on the "Stranger" series. But the critics didn't have anything to say about my heroin addict reports. The irony was that I received print journalism's prestigious Sigma Delta Chi awards for both the "Stranger" and the "Black Mark" series.

We stunk things up pretty well with the "Black Mark" series—even more so than with the "Stranger" series. But my private opinion, once again, was that this was a rotten way to be earning a living. Description of what an addict looks like is pretty sickening stuff to be putting on the air, I know. Even my bosses at NBC-Chicago were in distress when I used stuff like this. Our newsroom phones were tied up with calls of listener protest the evening that I ran an interview with a black prostitute who explained her method of putting the powder and a few drops of tap water into the scraped-out cap of a Coca-Cola bottle and holding a lighted match underneath. An editor at the *Evening American* called up after hearing this interview to thunder, "Your nigger whore story was revolting!" I thought it revolting, too—but I also thought the so-called decent folks should be told what was going on in this city in which they lived. I had moved into a new dimension of reporting—quite beyond the quasirespectable areas of gangster murders, hotel fires, school bus accidents, and other misfortunes of urban living.

We had had one big racial story that the major newspapers had not been able to ignore. In 1951 a black family committed the incredible gaffe of renting an apartment in lily-white Cicero, which borders Chicago's Southwest Side. The apartment was vandalized, and the black family's possessions thrown out the window. On two successive summer nights white people living in that section of Cicero poured out to hoot and holler death threats to the nonwhites. Governor Stevenson, faced with all hell breaking loose, hastily sent in units of the Illinois National Guard to restore order. With all of this happening and with the national press sending in reporters and photographers to cover the story, the Chicago papers couldn't sweep this one into the back pages.

Bill Ray had expressed grave doubts about my prudence

when, as the riot broke out, I said I was going to Cicero. I suppose I had some misgivings about going out in so conspicuous a thing as our mobile unit to cover a race riot. I don't remember whether I was frightened or not; I suppose I was, but this was the kind of thing I was hired to do. Heading out to Cicero on the first night of the riot with a radio engineer driving, I stayed in touch with the newsroom on the mobile phone. All I could gather from the guys in the newsroom and from the constant reports on the police radio, was that there was a mob of raging whites milling around in one area of Cicero—in the neighborhood where the black family's apartment had been torn apart. As we neared Cicero, one of the guys in our newsroom surprised me with the news that the mobile unit of WGN Radio had beaten us to the scene. I knew that WGN, the *Chicago Tribune* station, had started using a mobile unit, but I hadn't expected that WGN would get into something like a race riot. I got an even bigger shock when our guy at the Mart told me a mob of whites had overturned the WGN mobile unit and set it afire. Bill Ray got on the phone to press his opinion that I should get the hell out of there while I could. My recollection is that the NBC engineer with me was my regular companion, Dan Hozak. I asked him if he were willing to stay or whether he thought we should clear out. When he shrugged and said it was up to me, I told Ray we would be sending him something on short wave and we would like to have a line patched up to the recording room. We stayed.

Cicero, Illinois, is a contradictory place. At least in those days it was comprised of three nonsynergistic elements: hardworking, foreign-born immigrants who lived in neat-as-a-pin homes, where the grass was green and nicely cut and the bushes always trimmed; the giant industrial plants of major companies that provided steady work, at good wages, for the men who had settled here to raise their families; and the crime syndicate gambling houses, whorehouses, and all-night drinking places. Cicero was the place where the Scarface Al Capone mob had centered its operations. The big-corporation executives didn't concern themselves with the Capone gangsters, the Capone gangsters were meticulous about not causing the slightest trouble for the corporate giants, and the old-country working people retained an indifference toward both the wealthy factory operators and the girlie joint-gambling hall underlings of Al Capone. The corporations were regular contributors to all worthy causes and quick to write out a check when funds were needed for civic improvements. Nonresidents who drove to Cicero for a big night ran the risk of getting fleeced or beaten up in a whorehouse or something like that. The homicide guys in Chicago were certain that they were getting the bullet-torn bodies of guys who had suffered the misfortune of getting murdered by the Capones in Cicero. The Capones were pretty discreet about not shooting up somebody in front of witnesses, nor were they so untidy as to clutter up Cicero streets with the remains of those who got murdered. Yeah, Cicero was quite a place.

I had rather expected, when Hozak inched the mobile unit into the mob that was gathered in front of the apartment building, that the people who crowded in on us were intent upon putting the torch to our unit. But when I got out to confront the most voluble of these irate folks, they seemed to regard the microphone I held in my hand as providing the fortuitous opportunity to let the outside world know of the terrible injustice that the black family had tried to work on them. Apart from having a sense of relief that they were not going to wreck our unit, I was pleased that those who wanted to speak their thoughts were so mouthy. My recollection is that it was strong stuff—made worse, I guess, by the accents that must have raised the question in the minds of listeners as to just who in hell these people thought they were that they should be telling the rest of us how to run our country.

Hozak had set up the short wave, and NBC had hustled a couple of engineers over to the Civic Opera facility to receive the transmission and put it on a line to the recording studio. Cicero folks crowded in on me to speak their minds, and it was only when I got a "cut" sign from Hozak that I told the Cicero libertarians I had all I could handle at this moment. Bill Ray had called me on the mobile phone and, closing the windows to shut out the mob's howling, I gave some of my personal impressions—with full awareness that what I said was being recorded and would be used on the ten o'clock news. When we finished up with this, Ray said something complimentary about the stuff I had given them. Then he said something that gave me pause.

"How long will it take you," Bill Ray asked, "to get out of there? How long will it take you and Hozak to get clear of that mob and get safely on the way back here?"

"Oh, I don't know," I replied. "We're a couple of blocks from 22nd Street, and I think we'll be in the clear when we get there. They had state coppers all over the place when we came in. Having to worm our way through this mob, it would take about fifteen or twenty minutes, I imagine. What's so important about our getting out of here? You've got the stuff. It's recorded. I can't get you anything better than that."

"My God, man!" he exploded. "Don't you understand we'll be putting this stuff on the air in fifteen minutes? You've got to get out of there. Those people out there are going to be mad as a son of a bitch when they hear this stuff on the air. I'm not fooling," he said, "I am ordering you to get out of there!"

I laughed. I had been working for Bill Ray for a long time, and he had never "ordered" me to do anything. Besides, I thought he was overly concerned about Hozak and me; maybe the people who lived in Cicero might be a little offended by some of the personal observations I had recorded, but basically our stuff consisted of the outrageous things they had said and had *wanted* to say. Even so, Hozak pushed his short-wave stuff into the unit and we took off, barely able to inch forward down the block or two to 22nd Street. We had reached that heavily policed main thoroughfare and had gunned the unit to get us back to Chicago when the ten o'clock news came in on our receiver. Listening to it, I had to agree with Bill Ray's assessment; it was a lot stronger than I had thought it was. When he called me on the mobile phone to find out if we were all right, I felt that I owed it to him, after assuring him that we were free and clear, to admit he had probably been right that the white mob would have torn our unit apart after hearing our broadcast on the race riot.

It is immodest to say so, and this Cicero race riot happened a long time ago, but I thought that Hozak and I had done a damned good job under difficult circumstances. I remember hoping that the radio-TV critic who had expressed sadness that I had lost my zip had heard our report and that he might do a follow-up, saying "Well, he ain't dead yet"—or something flattering like that. I'd have to say that the Chicago newspapers did a good clean job in their coverage of the Cicero race riot. It would be a reasonable guess that the guys in the city rooms—at least at the *Evening American*, where the guys knew me—would have gathered around a radio to listen to what I had been able to turn up, snitching a few quotes out of our best interviews for inclusion in their stories. This was the biggest story of its kind to have popped up in the Chicago area in more than a generation, and some of the newspaper guys I knew were nice enough to tell me that I had beaten the hell out of the dailies.

As with any major story, the Cicero race riot died out pretty fast. The black folks seemed to have decided, when things cooled down, that they had been a little premature in thinking that the working stiffs of Cicero, Illinois, might be ready to accept them as neighbors. The white folks who had settled down in Cicero to enjoy the freedoms of this new land responded with looks of, "Who, *me?*" when newspaper reporters came in search of follow-up stories. There isn't all that much to talk about, really, after the act has been done; it's like standing in front of the rubble of a building that has been bombed, trying to describe what it used to look like.

It didn't bother me that the Cicero riot story quickly passed out of our area of interest; it is part of the nature of radio and TV news to skim the cream off the big stories and move on to something else, leaving the print people to splash around in the skimmed milk for a while, if that is what they want to do. But as I remember it, the Chicago newspapers didn't do much splashing around when the Chicago area discovered that the sport of white folks making life miserable for black folks was not confined to such states as Alabama. Perhaps with thoughts of what the Cicero riot might portend for sweet Chicago, the newspaper editors were not eager to keep the Cicero story alive.

Cicero itself set a sterling example of how a troubled city should put its troubles behind it. It annoyed the power center of Cicero, I think, that Governor Stevenson delayed ordering the Illinois National Guard to pack up and get out. But such big employers as Western Electric went right back to work. The Capone mob faced no interrupttion in the operation of its profitable whorehouses and gambling joints. The God-fearing immigrants went back to their well-scrubbed little bungalows, going off to catch the bus to work in the morning, with a paper bag of lunch in hand. Thoughtful people with long memories might have brooded that the Chicago area had not seen this kind of racial violence for thirty years, going back to the time when the Back-of-the-Yards white folks had beaten up on blacks, in a four-day rampage that left 38 dead—white as well as black—and 500 injured. But the bottom line of this new outbreak of racial violence seemed to be that the ethnic resisters of Cicero had turned back a black invasion and that life should now be comfortable again.

As objectively as I had been able, I had covered a tough story, and I was as anxious as anyone else to get it out of my mind. But, unavoidably, it sharpens your interest in the status of racial justice in your city when you witness racial conflict in a nearby town.

If you checked back, you would discover, I think, that the manpower needs that arose in the industrial centers of the nation during World War I induced the heavy black migration that brought massive change to the racial makeup of Chicago and other cities; with so many young men off fighting the Hun, there was a need to replenish the work force that produced the steel and butchered the hogs. A thousand or more blacks came into Chicago every day on the grubby day coaches of the Illinois Central Railroad. And these new arrivals had no desire to go back to the plantation states they had come from once the war was over and their job opportunities died out.

As the black population continued to bulge, white house-holders on the fringe of the ghetto sold their property and moved out, grudgingly giving way to the blacks block by block. The only neighborhood that stood fast was the area called Bridgeport, in which a variety of white ethnic groups had set-tled. Someone of dark complexion dared not tread, much less live, in Bridgeport. This place called Bridgeport, populated by immigrants who had found work in the steel mills and the Chicago Stock Yards, became a white enclave in a black sea. Mayor Daley, Bridgeport's favorite son, had reason to fear the potential for racial conflict. As a youth, he had witnessed the 1919 race riots, in which Bridgeport boys manned the front lines.

I would claim to no special insight into what was happening in Chicago—except that I was out on the street every day, going into black neighborhoods as well as white ones. I would have been dense if I had not become aware that Chicago was philo-sophically, as well as geographically, a segregated city.

Confinement of black kids to their own schools, common practice in the South, was the by-product in Chicago of the business and political establishment's policy of confining blacks to their own neighborhoods. The public schools in the South Side ghetto crowded up. Forbidden by arbitrary school district boundaries from spilling over into less crowded white schools, the black kids started to jam up in the buildings designated for them. Because of the overcrowding, textbooks and other learn-ing materials were in short supply, disciplinary problems in-creased, and the best qualified teachers exercised their senior-ity rights to transfer to less crowded white schools. The growing crisis of segregation in the public schools of Chicago began quietly to tick away like a bomb in Mayor Daley's paradise.

A couple of the newspapers' education writers dug up some damaging stuff on the public school system. How could they miss finding out what was going on when they were covering the Board of Education on a regular basis? But most of the exposés wound up "on the spike"—which meant that by edi-torial degree it wasn't getting into the newspaper. I suppose I would never have gotten into the sensitive school stories if the newspapers had been making a genuine effort to tell the story. But they studiously avoided saying much that was derogatory about the public schools' administration. I had gotten into the practice of looking around for virgin subject matter, in order that radio-TV reporting might win recognition as a source of significant information. Consequently, I got involved in the otherwise-not-reported story of the deliberate segregation of the Chicago public school system. And as far as audience resentment could be measured, even the narcotic-addict stories were kid stuff compared to stories that dug into the guts of racial segregation.

I got into the business of pounding away at School Superintendent Benjamin Willis, accusing him of gerrymandering school district boundaries to prevent black kids from attending all-white schools. The sullen resentment on both sides of this intense racial controversy was probably fed by the frequency of my going on the air with documentation that I think supported the argument that Chicago was the most bigoted of all the northern cities. My news reports and commentaries galled the hell out of my white brethren. I received unsigned mail that called me every vile word I had ever heard, and anonymous telephone threats. The newspapers reported any story pertaining to Dr. Willis with admiration and respect. Newspaper editors I knew gazed coolly at me when it chanced that our paths would cross, making it pretty obvious that they regarded me now as a pariah. Even the broad-minded guys at the *Evening American* made a point of not wanting to be too close to me.

The better element of Chicago was quick to express displeasure at the school stories I began putting together. It became obvious to me that our general manager was getting a little heat, in a polite way, from the affluent folks who had attained a degree of social status. Sometimes, someone who was part of the community that holds itself to be superior to everybody else would make an effort to search me out at a social affair—to make a genteel rebuttal of something I had said on the air. Quite a number of the "cultivated" set who made an effort to straighten me out in my views of racial and economic injustice would precede their argument by saying, "I want you to know that, personally, I am not 'prejudiced' or anything like that, but—"

I suppose someone reading this might come to the conclusion that I regarded myself, during the '50s and the '60s when I was pounding away at segregation of Chicago's public schools, as a heroic "crusader" or something like that. It wouldn't be correct to assume this. No way. There is a considerable distinction between reformer and reporter; the reformer has a "cause," and the reporter is merely trying to lay out the best information he can get on what is going on. But it seemed to me that our nation had come to the point where it would have to face up to the likelihood that things were going to get a lot worse, if we continued to regard the principle that all men are created equal as a prayerful thing intoned on Abraham Lincoln's birthday—but a precept, that, realistically, wasn't to be taken seriously. I came, in short, to a private conviction that if the white folks sincerely required the black folks to merit equality by lifting themselves up by their bootstraps, the least that the white folks must do is provide the black kids with schools where they could learn how to spell *shoe*.

Willis persistently denied that he was cavalierly perpetuating racial segregation in Chicago's public schools. And then, in the early '60s, a black lawyer from New York came to Chicago and started to stink things up for Ben Willis.

I was at home working on the day's radio-TV commentaries—finding it easier to write my copy at home than in my office at NBC—when my "associate" Val Press called to ask if I knew a guy named Paul Zuber. The name sounded sort of familiar, but I just couldn't recollect who this guy Zuber might be. So she told me. Zuber had been the attorney who won one of the first historic school desegregation cases—in New Rochelle, New York. Well, I didn't see the connection, but Val Press said he wanted to have lunch with me—and, was I willing? I said sure, I would meet the guy and buy him lunch at the Merchants & Manufacturers Club at the Merchandise Mart.

It wasn't until I was walking into the M & M Club that it dawned on me that I had no idea what this fellow looked like and that it might be a little difficult to spot him. But I had no trouble; as Zuber said, when we sat down at a table, "I knew you would find me right away, because I figured I would be the only black man in the place."

Well, it was true. You hardly ever saw a black man, unless he were the porter in charge of the men's room, at the M & M Club. The carpet and furniture people who were members of the M & M Club did not like Negroes showing up for lunch. I told Zuber about this, by way of explaining why the captain had marched us to a far corner of the dining room, while club members halted their forks in midair and gawked at us. Zuber grinned.

"It's kind of ironic," I said. "This is a club that is controlled by the building—and the Kennedy family owns the building."

Zuber nodded good naturedly. "It's the old story," he said, "Don't do as I do. Do as I say."

I was immediately impressed by Zuber. He was quite well informed about the makeup of Chicago's power structure. But Zuber didn't seem to appreciate that the ruling coalition of politicians, financiers, merchandisers, and labor bosses—though philosophically divided—pragmatically held together because there was a little something in it for every group that had a part in controlling the city. I was not surprised that this black lawyer from New York had not figured out why it was that Chicago was able to gloat, and not without reason, that it was "the city that worked." Eventually, he figured it out.

Zuber was exceedingly confident that he could bring an end to Chicago's practice of maintaining a segregated school system. Sitting at an isolated luncheon table in the M & M Club on the day we met, I had a question for Zuber: "How is it that a fellow like you, from New York, has come out here to make the Chicago Board of Education mend its ways?"

"If you're asking me if I want to be here," he said, "or if I regard this as a 'sacred cause,' the answer is 'no' on both counts. I took on the New Rochelle case because important people, white and black, put pressure on me to do so. I wasn't eager to get into it, but when I reviewed the evidence I decided that if the U.S. Constitution meant anything, New Rochelle's school segregation was legally indefensible. So I took the case. And I won. The court couldn't have ruled any other way. The evidence was too strong. But the case took more than two years out of my life. I didn't make any money. I had to pay a lot of expenses out of my own pocket. It was hard on my family life. When it was over I went back to earning a living—and I sure wasn't looking to come to Chicago."

"So how did you get here?" I asked.

"Civil rights groups asked me to take on the Chicago case," Zuber replied. "But I turned them down. My priority was to start earning my family a decent living."

"But you came out here anyway," I said.

"I got a call from Thurgood Marshall," Zuber said, "and I was back into it again."

"What did he say?"

Zuber studied me for a moment, then replied, "There is no black man in the legal profession who has achieved more for civil rights than Thurgood Marshall. He didn't pressure me; he had been told that I had refused the Chicago case. But he asked me why I had come to that decision. I told him what I've told you. A man has to provide for his family. And I told him that Chicago seemed to be a clear-cut case, but it would take a lot of somebody's time to prove it, and I simply did not have the time."

"So what changed your mind?" I asked.

"Thurgood Marshall changed my mind," replied Zuber. "He asked me, 'Who is the most qualified lawyer to pursue a suit against the Chicago Board of Education?' I had to say, 'Having had the experience of two years on the New Rochelle case, I'm best qualified to handle the Chicago case.'"

So that was how Paul Zuber happened to be in Chicago. But why have lunch with me?

"I'm trying to get the lay of the land." Zuber said. "I heard you're on Willis' tail, so I thought it would be a good start if I could sit down and talk to you."

Zuber kept in touch. I shocked the carpet merchants at the M & M Club a few more times—inviting Zuber and two smart black Chicago lawyers over for lunch. Invariably, my fellow club members stopped eating to stare at me and my guests, and invariably, we were marched to a distant table. But as Zuber and the two local guys would discuss the details of their case against Ben Willis & Co., it was helpful to be isolated. The two local black guys who went to work for Zuber were James D. Montgomery and Raymond Harth. Zuber and his colleagues hoped to prove that the Chicago Board of Education was deliberately setting arbitrary school district boundaries to keep white children and black children in separate schools. They also sought to prove that black schools were overcrowded, while white schools had empty classrooms, and that black students were receiving an inferior education.

It was apparent to me that Dr. Willis and his school board were cynically indulging in gerrymandering; even *he* might have conceded that school districts' conforming to racial housing patterns creates a basis for the conclusion that white kids were deliberately separated from black kids. But he never did concede it. In Chicago, school superintendents don't give aid to the enemy by admitting violations of the U.S. Constitution. Proving a case of segregation is more difficult than making the charge of segregation, and Zuber wryly observed to me, early in the game, that he had a tiger by the tail on the Chicago school map matter. Nonetheless, Zuber believed he would win his case. In Chicago it wasn't all that easy.

Zuber had not the slightest doubt that he could prove his case in federal court. I began to think that Zuber was in a can't-miss situation. City Hall began to think so, too. So did some of the leading citizens in Chicago's white establishment. The politicians and the politically connected businesspeople tried to put Zuber down as a "professional rabble-rouser." The establishment's line was that Zuber was an "outsider" intent on "causing trouble."

I never saw any evidence to support this. The Chicago school segregation case was clearly a personal burden to him. One time I asked who was compensating him for his labors, and he told me that all he had received were vague promises that he would be paid for his expenses—his travel costs and his living expenses in Chicago—but he hadn't seen any money yet, and he didn't know who was supposed to compensate him. Zuber told me that Chicago's do-gooder organizations seemed to resent his being here, that only two civil rights groups were making gestures of helpfulness, and that, aside from myself, nobody was buying him a meal. "Chicago," he quietly observed, "strikes me as a very strange place."

Having suffered for two and a half years the burden and indignities of preparing for battle with a minimal staff, and having impressed attorneys I knew with the skill he brought into federal court, Zuber seemed on his way to victory—even though the federal judge in the case was a dear friend and confidant of Richard J. Daley. But Zuber suddenly and inexplicably pulled out and went back to New York. I was amazed at the news that he was walking out.

I can't remember just where it was that he grimly told me the story; at lunch perhaps, or in my office. Wherever it was, I quite clearly remember that he looked at me accusingly and said, "What kind of a city is Chicago? What kind of a place is this, where blacks are in collusion with the whites who are putting them down? This is the damnedest place I've ever seen. Natural enemies cooperate with each other. Everybody's kept quiet by getting a little piece of the action. Chicago—you can have it!"

I was astounded. Clearly, Zuber was mad as hell about something, but I didn't have the faintest idea what he was talking about. When he told me, I could only shake my head; yeah, I admitted to myself, his story had the flavor of Chicago about it.

Zuber told me he had gone back to New York to attend to other matters that needed his attention while waiting for the federal court to set a date for a hearing. On short notice the court set the date, and he got a call from Chicago, telling him to come back right away.

"It was a surprise," Zuber said, "to get word like this, when I expected it would be a while before we were to be back in court. But these things happen, so I told the people who called me that I would be on a plane in the morning. Then they tell me, 'Don't forget to bring your wife with you.' I was confounded. I said, 'What the damned hell is that—bring my wife with me?' And they tell me there are stories going around in the black community about me—stories that I'm cattin' around with women in Chicago. It would be 'wise,' they said, to bring my wife with me. Now the people who called me knew damned well I was not cattin' around in Chicago; they knew damned well that when I was out here I worked all day and well into the night and was lucky to sneak off for an occasional sandwich."

"So what did you tell them?" I asked, "these people who called from Chicago?"

Zuber smiled and said, "I thanked them for the warning. I told them I would follow their advice and bring my wife with me. And that's what I did; she's at the hotel right now. My wife was furious. When I told her about the rumors of my womanizing, she said it sounded like a frame-up."

"What do you think?" I asked Zuber.

"What would any man in my position think?" he replied. "You give your people your time, you work your ass off for them, you pay your own expenses—then they give you the story you're playing around with women. Yeah, it's a frame-up. It hurts a man's pride to confess that his wife understands a situation quicker than he does, but her first impression was right."

"Who do you think was trying to frame you?" I asked.

He shook his head. "I don't know," he said. "The case has been heating up, and it's obvious the power structure is going to be bitter if the court holds against Dr. Willis and the school board. It would have to be somebody who has a hold on people on our side of the argument."

"You're saying that the power people have come up with a scheme to get you to drop the segregation case?"

"Maybe there's another explanation," he replied. "But, yeah, I think the people in charge of things around here would like to see me clear out. Chicago folks are cunning; you know that?"

"I'm surprised you're ready to capitulate," I said.

"I wouldn't be capitulating, as you say, if it weren't for one element of this affair: the evidence that Chicago's white power structure controls black people," Zuber said. "I've never seen anything like Chicago!"

Zuber was gone. The Federal Justice Department made a few motions of disapproval about the Ben Willis plantation policy, but the government didn't seem too sincere about getting Dr. Willis to mend his white-supremacy ways. And whatever fear Paul Zuber had instilled in Chicago's establishment was soon dislodged by the foreboding arrival of Dr. Martin Luther King, Jr.

So long as Martin Luther King, Jr., marched in Mississippi or Alabama, there was a degree of sympathy for him to be found in some, but certainly not all, of the white areas of Chicago. When King came to Chicago in 1965, those in the city's white power structure were pointedly reserved, except in private conversation among themselves, about Martin Luther King, Jr. A deep-seated fear seemed suddenly to settle on those who harbored a suspicion that blacks might someday muscle their way into greater domination of the public affairs of the city. If there were one vital element that Chicago's blacks were lacking, it was leadership. In an ominous way, the Reverend Martin Luther King, Jr., was viewed as the man who could fill the void. There was serious concern in the better areas of white Chicago and its suburbs that Martin Luther King, Jr., was plotting a black takeover. Well-rooted white Chicagoans, in short, had the hell scared out of them by King's arrival.

Even before King arrived from the South, I was catching a good deal of flak from people I would meet at social affairs—dinners, cocktail parties, and fund-raisers for various "worthy causes." People I knew as friends had increasingly become upset with me. Affluent people who had fled to the suburbs to escape such urban crises as segregated schools and ghetto neighborhoods got to arguing "the other side" of the city's problems—especially after three or four martinis. "For the good of the decent kids," they would say, "it makes a lot of sense not to put them in the same schools as Negro kids who just can't learn as fast as white kids." Generally, I would just nod and walk away. But sometimes, one of these white-supremacy guys would pursue me, saying, "Come on, let's be reasonable."

When the Rev. Dr. King made his appearance in Chicago, men of position sneered, "This King is just another dumb nigger."

In a city where the first question to be asked about someone who's causing trouble is, "What does he want?"—meaning, What is this guy's price?—Martin Luther King, Jr., gave no sign that he could be bought off. It frustrated the politicians who talked to me that this "nigger preacher" wouldn't state his price for getting out and leaving City Hall to parcel out social justice as it chose. How can you deal with a guy who is not willing to make a deal? Some of the blacks that I knew displayed little tolerance, much less affection, for the solemn-looking preacher who had come up from the South to lead his people in Chicago out of racial bondage. As far as I was able to determine, black politicians in Chicago—not partial to anyone who might jeopardize what power they had grasped—were discreetly noncommittal about Brother Martin. There were many times I wished I were earning my living selling insurance or dealing in used cars or something comfortable like that. It didn't help any when Martin Luther King, Jr., came to Chicago, because I didn't make it with him, either.

My personal view of the black preacher's arrival was that he was not likely to bring social disaster. I figured that King's presence in Chicago might inspire those in charge of things to give minority folks a little better deal than they had been getting. That was Chicago's style; somebody hollers, you give him a little something to keep him quiet. But not for an instant do you contemplate total surrender to anybody who demands for himself whatever it is you have put together for yourself. Not in Chicago, certainly. In my commentaries I raised the question of whether King had the moxie to deal with the cunning resistance of Chicago. Privately, I didn't think he was up to the new kind of challenge he faced in our city. Chicago was too set in its ways to permit a Southern preacher to effect any radical changes. But I used to wonder if King had heard the remark of Alderman Paddy Bauler, when Jake Arvey slated Martin Kennelly as the Democrats' reform candidate for mayor: "Chicago ain't ready for reform." And I toyed with the idea that Chicago might be ready for a little bit of this nonviolent reform that Martin Luther King espoused.

I got a phone call one day from one of King's disciples, who said King would like to talk to me. I don't remember who it was who phoned me; maybe it was a zealous, loquacious young man named Jesse Jackson. Jackson was a handsome, articulate young preacher who had impressed me as being a realist. Jesse seemed to be aware that Chicago's white establishment was not going to cave in, simply because a band of black ministers threatened to mount a parade of protest along State Street. If that first call didn't come from Jesse Jackson, it probably came from a soft-spoken public school teacher named Al Raby. The thoughtful Al Raby was hopeful, yet he struck me as having grave reservations about King's chances of bringing about racial equality in Chicago. Raby was another realist. He knew how tough it would be to convert nonbelieving Chicago to the precept that the U.S. Constitution was intended to provide and protect everybody's freedom.

It caused quite a bit of commotion when Martin Luther King, Jr., arrived at NBC-Chicago and marched through the hallways to my office off the newsroom. He was gracious when we met, but I instantly got the impression that he was intent upon sizing me up. This kind of tickled me. And I wondered if he had tried to get a reading on the important people of our city— the movers and shakers with whom he had been having preliminary discussions. As he looked me over, I looked him over. I was surprised to detect fatigue and a subtle kind of fear in this celebrated civil rights leader. He spoke softly, and he seemed to be weighted down by the cross of racial justice that he carried. I suppose I had expected him to come at me with the evangelical zeal of a bible-thumper. But he seemed to exude a great sadness—and, discovering him to be like this, I was disconcerted. It threw me off balance, I think, to discover that this heroic black preacher who brought foreboding to the white folks of our city was a gentle, sort of frightened man, who seemed to have resigned himself to verbal abuse and threats of physical harm—because no one else had come forward to carry this cross.

It would have been easy to get something interesting out of
the Rev. Dr. King if he had attacked me with a verbal fusillade
of hell fire and brimstone; I had been at this a long time, and
I had a reputation for being able to get a good radio or television piece out of somebody who hollered, or pounded the
table, or threatened me. I was the first white reporter to get
into the then-chancy business of covering the sect known as
"the Black Muslims," a black isolationist group that scornfully
referred to whites as "blue-eyed devils." Its members all vowed
submission to a cute little fellow who had changed his name
from Elijah Poole to Elijah Muhammed. Little Elijah and his
"elite guard" of karate experts, in black silk suits, black ties,
and white-on-white shirts, had not known what in hell to do
with me when I showed up at the Coliseum in the early '60s
to cover their annual national conventions. The silk-suited
bodyguards had escorted me to an isolated center seat in the
first row. Little Elijah Muhammed pleasantly insulted me—the
only white in the place—in a seemingly endless sermon, as a
dozen of the black-suited guys stood shoulder to shoulder at
the foot of the podium, not for a second averting their eyes
from me. What I mean is, I had had a little experience in trying
to get a story in a difficult situation; I had had some experience
in these white-reporter encounters with an important black
guy. But I found that trying to interview Martin Luther King,
Jr., under agreeable conditions was much more difficult than
doing those original Black Muslim stories. With Elijah Muhammed and Malcolm X, I never felt I was coming up empty,
as was the case that first time I tried to interview Martin Luther
King, Jr.

It exasperated me that I struck out with the nationally known
Reverend King. I didn't call in the technicians to film and tape
an interview with this man, though that is what I had planned
to do. When King left my office, I tried to figure out what had
gone wrong. What went wrong, I think, was that I hadn't been
able to interview him—because *he* had interviewed *me*.

I interviewed hundreds of people over the years; thousands,
I guess, would be more accurate. But only on rare occasions
did I allow myself to get knocked off stride by the other party's

problems, because you can't get information out of anyone who succeeds in shifting his woes onto you. It always bothers me when some big wheel I am interviewing puts a question to me as to what my judgment would have been, were I forced to deal with the problem he faced. Chicago's Mayor Daley frequently responded to a direct question with "What would you have done?" or "What do you think?"—his intention being to weasel out of answering a reporter's question. And it had annoyed me when the Reverend Dr. King started lobbing his problems to me. What was my judgment, he wanted to know, of a Southern black preacher's chances for spreading the "good news" of racial justice in a large Northern city?

Reverend King intoned a litany of abuses. One by one, he had counted off the terrible conditions he found in Chicago: segregation and inequitable education in the public schools; confinement of blacks to slums where rents were exorbitant and the poor were overcharged at white-owned grocery stores; the Daley administration's stubborn refusal to adopt a fair housing ordinance; police brutality; and restricted job opportunities for blacks. "You seem to have a good understanding of what goes on in Chicago," I told King. "But I get the impression that you think racial justice can be negotiated here."

In reply, King said, "I believe you underestimate the changes that are occurring in this city. Mayor Daley intends to call for a 'Conference on Race and Religion.' The religious leaders of the city and myself will air our grievances and seek a program for the solution of the problems existing in Chicago."

"This is the first I've heard about it," I said. "It sounds, somehow, like they're getting set to give you a snow job. You'll have some meetings and maybe a big lunch or two, and they'll all get together on a racial justice position paper that'll sound great but won't mean a damned thing."

"I am disappointed," Reverend King replied, "that you so little estimate this opportunity to take a giant step in bringing justice and fairness to the men and the women and the children of Chicago's slums."

"Daley says there are no slums," I responded.

The Reverend Martin Luther King said, "We will do whatever we must, to bring racial justice to Chicago. We will march! We will march in the white ghetto of your Southwest Side! In your segregated Marquette Park! We will march in Cicero!"

There was a firmness now in the set of his jaw. There was a zealot's look in his eyes. "What will Mayor Daley say to that?"

I shook my head. "I don't know what Daley would say to that," I replied, "but I was in Cicero when the white ethnics blew up when a black family tried to move in—about fifteen years ago. I don't imagine Cicero's white folks have changed much. I'm afraid that somebody is going to get killed, if you bring a lot of blacks in to march in Cicero."

Life had changed for me in the fifteen years or so since I had covered the race riots in Cicero. I was in the protected role of doing commentaries for radio and television, turning out about twenty-five hundred pearls of wisdom every working day. I was pretty much phased out of the exciting business of covering the news. But the assignment to figure out why something happened and what it portends—the function of commentary—is much more difficult than simply gathering up the facts. It was murder to write objective commentary on so volatile a matter as racial justice—especially during the year and a half or so when Martin Luther King, Jr., was so much a part of the news in Chicago. Protagonists on both sides of every sensitive story protested my every opinion. Val Press, my former right hand—who had moved up to the NBC assignment desk—used to drop into my office to ask, "How is it going?" But Val Press was sort of militant on the side of those who struggled for social justice, and even she would boil when something in one of my commentaries offended her prejudices. The Chicago area was divided: one side held hands and sang "We Shall Overcome," and the other side muttered that Daley or somebody should wake up and run this black revolutionary out of town. Not infrequently, my commentaries provoked bitter protests from both groups. When I did some tongue-in-cheek opinionating, for example, on the Reverend Dr. King's sanctimonious statement, "We do not seek to precipitate violence," the switchboard lit up with the angry phone calls of those who claimed I had maligned King and those who charged that I was partly responsible for his being in Chicago. Rev. King's presence in Chicago gave me a lot to talk about, but I really took the heat for whatever I said.

Martin Luther King, Jr., raised a pretty big stink in Chicago. He led a melodramatic march to City Hall—where he posted his demands on the La Salle Street door. King took up residence in a West Side ghetto called Lawndale, which rated with the city's blacks as the worst of the ghettos. It impressed me that King had chosen to live with the most underprivileged of his adopted flock. He made a grand speech to newspeople about locating in "an island of poverty that rests in an ocean of plenty," but white Chicago snickered at news reports that the great black emancipator had been reduced to scrubbing his own floors, clearing out dirt and debris, and setting out poison to rid his flat of the fat gray rats that infested his tenement.

King had appeared to me to be profoundly frightened when Lawndale erupted in arson and shooting and looting. The white establishment grimly cursed Martin Luther King, Jr., for having inspired the rioting—but it was not King who set off the Lawndale riot. On sweltering nights kids all over Chicago turn on hydrants to frolic in the water that pours out, by way of getting cooled off. And city officials—cops, or streets and sanitation workers, or whatever—move in to shut off the hydrants. One hot night in July 1966, the kids in Lawndale opened up the hydrants. And in a classic display of stupidity, with racial tension so high, squads of policemen moved in to close the hydrants. The black kids responded with rage, and all hell broke loose.

Martin Luther King, Jr., continued to rub Daley raw, after Governor Kerner's National Guard put down the Lawndale riot. King cooled off on his pledge to lead a march through Cicero, deciding, I guess, that there would be a bloodbath if he tried it. But with about a thousand Chicago policemen for escort, he and five hundred of his followers marched through lily-white Marquette Park on the Southwest Side. Amid a relentless chorus of racial insults and a barrage of bricks and stones, he warily walked through this neighborhood of working-class whites who were bitterly antiblack. A couple of weeks later he went back and did it again—and this time Rev. King himself was felled by a rock. King's followers had a look of fright on their faces. So too, I thought, did King. But somehow the crisis passed, and the black marchers cleared out of Marquette Park.

And that, I think, was Martin Luther King's last hurrah in Chicago. Oh, he stayed around for a while—attending meetings, making speeches, and so on. He came up to affluent Winnetka, a waspish suburb on Chicago's North Shore, to put on one of his rallies. I lived only a few blocks from the park where he was to speak, and I walked over to see how he would make out with the well-heeled folks. It intrigued me that the crowd of upper-income people who had turned out to get a look at Rev. King were gracious and cordial; the Reverend Dr. King clearly was perplexed. *This* crowd didn't howl insults at him. *This* crowd didn't throw rocks at him and call him "nigger." *This* crowd perhaps treated him as a curiosity, but nonetheless applauded him. I don't know what he expected, coming into racially restricted Winnetka. Maybe he expected that the black youths who accompanied him would get beaten up, as had happened in all-white neighborhoods of Chicago. But I didn't observe the slightest sign of resentment among the upper-income residents of Winnetka. King recognized me and gave me a smile—pleased, I guess, that I was there. But the Reverend Dr. King looked puzzled at finding that the people of Winnetka were docile and agreeable. He should have known that the people of Winnetka would be civil toward him. Why not? They didn't have any wild dreams of "overcoming" anything; they had already done it—or were well on their way to doing so.

Urbanologists and sociologists and political scientists might argue that Martin Luther King had a profound influence on Chicago. Maybe he did, but I don't know. A black man has a better chance of buying a house in a predominantly white neighborhood—and living there in peace—than he had before the Rev. Dr. King came to town to evangelize for racial justice. It is no longer amazing if a reporter contacts an upper-level executive of a major corporation and finds the big shot is a black man. There are black and Hispanic and Oriental faces on television—and not too long ago, there were none. Some efforts have been made to reduce the extent of segregation in the city's public schools. Chicago has a black mayor now, and Harold Washington's election demonstrated that blacks have emerged as a powerful political force. But the mayoral contest that put the first black in the city's highest office also demonstrated that racism runs strong still in Chicago.

The Rev. Martin Luther King, Jr., was a special kind of man. He carried the load in the struggle for racial justice—and got assassinated for it. Martin Luther King, Jr., had great influence in waking up America to the meaning of the principle that all men are created equal. But you take a drive down a Chicago thoroughfare called "Martin Luther King Drive"—meager tribute to the man's memory—and it is a little painful, because you are driving through the South Side ghetto. The black ghettos are still there. Yes, Martin Luther King changed things. But profoundly? I don't know about that.

That's the hell of it, when you spend your life doing stories on the people who make news. How do you measure the value of what a man has done with his life?

EPILOGUE: BIRTH OF HORROR IN THE LAND OF ENCHANTMENT

WHEN ALL YOU CAN CLAIM FOR YOURSELF is that maybe you are a pretty good reporter, the wise thing to do, I suppose, is to put it down and let it go to press and have done with it. Spending your life as a reporter is not much, I guess—but then, what is? The worst part of it, in these times, is winding up with a quiet little dread inside of you that you might have been there without even knowing it to see the beginning of the big finale. It is a lonesome kind of remorse that seems to possess you when you get to thinking that there is a real possibility that while you were out covering this and that in the human adventure, you missed the big story that the lights might be going out, never to be turned on again. You would be some kind of a reporter, if you blew this one.

It has always offended me that of all the dreary places on earth that might have been requisitioned for the building of the atomic bomb, an incomparably beautiful place in northern New Mexico was the choice. It was not for its beauty but for its promise of security that the area where the San Ildefonso

Indians had scratched out their existence for centuries was chosen as the site where men of science could work out the recipe for the weapon that would place all living things in perpetual jeopardy.

The scientific barn boss of the Manhattan Project, J. Robert Oppenheimer, had owned a little vacation spot in the Pecos Valley, down around Santa Fe. He knew the area well. He had ridden horseback across the grandeur of New Mexico, which aptly proclaims itself the "Land of Enchantment." It seems to have been Oppenheimer who urged the selection of Los Alamos for the construction of the atomic bomb. On Oppenheimer's recommendation, the Government took over the town—and a boys' boarding school, the prestigious Los Alamos Ranch School, to house the scientific cadre that would put together a new kind of explosive that would dwarf every bomb previously conceived in the mind of man.

It was sacrilege of the highest order to build such a thing in so peaceful a place. It revolts me to drive into Los Alamos and find service stations merchandising bags of fertilizer to make red roses grow. I am offended by the neatly cut lawns and trimmed hedges. In the center of the posh, suburban-looking town is a beauty parlor for the dogs of nuclear scientists. My God, you wonder, what has man wrought?

I spend a great deal of time these days in northern New Mexico, in a little town called Taos. Fifteen years ago all I knew about Taos was that D. H. Lawrence, lured into the place by Mable Dodge, and some notable artists like Joseph Henry Sharp, Nicolai Fechin, and Ernest L. Blumenschein had made this little place famous. I had an old friend down there—Steve Mitchell—former counsel to Mayor Edward J. Kelly, former campaign manager of Adlai Stevenson II, former national chairman of the Democratic party. He had pulled up his stakes in Chicago, severed most of his old ties—save for his place on the Democratic National Committee—and gone off to New Mexico.

Steve invited me to visit his adobe home one time. I had a couple of days, and I figured it would be interesting to see Taos. So I rented a car at the Albuquerque airport, asking the

Hertz girl, "Which way to Taos?" and I took off. Forty-eight hours later I was back at the airport—getting on a flight to Chicago. Looking out the window at the lovely mountains and desert as the plane took off, I told myself: "You've got to be nuts!" And maybe I was. Having looked at a condominium that hadn't even been built but was only roughed out—in a place that I had never seen before—I had bought it! Mitchell had said, "Well, I don't think you'll ever regret it." I never did.

An old roughneck named Kit Carson, who got famous in the long ago for fighting Taos Pueblo Indians—the Navajos not taking kindly to the Anglos' grabbing their land—is buried in a little cemetery in a modest site called Kit Carson State Park. The portal of my little place faces this park. Navajos, with J. C. Penney blankets draped over their heads and wrapped around their bodies, sometimes gather there to play drums and chant songs. My kind of folks, I guess. At least I understand their quiet regret that a famous Indian chief doesn't have his name on this park.

Two miles north of Taos is the pueblo that has stood for almost five hundred years. The Taos Indians with their Penney blankets have the forlorn look of a crushed people. Some of them have succeeded in making it in the white man's world, but the Indians are a distant third to the Spanish-speakers who are in charge of things and the Anglos who have put their roots down in New Mexico to enjoy the gorgeous setting that nature has produced.

As a raven flies, but longer by winding, mountainous road, Taos is a hundred miles northeast of Albuquerque and fifty miles north of Santa Fe. You are getting close to the southern boundary of Colorado when you reach Taos. It lies close to the lower reaches of the Sangre de Cristos mountains at an altitude of seven thousand feet. Hidden away on a mesa in the Sangres north of Taos, at an altitude a thousand feet or more higher, is a treasure of nature called Blue Lake. This lake is said to be calm and clear and deep and beautiful. Only for very special reasons does a white man get permission to make the difficult journey up there to see it, for it is a sacred place to the Navajos. It is the private property of the Taos Indians, the

U.S. Congress having had the decency about a decade or so ago to deed it to its original owners.

The Sangre de Cristos, capped with snow for much of the year, are simply beautiful. The snow is dry, and experts come from distant parts of the world to ski on it, testing their skills on a powder that nature does not seem to endow on any other place on earth. There are piñon trees, stubby little pines that live for eighty years or more. There is an entrancing odor to piñon burning in a fireplace. On the mountainsides are groves of aspens that turn golden in autumn. The aspens are spoken of by botanists as "nurse trees," because they are the first to sprout after fire sweeps a forest. The aspens provide shelter from the sun for the seedlings of the spruce and fir. The aspens die when the shade-tolerant trees reach up to the sun, closing out its rays to the short-lived aspen that have made it possible for the forest to live again. Nature can be as unmerciful as man.

The snow-capped Sangre de Cristos can be seen from the isolated mesa of Los Alamos, fifty miles southwest of Taos. Two hundred thirty miles south of Taos is Alamogordo, the desert wasteland on which the ultimate weapon was first tested.

At a party one night in an adobe house in Arroyo Seco, just north of Taos, I got to talking with a knowledgeable senior citizen named John Brandenburg. Brandenburg was an Oklahoman who had come to Taos in the dire days of the Great Depression and had become one of the town's leading citizens. A respected banker, he had provided much of the funding when Taos put in streets and sidewalks and small businesses got started as the town expanded as a center for music and the other arts. In the course of our conversation I asked Brandenburg if he had any recollection of the day the scientists tested their bomb at Alamogordo.

Brandenburg looked at me in surprise—not expecting a question like this, I guess. Then he said, "I can give you the date—July 16, 1945. I was here, in Taos. We hadn't been expecting it. No one knew what they were up to at Los Alamos. I was getting down there occasionally because I was financing some of the contractors who were doing work down there of one kind or another. But the Army didn't let you see much.

"The Government had to employ a great number of local firms—New Mexico firms—to get the construction done on all that was needed to get the project moving," Brandenburg told me. "People in lumber and plumbing and concrete and electricity—it was a boom for firms in Santa Fe and Española and Taos and the entire area. But no one was ever told the purpose of all this construction. No one was ever told the purpose of all the expense and effort. And if you wanted a contract on this job, you had better not ask.

"I was providing the financing for some of these contractors, tiding them over until they got paid by the Government. There was a local man, a Taos man, who was called down to Los Alamos and given a contract and the specifications to build an eighteen-square-foot box of concrete, with four-foot-thick walls and the same on the roof and the flooring. They didn't tell him what the purpose of this box would be and, naturally, he didn't dare ask. He needed capital to pay for his materials and labor and so on, and I financed him. The Government's standing behind him made this a very safe loan. So he built the concrete box and he told me that the Army people told him that he had done fine. He had a satisfied customer, you might say. But then he got a surprise—and I was surprised, too.

"This fellow comes into the bank one day, crestfallen, and he says, 'Mr. Brandenburg, the guys at Los Alamos wrecked my box. They call me down there this morning and they sit me down and they put the specifications for the concrete box in front of me and they say that they want me to build them a box. I looked at the specs, and then I looked at these Army guys and I tell them they seemed to be mixed up; I tell them I already built them this box and that they said they were satisfied and that I was waiting for the check. They say yeah, they know. They say don't worry, I will get the check. And they hand me a fountain pen, and they point at the place on the contract where I'm supposed to sign. I sign it all right, Mr. Brandenburg, and that's why I'm here—to borrow some more money to build it. Isn't that the craziest thing you ever heard of in your life?' And all I can add to that," Brandenburg said, "is that this is a true story of what happened and how much any of us knew about what was going on at Los Alamos."

"Did they give him any clue as to what had happened to the first one?" I asked.

Brandenburg shook his head. "They didn't tell outsiders anything at Los Alamos," he replied. "This local man said he thought that, for some reason or other, they had blown up the first one. He thought they were planning to blow up the second one, too. But whether they did or not, I can't say."

I mentioned that some people in Santa Fe had told me that, while the project was kept totally secret, there was a hot guess in Santa Fe that the Government was trying to produce a phenomenal new submarine. I said it sounded pretty crazy to me, the Government secretly building a submarine in the mountains of a desert state so distant from deep waters. But it had been wartime, I said, and you hear a lot of crazy talk during wartime. Had the Taos banker ever heard anything like this?

I thought this banker, who had been cordial to me, would write me off as crackers and get away from me fast. But he simply got pensive and replied, "I'm not sure I heard that one, but there was an awful lot of speculation at that time about what could possibly be going on at Los Alamos. On a straight line Los Alamos is not twenty-five miles from Santa Fe—to the northwest. The elevation is a little higher at Los Alamos, maybe a thousand feet higher. And the laboratory people kept the lights burning all night as they went about doing whatever it was they were up to. The lights were visible in Santa Fe, and this had a great deal to do with all of the stories that got spread around as to what was going on up there. Submarine? Well, I'm not surprised that some people in Santa Fe thought that was the secret project. We all found out, in due course, that it was a new kind of bomb they had been working on."

"When did you, personally, find out about it, Mr. Brandenburg?"

He rubbed his chin as he thought that over. Then he said, "In all honesty, I don't believe that anyone around here—except for the insiders who were in on the project—had any advance information. Some of us, those who had had business down there and had personal experience with the extremely tight security, realized that something of great importance was going on. We were all provided with a great clue when they had the bomb test at Alamogordo. But not until the bomb was dropped on Japan and announcement was made of what kind of bomb this had been—not until then could anyone here say with certainty what the project had been at Los Alamos."

"What happened the day they tested the bomb?" I asked.

"I was right here—in Taos," he replied. "The test bomb was exploded before dawn. I was up, although this was not my habit. For some reason, I couldn't sleep, and I got to see the aftereffects of this new bomb.

"The testing at Alamogordo came in the darkness of the morning of July 16, 1945. Alamogordo is Government-owned wasteland and, when I learned about this later, I thought it had been a wise selection of a location to test the bomb.

"I was gazing out a window at the nighttime sky. I had not turned on any lights in my house. Suddenly there was this incredible sight of the night turning to day. I couldn't believe such a thing could be happening.

"I don't know what the testimony of others might be. But I am certain there was no sound of an explosion. There was no convulsion of the earth that I was aware of. There was no surface concussion that I was conscious of. The glass panes of the windows didn't rattle. It was simply a matter of having witnessed the darkness of the predawn being instantly lighted up with the brilliance of a bright sun on a cloudless day. It was an incredible sight.

"Many people in the area saw what I had seen. The mysteriously lighted sky was all anyone around here talked about in the morning. People were frightened. There was no explanation on the radio of what had caused this extraordinary thing. The newspapers—the *New Mexican* in Santa Fe, the *Journal* in Albuquerque, and I don't remember what others—later carried an account of the Army having announced that an explosive accident had occurred in the southernmost part of the state, the explosion being of such magnitude that the flash had been seen across the state.

"Most of us who read this in the newspapers accepted the explanation as true. Some people criticized the Army for being so careless in handling its munitions that an accident of this kind could occur. But most of us, I believe, were greatly relieved to learn that what we had seen was the result of the accidental detonation of a huge storage of explosives.

"The next we heard, the Air Force had dropped an atomic bomb on Hiroshima. We understood then what had happened at Alamogordo, lighting up the sky. Our scientists had carted the test bomb to Alamogordo to find out whether it worked or not."

There is, in Taos, a grand old gentleman named Paul Bigelow Sears, with whom I have discussed a great many things: the function of worms that crawl in the earth, the fundamental need for animals to share with man the responsibility for keeping soil sweet and productive, the urgent necessity to keep water pure to preserve the chances of survival of plants and fish and humans and other living things. Paul Sears is a scholarly gentleman of the old school. He is now very well up in years—with only God knows how much longer to share his wisdom of the forests and the birds and the land. I met him the first day that I set foot in Taos. He was there in retirement—articulate, alert, knowledgeable about many things, professor emeritus of Yale, former head of the School of Botany at the University of Oklahoma and then at Oberlin. He is a gifted writer who has written four books—including the botany classic *Deserts on the March*, which begins with the line, "All the earth is a graveyard. . ." He is a dear man and my good friend.

I have had, in Taos, many talks with Paul Sears about many areas of inquiry—including this matter of the physicists who, in jerry-built laboratories on a gorgeous, isolated mesa of northern New Mexico, invented the bomb that threatens to visit extinction upon every last thing in creation. Though concerned not for himself, for he calmly accepts that the sands of his hourglass are running out, Paul Sears seems weighted with a subtle despair that his colleagues in science have schemed up a way to obliterate all life.

One time, he looked at me and said; "Are you familiar with the comment of L. O. Howard?"

I shook my head and said "Who is *he*?"

Sears told me that I should read L. O. Howard. "He was an entomologist of great renown."

I nodded and said, "And what is this comment that you mentioned?"

With a sad little smile, Paul Sears said, "Someone asked L. O. Howard—with reference to the possibility of the extinction of all living things—what his judgment would be on what is likely to be the last living thing to remain on earth. L. O. Howard replied, 'That is hard to say, but if I had to hazard a guess, I would think it would be the sole-surviving cockroach on a dead twig.' What do you make of that?"

"It would be a hell of a story to cover," I replied, "The last living thing."

Paul Sears nodded. He smiled. "Yes, I guess it would," he said. "But who would be here to write it—or read it?"

INDEX

427